Economic Analysis
of Environmental Policy
and Regulation

Economic Analysis of Environmental Policy and Regulation

FRANK S. ARNOLD

John Wiley & Sons, Inc.
NEW YORK • CHICHESTER • BRISBANE • TORONTO • SINGAPORE

Acquisitions Editor   Whitney Blake
Marketing Manager   Debra Riegert
Senior Production Editor   John Rousselle
Designer   Lee Goldstein / Kevin Murphy
Manufacturing Manager   Susan Stetzer
Senior Coordinator Illustration   Jaime Perea
Digital Production Manager   Jennifer Dowling

This book was set in 10 / 12 Palatino by Digital Production /
Justine Burkat Trubey and printed and bound by Malloy
Lithographing. The cover was printed by Phoenix.

Library of Congress Cataloging in Publication Data:
Arnold, Frank S.
    Economic analysis of environmental policy and regula-
tion / Frank S. Arnold. -- 1st ed.

            p.   cm.
    Includes bibliographical references (p.).
    ISBN 0-471-00084-1
    1. Environmental policy--Economic aspects. 2. Environ-
mental law. 3. Environmental policy--Economic aspects--
United States--Case studies. 4. Environmental law--United
States--Case studies.
I. Title

HC79.E5A76 1994
363.7--dc20   94-23146
                                                      CIP

Printed in the United States of America

10 9 8 7 6 5 4 3 2 1

Printed and bound by Malloy Lithographing, Inc.

Preface

In my years of experience conducting economic analysis of environmental policy and regulation, I have noticed a scarcity of teaching and research materials bridging the gap between environmental economics as taught in the classroom and the world of practical regulatory policy evaluation. To be sure, there is a wide variety of literature on environmental economics, ranging from basic and advanced textbooks and several journals devoted to the subject to collections of case studies summarizing practical applications. But what I have in mind is different both in its content and objectives from what is currently available to students and practitioners from these sources.

Largely missing from the existing literature on environmental economics is material that conveys the texture and context of actual policy issues, the nature of the questions that analysts typically confront in practice, and the way to bring the basic tools of environmental economics to bear on those questions. A book on these issues and topics would be useful to many students and analysts in reconciling the apparent disparity between environmental economics as taught in texts and the way it is actually applied in real-world regulatory and policy analysis.

I use the term *apparent* because many of the differences between environmental economics theory and practice are not as significant as they at first appear. Indeed, most of the dissimilarities can be traced to the fact that real-world pollution problems and the statutory mandates under which environmental policy is conducted were not designed to provide ready-made applications of textbook lessons. Many actual environmental problems are causally related to economic activities in complex ways, and most pollution damages are difficult to measure and often highly location-specific. In addition the goals and constraints that characterize practical environmental policy are frequently different from, and more diverse than, those that a purely economic efficiency-based perspective might suggest. These and other considerations substantially shape the character of the central questions in environmental policy, and the nature and content of the analyses practitioners undertake to provide answers. My primary purpose in writing this book is, therefore, to try to convey to students and others a deeper understanding of environmental economics as it is actually applied in regulatory policy analysis.

While many topics and issues are canvassed here, overall the book pursues three fundamental themes. First, it focuses on why environmental economics in practice is not primarily an exercise in estimating the value of pollution damages and then promulgating taxes to make polluters internalize those harms, but consists mainly of applied cost–benefit analysis. Of course, many researchers are occupied with valuing environmental damages using a variety of techniques, but that is not the central analytical support environmental economics contributes to the regulatory and policy-making process. Second, the material presented in this book shows that much of the hard work in practical applications of environmental economics involves fashioning a coherent set of questions for analysis, questions that reflect multiple policy goals and constraints, the complexity of real-world pollution problems, and the limitations of available information. The third and somewhat different emphasis of the book is on how practical environmental policy analyses often pose some deceptive theoretical questions, particularly problems in measuring the social costs and benefits of environmental regulations. Analysts often find these puzzles challenging at first, but transparently obvious after solving them. The book offers students and practitioners a glimpse of the nature of these questions and problems, and tries to show why their correct solution can be somewhat elusive in real-world contexts.

It seemed only natural to pursue these themes using actual applications of environmental economics, for it was in the course of analyzing a number of real environmental policies that much of what is contained in this book arose. My hope is that the book's attempt to communicate the richness of practical economic analysis of environmental regulatory policy through a collection of examples will be useful to readers both for the analytical and empirical issues it explores, and for the window it provides on the nature of environmental policy and regulation.

I owe a significant debt to ICF Incorporated, where I conducted the projects upon which much of this book is based, and to the many talented individuals with whom I collaborated over the years. Throughout the book I have tried to highlight the contributions of my colleagues at ICF and other organizations, and apologize for the inevitable omissions. I also owe thanks to several individuals of the Environmental Protection Agency: Christine Augustyniak, Michael Shapiro, and Al McGartland who oversaw several of the large research projects on which significant portions of this book are based.

A number of other individuals were very helpful during the process of writing this book. Arun Malik of The George Washington University, Mario Rizzo of New York University, and Robert Shapiro of the Progressive Policy Institute, and Anne Forrest of the Environmental Law Institute offered insightful comments and much-appreciated encouragement along the way. Thanks are due as well to the many technical reviewers of the manuscript who provided valuable advice and suggestions: Donald Cell, Cornell College; Ronald Cummings, Georgia State University; Charles W. Howe, University of Colorado at Boulder; Jeffrey A. Krautkraemer, Washington State University; Lloyd Orr, Indiana University; Clifford Russell, Vanderbilt University; Michael K. Taussig, Rutgers University; and Walt Hecox, Colorado College.

I would also like to thank everyone at John Wiley & Sons, Inc. involved in the production of the book, particularly John Rousselle and Justine Burkat Trubey. Special thanks go to Joanne M. Still, the indexer. Finally, I must express my gratitude to the Environmental Law Insitute and its staff for hosting me as a Visiting Scholar while I drafted the book, and to Dean Wagnon for his constant encouragement throughout this process.

Frank S. Arnold
Environmental Law Institute
Washington, D.C.
October, 1994

Brief Contents

CHAPTER 1

Purpose, Technical Level,
and Scope   1

CHAPTER 2

Environmental Policy Analysis
in Practice   7

CHAPTER 3

Design of Appropriate Models for
Policy Analysis   45

CHAPTER 4

Reconciling Conceptual Tools
and Available Data   66

CHAPTER 5

Modeling and Interpreting Social
Welfare Changes   84

CHAPTER 6

The Analytical Significance
of Baselines   103

CHAPTER 7

The Importance
of Anticipatory Responses   126

CHAPTER 8

Incidence of
Regulatory Costs   152

CHAPTER 9

Intertemporal Issues   177

CHAPTER 10

Recent Trends in Environmental
Policy: Some Cautionary Notes   198

CHAPTER 11

Environmental
Policy in Theory and Practice   219

Contents

CHAPTER 1

Purpose, Technical Level, and Scope   1

Purpose of the Book   2
Technical Level of the Book   3
Scope of the Book   4

CHAPTER 2

Environmental Policy Analysis in Practice   7

Case Study of the Asbestos Products Ban   8
  The Question   9
  The Analysis   10
  Asbestos Markets and Uses   11
  Addendum   40

CHAPTER 3

Design of Appropriate Models for Policy Analysis   45

Options for Enhancing Used-Oil Recycling   45
  The Question   46
  The Analysis   50

CHAPTER 4

Reconciling Conceptual Tools and Available Data   66

Restrictions on Formaldehyde Use in Textiles Manufacturing   66
  The Question   67
  The Analysis   68
Cancellation of a Pesticide Registration   75
  The Question   76
  The Analysis   77

CHAPTER 5

Modeling and Interpreting Social Welfare Changes   84

Cost–Benefit Analysis and Related Markets   84
  The Question   85
  The Analysis   85
Information Provision, Market Adjustments, and Net Benefits   93
  The Question   94
  The Analysis   94
Product Bans, Regulatory Cost Savings, and Social Cost Accounting   99
  The Question   99
  The Analysis   99

CHAPTER 6

The Analytical Significance of Baselines   103

Mandatory Recycling under the CFC Phaseout and Tax   104

The Question   106
The Analysis   106
Overlapping Regulations for
Hazardous Waste Disposal   111
The Question   112
The Analysis   113

CHAPTER 7

The Importance
of Anticipatory Responses   126

Carbon Storage through Government-
Sponsored Tree Planting   126
The Question   128
The Analysis   128
Low-Income Household Weatherization
Program   133
The Question   134
The Analysis   134
Impact of Accelerated Sea-Level
Rise on Yap   138
The Question   139
The Analysis   140

CHAPTER 8

Incidence of Regulatory Costs   152

Assessing Regulatory Cost Incidence in
Practice   152
The Question   153
The Analysis   154
Summary   163
Differential Regulatory Impacts on
Small Firms   164
The Question   164
The Analysis   165
Cost Incidence of Mandatory CFC
Recapture and Recycling   173

The Question   174
The Analysis   175

CHAPTER 9

Intertemporal Issues   177

Discounting from a Social Perspective:
First Principles   177
The Question   178
The Analysis   179
Does the Value of Risk Reduction
Increase over Time?   193
The Question   194
The Analysis   194

CHAPTER 10

Recent Trends in Environmental
Policy: Some Cautionary Notes   198

Evaluation of Environmental Life-Cycle
Assessment   199
The Question   199
The Analysis   200
Mandatory Solid Waste Separation and
Recycling   212
The Question   213
The Analysis   214

CHAPTER 11

Environmental Policy in Theory
and Practice   219

Why Policy Makers Don't Use
Environmental Taxes   219
The Question   220
The Analysis   221

Index   247

Economic Analysis
of Environmental Policy
and Regulation

Chapter 1

Purpose, Technical Level, and Scope

This book presents a wide variety of practical applications of microeconomics to environmental regulatory and policy analysis. Contrary to what some might expect, the examples and illustrations the book contains form a body of material quite different from a traditional collection of case studies in applied environmental economics. Although some of the applications presented do provide comprehensive technical and empirical encapsulations of entire research projects and therefore would be considered case studies in the conventional sense of the term, the book's scope, content, presentation, and ultimate purpose all distinguish it from existing collections of case studies on environmental policy analysis.

At its core, the fundamental motivation for presenting these examples of applied environmental economic analysis is to help teach students and practitioners how to use the basic tools of microeconomics to address the myriad of problems and circumstances that commonly arise in practical applications of environmental economic analysis. Thus, the primary interest here is the development and application of basic methodological elements—model building and selection, economic logic and tools, the modeling/data interface, and the potential pitfalls,

given real-world complexities and uncertainties. This book's purpose is therefore more akin to that of a text on environmental economics in that the ultimate goal is not to arrive at answers for specific policy questions but rather to explore the nature of the problems and the structure of the analyses that characterize practical applications of environmental economics.

As a result, while several of these examples of practical economic analysis of environmental policy are case studies in the traditional sense, many of these applications focus more closely on specific theoretical issues that arise routinely in the course of conducting practical analyses. Others seek to illustrate how policy and information constraints fundamentally shape environmental economic analysis in the real world, exploring the interface between economic analysis on the blackboard and environmental regulatory policy as made. The content of this book is therefore different from most of what is available to researchers, practitioners, and students of environmental economics in textbooks, journals, and existing collections of case studies. Hence, it is worth being explicit at the outset about the place this book occupies among these other resources, as well as its intended audience, technical level, and scope.

Purpose of the Book

The theory and practice of environmental economics have experienced what can only be described as explosive growth during the past 25 years. At least in part, this has been due to the greater importance of environmental considerations in public policy making. The advances made in the economics of the environment span the entire spectrum from extremely technical and theoretical to highly empirical and practical.

This growth in the field of environmental economics has produced a wide variety of resources on the subject that researchers, teachers, students, and practitioners can consult. A number of texts now cover the area at various technical levels; these texts include Tietenberg,[1] Fisher,[2] Field,[3] Pearce and Turner,[4] and Baumol and Oates.[5] In addition, several scholarly journals are devoted to publishing both theoretical and quantitative research on environmental economics; among them is the *Journal of Environmental Economics and Management*, and the field recently has been summarized by Cropper and Oates in the *Journal of Economic Literature*.[6] Taken together, the various branches of the environmental economics literature provide comprehensive coverage of the host of issues and topics in the field, which range from the welfare economic foundations of theory of externalities and common property resources, natural resource management, valuation of non-market goods, and the many relevant features of cost–benefit analysis, such as social discounting, that play an important role in the environmental arena.

The purpose of this book is therefore not to duplicate what is available in the existing literature, but instead to fill several gaps in the coverage of those materials relating specifically to applying textbook lessons to practical analysis of environmental regulation and policy. As such, the central focus of the examples in this book is on how the basic tools of microeconomics can be used to analyze real-world environmental regulatory issues.

A number of features of the book's approach and contents make it somewhat different from the existing literature on environmental economics. First, the book's applications stress the importance of translating complex questions into tractable analytical constructs. Most texts on microeconomics and environmental analysis emphasize the fundamental partial equilibrium apparatus of supply and demand functions, and its correct use. In reality, it is not always easy to transform the question asked into a familiar diagram recalled from the classroom. One purpose of the book, therefore, is to show through its illustrations and examples how to translate a complex public policy issue or problem, often presented by a person without any economic training, into a theoretically coherent microeconomic framework that can then be used for practical qualitative and quantitative analysis. An analogy would be that existing texts teach how to solve equations, whereas the practical world of policy analysis consists of "word problems" in which the challenge is formulating a tractable question or problem to be solved. Hence, the book demonstrates that flexibility and creativity in structuring questions and analyses are key components of practical environmental policy analysis.

This book also emphasizes the fact that in the realm of practical applications of microeco-

---

[1] T. H. Tietenberg, *Environmental and Natural Resource Economics*, Third Edition, (HarperCollins, New York), 1992, and *Environmental Economics and Policy*, (HarperCollins, New York), 1994.

[2] A. C. Fisher, *Resource and Environmental Economics*, (Cambridge Univ. Press, Cambridge, U. K.), 1981.

[3] B. C. Field, *Environmental Economics: An Introduction*, (McGraw–Hill, New York), 1994.

[4] D. W. Pearce and R. W. Turner, *Economics of Natural Resources and the Environment*, (Johns Hopkins Press, Baltimore),1990.

[5] W. J. Baumol and W. E. Oates, *The Theory of Environmental Policy* (Cambridge Univ. Press, Cambridge, U.K.),1988.

[6] M. L. Cropper and W. E. Oates, "Environmental Economics: A Survey," *Journal of Economic Literature*, Vol. XXX, June 1992, pp. 675–740.

mics, the complexities of actual circumstances must be incorporated into the analysis. This stands in contrast to the process of learning economics and public policy, where it is extremely useful to simplify the world in order to understand and appreciate the powerful propositions and analytical techniques being studied. Yet, applying these lessons requires one to tailor them to the actual circumstances, intricate as they may be, of the problem to be addressed. Hence, a second emphasis is on assisting readers in extending theoretical analysis into the practical world by showing how to incorporate often complex features of real-world environmental problems. The examples in the book also identify some of the more important limitations often encountered. To a large extent, one of the fundamental challenges in conducting applied environmental economic analysis is to tailor the theoretical constructs to the inevitably less-than-ideal set of information available.

The many examples in this book also highlight a number of technical issues that often arise in practical applications of economic analysis. Many of these questions are "puzzles" whose solutions, after some careful thought and a bit of diagramming, ultimately involve the most fundamental properties of applied welfare analysis. But because in practice these questions are not formulated initially in the language of textbooks, their solutions can often be elusive. The aim here is to illustrate the nature of these problems and show how they can be thought through logically.

One final useful feature of the examples in the book is their focus on real-world policy issues, such as global climate change and ozone depletion, toxic chemicals, and solid and hazardous wastes. By motivating each application with the nature of the regulatory process involved and the specific environmental issues of concern, it provides readers with more of the texture and circumstances of practical environmental policy analysis.

Exploring the world of actual environmental policy making also reveals why applications of environmental economics are often so different from what textbooks present. Such factors as regulatory goals that are dictated by considerations other than economic efficiency, the political difficulties and dilemmas surrounding attempts to place monetary values on environmental harms, and the inherent complexity of real-world environmental problems, among many others, all make practical economic analyses of environmental policies considerably different, if not richer in scope and detail, than what one might expect based on purely economic considerations.

Overall, the book is intended to be a useful supplement to the teaching and research materials already available on environmental economics, thereby providing at least a partial bridge from the blackboard to everyday practice. Hence, the scope of the book's topical coverage was guided primarily by the prevalence of different analytical issues in practice. As a result, much of the focus is on fairly traditional environmental economics and cost–benefit analysis, this to the exclusion of some other areas and topics, such as natural resource economics and environmental damage valuation techniques. But there are many materials available on those and other topics, from narrow to comprehensive in focus. The purpose of this book is to examine the analytical and empirical topics that it explores from a different perspective than do existing texts, emphasizing particularly the practical context of real-world environmental economic analyses, as well as a number of technical issues and other challenges that arise frequently in applying basic theory.

Technical Level of the Book

The technical level of presentation in all of the examples is extremely basic, employing only graphs and text. That is not to say that the material presented here is simple, for readers will require a firm grounding in the fundamentals of microeconomics, particularly supply and demand analysis and measurement of welfare effects through consumer and producer surpluses. While many of the issues addressed in the book clearly could be more formally presented and analyzed, a number of considerations suggested the nontechnical format adopted here.

Probably most important is that the book attempts to convey the general nature of the questions and the overall character of economic analyses of environmental policies in the real world. These applications therefore seek to describe actual projects and analyses that were undertaken to evaluate environmental regulatory policy, and a number of analytical issues that arose in the course of conducting them, as they really occurred. To dress them up in different technical clothing would largely defeat this objective.

Another reason for presenting the contents of this book using the most basic of tools in the economist's portfolio—logical argument and graphics—is that for many practitioners and students of applied microeconomics, the ability to describe a phenomenon or analysis in words and diagrams is the quintessential indicator of understanding. A number of the issues raised in the studies and applications in this book are not necessarily simple, despite the fact that they are handled in a fairly nontechnical way. The intention in making it so is to show that complex questions can be addressed using terms and methods that facilitate the use of practical environmental economics in the policy-making process, which operates for the most part on the level of what many would call economic common sense.

One final reason for presenting these examples of applied environmental economics at a fairly basic and accessible level has to ultimately with the intended audience. To a large extent, those who will benefit most from the material in this book are undergraduate students with solid microeconomics skills, graduate students in economics, public policy, and business, and students in related fields of study that have arisen recently as interest in environmental policy has grown. Practitioners with a variety of different academic backgrounds also stand to benefit from the material in this book.

This is not to say that those with advanced economics degrees will not also find the applications helpful. Some of what is covered in several chapters of the book may in fact be new even to the most seasoned environmental economist. Nevertheless, the central goal in presenting these materials is to assist in teaching environmental economics to those who now or in the future will observe, analyze, or formulate environmental public policy—a diverse audience whose common denominator is basic economic logic.

Scope of the Book

The examples and illustrations in this book are based on projects that originated mostly in the course of evaluating federal environmental regulatory policy. Because they are based on the experience of primarily one policy analyst, they necessarily reflect the mix of problems and areas of environmental regulation seen by the author over a number of years. Hence, the primary environmental problems that provide the factual backdrop for the analyses presented here are hazardous and solid wastes, toxic substances, air and water pollution issues, and stratospheric ozone depletion.

As a result, the scope of environmental regulatory programs discussed in these applications is not comprehensive in the sense of spanning all of the nation's environmental laws, regulations, and other programs. It is nevertheless representative of the kinds of questions, theoretical problems, and empirical analyses one typically encounters in applying microeconomics to environmental issues, a scope that is consistent with the book's underlying objective—highlighting how to apply textbook lessons in practice.

All of the applications of economics to environmental policy analysis in this book were motivated by actual regulatory issues. All of the questions posed are real, as are all of the circumstances described, which often complicate, but ultimately enrich the resulting analysis. The examples in this book are therefore based on often fairly extensive research projects, with some chapters presenting complete case studies, and others offering summaries, adaptations, or specific features of larger projects that are particularly relevant to the book's objectives. Each application therefore begins with a discussion of the policy context and background from which the particular question of interest arose, and then encapsulates the central issues to be examined and the analysis that was developed to address the question.

Finally, a brief review of what the various chapters seek to accomplish may help guide readers through the volume. First of all, the applications can be taken up in any order, because the environmental topics and analytical points addressed in each are, to a great extent, independent of those discussed in others. Hence, the reader keenly interested in the topic of discounting from a social perspective, for example, can proceed directly to that chapter, because it more or less stands on its own.

Nevertheless, the ordering of the material in this book reflects an overall plan to introduce readers to the world of practical applications of environmental economics. The book begins in Chapter 2 with a single comprehensive case study of the cost–benefit analysis conducted for an environmental regulation targeting the risks associated with asbestos use. The theoretical and empirical features of this case study are fairly typical of practical applications of the basic framework of cost–benefit analysis to environmental regulatory deliberations. This case

study therefore sets the stage and the overall tone for the book by showing how basic textbook constructs can be used, perhaps with some simplifications and adaptations, to address practical policy issues. Following this, Chapters 3 and 4 contain three applications that build on the basic approach presented in the asbestos analysis. The objective of these studies, however, is to illustrate the central importance of tailoring economic analyses of environmental regulatory policies to the available information, showing how the results of an analysis often depend critically on the facts and circumstances of the real world.

Next are five chapters containing a variety of studies that explore a host of technical and other issues that occur frequently in microeconomics to practical environmental policy analysis. Chapter 5 reviews some welfare effects measurement issues that are fairly representative of the types of analytical questions that occur frequently to actual environmental policy evaluation. Chapter 6 focuses on the importance of baseline specification in applied economic modeling. Chapter 7 highlights the profound impact that anticipatory responses to a regulatory program can play in either advancing or hindering the attainment of the policy's ultimate goals. Chapter 8 explores the incidence of environmental regulatory costs, an important issue in practical policy making. Finally, Chapter 9 focuses on various intertemporal issues that are often critical in practical environmental economic analyses.

The book concludes with two chapters that focus more deeply on the interplay and, to some degree, the conflicts between the purely economic perspective on environmental policy evaluation and regulatory policy analysis in practice. Chapter 10 raises serious doubts whether a recent "advance" in environmental policy analysis—what is referred to as *environmental life cycle assessment*—is of any practical or policy-making value. Chapter 11 explores why public policy makers rarely actually use corrective environmental taxation, the approach for handling externalities that dominates texts and the journals. As the reader will see, this chapter suggests that analysts need more than the concept of economic efficiency to describe practical environmental policy making, and, perhaps more importantly, to participate effectively in its formulation.

Chapter 2

Environmental Policy Analysis in Practice

This chapter presents a summary of a detailed cost–benefit analysis conducted for a major environmental regulation—a rule banning almost all manufacturing and importation of asbestos-containing products. As the first major chapter of the book, it serves two overall purposes. One is to set the stage for the rest of the book by reviewing all of the technical and empirical efforts that go into typical economic analyses of environmental regulatory policies in practice. As such, this chapter presents what many would consider to be a traditional "soup-to-nuts" case study. This is a useful point of departure, because a fairly complete review of an entire cost–benefit study as conducted in practice conveys the overall flavor of environmental policy and the economic component of the analyses normally undertaken to support specific regulatory actions. In addition, this chapter indicates the technical level of the analyses in this book and of most real-world environmental policy studies. Finally, as an overview of practical economic analysis of environmental policy and regulation, this chapter introduces a host of concepts that the remainder of the book explores in greater detail. Many of the topics and themes analyzed in other chapters are extensions and further illustrations of analytical and policy issues either explicitly or implicitly present in this asbestos study.

The second purpose of this case study is to show that the basic techniques of applied microeconomics can be used quite successfully in practice, but that real environmental problems and their solutions are often technically and factually complex. In learning the basic methods for analyzing public policy issues, many simplifying assumptions are made in order to highlight the central techniques and results of interest. In particular, most illustrations of the fundamentals of applied cost–benefit and environmental policy analysis normally assume that risks and damages are fairly easily measured and valued, that the regulator is more or less free to select whatever option seems best from a purely economic point of view, that enforcement and administration of regulations are straightforward, and that the quantitative information necessary to conduct empirical analyses generally is available in the form required by the theoretical constructs.

While these assumptions are very useful in teaching the analytical techniques and empirical methods of environmental economics, when one tries to apply these basic tools and concepts to actual regulatory and policy settings, most of these conveniences rarely hold. Hence, in addition to providing a fairly complete review of the many features of practical environmental economic analysis, this case study highlights how one can still use the fundamental concepts and tools learned in the classroom despite the complexities of actual regulatory circumstances. For example, the asbestos regulatory analysis had to account for the fact that human health risks varied tremendously across different products depending on the nature and composition of particular asbestos uses. Moreover, there was no general agreement on the exact social value of avoiding those exposures, and the analysis was confined to a fairly narrow set of regulatory options and acceptable policy outcomes. Finally, there were no detailed and reliable sources of demand and supply elasticities that easily could be applied in a conventional cost–benefit framework.

While the analysis described in this case study focuses on regulations that sought essentially to ban a toxic substance, the essential characteristics of theoretical and empirical analyses for environmental regulations targeting other sources of pollution risks are similar to those presented here. Thus, the complexities and constraints inherent in applying microeconomics to actual environmental problems, as illustrated by this asbestos case study, are the rule, not the exception.

Case Study of the Asbestos Products Ban[1]

Asbestos is a naturally occurring substance whose unique physical properties have made it an important component in many diverse manu-

facturing activities. Used for thousands of years, asbestos became increasingly important after 1850 because of two characteristics for which it is probably best known: extremely effective insulation properties and resistance to wear. Hence, asbestos traditionally has been used where heat protection is important, such as fire-resistant clothing, and in friction materials, such as automobile brakes.

Despite its desirable industrial properties, the unfortunate fact is that asbestos kills people. Indeed, throughout the twentieth century evidence of the adverse health effects of asbestos has been mounting. Exposure to asbestos dust has been shown to increase significantly an individual's risk of contracting a number of potentially serious diseases. These diseases frequently end in death, and when they do not, individuals' activities are circumscribed because respiratory function typically is significantly impaired.

Over the years, a variety of federal regulations have been enacted targeting relatively high levels of worker exposure to asbestos. But recent medical studies point to the likelihood that even the low doses of the nonoccupationally exposed are potentially hazardous. In response to this information, the Environmental Protection Agency (EPA) sought to address the remaining asbestos exposure and risk problems using one of its many enabling statutes—the Toxic Substances Control Act, or TSCA. This legislation is perhaps unique among the many that EPA enforces in that its reach is broad and the powers conferred on the agency are significant. Many U.S. environmental protection statutes focus on pollution control and risk reduction associated with a particular exposure medium or with specific types of sources. For example, the Clean Air Act targets risks to human health and the environment that are posed by pollutants that impact the troposphere and stratosphere. Similarly, the Federal Insecticide, Fungicide, and Rodenticide Act (FIFRA) focuses on occupational, consumer, and other sources of risks due to the use of a variety of toxic pest-management substances.

[1] This case study is based on the asbestos regulatory impact analysis ICF Incorporated conducted for the Environmental Protection Agency. While many people contributed to the project, four deserve special mention. Vikram Widge of ICF designed and oversaw the project's simulation modeling component. Josephine Mauskopf of Research Triangle Institute conducted the risk modeling for the analysis including designing a large demographic simulation model for the benefits assessment. Nora Zirps of ICF supervised the project's exposure assessment portion. Finally, Christine August-yniak of the Environmental Protection Agency provided overall project direction and technical guidance.

TSCA, on the other hand, authorizes several different programs regulating toxic substances, regardless of the medium of potential exposure or the nature of the economic activities that impose these environmental risks. Section 6 of TSCA, in particular, authorizes the administrator of EPA to undertake whatever regulatory actions are deemed necessary to address a risk that is determined to be unreasonable. Under this provision, virtually any regulatory action can be taken, from banning a substance to requiring exposure controls, and these remedies can apply across the entire nation or only to a specific process in a particular plant. Section 6, however, does require the administrator to adopt the "least burdensome" approach for addressing unreasonable risks.

Because of EPA's broad regulatory authority under TSCA and the fact that the remaining uses of asbestos included quite diverse products and activities that posed a wide variety of risks to human health, EPA began the lengthy process of regulatory development and implementation for asbestos under this statute. Many different analyses in support of such a proposed rule are required, including hazard assessment (toxicity of the substance), exposure evaluation, regulatory options development, a cost–benefit analysis, and various ancillary impacts assessments. These studies are normally summarized in what is referred to as a regulatory impact analysis (RIA). This case study reviews the cost–benefit analysis conducted for the asbestos regulation, and, in doing so, identifies a number of analytical and empirical aspects of practical environmental economics applicable to a wide range of environmental and other regulatory program settings.

The Question

The central task in this case study is to quantitatively estimate the costs and benefits of various proposed regulatory options for addressing human health risks from remaining asbestos production and products. But before turning to the theoretical apparatus used in doing so and the various data collection and modeling exercises that were required, it is worth pausing first to examine the set of regulatory options that were developed and evaluated.

Essentially two different strategies were proposed for asbestos products: a "staged" asbestos-containing product ban in which groups of products are banned at various points in time, and a phaseout of asbestos fiber use over time, perhaps with some specific product exemptions. A few other types of regulatory options were considered at one time or another during the asbestos regulatory development process, such as information provision through mandatory product labeling, and various engineering exposure controls, primarily for additional worker protection. Throughout the analysis, however, only the staged product ban and the fiber phaseout options were realistic contenders.

One might legitimately ask why the set of regulatory options was so limited and, perhaps more significantly, why wasn't the classic economic tool to correct externalities—environmental taxes or charges—considered? There are both long and short answers to these questions. Indeed, the final chapter of this book provides an in-depth discussion of the use of incentive systems in actual environmental policy making, of the nature of the public policy decision-making and priority-setting process, and of the role of economics and economists in the whole affair. But the emphasis of this case study is on the theoretical and empirical questions and analyses that one normally conducts in practical cost–benefit evaluations of environmental policies, so the short answer will have to suffice here.

There are several reasons for the relatively circumscribed and fairly stringent set of regulatory options considered for addressing the risks of remaining asbestos-containing products. Probably the most important is that EPA rarely uses any methods of regulation other than what one may call "command and control." The most common types of regulations are technology-based controls, concentration or emission limitations, treatment and disposal requirements, and selective or complete bans of substances or practices. Only very recently has EPA seriously tried to use tradeable emission systems in a few instances, and true corrective environmental taxes have rarely, if ever, been used. Hence, one reason for the absence of the quintessential economic approach for addressing environmental problems—an externality tax—is the regulators' lack of experience with that tool.

There are other reasons why EPA seriously considered only banning asbestos products and phasing out asbestos fiber use. While the language of TSCA Section 6 is expansive and powerful, it nevertheless mostly refers to measures to *restrict* a substance's use in the chain of commerce. The term "restrict" normally is interpreted fairly rigidly by regulators. Along similar lines, EPA had already reached the determination that the risks attributable to exposures to remaining asbestos-containing products were unreasonable, in line with the statute's requirements for intervention. Any regulatory response that did not ultimately rid the nation of these risks, perhaps allowing for the most modest of exceptions or exemptions, would seem to imply that the risks in question are not really unreasonable.

Yet another reason why EPA did not consider an externality tax to be a strong contender flows from the nature of the risks asbestos poses. In the usual stylized examples of environmental corrective taxation, a risk is isolated in a single market and is easily measured and valued, and continued pollution and environmental harm can be tolerated in exchange for payment of the penalty imposed by the externality tax. Asbestos exposure, on the other hand, causes cancer in humans (which is an extremely incendiary public policy issue), the exposures and risks are quite heterogeneous depending on the product and activity in question (so that many different tax rates at a number of different points in the economy might be necessary), and the precise

value of avoiding these exposures and harmful effects was the subject of considerable dispute.

In light of all of this, it would be difficult for even an innovative regulator to advocate an externality tax instead of interventions that would clearly and convincingly reduce to a minimum the risks of asbestos-related harms. Instead, EPA attempted to apply the "least burdensome" recommendation of the statute to the product ban and fiber phaseout regulations by systematically examining the availability and cost of substitutes for asbestos, product by product, and by considering a host of different timing options and exemptions to lower compliance costs by allowing certain industries more time to adjust and avoiding a few cases in which the burden of regulation would be extremely heavy.

Regardless of one's perceptions of the virtues or defects of the policy-making process behind the asbestos ban–phaseout regulation, these objectives and constraints are more the rule than the exception. It is within these confines that practical economic analysis of environmental policy mostly operates. It is often appreciated that the options considered are not necessarily "first-best" approaches, but that rarely results in significant changes in the class of regulatory options on the table. In practical policy analysis, one makes progress in small increments on the fundamental issue of moving actual policy development in the direction of the economist's view of optimality while spending a great deal of time analyzing, to the best of one's ability, the regulatory options and market circumstances that are the standard fare in the policy-making process.

The Analysis

As indicated earlier, this first case study attempts to be reasonably comprehensive in order to introduce a variety of topics and themes that later chapters explore in greater depth. Hence, a considerable number of technical and empirical issues are explored here. These are organized more or less according to the way these topics are pursued in practical environmental policy evaluations. This structure is notably different from how one might expect to conduct the analysis if one were setting out to promulgate an environmental tax. Indeed, the latter approach would focus primarily on estimating the social costs of the externalities asbestos use causes, and then computing the appropriate tax rates. In most practical environmental analyses, however, the evaluation of the *costs* of various regulatory interventions is where economics mostly applies, and this is largely separated from the study's benefits portion. Why this is so will become clear as the case study unfolds.

This summary of the cost–benefit analysis for the asbestos ban and fiber phaseout regulatory options proceeds as follows. First, the overall structure of the markets for asbestos fiber and the many products that use asbestos is reviewed briefly. This information suggests a specific theoretical structure for analyzing the regulatory options' costs and benefits. A graphical presentation of how one can estimate the costs of the regulatory options is presented first. While this general overview of the microeconomic framework for the analysis reveals how one can compute the regulatory options' welfare effects, how to render the model operational so that quantitative estimates of costs and benefits can be calculated is the real challenge in practice. Hence, the analysis next turns to how numerical estimates of all of the inputs necessary to obtain empirical estimates of the costs were derived. This reveals some of the necessary shortcuts one makes in practical quantitative cost–benefit analysis and some of the inherent limitations one confronts. Following the presentation of the cost-side modeling, the general methods used to calculate the benefits of the asbestos regulatory options are reviewed. This discussion first indicates why the analysis of benefits usually is carried out independently of the costs, at least up to a certain point in the process. The section then reviews the basics of typical benefits assessments for environmental regulations. The case study concludes

with some representative cost–benefit results obtained in the analysis and a brief postscript.

ASBESTOS MARKETS AND USES

Asbestos fibers have been used in manufacturing a variety of products for industrial and consumer use. The concentration of fiber within the final product depends on the application, but all products are formulated by mixing asbestos fiber from domestic or imported sources with other ingredients by a *primary processor* to form an asbestos mixture. This mixture is then processed further by a *secondary processor* to form a product that can be used in one or many applications. Significantly, the vast majority of asbestos fiber is imported to the United States.

Asbestos-containing products are normally classified according to the 37 product categories identified in the left column of Table 2-1. These products generally fall into several broad categories including construction-related goods, such as piping, shingles, tiles, and roofing materials; friction products, such as vehicle brakes and clutch parts; a variety of heat-resistant applications, such as gaskets and textiles; and a host of miscellaneous uses, such as linings for acetylene cylinders and missiles, and various extruded products. Table 2-1 reports asbetos fiber consumption for all of these product categories and their outputs in appropriate units.

Two features in the table deserve comment. First, several products' production volume in 1985 was zero; they were nevertheless carried through the analysis and were explicitly included in the asbestos regulatory options because it was possible for production of these products to be resumed. Second, the original equipment market (OEM) and the aftermarket (A/M) for drum brakes and light motor vehicle (LMV) brake pads are modeled separately. This allows several differences between these two brake markets to be reflected in the analysis. One is that the evolution over time of the original equipment and aftermarket during the timeframe of the analysis are very different, with

Table 2-1
ASBESTOS FIBER USE AND PRODUCTION OF ASBESTOS PRODUCTS, 1985

TSCA Number	Product Category	Asbestos Fiber Consumed (short tons)	Production Volume
1	Commercial Paper	0.0	0 tons
2	Rollboard	0.0	0 tons
3	Millboard	435.8	581 tons
4	Pipeline Wrap	1,333.3	296,949 squares
5	Beater-Add Gaskets	12,436.4	16,505 tons
6	High-Grade Electrical Paper	744.0	698 tons
7	Roofing Felt	0.0	0 tons
8	Acetylene Cylinders	584.1	392,121 pieces
9	Flooring Felt	0.0	0 tons
10	Corrugated Paper	0.0	0 tons
11	Specialty Paper	92.1	434 tons
12	V/A Floor Tile	10,374.0	18,300,000 square yards
13	Asbestos Diaphragms	977.0	9,770 pieces
14	A/C Pipe	32,690.8	15,062,708 feet
15	A/C Sheet, Flat	2,578.8	22,621 squares
16	A/C Sheet, Corrugated	0.0	0 squares
17	A/C Shingles	3,893.0	176,643 squares
18	Drum Brake Linings (OEM)	6,642.3	34,713,675 pieces
19	Disc Brake Pads, LMV (OEM)	1,089.2	10,077,464 pieces
20	Disc Brake Pads (HV)	117.6	156,820 pieces
21	Brake Blocks	2,643.6	4,570,266 pieces
22	Clutch Facings	993.5	7,237,112 pieces
23	Automatic Trans. Components	2.5	585,500 pieces
24	Friction Materials	1,602.5	8,719,541 pieces
25	Asbestos Protective Clothing	0.0	0 tons
26	Asbestos Thread, etc.	558.0	1,125 tons
27	Sheet Gaskets	5,441.1	3,607,408 square yards
28	Asbestos Packing	2.1	3 tons
29	Roof Coatings	29,551.2	75,977,365 gallons
30	Non-Roofing Coatings	2,951.4	9,612,655 gallons
31	Asbestos-Reinforced Plastics	812.1	4,835 tons
32	Missile Liner	700.0	4,667 tons
33	Sealant Tape	1,660.2	423,048,539 feet
34	Battery Separators	1.0	2,046 pounds
35	Arc Chutes	13.5	900 pieces
36	Drum Brake Linings (A/M)	18,049.4	94,328,903 pieces
37	Disc Brake Pads, LMV (A/M)	6,030.0	55,791,708 pieces
		145,000.5	

Source: ICF Incorporated, 1989. "Regulatory Impact Analysis of Controls on Asbestos Products," Volume I, Table I-1.

the former tracking new vehicle sales and the latter governed by replacement brake jobs. The other reason for separating these two brake markets is that substituting nonasbestos brakes for asbestos ones is more difficult for the aftermarket than for new vehicles, because entire braking systems are designed for particular types of friction materials. Hence, it is not clear that "drop-in" substitutes for asbestos brakes in the aftermarket will satisfy fairly strict safety standards.

This background information suggests that the theoretical apparatus used to compute quantitative costs and benefits of the various asbestos regulatory options should account for several important features of the problem. First, asbestos fiber and asbestos-containing products are imported to the United States, so the analysis should divide the welfare effects of the regulatory options into domestic and foreign components. Indeed, because nearly all asbestos fiber is imported, to the degree that asbestos mining operations bear any of the regulatory costs or enjoy any of the benefits, these generally will accrue to foreign entities. Second, because products that contain asbestos are used in a variety of applications, they are likely to vary widely in terms of the social costs of substituting other materials for asbestos and the levels of risks posed. The approach for estimating the costs and benefits of asbestos controls should therefore explicitly model both the "upstream" asbestos fiber supply and the many "downstream" asbestos-containing products themselves. This disaggregation and explicit modeling of these "vertically related" markets is doubly important, because the asbestos product bans to be analyzed will affect not only the products directly targeted, but also the market for asbestos fiber; this in turn affects the other nonbanned asbestos-containing products. None of this detail would be necessary if the risks posed by asbestos were the same regardless of the use to which it is put and if substitution costs were uniform, for then the entire analysis could

be conducted exclusively in the upstream fiber market. The fact is, however, that risks and costs do vary dramatically across the different asbestos-containing products, so this more complete vertically related market structure is appropriate.

BASIC STRUCTURE OF THE REGULATORY COST ANALYSIS

The primary task for the cost side of the analysis is to model the economic interactions between the asbestos fiber market and the numerous asbestos-containing product markets to calculate changes in producer and consumer surpluses that result from the various regulatory options. The essence of the approach for modeling these vertically related asbestos markets is as follows. In each asbestos-containing product market, demand and supply depend on many factors, such as the prices of alternatives and the costs of inputs used to make the product.

One input for each product of particular importance is asbestos fiber. Each product market can be thought of as generating a *derived demand* for fiber, based on the shapes and positions of the product's demand and supply functions. Conceptually, a product's derived demand for asbestos fiber can be drawn by (1) hypothetically raising and lowering the price of asbestos fiber, (2) tracing out alternative product supply functions associated with different underlying fiber prices, (3) translating the resulting product quantities into the implied quantity of asbestos fiber demanded at each fiber price, and (4) plotting the resulting pairs of asbestos fiber prices and quantities for the particular product market. This exercise is shown graphically in the bottom portion of Figure 2-1.[2]

[2] This procedure assumes that asbestos and other inputs are used in fixed proportions to manufacture asbestos-containing products, although these proportions differ from product to product. This is a restrictive form of derived demand, but one that largely fits the physical realities of asbestos products manufacturing.

FIGURE 2-1

Derived Demand and Price Determination in Vertically Related Asbestos Markets

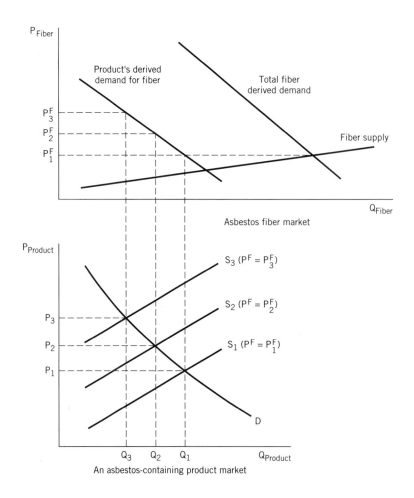

The bottom panel shows the demand for an asbestos-containing product and alternative supply functions for that product, depending on the price of asbestos fiber. The top panel depicts the market for asbestos fiber, including the derived demand for fiber for manufacturing the product shown in the bottom panel, the total asbestos fiber derived demand, and the supply of fiber.

Once the derived demand for asbestos fiber for each asbestos-containing product market has been estimated, these can be summed horizontally to yield the total demand for asbestos fi-ber, as shown in the top portion of Figure 2-1. The total derived demand for fiber and its supply determine the fiber price, P_1^F in this case. Once the price of fiber is known, the actual supply functions in each of the asbestos-containing product markets can be located. For the particular product market shown in the bottom portion of Figure 2-1, the supply function is S_1, which is the supply function consistent with the market price of asbestos fiber, P_1^F.

Given this construction of the vertically related asbestos markets, the influence of changes in one market on others is easy to see. Consider a decline in the demand for one asbestos-containing product. This will reduce the demand for asbestos fiber, resulting in a decrease in the market price of fiber and thereby translates to lower product prices in other downstream asbestos-containing product markets. Thus, changing conditions in one asbestos-containing product market, either exogenous or caused by some policy intervention, will affect all of these related markets.

Asbestos Fiber Phaseout: Applying this vertically related markets framework to the specific asbestos regulatory options is relatively easy, at least on a conceptual level. Figure 2-2 shows the asbestos fiber market (top panel) and one of the many markets that use fiber at a particular point in time (bottom panel). The fiber market panel shows the impact of a cap on the total usage of fiber (a one-year snapshot of the entire phasedown procedure), which reduces fiber consumption and production to $\overline{Q}$ from Q_0.

The result of this restriction of fiber usage translates into two effects of interest. First, the value of the right to purchase or use a unit of asbestos fiber—a *permit*— is positive if the quantity limitation in the fiber market is effective in reducing consumption.[3] That is, as long as $\overline{Q}$ is less than Q_0, these rights will be scarce. In fact, the value of a permit for one unit of asbetos fi-

FIGURE 2-2

Asbestos Fiber Use Phaseout

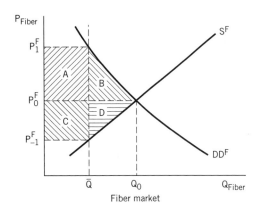

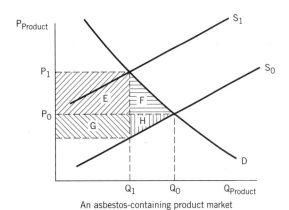

An asbestos-containing product market

In the top panel surplus losses due to a phaseout of asbestos use are measured in the asbestos fiber market. Asbestos demanders lose areas A and B, and supplies of fiber lose areas C and D. Areas A and B can also be measured in the many asbestos-containing product markets as consumer (areas E and F) and producer (areas G and H) surplus losses, as shown in the bottom panel.

---

[3] Permits are thought of here as rights to use or purchase asbestos, but they could just as well be defined as rights to sell asbestos fiber. Deciding which side of the market must possess a permit is a matter of transactions costs, administration, and enforcement. A slightly different issue is deciding which parties will initially reap the value of these permits. Depending on how the permits are distributed, their value could accrue to those who mine or import fiber, to those who purchase and use the fiber, or even to the government if it decides to sell the permits instead of allocating them to private sector entities.

ber is equal to the difference between P_1^F and P_{-1}^F. As shown in the top panel, P_1^F represents the value to users of the marginal unit of fiber— where total demand for fiber intersects the quantity limitation—and P_{-1}^F measures the marginal fiber supply price. The competitive producers of asbestos fiber bid down the supply price of fiber according to their particular cost conditions, given that asbestos fiber demanders now face the cost of having to possess permits in addition to the explicit price of asbestos fiber.

The second consequence is that the total cost of producing asbestos-containing products rises, which reflects the higher *full* price of fiber (where the full price equals the price of asbestos fiber itself plus the value of the permits to use fiber). This increased cost of production of asbestos-containing products is represented as an upward shift of the supply schedules in these output markets (S_0 to S_1 in the bottom panel).

This analysis assumes that the supplies of the output goods using asbestos fiber, at least in the short run and for the duration of the time horizon of the analysis, can be upward sloping. This reflects the fact that there can be *quasi rents*, or producer surpluses, that accrue to factors in these markets and that can be forfeited in the short run if the price that producers receive falls. For example, financial returns on assets such as a factory building or long-lived equipment specific to making asbestos-containing products are quasi rents that might be foregone for some period of time if no other economically viable use for these assets exists. Some asbestos-containing product supply curves could also be effectively perfectly elastic, especially if assets devoted to making these products are easily redeployed to alternative uses. In these cases, no producer surpluses exist to be lost in these markets. Instead, any regulatory costs borne in these markets will be shouldered by consumers alone.

Several shaded areas in these graphs are the central focus in determining the net cost of the fiber phaseout's quantity restriction as depicted in Figure 2-2. First of all, areas C and D in the asbestos fiber market measure the gross loss of producer surplus imposed on suppliers of fiber in their capacities as miners and millers of asbestos. This loss occurs because fiber supply is restricted and the received price is lower . Hence, relative to the unregulated situation, fiber suppliers are worse off by areas C and D. Of course, because the vast majority of asbestos fiber is imported to the United States, most of these losses are borne by foreign entities. This will be ignored, however, until the empirical results are presented. Hence, in this section the term *social* means, strictly speaking, the United States and the rest of the world.

Areas A and B in the fiber market measure the losses of producer and consumer surpluses in all of the downstream asbestos-containing product markets because of the higher full price of asbestos fiber. In the context of vertically related markets, areas under the upstream derived demand function for fiber are more than conventional consumer surpluses, because they measure both consumer surpluses and producer surpluses in downstream markets together. That is, areas E, F, G, and H in the product market shown in the bottom panel of Figure 2-2, summed over all such asbestos-containing product markets, exactly equal areas A and B in the asbestos fiber market.

The equivalence of areas A and B in the fiber market to the sum of all of the areas E, F, G, and H in the many product markets is reasonably intuitive. Recall that in constructing the derived demand for asbestos fiber, one imagines "calling out" higher and higher fiber prices and then summing up the quantities of fiber desired in each product market. The willingness to pay higher prices for asbestos fiber in a particular product market, however, depends not only on the demand for the product (consumer surplus), but also the potential losses producers might bear if they were unable to use asbestos (producer surplus). Hence, both of the sources willing to pay higher prices for fiber—consumer and producer surpluses—will be captured by the area below the derived demand function in the asbestos fiber market. Of course this also means that one should use either areas A and B in the fiber market *or* the sum of areas E, F, G, and H in all of the product markets to measure the downstream producer and consumer surplus losses caused by the asbestos phaseout restrictions, but not both, to avoid double-counting.

Not all of the gross losses of producer and consumer surpluses as measured by areas A, B, C, and D in the asbestos fiber market are necessarily net social welfare losses. In fact, areas A and C together measure the value of the permits that authorize the use of asbestos fiber up to the phaseout's quantity limitation. This area is simply the value of a permit multiplied by the number of permits. As a result, those to whom the permits are given, or the government if the permits are sold, are better off by the amount measured by areas A and C. Hence, the net cost to society in this particular year of the asbestos phaseout is simply areas B and D in the fiber market.

Asbestos-Containing Product Bans: Figure 2-3 shows the impact of banning one or more asbestos-containing products on the fiber market (top panel) and a banned market (bottom panel). The product ban regulatory option's mechanics are fairly easy to demonstrate. First, as shown in the bottom panel depicting a banned asbestos-containing product market in a particular year, all of the consumer and producer surpluses are lost for banned products. Areas A and B across all banned products are thus the first component of this year's social costs of the product ban regulatory option.

Next, the price of asbestos fiber falls because the derived demand for fiber for banned prod-

FIGURE 2-3

Asbestos Product Ban

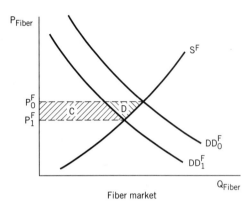

Fiber market

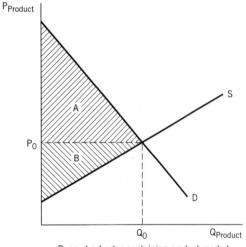

Banned asbestos-containing product market

Net surplus losses caused by a ban on an asbestos-containing product are the consumer and producer surplus losses, shown in the bottom panel areas A and B, and area D in the top panel, which reflects the total fiber supplier–producer surplus loss of areas C and D, minus area C, which is gained by remaining asbestos fiber users because of the asbestos price decline.

ucts declines to zero. In the top panel of Figure 2-3, the fiber-market derived demand is shifted inward to reflect this.[4] Because asbestos fiber supply is upward-sloping, the price of fiber falls from P_0^F to P_1^F. This decline in the price of fiber generates a gross loss of fiber market producer surplus, measured by the sum of areas C and D. But some of this lost producer surplus is regained by consumers of nonbanned asbestos-containing products. Following the earlier discussion of the construction of derived demand functions, area C measures the gain in surpluses in nonbanned downstream markets, so this area represents a transfer. Hence, the total social cost of the asbestos product ban option in the year depicted is the sum of all of the areas A and B in the banned markets plus area D in the asbestos fiber market.

Combinations of Asbestos Fiber Phaseout and Product Bans: Figure 2-4 shows the impact in a particular year of combining the two types of policies by banning one or more asbestos-containing products and, at the same time, imposing a quantity limitation on total asbestos fiber use. As before, banning some products shifts the derived demand for fiber downward, as shown in the top panel. A limitation on the total fiber usage is then imposed on the recomputed derived demand (DD_1^F), shown as $\overline{Q}$. The product bans by themselves would reduce the quantity of asbestos fiber sold from Q_0 to $\hat{Q}$, while the phaseout's quantity cap further reduces fiber consumption and production from $\hat{Q}$ to $\overline{Q}$.

Measuring surplus changes for this combination of the two types of regulations can be done in two stages. First, impose conceptually the product ban portion of the combined regulatory option and measure the losses of consumer and producer surpluses in the banned product mar-

kets as areas E and F, as shown for a representative banned market in Figure 2-4. At this point, one could then elect to measure the loss in asbestos fiber producer surplus and the transfers

FIGURE 2-4

Combined Fiber Phaseout and Product Ban

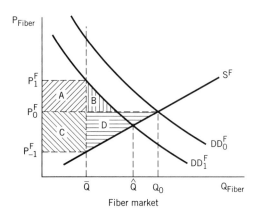

Fiber market

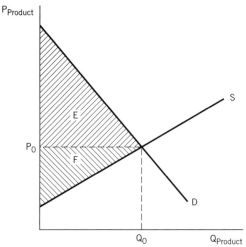

Banned asbestos-containing product market

The product ban causes the surplus losses in the bottom panel and the shift of the asbestos fiber derived demand in the top panel. The additional welfare losses in the fiber market are shown in the top panel as areas B and D. Areas A and C are transfers from asbestos demanders and suppliers to permit owners.

[4] The area between the pre- and post-ban asbestos derived demand functions in the top panel down to the original fiber price is another (redundant) way to measure the loss of producer and consumer surpluses in the banned asbestos-containing product markets.

from them to producers and consumers of nonbanned asbestos-containing products. However, because the phaseout restriction will erase any welfare gains for nonbanned markets and induce further fiber market producer surplus losses, it is simpler to bypass this intermediate step and to directly impose the fiber quantity restriction and then measure the welfare effects felt in the fiber market.

The top panel of Figure 2-4 shows the total impact of both the product bans and the phaseout restriction on producers of asbestos fiber and producers and consumers of nonbanned products. Fiber market producers lose areas C and D because the net price they receive drops from P_0^F to P_{-1}^F and the quantity they supply declines from Q_0 to $\overline{Q}$. Producers and consumers of nonbanned products lose areas A and B because of the increase in the full price of asbestos fiber from P_0^F to P_1^F, reflecting the need to possess permits to purchase asbestos fiber under the phaseout. As before, areas A and B in the fiber market can be measured equivalently in all of the nonbanned asbestos-containing product markets. Finally, those who own the permits that enforce the phaseout, or the government if permits are auctioned rather than allocated to market participants, gain areas A and C. Hence, the net cost in this year of the combined regulatory intervention is the sum of the banned markets' areas E and F and areas B and D in the fiber market.

Regulatory Cost Simulation Model: To this point, all that has really been presented is the basic welfare measurement apparatus to be used in estimating changes in producer and consumer surpluses caused by the alternative asbestos regulatory approaches. These procedures, however, must be applied in each year of the timeframe of the analysis, which was over ten years in the case of asbestos. Furthermore, as indicated above, there are numerous different asbestos-containing product markets with different substitution, risk, and other characteristics. It is also possible to specify many unique

regulatory policies by varying the years in which individual products are banned, by beginning and ending the fiber phaseout at different times, and by allowing for specific product exemptions to the phaseout. Finally, the baseline conditions in the various asbestos markets can change over time as markets grow or contract, thereby changing the underlying asbestos fiber price and the producer and consumer surpluses in the many asbestos-containing product markets.

Clearly, there are too many variables and policies for simple hand calculations of the welfare impacts of the many possible asbestos regulatory options to be feasible. To overcome this computational difficulty, a computer simulation model of the asbestos markets and the effects of regulatory policies on them was developed. This model's operation is fairly easy to describe. Conceptually speaking, the model begins by using the shapes and positions of the demand and supply functions for each asbestos-containing product to develop a derived-demand function for asbestos fiber for each market. These are then summed horizontally to generate the total asbestos fiber derived demand, which, along with the asbestos fiber supply function, yields the baseline equilibrium price of fiber, and hence the prices of all of the asbestos-containing products. This computation is done for each year of the simulation period after accounting for underlying rates of increased or decreased production in each product market.

This entire process is then repeated, but with the addition of any regulatory policies in effect in each year. For example, if some markets are banned in a particular year, the total asbestos fiber derived demand will be lower than for the same year in the baseline simulation. This results in a decrease in the asbestos fiber price and a decline in the quantity of fiber purchased; this in turn feeds back into the nonbanned product markets. Similarly, a fiber quantity restriction's effects on prices and quantities can be computed directly, based on the relevant asbestos fiber derived-demand function (accounting for any product bans) and the allowed fiber supply. The higher full price fiber is then fed back to the as-bestos-containing product markets to determine their new prices and quantities.

Finally, the model compares the baseline and policy-scenario price and quantity results for all markets in each year of the simulation and computes all of the various areas of surplus gains and losses as enumerated above. These results are then summed and discounted to generate various disaggregated and summary regulatory cost results.

Of course, welfare measurement apparatus and simulation modeling cannot generate empirical results without accurate input information. Hence, before turning to the benefits portion of the analysis, it is instructive to explore the sources and nature of the data available for this type of modeling.

DATA INPUTS FOR THE COST ANALYSIS

In practical applications of environmental economics to policy issues, developing the data required to make a theoretical framework yield quantitative results is often a far larger task than constructing the measurement apparatus in the first place. The familiar expression "garbage in, garbage out" is a crude way of emphasizing the importance of accurate input information for obtaining reliable empirical results. However, moving from the purely technical aspects of how to measure welfare changes to actually obtaining quantitative results is not nearly as simple as one would hope. The theoretical apparatus for measuring surplus changes as developed above would be disarmingly simple to apply in practice if one really could always open a *Book of Elasticities*, copy down those needed, and then place them in the demand and supply framework and simulation model to generate numerical results. The problem is that this *Book* does not exist, and in many cases there is really no hope of ever estimating the required elasticities. While one does have access to elasticities in some areas of interest in public policy, such as agri-culture and labor, environmental regulations often target substances or activities such as industrial emissions to air and water, which are not tracked by market transactions, so that data on quantities are frequently sparse and prices rarely mean anything concrete and recordable.

But if one cannot expect to find or estimate the elasticities needed to obtain quantitative results using the theoretical framework, what does one do? The asbestos analysis provides at least one answer to this question, perhaps a crude substitute for having reliable elasticities, but certainly better than no input information at all. It is also indicative of what sorts of rough edges one must accept in most practical applications of cost–benefit analysis.

Asbestos-Containing Product Demand Functions: One of the most important of the many empirical inputs needed to generate quantitative estimates of the impacts of the various asbestos regulatory options is the demand functions for the asbestos-containing products. Given the types of products that use asbestos, such as friction materials, concrete products, and a wide variety of coatings and related goods, published elasticities of demand are unlikely to exist and would be extremely difficult to try to estimate. For example, imagine trying to estimate the demand for asbestos-based vehicle brake pads. Even if quantity and price information were available, one would still not expect any significant demand variation related to brake pad prices, given the very small portion of the cost of a vehicle, or even the cost of a brake servicing job, that the pad represents. Any brake pad quantity variation would be related mostly to changes in the historical volumes of vehicles produced, not to changes in the price of asbestos brake pads. Econometric estimation of the price elasticity of brake pads would tend to find it infinitely inelastic within the range of historical variation of prices and quantities of pads. But the price elasticity of brake pads cannot really be infinitely inelastic for large increases in prices, especially for those that might be caused by the asbestos phaseout, much less the implicitly infinite price increase associated with a brake pad product ban. These price increases are outside the historical variation of brake pad prices, so econometric estimation is not useful.

In place of elasticities, one often uses the results of a *use-and-substitutes* analysis. This is an in-depth examination of each significant use of the substance in question, asbestos in this case, and an assessment of the costs, performance, and useful life of substitutes, on a product-by-product basis. For example, one use of asbestos is in making asbestos cement (A/C) pipe. The asbestos use-and-substitutes analysis for this product identified a number of specific applications of A/C pipe, based on the characteristics of the particular use of the pipe. Two major substitutes for A/C pipe were also identified, based on the ability of each substitute to satisfy specific requirements asbestos-based piping currently fulfills. One, polyvinylchloride (PVC) pipe, could be used in place of A/C pipe in most segments, and costs some $2 more per foot, or 20 percent more than A/C pipe. The other substitute, ductile iron pipe, would be required in some uses because of high-pressure requirements. This ductile iron substitute costs almost $7 more per foot, or 70 percent more than A/C pipe.

Thus, the task of the asbestos use-and-substitutes analysis was to define markets and segments of markets that are relatively homogeneous, assess the cost of the asbestos-based products, identify the most appropriate substitutes, and estimate the incremental cost of the substitutes in each specific application. In general, it is fairly labor intensive to gather the necessary information on uses and substitutes for a substance such as asbestos or for alternatives to, or controls for, any potential regulatory target. One must explore the products and technologies in some detail and consult a variety of published sources as well as engage in primary data collection, and in some cases communicate directly with industry sources to obtain whatever data exist.

One can then use the results of a reasonably comprehensive use-and-substitutes analysis to generate crude demand functions, as was done for each asbestos-containing product market. Essentially, a *step function* was plotted for each product based on the incremental cost of each segment's substitute and the portion of the overall product market for which each substitute would be used if the price of the asbestos product were to rise enough to cause producers and consumers to switch to the substitutes. Figure 2-5 shows such a stepped demand function for the A/C pipe market. As shown, the baseline quantity of A/C pipe produced is some 15 million feet at a cost of about $9 per foot. The figure shows that most A/C pipe could be replaced by PVC piping if the price of A/C pipe were to rise to the $11 per foot range. The remaining segment of the market would then adopt ductile iron pipe if the price of A/C pipe were to increase even more to the $16 per foot range.

A few comments about this procedure are in order. First, if this seems somewhat crude, given the many details and nuances of demand theory, indeed, it is quite primitive, but it is better than nothing at all, which is the relevant alternative. The method is also broadly consistent with the spirit of demand functions in that it does try to determine what substitution away from particular products will occur at different price increases. This is the nature of demand functions, except that in theoretical or econometric formulations, smooth substitution for a product is normally allowed. The stepped demand function formulation allows for substitution in blocks, rather than smoothly along a downward-sloping curve.

What this means is that the actual losses of surpluses due to a product ban or a fiber phaseout will probably be less than those estimated using this rougher method. There are limits to the amount of information one can gather and practical limitations to providing ever increasing details and subdivisions for each market, so it is inevitable that the smoother substitution

FIGURE 2-5

Stepped Demand Function for A/C Pipe Based on Use-and-Substitutes Analysis

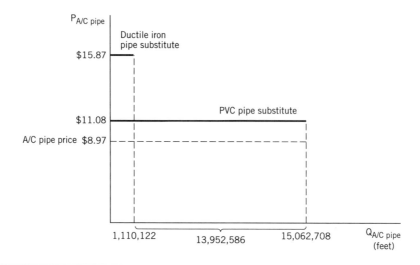

A "stepped" demand function for A/C pipe resulting from a use-and-substitutes analysis reflects the "lumpi-ness" of demand-side information in many applications. If A/C pipe were banned, the lower cost substitute, PVC pipe, would capture most of the market, with the remainder serviced by ductile iron piping.

possibilities that will actually occur cannot be measured and incorporated. But at least the error is on the side of higher costs rather than underestimated costs.

Second, while the method is fairly basic, it is less crude than one might think given that the asbestos products in question are mostly pro-ducer goods or small components of far larger and more costly products. Brakes for an auto-mobile are a very small component of the total cost of the vehicle. Moreover, without significant innovations in automobile design, the need for friction-based braking systems is unlikely to dis-appear. Hence, one would not expect significant incremental substitution away from asbestos-based braking systems as the price of asbestos increases. Many environmental regulations tar-get producer activities and intermediate goods rather than final consumer goods; therefore rela-

tively straightforward stepped demand func-tions based on use-and-substitutes analyses are not necessarily as inaccurate as one might at first think.

Third, there is one less-obvious advantage to conducting a use-and-substitutes analysis and then using the results to generate rough demand functions for products or activities. In most cases of real-world regulatory analyses, decision mak-ers want some idea of what producers and con-sumers are going to use or do after the regula-tions are promulgated. In the case of asbestos this was especially important because of the pos-sibility that some of the substitutes for asbestos could be more harmful than asbestos itself, de-pending on use conditions. Regulators are asked to predict "who will do what differently" in re-sponse to a regulation, in addition to being re-quired to calculate its economic costs and benefits. Having to conduct a use-and-substitutes analysis to define markets and substitutes and to develop demand functions provides this extra information for decision makers as a byproduct.

Conversely, a hidden cost of using whatever econometric estimates of demand elasticities one can find is that they do not reveal what alternatives are supposedly being adopted as substitution occurs. While using existing or estimated elasticities of demand is very convenient in obtaining quantitative results from a theoretical apparatus, this does not eliminate the necessity of "going behind" the elasticities to determine what the regulated parties are doing differently as they substitute away from the targeted activity.

Finally, constructing demand functions for products based on substitution costs and characteristics is clearly the standard approach for analyzing regulations that target substances or activities that feed into many products or other activities, as does asbestos, and in which the regulatory options contemplated mostly seek to eliminate the substance. But other types of regulations often require emission treatment technologies, limit effluent, or otherwise regulate practices rather than banning them. Nevertheless, the same basic idea applies. Suppose a regulation seeks to place maximum concentration limitations on an effluent from an industry or plant. In this event, one would set about assessing what the industry or plant can do to comply with the regulation. Alternative treatment technologies, waste reduction activities, and various other methods of satisfying the regulation's requirements would be identified and analyzed to determine their feasibility, effectiveness, and cost, so the fundamental approach for the analysis is the same.

A summary of the quantitative results of the asbestos use-and-substitutes analysis is presented in four extensive tables. Table 2-2 lists the 1985 values for a number of asbestos-containing product market characteristics using the cat-

egories identified earlier in Table 2-1. Particularly relevant for the analysis are production volumes, prices, product lifetimes, the ratio of consumption to production (to measure product imports), and the amount of asbestos in tons per unit of the product (the asbestos product coefficient). Several of the products are listed as "not modeled" due to lack of sufficient information about substitutes. Hence, these are not included in the cost model simulations.

The information in Table 2-2 is for the year 1985, the first year of the modeling time horizon. But because the analysis extends through to the year 2000, the cost-modeling process requires information about the future baseline values for the items contained in Table 2-2. In essence, the asbestos product market characteristics must be projected into the future under the assumption that no regulations on asbetos use are promulgated. Asbestos product baseline projections reflect both assumptions about future growth rates and additional data indicating that between 1985 and the time the analysis was completed (1988), declines in the production volumes of some asbestos-containing product categories had occurred. For example, production of vinyl-asbestos floor tile, flooring felt, and corrugated paper had all declined to zero over that period, and volumes for the coatings, plastics, and packings had fallen substantially.

Future production volumes for all of the asbestos products, with the exception of the vehicle brake categories, were therefore projected in several ways, reflecting either an assumption of no change or a simple time trend for each product, based on the observed change from 1981 to 1985. Product growth rates between 1981 and 1985 were negative in virtually every case, but it was unclear how to allocate responsibility for these trends to the threat of regulation versus other truly baseline, nonregulatory factors. Hence, in addition to a scenario based on the observed 1981 to 1985 rates of production volume decline for asbestos-containing products, a *moderate decline* scenario was used under which

Table 2-2
ASBESTOS-CONTAINING PRODUCTS DATA

Product Category	1985 Quantity	1985 Price ($/unit)	Consumption/ Production Ratio	Product Asbestos Coefficient	Life of Asbestos Product (years)
1. Commercial Paper	0 tons	n/a	n/a	n/a	n/a
2. Rollboard	0 tons	n/a	n/a	n/a	n/a
3. Millboard	581 tons	1,760.00	1.0050	0.7500861	25.0
4. Pipeline Wrap	296,949 squares	5.80	2.5000	0.0044900	25.0
5. Beater-add Gaskets	16,505 tons	1,500.00	1.0200	0.7534929	5.0
6. High-grade Electrical Paper	698 tons	5,060.00	1.0000	1.0659026	3.0
7. Roofing Felt[a]	283,200 tons	6.65	Imports Only	0.0045000	18.0
8. Acetylene Cylinders	392,121 pieces	90.00	1.0000	0.0014896	1.0
9. Flooring Felt	0 tons	n/a	n/a	n/a	n/a
10. Corrugated Paper	0 tons	n/a	n/a	n/a	n/a
11. Specialty Papers	434 tons	4,300.00	1.0000	0.2122120	1.0[b]
12. Vinyl-Asbestos Floor Tile	18,300,000 sq. yards	n/a	1.0000	0.0005700	[c]
13. Asbestos Diaphragms	9,770 pieces	215.87	1.0000	0.1000000	1.0[b]
14. Asbestos-Cement Pipe	15,062,708 feet	8.94	1.0128	0.0021703	50.0
15. Flat A-C Sheets	22,621 squares	181.00	1.1500	0.1140003	25.0
16. Corrugated A-C Sheets[a]	3,859 squares	277.00	Imports Only	0.0855000	30.0
17. A-C Shingles	176,643 squares	113.00	1.3700	0.0220388	40.0
18. Drum Brake Linings (OEM)	34,713,675 pieces	0.63	1.1500	0.0001913	4.0
19. Disc Brake Pads, LMV (OEM)	10,077,464 pieces	0.42	1.1900	0.0001081	4.0
20. Disc Brake Pads (HV)	156,820 pieces	10.00	1.0000	0.0007499	0.5
21. Brake Blocks	4,570,266 pieces	5.74	1.0100	0.0005784	0.5
22. Clutch Facings	7,237,112 pieces	1.71	1.1200	0.0001373	5.0
23. Automatic Transmission Components	585,500 pieces	1.60	1.0000	0.0000043	5.5
24. Friction Materials	8,719,541 pieces	34.65	1.0000	0.0001838	0.5
25. Asbestos Protective Clothing	0 tons	n/a	n/a	n/a	n/a
26. Asbestos Thread, Yarn, and Other Cloth	1,125 tons	3,300.00	1.5110	0.4960000	1.0
27. Asbestos Sheet Gasketing	3,607,408 sq. yards	5.69	1.0700	0.0015083	5.0
28. Asbestos Packing	3 tons	60,400.00	1.0000	0.7000000	1.0
29. Roof Coatings and Cements	75,977,365 gallons	2.49	1.0000	0.0003889	10.0
30. Non-Roofing Coatings, Compounds, and Sealants	9,612,655 gallons	13.90	1.0000	0.0003070	10.0
31. Asbestos-Reinforced Plastics	4,835 tons	5,260.00	1.0300	0.1679628	1.0
32. Missile Liner	4,667 tons	14,000.00	1.0000	0.1499893	1.0[b]
33. Sealant Tape	423,048,539 feet	0.07	1.0000	0.0000039	20.0
34. Battery Separators[d]	—	—	—	—	—
35. Arc Chutes[d]	—	—	—	—	—
36. Drum Brake Linings (A/M)	94,328,903 pieces	0.63	1.1500	0.0001913	4.0
37. Disc Brake Pads, LMV (A/M)	55,791,708 pieces	0.42	1.1900	0.0001081	4.0

Source: ICF Incorporated 1989. "Regulatory Impact Analysis of Controls on Asbestos Products," Volume I, Table III-8.
[a] Quantity reported for 1985 is imports only.
[b] Life is one use.
[c] Product is no longer made or sold in the United States.
[d] This product is not included in the simulations.

these rates of production volume declines were halved. Table 2-3 lists the low-, moderate-, and high-decline baseline growth rate scenarios for asbestos products. The vehicle brake baseline production volume growth rates, in contrast, were derived using projections of new vehicle sales and recent trends in asbestos brake component sales, and estimates of future aftermarket brake repair volumes, based on the stock of existing vehicles, brake lifetimes, and vehicle retirement rates. These are shown in Table 2-4.

Finally, the substitutes information for asbestos products generated by the use-and-substitutes analysis is summarized in Table 2-5, where nonasbestos product substitutes are listed along with their costs, useful lives, and the proportion of the asbestos-based product market for which each is considered the most viable technical substitute. Where the useful life of a particular alternative is different from the asbestos version of the product, its cost is adjusted to an annualized equivalent cost over the life of the asbestos product.

Producer Surplus Estimation: As with demand elasticities, the general rule is that elasticities of supply for the products or activities subject to regulatory intervention will be unavailable in practice. One common response to this situation is to assume that the supplies are all infinitely elastic. For purely theoretical or expository purposes this is often satisfactory, but for actual quantitative modeling of the impacts of regulations, such an assumption often cannot be justified. But if one has no supply elasticity estimates, how can potential producer surplus losses be calculated?

The solution in practice is normally to carefully consider exactly what gives rise to producer surpluses in the first place. Analytically, producer surpluses are depicted as areas above supply functions and below the market price, as shown in the figures earlier in this chapter. Those areas mean that the owners of some inputs involved in supplying the product or activity in question are willing to accept lower compensation and still remain devoted to that use. Hence, in the absence of estimated supply elasticities, one should search directly for the inputs that would be willing to accept lower compensation—this is all that an upward sloping supply function really means.

Applying this direct approach in the asbestos analysis revealed that of the inputs involved in supplying the various products, the most likely source of producer surplus was the capital equipment devoted to making asbestos-containing products and the suppliers of asbestos fiber itself. Focusing on the asbestos-containing product suppliers, a central issue in computing producer surpluses was whether or not the capital equipment could be converted to alternative uses and, if so, at what cost and potential loss of productivity.

For example, an asbestos-cement pipe factory could be converted to producing non-asbestos piping products, but doing might require some additional investment and asbestos clean-up and removal, and the equipment might be less productive in making non-asbestos products. These are the sources of potential producer surplus losses in the A/C pipe product market, for otherwise, A/C pipe producers would redeploy their capital equipment without suffering any decreased profit. Equipment in other product markets, however, might be completely specific to making asbestos-based products. In this case, owners of the equipment would be willing to continue to produce using the equipment as long as their variable costs are covered, so that here potential producer surplus losses are essentially the current value of this stock of capital equipment.

Through a variety of engineering process and equipment cost modeling and data collection, the transferability of equipment in each asbestos-containing product market was evaluated. Where equipment was deemed to be convert-

Table 2-3
BASELINE GROWTH RATES OF ASBESTOS PRODUCTS: 1985–2000

	Growth Rates, 1985–2000 (%)		
Product Category	Low Decline	Moderate Decline	High Decline
1. Commercial Paper	n/a	n/a	n/a
2. Rollboard	n/a	n/a	n/a
3. Millboard	0.00	-16.15	-32.31
4. Pipeline Wrap	0.00	-19.51	-39.03
5. Beater-Add Gaskets	0.00	-5.39	-10.77
6. High-Grade Electrical Paper	0.00	-0.14	-0.28
7. Roofing Felt	0.00	0.00	0.00
8. Acetylene Cylinders	0.00[a]	-8.41[a]	-16.82[a]
9. Flooring Felt	n/a	n/a	n/a
10. Corrugated Paper	n/a	n/a	n/a
11. Specialty Paper	0.00	-16.25	-32.50
12. V/A Floor Tile	n/a	n/a	n/a
13. Asbestos Diaphragms	0.00	0.00	0.00
14. A/C Pipe	0.00	-5.98	-11.95
15. A/C Sheet, Flat	0.00[b]	-26.36[b]	-52.72[b]
16. A/C Sheet, Corrugated	0.00	0.00	0.00
17. A/C Shingles	0.00	-4.89	-9.78
18. Drum Brake Linings (OEM)	[c]	[c]	[c]
19. Disc Brake Pads, LMV (OEM)	[c]	[c]	[c]
20. Disc Brake Pads (HV)	0.00	-17.67	-35.33
21. Brake Blocks	0.00	-15.96	-31.93
22. Clutch Facings	0.00	-0.27	-0.54
23. Automatic Transmission Components	0.00[d]	0.00[d]	0.00[d]
24. Friction Materials	0.00	-8.13	-16.26
25. Asbestos Protective Clothing	n/a	n/a	n/a
26. Asbestos Thread, etc.	0.00	-16.96	-33.92
27. Sheet Gaskets	0.00	-11.59	-23.17
28. Asbestos Packing	0.00[e]	-14.92[e]	-29.84[e]
29. Roof Coatings	0.00[f]	-0.76[f]	-1.53[f]
30. Non-Roofing Coatings	0.00[g]	-13.94[g]	-27.89[g]
31. Asbestos-Reinforced Plastics	0.00[h]	-10.48[h]	-20.96[h]
32. Missile Liner	0.00	0.00	0.00
33. Sealant Tape	0.00	3.27	6.54
34. Battery Separators[i]	—	—	—
35. Arc Chutes[i]	—	—	—
36. Drum Brake Linings (A/M)	[c]	[c]	[c]
37. Disc Brake Pads, LMV (A/M)	[c]	[c]	[c]

Source: ICF Incorporated, 1989. "Regulatory Impact Analysis of Controls on Asbestos Products," Volume I, Table III-9.
[a] Growth rate for 1985–86 is -21.42%.
[b] Growth rate for 1985–86 is -77.17%.
[c] Growth rates for this category are based on the Brakes Model and are different for each year. See Table 2-4 for all growth rates.
[d] Growth rate for 1985–86 is -54.70%, 1986–87 is -78.30%, and 1987–88 is -4.40%.
[e] Growth rate for 1985–86 is -66.67%.
[f] Growth rate for 1985–86 is -26.33%.
[g] Growth rate for 1985–86 is -19.41%.
[h] Growth rate for 1985–86 is -12.10%.
[i] This product is not included in the simulations.

Table 2-4
BASELINE GROWTH RATES FOR OEM AND A/M BRAKE MARKETS: 1985–2000

Growth Rates, 1985–2000 (%)

Year	18. Drum Brake Linings (OEM)			19. Disc Brake Pads, LMV (OEM)			36. Drum Brake Linings (A/M)			37. Disc Brake Pads, LMV (A/M)		
	Low Decline	Moderate Decline	High Decline	Low Decline	Moderate Decline	High Decline	Low Decline	Moderate Decline	High Decline	Low Decline	Moderate Decline	High Decline
1985–1986[a]	1.52	1.52	1.52	-54.05	-54.05	-54.05	-3.54	-3.54	-3.54	-6.25	-6.25	-6.25
1986–1987	3.56	-7.94	-17.15	3.57	-17.14	-30.95	-8.66	-8.66	-8.66	-7.04	-7.04	-7.04
1987–1988	0.59	-11.98	-24.56	0.54	-24.60	-49.73	6.46	6.46	6.46	-1.36	-1.36	-1.36
1988–1989	-1.94	-15.95	-34.63	-1.92	-34.62	-100.00	-0.16	-0.16	-0.16	-4.07	-4.07	-4.07
1989–1990	-7.87	-23.22	-53.93	-7.89	-53.94	0.00	-1.45	-1.45	-1.45	-18.35	-18.35	-18.35
1990–1991	-3.18	-22.55	-100.00	-3.16	-100.00	0.00	-1.95	-6.48	-10.11	-6.64	-9.13	-10.79
1991–1992	11.51	-16.37	0.00	11.57	0.00	0.00	4.85	0.18	-3.90	-4.15	-7.03	-9.04
1992–1993	6.46	-29.03	0.00	6.44	0.00	0.00	-0.02	-4.61	-8.98	-8.57	-11.87	-14.29
1993–1994	-5.83	-52.92	0.00	-5.92	0.00	0.00	-3.45	-7.40	-11.53	-22.28	-26.73	-24.82
1994–1995	-3.23	-100.00	0.00	-3.27	0.00	0.00	-0.80	-9.93	-20.35	-5.83	-14.25	-13.31
1995–1996	6.89	0.00	0.00	6.95	0.00	0.00	7.26	-4.84	-7.58	-1.93	-9.86	-13.39
1996–1997	8.68	0.00	0.00	8.69	0.00	0.00	2.70	-10.37	-12.65	-6.99	-16.47	-21.18
1997–1998	-2.40	0.00	0.00	-2.47	0.00	0.00	-4.62	-16.05	-16.39	-19.60	-32.36	-29.38
1998–1999	-5.26	0.00	0.00	-5.31	0.00	0.00	-1.59	-19.15	-26.97	-4.02	-18.12	-14.70
1999–2000	4.61	0.00	0.00	4.59	0.00	0.00	7.43	-7.92	-11.25	1.77	-12.76	-18.05

Source: ICF Incorporated, 1989. "Regulatory Impact Analysis of Controls on Asbestos Products," Volume I, Table III-10.
[a]Growth rates for 1985–86 are based on actual information.

Table 2-5
SUBSTITUTES INFORMATION FOR ASBESTOS-CONTAINING PRODUCTS

Product Category / Substitute Name	Price	Useful Life	Market Share
1. *Commercial Paper*	n/a	n/a	n/a
2. *Rollboard*	n/a	n/a	n/a
3. *Millboard*			
Standard Board	$2,560/ton	25 years	80%
Premium Board	$6,800/ton	25 years	20%
4. *Pipeline Wrap*			
Mineral Felt	$5.80/square	25 years	48%
Safelt(R)	$6.20/square	25 years	32%
Duraglass(R)	$5.80/square	25 years	20%
5. *Beater-Add Gaskets*			
Cellulose	$1,800/ton	5 years	25%
Aramid	$3,380/ton	5 years	30%
Fibrous Glass	$3,000/ton	5 years	20%
PTFE	$5,240/ton	5 years	10%
Graphite	$3,000/ton	5 years	10%
Ceramic	$4,500/ton	5 years	5%
6. *Electrical Paper*			
Aramid Paper	$10.48/lb.	3 years	80%
Ceramic Paper	$7.04/lb.	3 years	20%
7. *Asbestos Felt*			
Fiberglass Felt	$3.85/square	18 years	40%
Modified Bitumen	$7.48/square	18 years	50%
Single-Ply Membrane	$29.26/square	18 years	10%
8. *Acetylene Cylinders*			
Glass Fiber Filler	$93.00/ton	1 per cylinder	100%
9. *Flooring Felt*	n/a	n/a	n/a
10. *Corrugated Paper*	n/a	n/a	n/a
11. *Specialty Papers*			
Diatomaceous Earth and Cellulose Filter Paper	$4,000/ton	1 use	50%
Loose Cellulose Fiber Filter Paper	$2,000/ton	1 use	50%
12. *Vinyl-Asbestos Floor Tile*	n/a	n/a	n/a
13. *Asbestos Diaphragms*			
Mercury and Membrane Cells	n/a	n/a	n/a
14. *A/C Pipe and Fittings*			
PVC Pipe	$11.08/foot	50 years	92.63%
Ductile Iron Pipe	$15.87/foot	50 years	7.37%
15. *A/C Flat Sheet*			
Calcium Silicate Construction/Utility Flat Sheet	$182/square	25 years	76%
Non-Calcium Silicate Construction/Utility Flat Sheet	$417/square	25 years	4%
Substitute Laboratory Work Sheet	$217/square	25 years	20%

Table 2-5 (Continued)
SUBSTITUTES INFORMATION FOR ASBESTOS-CONTAINING PRODUCTS

Product Category / Substitute Name	Price	Useful Life	Market Share
16. *Corrugated A/C Sheet*			
FRP	$246 / square	20 years	48%
Aluminum	$188 / square	20 years	32%
Steel	$157 / square	15 years	11%
PVC	$301 / square	20 years	9%
17. *A/C Shingles*			
Wood Siding and Roofing	$162 / square	30 years	32%
Vinyl Siding	$106 / square	50 years	27%
Asphalt Roofing Shingles	$49 / square	20 years	20%
Aluminum Siding	$128 / square	50 years	19%
Tile Roofing	$173 / square	50 years	2%
18. *Drum Brake Linings (OEM)*			
NAO	$0.79 / piece	5 years	99%
Semi-Metallic	$1.09 / piece	4 years	1%
19. *Disc Brake Pads, LMV (OEM)*			
Semi-Metallic	$0.67 / piece	7.4 years	100%
20. *Disc Brake Pads (Heavy Vehicles)*			
Semi-Metallic	$12.50 / piece	0.75 years	100%
21. *Brake Blocks*			
NAO	$8.04 / piece	0.65 years	99.5%
Full-Metallic	$6.89 / piece	0.5 years	0.5%
22. *Clutch Facings*			
Woven Fiberglass (European Product)	$2.92 / piece	7.5 years	50%
Woven Fiberglass (U.S. Product)	$2.92 / piece	7.5 years	30%
Molded Aramid Fiber, Fiberglass, Cellulose and Ceramic Fiber (Nuturn's Product)	$2.55 / piece	6.25 years	10%
Molded Fiberglass	$2.55 / piece	6.25 years	10%
23. *Automatic Transmission Components*			
Cellulose	$2.00 / piece	4–7 years	100%
24. *Friction Materials*			
Fiberglass and Kevlar(R)	$34.65 / piece	0.5 years	100%
25. *Protective Clothing*	n/a	n/a	n/a
26. *Asbestos Textiles*			
Glass Fiber Mixtures	$ 3,460 / ton	1 year	50%
Ceramic Fiber Mixtures	$ 7,920 / ton	1 year	15%
Aramid Fiber Mixtures	$19,800 / ton	1 year	15%
Carbon Fiber Mixtures	$52,800 / ton	1 year	10%
PBI Fiber Mixtures	$79,200 / ton	1 year	10%

Table 2-5 (Continued)
SUBSTITUTES INFORMATION FOR ASBESTOS-CONTAINING PRODUCTS

Product Category/ Substitute Name	Price	Useful Life	Market Share
27. *Sheet Gaskets*			
Aramid	$9.72/sq. yd.	5 years	30%
Fibrous Glass	$11.38/sq. yd.	5 years	25%
Graphite	$11.38/sq. yd.	5 years	15%
Cellulose	$6.83/sq. yd.	5 years	15%
PTFE	$19.91/sq. yd.	5 years	10%
Ceramic	$11.38/sq. yd.	5 years	5%
28. *Asbestos Packings*			
Aramid	$135,900/ton	1 year	30%
Fibrous Glass	$120,800/ton	1 year	30%
PTFE	$211,400/ton	1 year	15%
Graphite	$120,800/ton	1 year	10%
PBI	$181,200/ton	1 year	15%
29. *Roof Coatings*			
Cellulose Mixture	$2.95/gal.	10 years	87.42%
Polyethylene Mixture	$3.36/gal.	10 years	7.62%
Other Mixtures	$3.03/gal.	10 years	4.95%
30. *Non-Roofing Coatings*			
Fiber Mixture	$15.10/gal.	10 yrs	70%
Non-Fiber Mixture	$14.42/gal.	10 yrs	30%
31. *Asbestos-Reinforced Plastics*			
Glass-Reinforced Plastic	$1.40/lb.	1 year	47.9%
Teflon-Reinforced Plastic	$2.25/lb.	1 year	42.5%
Product X	$11.22/lb.	1 year	7.4%
Porcelain	$4.08/lb.	1 year	1.4%
Silica-Reinforced Plastic	$3.00/lb.	1 year	0.5%
Carbon-Reinforced Plastic	$47.25/lb.	1 year	0.3%
32. *Missile Liner*			
Kevlar(R) Liner	$ 29,000/ton	1 use	80%
Ceramic Fiber Liner	$140,000/ton	1 use	20%
33. *Sealant Tape*			
Cellulose Tape	$0.05/ft.	15 years	56.4%
Structural Urethane	$0.07/ft.	20 years	36.8%
Carbon-Based Tape	$0.32/ft.	20 years	6.6%
Non-Curing Tape	$0.10/ft.	n/a	0.2%
34. *Battery Separators*	n/a	n/a	n/a
35. *Arc Chutes*	n/a	n/a	n/a
36. *Drum Brake Linings (Aftermarket)*			
NAO	$0.79/piece	5 years	99%
Semi-Metallic	$1.09/piece	4 years	1%
37. *Disc Brake Pads, LMV (Aftermarket)*			
Semi-Metallic	$0.67/piece	7.4 years	100%

Source: ICF Incorporated, 1989. "Regulatory Impact Analysis of Controls on Asbestos Products," Volume I, Table III-8.

ible, any added costs of converting were calculated as the potential producer surplus for that equipment. When equipment was deemed not feasible to convert, the value of the capital was used as the producer surplus in these markets.

Another source of potential producer surplus loss in the asbestos-containing product markets is the possible need to engage in costly product reformulation efforts to eliminate the need for asbestos. This is relevant for such products as coatings and friction materials. From an analytical perspective, these reformulation expenditures can be treated in the same way as are potential producer supluses that arise from capital equipment dedicated to producing asbestos-containing products. That is, reformulation costs are expenses incurred to shift away from using asbestos, just as are conversion costs for capital equipment.

Of course, these computations yield the maximum potential producer surplus losses in these markets, because the actual producer surplus lost will depend on the impacts of the regulatory options. A market that is unaffected by a regulatory intervention will experience no producer surplus loss, while one immediately banned will suffer the entire loss in the year of the ban. Moreover, under the asbestos fiber phaseout regulatory option, producers who face either the loss of value of their equipment, the costs of converting it to another use, or product reformulation costs, will accept lower product prices year by year only as long as the present value of the stream of current and future reduced profits is less than the entire potential producer surplus loss. Equivalently, producers will accept lower profits in a given year rather than converting or liquidating their capital, or incurring product reformulation costs, as long as this fall in profitability is less than the relevant maximum producer surplus loss multiplied by the interest rate, which is called a *cost perpetuity* in this analysis. Translating potential producer surplus losses into these cost perpetuities is necessary because the cost modeling is based on yearly construc-

tion of market supplies and demands, and under the asbetos phaseout, producers must decide each year whether to accept lower returns or cease using asbestos altogether. In light of this, Table 2-6 lists producer surplus cost perpetuities for converting equipment or for engaging in product reformulation, and the maximum producer surplus losses on which the perpetuities are based. The table also distinguishes maximum surplus losses for domestic producers from the totals, market by market, to account for the importation of some products.

The other major source of producer surplus in the asbestos markets relates to the supply of fiber itself. Asbestos is a naturally occurring mineral that is mined and then processed before being incorporated into products. As with most mining operations, there is little alternative productive use for an asbestos mine if the demand for asbestos falls. Hence, one would expect to find long-run producer surpluses associated with asbestos mining operations, given that nothing else can be done economically with the mine.

It obviously will not work here to estimate the level of asbestos mining producer surplus using the foregoing method of valuing capital equipment or computing equipment conversion costs, because the relevant surplus flows both from the land itself and from manmade asbestos mining capital. Two alternative methods are possible. One is to model the capital and variable costs of asbestos mining and then subtract these costs from actual mining revenues to arrive at a crude estimate of the returns to the mine itself. The other method is to reconsider using econometric estimates of the asbestos fiber supply function. It turns out that fairly detailed information normally is available for both mining activities in the United States and for imports and exports. Because almost all of the asbestos used in the United States is imported from Canada, reasonably accurate statistics on asbestos fiber production and importation were available.

Table 2-6
MAXIMUM PRODUCER SURPLUS LOSSES AND COST PERPETUITIES FOR ASBESTOS-CONTAINING PRODUCTS

Product Category	Industry Segment Classification	Conversion Cost Perpetuity ($/unit)	Reformulation Cost Perpetuity ($)	Domestic Producer Surplus Loss (1,000 $)	World Producer Surplus Loss (1,000 $)
1. Commercial Paper	Papers and Felts	0.19	0	0.00	0.00
2. Rollboard	Papers and Felts	0.19	0	0.00	0.00
3. Millboard	Papers and Felts	0.19	0	1.58	1.58
4. Pipeline Wrap	Papers and Felts	0.001	0	4.24	10.61
5. Beater-add Gaskets	Papers and Felts	0.19	0	44.80	45.70
6. High-Grade Electrical Paper	Papers and Felts	0.19	0	1.89	1.89
7. Roofing Felt	Asbestos Roofing Felt	0.00	0	0.00	0.00
8. Acetylene Cylinders	Acetylene Cylinders	0.00	0	0.00	0.00
9. Flooring Felt	Papers and Felts	0.19	0	0.00	0.00
10. Corrugated Paper	Papers and Felts	0.19	0	0.00	0.00
11. Specialty Papers	Papers and Felts	0.19	0	1.18	1.18
12. Vinyl-Asbestos Floor Tile	Vinyl-Asbestos Floor Tile	0.00	0	0.00	0.00
13. Asbestos Diaphragms	Chlor-Alkali Industry	19,801.60	0	2,763,737.60	2,763,737.60
14. Asbestos-Cement Pipe	Asbestos-Cement Pipe	0.21	0	45,188.12	45,766.53
15. Flat A-C Sheets	Asbestos-Cement Sheet	19.27	0	1,421.68	1,634.93
16. Corrugated A-C Sheets	Asbestos-Cement Sheet	19.27	0	0.00	1,062.33
17. A-C Shingles	Asbestos-Cement Shingle	3.31	0	8,352.69	11,443.19
18. Drum Brake Linings (OEM)	Friction Products	0.005	248,500	5,693.81	6,547.88
19. Disc Brake Pads, LMV (OEM)	Friction Products	0.005	308,000	4,040.04	4,807.65
20. Disc Brake Pads (HV)	Friction Products	0.005	24,500	361.20	361.20
21. Brake Blocks	Friction Products	0.005	154,000	2,504.67	2,529.71
22. Clutch Facings	Friction Products	0.005	31,500	918.72	1,028.97
23. Automatic Transmission Components	Friction Products	0.005	10,500	154.11	154.11
24. Friction Materials	Friction Products	0.005	105,000	2,122.82	2,122.82
25. Asbestos Protective Clothing	Textiles and Packing	0.00	0	0.00	0.00
26. Asbestos Thread, Yarn, etc.	Textiles and Packing	0.00	0	0.00	0.00
27. Asbestos Sheet Gasketing	Sheet Gasketing	0.16	0	8,245.50	8,822.69
28. Asbestos Packing	Textiles and Packing	0.00	0	0.00	0.00
29. Roof Coatings and Cements	Coatings and Sealants	0.00	40,600	580.00	580.00
30. Non-Roofing Coatings, etc.	Coatings and Sealants	0.00	78,400	1,120.00	1,120.00
31. Asbestos-Reinforced Plastics	Asbestos-Reinforced Plastics	0.00	16,800	233.01	240.00
32. Missile Liner	Coatings and Sealants	0.00	12,600	180.00	180.00
33. Sealant Tape	Coatings and Sealants	0.00	7,00	100.00	100.00
34. Battery Separators[a]	Textiles and Packing	—	—	—	—
35. Arc Chutes[a]	Arc Chutes	—	—	—	—
36. Drum Brake Linings (A/M)	Friction Products	0.005	248,500	9,023.38	10,376.89
37. Disc Brake Pads, LMV (A/M)	Friction Products	0.005	308,000	7,170.51	8,532.91
				2,861,201.57	2,871,210.37

Source: ICF Incorporated, 1989. "Regulatory Impact Analysis of Controls on Asbestos Products," Volume I, Table III–11.
[a] This product is not included in the simulations.

Hence, the asbestos fiber supply elasticity was obtained econometrically using a fairly simple specification, producing an estimate of 1.46. Using this directly in the asbestos regulatory cost simulation model automatically generates estimates of producer surpluses in the asbestos fiber market. Of course, nearly all of these losses are shouldered by Canadian producers of asbestos.

FRAMEWORK FOR ESTIMATING BENEFITS OF ASBESTOS REGULATORY OPTIONS

The analytical steps in evaluating the costs of regulatory programs and options in practice are broadly consistent with the ways these analyses normally are cast in textbook treatments. The fundamental microeconomic apparatus of supply and demand functions and areas of consumer and producer surpluses used to estimate the costs of regulatory interventions are all familiar concepts. As shown above, some of the techniques necessary to obtain quantitative cost estimates using this technical framework are sometimes unconventional and "rough and ready," but the basic thrust of the approach is to find quantitative information to allow the framework to produce numerical results.

The benefits side of practical cost–benefit analysis, particularly evaluations of environmental policies, tends to have a slightly different complexion than typical textbook treatments of the subject. This is not because environmental benefits in *theory* and in *practice* are fundamentally different. Rather, the traditional depiction of the environmental benefits of regulation is the ultimate goal of the analysis, instead of its point of departure. Most of the focus in practical benefits analyses is on the "nuts and bolts" of estimating the risk reduction itself.

To see this, consider Figure 2-6, which shows a conventional graphical technique for analyzing the benefits of, say, a regulation banning an asbestos-containing product. Here the demand and supply functions are as seen before, and ar-

FIGURE 2-6

Conventional Benefits Analysis of Asbestos Product Ban

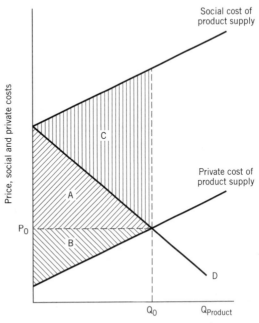

A banned asbestos-containing product market

The conventional graphical representation of the benefits side of the analysis shows the full social costs of— including the environmental harms caused by— producing a product. The net social benefits of banning this product is then the difference between the gross environmental benefits of banning it, areas *A*, *B*, and *C*, minus the consumer and producer surpluses received from the product, areas *A* and *B*.

---

eas *A* and *B* (ignoring losses in the fiber market) measure the producer and consumer surplus losses caused by banning the product. But the schedule in the top of the diagram measures the actual total social costs of supplying and using this asbestos-containing product, where the total social costs include both the explicit costs of supplying the product *and* the monetized value of the risks that the product's manufacture, use, and disposal pose to humans and the environment.

Using this diagram, the environmental benefits of banning the product are measured by areas *A*, *B*, and *C* together, because these represent the excess of the social costs of making, using, and disposing of the product over the purely privately perceived costs as measured by the product supply function. Thus, the net social welfare gain from banning this product is measured by area *C*, or the value of the environmental harms avoided minus the producer and consumer surpluses lost. Intuitively, the full social welfare effects—when benefits and costs are both counted—of banning this product are the environmental harms avoided minus the net private benefit of having the product in the first place, which is the sum of the producer and consumer surpluses provided by the product.

All of this is quite correct and eminently reasonable as long as the various environmental harms are known, quantified, valued, and fed back into the diagram to identify the full social cost schedule for a product. In practice, while there is a considerable volume of ongoing research seeking to value the many types of harms that are caused by the variety of environmentally damaging activities in the economy, most benefits analyses do not actually arrive at the point at which monetary values are placed on harms and then used to compute the net social gain from a regulation. This is not because public policy practitioners don't want to do so, but for other reasons.

Often there is considerable uncertainty regarding the magnitude of the environmental risks to be addressed by a regulation even in terms of physical units, such as cancer cases avoided or an effluent emission's impact on the chemistry of a water body. Similarly, there is considerable controversy in practice about the wisdom of basing public policy on economists' estimates of the social values of reducing most types of environmental damages. Simply because someone has estimated the value of a particular amount of risk reduction does not mean that everyone will agree with the estimate. There is always considerable variance in the estimates of risk-reduction benefits, so it is often unclear exactly what value from a wide range should be used. For the most part, decision makers tend to be more comfortable with benefits analyses that stop short of distilling all of the relevant environmental effects into a single monetary social benefit number, and deal instead with risk estimates of many types in their natural units, such as cancer cases avoided. Monetizing risk-reduction benefits is done in some cases, but the central focus of decision makers is on more basic measures of benefits.

Probably more important than the empirical difficulties of monetizing benefits, or the political liabilities of committing to those valuations in policy discussions, is a slightly different and perhaps more fundamental issue. In most practical cost–benefit analyses, as in the asbestos ban–phaseout study, the sources of risks can be fairly complex and diverse. For example, the risks from manufacturing asbestos-containing automobile brakes may be due to worker and ambient exposures in asbestos mining and milling operations (to get the asbestos fiber in the first place) and in the brake manufacturing stage; general population exposures to air emissions as the brakes are used; worker exposures in the course of brake servicing; and worker and consumer exposures associated with the ultimate disposal of the brakes. From a risk assessment perspective and for policy makers, trying to represent all of these sources of risk as a single value-per-brake number obscures the complex texture of the problem.

In practical cost–benefit analyses, therefore, it often makes sense to tailor the cost assessment to the markets and activities targeted by regulatory policies, but to measure the benefits of these interventions beginning directly with the exposures avoided. The results of the two sides of the analysis must then be joined as best one can.

The analysis conducted for the asbestos ban–phaseout regulation is thus an instructive example of why, despite their common theoretical motivation, the empirical points of departure of the cost evaluation and the benefits estimation are normally very different. In measuring costs, one first develops a conceptual microeconomic framework in terms of the familiar supply and demand formulations and then tries to find the necessary data to define those functions to generate quantitative results in terms of producer and consumer surplus changes. In practical benefits analyses, however, most of the real work is focused on the basic tasks of measuring exposures and estimating the resulting health and environmental harms. Definitive monetization of harms and other computations necessary to depict the benefits as shown in Figure 2-6 are the exception rather than the rule.

This seems to imply that practical benefits analysis is really a matter left to risk and exposure assessment specialists. If so, one might legitimately ask why economists or public policy analysts should concern themselves with activities conducted by researchers in completely different fields. At least part of the answer is that often the economic or policy analyst is responsible for incorporating the benefits estimates into the cost modeling results to produce the cost–benefit and regulatory impact analyses. This effort almost always raises issues of consistency between the cost side and the benefit side of the analyses, of the economic and policy interpretation of the types and magnitudes of the risk reduction estimates, and of correctly matching or linking the benefits side to the cost results. It is therefore important for public policy analysts to gain at least some sense of the nature and content of the risk-reduction, or benefits side, of practical environmental economic analysis.

What is provided here is merely an encapsulation of the basic methods used to estimate the benefits of the various asbestos ban and phaseout regulatory options. It is not intended to be exhaustive, for a complete and definitive review of all of the risk and exposure analyses conducted for the asbestos cost–benefit analysis would more properly belong in a text on risk assessment. Instead, it is intended to give the general flavor of the procedures used to estimate benefits and show how they dovetail with the structure of the cost analysis described above.

Just as the costs of the regulatory options are simply the net differences in producer and consumer surpluses with and without a regulatory intervention, the basic approach for estimating the benefits of reduced asbestos exposure is also based on subtracting risks with the regulatory option from those in the baseline. Risks in each case are measured essentially by estimating the populations exposed, the intensity and duration of exposure, and the degree to which exposures result in adverse health effects—cancer cases in this instance.[5]

Benefits analyses, especially for toxic and hazardous substances, typically begin with an assessment of the degree of hazard posed by exposures to a harmful substance such as asbestos. This assessment normally produces an estimated *dose-response function* that translates different levels of exposures to the substance into probabilities of experiencing the health effects of concern. Deriving dose-response functions is a complex matter best left to toxicologists and other scientists, but because dose-response functions lie at the core of most benefits assessments, especially those involving toxic chemicals and hazardous wastes, one should have at least a passing familiarity with them.

In practice, dose-response functions typically are estimated from animal or other nonhuman toxicological information, although occasionally human data are available. The essential task here

---

[5] Although asbestos causes a number of human health problems, only cancer cases were quantified in the analysis, primarily because these asbestos exposure risks are well-known and well-researched. Non-cancer asbestos health risks can also pose significant medical care expenses, reduced productivity, and deterioration of the quality of life.

is to gather data on exposures and the incidence of adverse health effects, such as cancers, in rats or other subjects. These can be used to estimate a mathematical relationship predicting probabilities of health effects for various levels of exposures. Naturally, a number of statistical and inference issues are involved in this effort and, of course, some dose-response functions often generate heated debates between various interested parties. For example, in rat studies, doses administered are often far higher than any normal exposures humans might face. This is done to make the cost of these toxicological studies manageable. At lower doses, more rats are needed to determine the toxicity of a substance, and at higher doses, fewer rats are required.

Using high doses in toxicological studies raises the obvious question of whether substances that are toxic at high doses are indeed toxic at far lower doses. Again, the technical procedures and methods health and environmental scientists use to derive dose-response functions are not the province of public policy analysts. Nevertheless, the applicability of high-dose toxicological information to lower-dose situations highlights a critical characteristic of dose-response functions in practical analyses. Many dose-response functions are estimated (or assumed) to be linear so that the probability of manifesting the health effects of concern rises proportionately with increased exposure. Linear dose-response functions tend to be of two types—*no-threshold* and *positive-threshold*. A no-threshold dose-response function assumes that health effects are caused by even the smallest of exposures to a substance so that the dose-response function predicts adverse health effects continuously beginning at near-zero levels of exposure. The positive-threshold dose-response function, on the other hand, assumes that health effects are caused only at exposures above a certain level, hence the term *threshold*.

In practice, whether or not the dose-response function has a threshold is very important. Exposure levels to many substances are sometimes fairly low, but are experienced by a very large number of people. For example, routine emissions from many industrial plants may expose a very large population in the entire region to extremely small doses. It then matters a great deal whether the dose-response relationship for these emissions is a no-threshold function, or a threshold function whose critical threshold level is above the population's per-person exposure. In the no-threshold case, estimated health effects could be quite large, while in the latter case they might be nil.

After settling on a dose-response function, the next step is to characterize the nature, intensity, and duration of exposures suffered by the many different sets of humans or other receptors exposed. This can be a challenging task, as it was for asbestos, because exposures can occur in a wide variety of ways, can extend over the entire life of a product, and can affect many different sets of people. In the asbestos analysis, the exposure estimation step was conducted separately for each asbestos-containing product, and was further subdivided into five occupational and nonoccupational exposure categories as follows: (1) primary manufacturing, (2) secondary manufacturing, (3) installation, (4) use, and (5) disposal or repair.

Occupational exposure occurs among individuals engaged in the manufacture, installation, use, and repair or disposal of asbestos products. Nonoccupational exposure can be subdivided into ambient exposure and consumer exposure. Ambient exposure occurs among people close to the sites of the manufacture, repair, or disposal of asbestos products, or their use, while consumer exposure occurs among people who personally install, use, repair, or dispose of asbestos products.

In addition to the activity that gives rise to asbestos-related risks, the timing of exposures is also important for the analysis. Exposures from releases during product installation, for example, are assumed to be contemporaneous with those from primary and secondary asbestos-containing product manufacturing; exposures during repair or disposal are assumed to occur during and at the end of the average product life, often many years after the products are first made. Exposures during product use, on the other hand, are assumed to be evenly distributed during the time from product manufacture to repair or disposal.

To quantify the relevant exposures for each asbestos-containing product and for each exposure setting, occupational and nonoccupational exposures were analyzed in different ways. For occupational exposures, the basic method used was to canvass the available sources of information on workplace concentrations of asbestos fibers during the various tasks required to manufacture, repair, or dispose of the different asbestos-containing products. Using this monitoring and survey information, data on the length of time for the relevant labor tasks, along with a considerable amount of professional process-engineering judgment, estimates of the amount of worker exposure for a given task, exposure setting, and product were calculated. For nonoccupational consumer exposures to asbestos during product installation, use, or repair of asbestos-containing products, the same measurement method was applied.

For ambient population exposures, two different methods were used. For computing the population exposed due to certain products' use, ambient concentrations of asbestos that result from their use and the associated number of exposed individuals were investigated. For example, exposures and risks due to the use of vehicle brake products were calculated based on the concentrations of asbestos fibers that result, the volume of vehicle miles driven in areas of different population densities, and the number of people so exposed. For ambient population exposures to asbestos associated with releases of asbestos during asbestos-containing product manufacturing, information on product manufacturing plants' emission control characteristics, production processes, and typical atmospheric conditions (e.g., winds that transport the asbestos fibers through the air) were combined with data on population densities in the surrounding region to arrive at quantitative exposure estimates.

After gathering all of this information on occupational and nonoccupational exposures and the points at which they occur over the lifetime of the various asbestos-containing products, the benefits analysis generated time profiles of asbestos exposures for each product; these profiles identified the amount of exposure, the numbers of people exposed, and the time at which the exposures take place per unit of the product. These profiles span many years to account for exposures that occur early in the process, say in manufacturing, and those that occur later during the product's use, repair, or disposal.

Using these product-by-product exposure profiles, total asbestos exposures over time due to a particular year's production and use of an asbestos-containing product can be estimated by multiplying the product's per-unit exposure profile by the amount of the product supplied. Repeating this procedure for each product and year in the analysis yields total asbestos exposures for the entire simulation, both in the baseline and under the various regulatory options.

The next step in the benefits analysis was to embed the estimated asbestos exposures in a population dynamic model to estimate actual cancer cases and cancer deaths attributable to them. This procedure essentially uses demographic information on the exposed population, the asbestos exposure profiles product by product, the dose-response function for asbestos-related cancers, and assumptions concerning latency (the lag between exposure and the onset or diagnosis of the cancer) to generate time profiles of cancer cases and deaths caused by asbestos exposures, both with and without the regulatory policies.

Finally, the benefits computational procedures were linked to the regulatory cost modeling results very simply. The benefits analysis operates in terms of the product-by-product asbestos exposure profiles and the host of other input information described above. The one piece of information the benefits analysis still requires, however, is the actual level of production of asbestos-containing products in the baseline and under the various regulatory policy scenarios. This must be supplied by the cost model, because it is that simulation that computes the evolution of the asbestos markets in the baseline and under the regulatory options Hence, the linkage between the cost and benefits analyses occurs by using estimates of asbestos fiber usage and asbestos-containing product supply over time from the cost analysis as an input for the benefits assessment. By estimating total asbestos-related cancers using the baseline and policy scenario cost model outputs, the benefits model can generate quantitative measures of the reduction in cancer cases provided by each of the various regulatory options.

COSTS AND BENEFITS OF THE REGULATORY OPTIONS

Numerous specific regulatory options were considered and simulated during the policy deliberation stages of the asbestos project. Indeed, the project explored hundreds of combinations of specific product bans at different dates, alternative schedules for phasing out asbestos fiber usage, and a variety of possible product market exemptions. Here only three specific options are shown to give the flavor of the numerical results and to indicate the reasoning behind EPA's ultimate decisions on asbestos. These are:

- *Option A:* a complete ban on all products immediately (1987 in the simulation modeling)
- *Option B:* a fiber phaseout starting in 1987 and ending in 1997, combined with an immediate ban on protective clothing and some construction products (except for A/C sheet and shingle), but with diaphragms and missile liner exempt

- *Option C:* a three-stage product ban with products 7, 9, 10, 12, 14, 15, 16, 17, and 25 banned in 1987, products 18, 19, 20, 21, 22, 23, 24, 36, and 37 banned in 1991, and all remaining products banned in 1997, except for diaphragms and missile liner

Quantitative estimates of the costs and benefits of these three regulatory options are presented in Tables 2-7 through 2-10. For each option, Table 2-7 lists the welfare effects by class of affected entity; the classes are foreign and domestic fiber suppliers, foreign and domestic product manufacturers, domestic product purchasers, and the government. The government is listed here because under the phaseout option, the permits that enforce the fiber use limitation are assumed to be sold by the government rather than allocated to private sector entities. Foreign asbestos fiber and product suppliers are also listed so that U.S. and total world effects can be distinguished. Tables 2-8 through 2-10 then disaggregate the domestic costs benefits of each option by product to show how these vary by market. For all of these tables, the *low decline* baseline for asbestos-containing product growth rates is used. In addition, costs and benefits are both discounted using a three percent real rate, although many different rates were used for computing the actual cost and benefit results reported in the original cost–benefit analysis.

Option A produces the largest costs and benefits of the three alternatives because it is the most stringent policy, imposing domestic costs of nearly $7 billion and avoiding some 266 cancer cases, as shown in Tables 2-7 and 2-8. While these results clearly represent the upper bounds for the costs and benefits of addressing the remaining asbestos risks, they are perhaps more instructive in determining the relative magnitudes of the product-by-product costs and benefits of eliminating asbestos use. For example, most of the risk reduction provided by an immediate ban is largely in the friction products categories. This is the direct influence of the

Table 2-7

COSTS OF ASBESTOS REGULATORY OPTIONS BY AFFECTED ENTITY

(Present values, in millions of dollars, at 3%)

Entity	Option A	Option B	Option C
Domestic Miners and Millers	12.32	10.55	9.21
Foreign Miners and Millers	134.29	115.04	100.42
Domestic Primary Processors	2,778.41	102.48	87.51
Foreign Primary Processors	9.81	10.94	8.93
Domestic Product Purchasers	4,143.77	1,228.62	911.54
Government	0.00	-262.69	0.00
U.S. Welfare Cost	6,934.49	1,078.96	1,008.26
World Welfare Cost	7,078.59	1,204.94	1,117.61

Source: ICF Incorporated, 1989. "Regulatory Impact Analysis of Controls on Asbestos Products," Volume IV.

no-threshold dose-response function used to translate asbestos exposures into estimated adverse health effects. Friction products expose numerous people, most of the U.S. population in fact, to small doses of asbestos over a long time horizon. Even small doses over time multiplied by some one-quarter of a billion people can amount to a non-trivial number of cancer cases.

The detailed results for Option A also reveal that there are some products with almost no cancer risk due to asbestos exposures whose banning imposes extremely large costs. A ban on asbestos diaphragms in particular generates virtually no risk reduction and is extremely costly, amounting to over $2.5 billion. This is because diaphragms are necessary for manufacturing chlorine using one of two processes. Diaphragms are integral to the process and, according to all available information, have no technologically feasible substitutes. If the continued production and use of these diaphragms were to be banned, about half of the U.S. chlorine manufacturing plants would be rendered essentially worthless. Similarly, banning missile liner also imposes very high costs, nearly $2 billion, due to the high cost of asbestos substitutes in this use.

The detailed cost and benefit results for the immediate and complete product ban indicate

that the risk-reduction benefits and the costs of eliminating asbestos use are quite different, depending on the availability and cost of substitutes and the types of exposures avoided. Moreover, there is no clear correlation between the magnitudes of the benefits and the costs other than through the volume of the products produced and used.

In light of these facts and findings, EPA considered many possible variations of the two primary regulatory strategies. The asbestos fiber phaseout's results were computed for numerous different phaseout periods, with and without exemptions for certain product categories, and with and without imposing specific product bans. Option B is one example of this. Under this ten-year fiber phaseout, the asbestos diaphragm and missile liner product categories are exempted from the phaseout, although a few specific products are banned immediately.

For several reasons, the results for Option B, as shown in Tables 2-7 and 2-9, are dramatically different from those of the immediate ban. First, by exempting the asbestos diaphragms and missile liner markets from the phaseout, the very large producer and consumer surplus losses for those uses are avoided. Second, whatever consumer and producer surplus losses are experi-

Table 2-8
COSTS AND BENEFITS OF OPTION A
(Costs and benefits discounted at 3%, millions of dollars)

Product Category	Domestic Consumer Surplus Loss	Domestic Producer Surplus Loss	Gross Domestic Total Loss	Total Cancer Cases Avoided	Cost per Cancer Case Avoided
1. Commercial Paper	.00	.00	.00	.0000	n/a
2. Rollboard	.00	.00	.00	.0000	n/a
3. Millboard	10.99	.00	10.99	.9286	11.83
4. Pipeline Wrap	1.96	.01	1.97	1.4052	1.40
5. Beater-Add Gaskets	310.13	.04	310.17	8.7628	35.40
6. High-Grade Electrical Paper	114.72	.00	114.72	.6410	178.97
7. Roofing Felt	8.90	.00	8.90	1.2196	7.30
8. Acetylene Cylinders	10.56	.00	10.56	.0000	—[a]
9. Flooring Felt	.00	.00	.00	.0000	n/a
10. Corrugated Paper	.00	.00	.00	.0000	n/a
11. Specialty Paper	.02	.00	.03	.0414	.62
12. V/A Floor Tile	.00	.00	.00	.0000	n/a
13. Asbestos Diaphragms	.26	2,683.24	2,683.50	.2686	9,991.41
14. A/C Pipe	438.45	43.87	482.32	5.0204	96.07
15. A/C Sheet, Flat	1.35	1.38	2.73	.8475	3.22
16. A/C Sheet, Corrugated	.62	.00	.62	.1158	5.33
17. A/C Shingles	63.31	8.10	71.42	.5160	138.42
18. Drum Brake Linings (OEM)	14.92	5.65	20.57	9.3392	2.20
19. Disc Brake Pads, LMV (OEM)	.16	3.94	4.10	1.1052	3.71
20. Disc Brake Pads, HV	.03	.35	.38	.2445	1.56
21. Brake Blocks	25.70	2.45	28.15	16.2894	1.73
22. Clutch Facings	36.85	.92	37.77	.6833	55.27
23. Automatic Trans. Components	.25	.15	.40	.0005	745.38
24. Friction Materials	.43	2.09	2.52	.5923	4.25
25. Asbestos Protective Clothing	.00	.00	.00	.0000	n/a
26. Asbestos Thread, etc.	303.38	.00	303.38	.7810	388.48
27. Sheet Gaskets	235.37	7.88	243.25	2.7854	87.33
28. Asbestos Packing	.99	.00	.99	.0143	69.00
29. Roof Coatings	319.92	.56	320.48	2.4015	133.45
30. Non-Roofing Coatings	87.79	1.09	88.88	.4811	184.75
31. Asbestos-Reinforced Plastics	78.49	.23	78.72	.8246	95.45
32. Missile Liner	1,961.33	.17	1,961.50	.3967	4,944.40
33. Sealant Tape	79.58	.10	79.67	.1399	569.53
34. Battery Separators	.00	.00	.00	.0000	n/a
35. Arc Chutes	.00	.00	.00	.0000	n/a
36. Drum Brake Linings (Aftermarket)	36.26	9.05	45.31	168.1760	.27
37. Disc Brake Pads LMV (Aftermarket)	1.05	7.13	8.18	40.4240	.20
38. Mining and Milling	.00	12.32	12.32	1.9145	6.43
Total			6,934.49[b]	266.3603	26.03

Source: ICF Incorporated, 1989. "Regulatory Impact Analysis of Controls on Asbestos Products," Volume IV.
[a] Exposure data not available.
[b] U.S. net welfare cost.

enced in this case occur later in time, so they are lower in present-value terms under a lengthy phaseout than under an immediate product ban. This gradual tightening of the phaseout also is responsible for the fall in the number of cancer cases avoided from the immediate ban's 266 to 208 cases under the phaseout. Finally, under this option, the government gains over $250 million in revenues from the sale of the permits that enforce the asbestos fiber use phaseout.

Option C is an example of tailoring the staged product bans to try to reduce the costs of asbestos controls while still generating much of the risk-reduction benefits. Under this option, protective clothing and construction products are banned immediately, friction products are banned some five years later, and all remaining products except diaphragms and missile liner are banned in ten years. This option was constructed more or less on the basis of the relatively low cost and immediate availability of substitutes for products banned earlier, and a concern to allow adequate time for the redesign of friction product uses to avoid any safety problems. The exemptions, of course, were included to avoid extreme cost burdens.

As shown in Tables 2-7 and 2-10, costs are slightly lower than for Option B, while the benefits in terms of cancer cases avoided are about 149, 50 cases less than under Option B. This disproportionate decline in the benefits relative to costs in moving from Option B to Option C is almost entirely due to the difference in the timing of substitution away from asbestos in the vehicle brakes aftermarkets. Under the Option B phaseout, substitution away from asbestos in brakes occurs relatively early because of the modest incremental costs of brake substitutes. Under Option C's staged ban, however, these markets are not required to substitute until fairly late in the regulation's timeframe. Again, EPA's concerns about the safety of using non-asbestos brakes in systems designed to use asbestos drove the decision to delay the brake aftermarket product ban under Option C.

In the end, EPA chose to promulgate the asbestos regulation as a variant of the staged ban strategy for several reasons. Probably most important was that the regulatory posture of the rule-making procedure was geared toward eliminating asbestos from the workplace and from products and to do so as expeditiously as possible. At the same time, EPA wanted to avoid any safety problems, especially in the friction product categories, due to the use of non-asbestos substitutes. Thus, the degree of control and timing offered by the staged product ban approach was superior to that offered by the phaseout approach. Under the phaseout strategy, substitution costs and the stringency of the production limitations determine when the various asbestos producers would adopt substitutes, not policymakers.

The phaseout approach also entailed establishing an entire regulatory infrastructure to design, initiate, administer, and enforce the asbestos phaseout production and importation limitations. While marketable permits schemes have certain desirable features in many regulatory situations, using one to accomplish what was effectively a desire to eliminate asbestos from the marketplace seemed cumbersome at best.

Addendum

After much study and deliberation, the asbestos staged product-ban rule was promulgated in 1989. As is quite common in the environmental regulatory arena, the rule was challenged in federal court. The suit filed by the asbestos industry association and others argued, among other things, that EPA had failed to allow adequate opportunity for public comment on the methods and data used to estimate the costs and benefits of the product-ban regulation. Challenging an environmental regulation on these grounds is rooted in the fact that the procedural law governing EPA and other rule-making agencies specifies numerous rules and guidelines to

Table 2-9
COSTS AND BENEFITS OF OPTION B
(Costs and benefits discounted at 3%, millions of dollars)

Product Category	Domestic Consumer Surplus Loss	Domestic Producer Surplus Loss	Gross Domestic Total Loss	Total Cancer Cases Avoided	Cost per Cancer Case Avoided
1. Commercial Paper	.00	.00	.00	.0000	n/a
2. Rollboard	.00	.00	.00	.0000	n/a
3. Millboard	5.32	.00	5.32	.4872	10.92
4. Pipeline Wrap	1.96	.01	1.97	1.4052	1.40
5. Beater-Add Gaskets	157.20	.06	157.25	3.5130	44.76
6. High-Grade Electrical Paper	34.62	.00	34.62	.1569	220.61
7. Roofing Felt	8.90	.00	8.90	1.2196	7.30
8. Acetylene Cylinders	5.81	.00	5.81	.0000	—[a]
9. Flooring Felt	.00	.00	.00	.0000	n/a
10. Corrugated Paper	.00	.00	.00	.0000	n/a
11. Specialty Paper	.02	.00	.03	.0414	.62
12. V/A Floor Tile	.00	.00	.00	.0000	n/a
13. Asbestos Diaphragms	-1.54	.00	-1.54	.0000	n/a
14. A/C Pipe	438.45	43.87	482.32	5.0204	96.07
15. A/C Sheet, Flat	.82	1.55	2.37	.5988	3.95
16. A/C Sheet, Corrugated	.40	.00	.40	.0769	5.18
17. A/C Shingles	30.67	9.34	40.02	.3345	119.65
18. Drum Brake Linings (OEM)	12.99	6.25	19.24	6.3090	3.05
19. Disc Brake Pads, LMV (OEM)	.10	3.88	3.98	.6751	5.90
20. Disc Brake Pads, HV	.02	.39	.41	.1641	2.49
21. Brake Blocks	17.11	2.92	20.03	9.6853	2.07
22. Clutch Facings	17.42	1.22	18.63	.2123	87.77
23. Automatic Trans. Components	.06	.11	.17	.0001	1,341.00
24. Friction Materials	.43	2.09	2.52	.5923	4.25
25. Asbestos Protective Clothing	.00	.00	.00	.0000	n/a
26. Asbestos Thread, etc.	78.96	.00	78.96	.3576	220.80
27. Sheet Gaskets	98.40	10.44	108.84	.9144	119.03
28. Asbestos Packing	.25	.00	.25	.0035	70.76
29. Roof Coatings	206.79	.73	207.52	1.1433	181.50
30. Non-Roofing Coatings	40.15	1.46	41.61	.1377	302.28
31. Asbestos-Reinforced Plastics	19.96	.23	20.19	.7680	26.29
32. Missile Liner	-1.10	.00	-1.10	.0000	n/a
33. Sealant Tape	20.78	.10	20.88	.1325	157.55
34. Battery Separators	.00	.00	.00	.0000	n/a
35. Arc Chutes	.00	.00	.00	.0000	n/a
36. Drum Brake Linings (Aftermarket)	32.62	10.46	43.08	136.4880	.32
37. Disc Brake Pads, LMV (Aftermarket)	1.05	7.37	8.42	36.3111	.23
38. Mining and Milling	.00	10.55	10.55	1.3468	7.83
Total			1,078.96[b]	208.0948	5.18

Source: ICF Incorporated, 1989. "Regulatory Impact Analysis of Controls on Asbestos Products," Volume IV.
[a] Exposure data not available.
[b] U.S. net welfare cost.

Table 2-10

COSTS AND BENEFITS OF OPTION C
(Costs and benefits discounted at 3%, millions of dollars)

Product Category	Domestic Consumer Surplus Loss	Domestic Producer Surplus Loss	Gross Domestic Total Loss	Total Cancer Cases Avoided	Cost per Cancer Case Avoided
1. Commercial Paper	.00	.00	.00	.0000	n/a
2. Rollboard	.00	.00	.00	.0000	n/a
3. Millboard	2.36	.00	2.36	.2274	10.40
4. Pipeline Wrap	-2.00	.00	-2.00	.3441	-5.81
5. Beater-Add Gaskets	66.48	.03	66.51	2.1456	31.00
6. High-Grade Electrical Paper	27.53	.00	27.54	.1569	175.45
7. Roofing Felt	8.90	.00	8.90	1.2196	7.30
8. Acetylene Cylinders	2.24	.00	2.24	.0000	—[a]
9. Flooring Felt	.00	.00	.00	.0000	n/a
10. Corrugated Paper	.00	.00	.00	.0000	n/a
11. Specialty Paper	-.06	.00	-.06	.0101	-6.10
12. V/A Floor Tile	.00	.00	.00	.0000	n/a
13. Asbestos Diaphragms	-1.26	.00	-1.26	.0000	n/a
14. A/C Pipe	438.45	43.87	482.32	5.0204	96.07
15. A/C Sheet, Flat	1.35	1.38	2.73	.8475	3.22
16. A/C Sheet, Corrugated	.62	.00	.62	.1158	5.33
17. A/C Shingles	63.31	8.10	71.42	.5160	138.42
18. Drum Brake Linings (OEM)	6.99	4.83	11.82	5.6962	2.08
19. Disc Brake Pads, LMV (OEM)	-.06	3.39	3.33	.6751	4.93
20. Disc Brake Pads, HV	-.01	.30	.29	.1454	1.99
21. Brake Blocks	14.54	2.11	16.65	9.6853	1.72
22. Clutch Facings	21.60	.79	22.39	.4063	55.12
23. Automatic Trans. Components	.15	.13	.28	.0003	877.15
24. Friction Materials	-.19	1.80	1.61	.3522	4.58
25. Asbestos Protective Clothing	.00	.00	.00	.0000	n/a
26. Asbestos Thread, etc.	73.66	.00	73.66	.1912	385.19
27. Sheet Gaskets	53.29	5.86	59.16	.6820	86.74
28. Asbestos Packing	.24	.00	.24	.0035	68.86
29. Roof Coatings	62.11	.42	62.53	.5880	106.34
30. Non-Roofing Coatings	19.72	.81	20.53	.1178	174.31
31. Asbestos-Reinforced Plastics	18.67	.17	18.84	.2019	93.30
32. Missile Liner	-.90	.00	-.90	.0000	n/a
33. Sealant Tape	18.25	.07	18.33	.0343	535.05
34. Battery Separators	.00	.00	.00	.0000	n/a
35. Arc Chutes	.00	.00	.00	.0000	n/a
36. Drum Brake Linings (Aftermarket)	16.65	8.21	24.85	101.6571	.24
37. Disc Brake Pads, LMV (Aftermarket)	-1.09	5.21	4.12	17.6734	.23
38. Mining and Milling	.00	9.21	9.21[b]	1.1014	8.36
Total			1,008.26[b]	149.8147	6.73

Source: ICF Incorporated, 1989. "Regulatory Impact Analysis of Controls on Asbestos Products," Volume IV.
[a] Exposure data are not available.
[b] U.S. net welfare cost.

which the government must adhere. In general, if these procedures are followed, the courts normally defer to the judgment of the regulators on matters of fact and on policy decisions that require weighing various alternatives and outcomes.

The basis of the asbestos industry association's ability-to-comment complaint stemmed from EPA's decision during the regulatory options evaluation process to use an asbestos exposures data set different from, and more extensive than, that used as the base case exposure information throughout most of the regulatory development process. The base case exposure data set, which underlies the quantitative estimates of the benefits presented above, was constructed using whatever exposure information was reasonably available. This data set necessarily did not include many exposures associated with asbestos-containing products for which quantitative information was unavailable. Hence, the larger benefits data set that EPA elected to use in support of the final rule was one in which some of these unknown, but strongly suspected, exposures were estimated by analogy to similar product exposure settings and circumstances for which quantitative information was available.

While this larger benefits data set had been used in a number of sensitivity analyses throughout the regulatory development process, the asbestos industry's suit was successful. The court held that the public had not been given adequate opportunity to comment on the use of the more expansive data set. This court went on to offer other comments on the rule and the supporting analyses, as well as its interpretation of TSCA's requirement that EPA adopt the "least burdensome" remedy and consider the risks of substitutes for asbestos. As a result, the asbestos-containing product staged-ban rule was returned to EPA for further consideration. To date, there is still no agreement on whether to proceed with another rule governing the remaining risks caused by asbestos-containing products.

Chapter 3

Design of Appropriate Models for Policy Analysis

The asbestos case study in the previous chapter illustrates how the basic apparatus of microeconomic analysis can be applied to theoretical and empirical evaluation of environmental policy and regulation. This chapter continues in that vein by exploring a theme implicit in the asbestos analysis. In particular, this study emphasizes that, quite often, developing even a rudimentary technical framework for analyzing a regulatory policy requires some real-world information about the environmental problem of concern and the economic activities that cause them. The central issue here involves the normally straightforward exercise of drawing a supply function, to be used in estimating the costs and effects of regulatory interventions. The specific subject matter underlying this study was an evaluation of alternative methods for increasing the recycling rate for used lubricating oil, so some background is important for understanding the analysis and conclusions.

Options for Enhancing Used-Oil Recycling[1]

Hazardous wastes are regulated in the United States primarily through the Resource Conservation and Recovery Act (RCRA). Under this statute, EPA has promulgated a number of regulations governing hazardous waste management, ranging from rules targeting waste handling, storage, and transport, to standards for proper waste disposal. Generally, the goal of this regulatory program is to achieve minimal human and environmental exposures to hazardous wastes. As a result, these rules tend to be fairly restrictive and impose significant costs of compliance.

In general, the body of rules and regulations relating to hazardous waste management applies to any waste listed by EPA, where wastes are identified by the processes from which they are generated, by particular constituents contained in them, or by their properties, such as flammability and corrosivity. Thus, there is an ongoing regulatory program at EPA to determine whether to list specific wastes as hazardous, or to "delist" wastes that are found not to be sufficiently hazardous to warrant continued inclusion in this classification.

[1] This analysis is based on a research project conducted by ICF Incorporated and Clayton Environmental. Principal contributors to the project were Vikram Widge and David Reiner, both of ICF Incorporated, Kevin Dietly of Clayton Environmental, and Frank Smith of the Environmental Protection Agency.

For a number of years, EPA has been in the process of deciding whether to list used lubricating oil as a hazardous waste. Lubricating oil is used in a variety of engines, machines, and devices to prevent wear on metal parts. Over time, lubricating oil loses its ability to provide adequate wear protection and it becomes contaminated with a variety of impurities. Hence, old lubricating oil routinely is replaced with new oil. Whether used oil is a hazardous waste is the central question EPA faces.

Those pressing for listing used oil as a hazardous waste argue that it contains toxic constituents, such as lead and other heavy metals, and various combustion byproducts. Much of the volume of used oil generated is burned for its fuel content in industrial and commercial boilers. To the degree that these hazardous constituents are not removed prior to burning, potentially harmful exposures may occur. Proponents of listing further note that large quantities of used oil are routinely dumped onto land or into sewers, rather than being properly disposed of or recycled.

Opponents of listing used oil as a hazardous waste assert that the risks posed by oil that is improperly disposed of are insignificant and diffuse, and that used oil is adequately processed to remove hazardous constituents prior to burning. Thus, opponents argue, the environmental case for listing used oil is weak. They further point out that the substantial costs of the many RCRA rules governing hazardous waste management that would apply to used oil if it were listed might cause a significant increase in improper disposal, by diverting used oil that is currently recycled or otherwise handled appropriately.

In an attempt to avoid imposing the substantial costs of numerous hazardous waste management rules on used oil, but still to increase the rate of used-oil recycling and decrease the amount of improper disposal, EPA examined the possible use of several alternative approaches to a more costly hazardous waste listing decision. Positive incentives of one type or another, or measures that make it easier to return used oil for recycling, might draw more used oil into the legal and environmentally safe recycling system. If so, they might perform better, both economically and environmentally, than the more problematic approach of listing used oil as hazardous waste. This study summarizes the preliminary economic analysis conducted for EPA of three nontraditional approaches—two of them market-based—intended to enhance the recycling of used oil.

The Question

Given that the goal is to increase the recycling rate for used oil, this discussion assumes throughout that the environmental concerns that motivate these policies are those associated with dumping and other inappropriate ways of disposing of used oil. Hence, the approaches examined here target increasing the recycling of used oil, not other potential risk sources, such as burning used oil that has not been adequately processed to appropriate standards of purity.

Before introducing and analyzing the three approaches for increasing used-oil recycling, it is worthwhile to review some information about used-oil generation and disposition in the baseline, largely unregulated circumstances. Lubricating oil is a widely used commodity applied primarily to reduce the friction and abrasive consequences of closely fitted metal parts in machines. Lubricating oil for automobile engines, for example, is a necessity to facilitate the up-and-down movement of the pistons within the cylinders. In an automobile engine, a very tight seal between the piston and cylinder wall is necessary to contain the combustion of the gasoline and air mixture and thereby exert as much force as possible on the piston.

Yet, the piston must also move down the cylinder wall during the combustion phase to transfer the resulting energy to the crankshaft and, ultimately, to the wheels of the vehicle. The tighter the seal between the piston and the cylinder wall, however, the more friction is generated, which reduces power transfer and abrades the cylinder. Lubricating oil, by providing a very thin and slippery film between the piston and cylinder, is a valuable solution to these tradeoffs. Unfortunately, oil breaks down over time, losing its lubrication properties. When the old oil is drained and replaced, used oil is generated.

Figure 3-1 shows the amounts of used oil estimated to be generated by three major aggregated economic sectors. Commercial transportation includes automobile service establishments, trucks and buses, construction and mining, farms, and other sectors engaged in transport activities. The industrial sector covers nontransportation processes, such as metalworking and other activities that involve equipment using lubrication oil. Finally, the DIY sector, which stands for "Do-It-Yourselfer," represents people who change the oil in their vehicles themselves. As Figure 3-1 indi-

cates, of the over 1.4 billion gallons of used oil generated each year (these data are estimates for 1990), the industrial and commercial transportation sectors accounted for roughly 85 percent, while the DIY segment generated about 15 percent.

Yet, it is not so much the act of generating used oil that causes potential environmental problems; it is what happens to the used oil afterward. A number of different used-oil management methods are practiced in the United States. The most prevalent, as indicated in Figure 3-2, is recycling through what is called the *used-oil management system*, or the UOMS. This system consists of numerous large and small collectors and consolidators who direct used oil flows to what are called reprocessors and re-refiners. Reprocessors essentially purify the used oil so that it can be burned for its fuel content in industrial, commercial, and even residential establishments. Re-refiners, however, generally pro-

FIGURE 3-1

Generation of Used Oil by Sector
(millions of gallons, 1990)

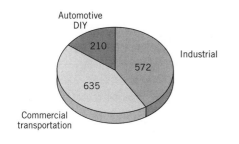

Used oil in the United States is largely generated by industrial and commercial sources, although a significant volume is generated by the automotive sector.
Source: ICF Incorporated, 1992. "Evaluation of Alternative Options for Enhancing Used Oil Recycling."

FIGURE 3-2

Disposition of Used Oil by Major Category
(million of gallons, 1990)

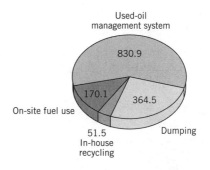

Disposition of used oil is mostly through on- and off-site reuse as fuel or lubricating applications. A substantial volume of used oil, however, is improperly disposed of mainly through dumping onto land and into sewers.
Source: ICF Incorporated, 1992. "Evaluation of Alternative Options for Enhancing Used Oil Recycling."

cess the used oil to the point at which it can be resold for its original lubrication purpose. Both re-refined and reprocessed used oil have a few other nonfuel and nonlubricating uses, but they are minor compared to these major applications. Non-UOMS disposition of used oil consists mainly of on-site recycling in the industrial sector, on-site use as a fuel in the industrial and commercial transport sectors, and dumping, which refers to disposal into sewers or onto land, mostly by generators of very small quantities.

All of this is useful and informative, but if the actual environmental concerns have to do with avoiding risks associated with inappropriate used oil disposal, tracing from generation to ultimate disposition is critical. Table 3-1 provides the best available estimates of how used oil is managed by the different generation sources identified in Figure 3-1. Table 3-1 allows several important observations for the analysis. For example, while the volume of used oil inappropriately managed is large, in percentage terms it is a far larger proportion of the DIY used-oil generation than of the other sectors. Similarly, in the commercial transport sector, farms and mining operations stand out as

Table 3-1
USED OIL GENERATION AND DISPOSITION BY SECTOR
(Millions of gallons in 1990)

Generator Sector	Disposition of Used Oil				
	Used Oil Generated	Used-Oil Management System	On-Site Fuel Use	In-House Recycling	Dumping
Automotive DIY:	210.0	69.9	0.0	0.0	140.1
Commercial Transportation:					
Light Vehicles	293.0	196.3	79.1	0.0	17.6
Trucks and Buses	101.0	67.7	31.3	0.0	2.0
Construction/Mining	127.0	55.9	7.6	0.0	63.5
Farms	84.0	21.8	6.7	0.0	55.5
Aviation	10.0	10.0	0.0	0.0	0.0
Other	20.0	14.6	5.4	0.0	0.0
Subtotal	635.0	366.3	130.1	0.0	138.6
Industrial:					
General Industrial	344.0	237.4	24.1	31.0	51.5
Industrial Engines	47.0	32.4	3.3	4.2	7.1
Metalworking	119.0	82.1	8.3	10.7	17.9
Processes	62.0	42.8	4.3	5.6	9.3
Subtotal	572.0	394.7	40.0	51.5	85.8
Total	1,417.0	830.9	170.1	51.5	364.5

Source: ICF Incorporated, 1992. "Evaluation of Alternative Options for Enhancing Used Oil Recycling."

relatively low-level recyclers. What distinguishes these generators from their higher recycling-rate counterparts appears to be the volume of used oil generated, which is very small in the case of DIYs, and their possible remoteness from the existing recycling infrastructure, especially mining and farm operations.

It is also possible to further disaggregate some of these sectors into regional and other subsets that display significant differences in recycling rates. For example, a few states now regulate used oil substantially more stringently than the federal government, so they recycle at a higher rate than do other states. In any event, the underlying baseline differences among these used-oil generation sectors clearly are important both for designing a framework to analyze the responsiveness of generators to enhanced incentives or opportunities to recover and recycle used oil, and for evaluating the cost and performance of the different approaches.

The central question for this analysis is to determine the relative performance of several alternative approaches for enhancing the recovery and recycling of used oil. Three options were specified for the analysis, representing somewhat different approaches for targeting used-oil recycling decisions. The first is a *product charge* on sales of lubricating oil, with the proceeds devoted to various programs to enhance used-oil recycling, such as collection centers and public education campaigns. A form of this approach was used in Germany during the 1980s and was quite successful at increasing the used-oil recycling rate.

The second, incentive-based option is a *recycling credit* arrangement under which sellers of virgin lubricating oil must recycle an amount of used oil equal to a certain percentage of their sales of virgin oil, 40 percent for example. The percentage would be established by the administrator of EPA and could be increased over time. In lieu of physically recycling the used oil themselves, sellers of virgin lubricating oil could purchase credits from recyclers who do the actual recycling, hence the term "credit" system.

The third approach considered, also incentive-based, is a deposit-refund system in which all or a subset of lubricating oil sales would be subject to a deposit, which would then be refunded upon the return of the used oil. These three alternative approaches are likely to perform differently in enhancing used-oil recovery and recycling because of baseline differences in recycling rates across generators, potentially different sensitivities of some generation sectors to the incentives posed by the systems, and the slight variations in the exact operation of the alternatives.

Before turning to the analysis, it is worth discussing which of the three approaches one might expect to be the most appropriate for reducing inappropriate disposal and enhancing used-oil recycling, based on the baseline used-oil information presented above. Prior to conducting any analysis, most economists would probably argue that the deposit-refund system is likely to enhance used-oil recycling more than the other two systems because its focus on a positive incentive to recycle should appeal to the generators whose recycling rate is lowest, the DIY sector. Indeed, it is almost a reflex for economists to recommend using a deposit-refund system for situations in which the target is millions of individuals, each of whom generates a very small amount of harm. The classic example of this approach is container deposit-refund systems covering plastic and glass bottles. Generally these systems are considered very successful. Given that it is impossible to enforce negative prohibitions, such as handing out fines to every person who litters, it makes sense to use a positive monetary incentive, a refund, to coax consumers to return containers for recycling, and to levy a deposit on the same individuals to provide the money to pay the refunds. A similar line of reasoning seems to point to the deposit-refund approach to solve the used-oil problem. Hence, in this analysis, a critical focus is on whether a deposit-refund system applies in the case of used oil, in which many people individually cause very small harms. Somewhat surprisingly, the answer turns out to be no.

The Analysis

The analysis of the operation and effectiveness of the three different approaches for enhancing used-oil recycling begins with structuring the baseline conditions in the used-oil generation and recycling system. This involves developing information on the supply of virgin lubricating oil, the demand for used oil, and the conditions surrounding the costs of recovering, transporting, and recycling used oil. Next, the basic operation of the three approaches is modeled using a fairly simple analytical framework. Finally, quantitative results for several of the alternatives are presented to demonstrate empirically the conclusions reached in the analysis.

BASELINE SPECIFICATION

Arguably, the most important part of the process of modeling the effects of the alternative approaches on used-oil generation, collection, and management is setting out the baseline conditions, the numbers and types of generators, and the way in which used oil makes its way (or not) into the used-oil management system.These are the tasks—both modeling and data driven—that ultimately determine the operation, impacts, and costs of the different systems. Hence, laying out carefully how the markets for used-oil generation are conceptualized, as well as how the various generation, collection, transport, and other relevant sectors function, are crucial steps in developing a coherent model for computing the effects of these policy alternatives.

To begin, assume the following structure for the market for lubricating oil itself and for the ultimate uses of used oil after it is generated. The simplest, and probably most accurate, representation of the lubricating oil demand func-

tion is perfectly inelastic, at least within the relevant range of price variations potentially caused by any of the policies considered in this analysis. Moreover, to the degree that demand is not perfectly inelastic, any minor changes in quantities simply ripple through the results with little or no effect from a policy perspective on the evaluation of the different approaches for enhancing used-oil recycling.

For used-oil demand, it is reasonable to assume that used-oil re-refiners and reprocessors are *price takers* in the sense that they cannot affect the prices of the substitutes for their products. Further, because of the relative magnitudes involved, within the range of quantity variation anticipated under the three policies, any additional used oil recycled will not affect the prices of the underlying products for which used oil substitutes. This is a reasonable assumption, because the additional flow of re-refined and reprocessed used oil to their respective markets possibly caused by the approaches considered here is very small relative to the volumes in the markets where it is used. Consistent with this assumption, the value of used oil of a given quality level is thus set by the price of its substitute. In the case of used oil that is re-refined, for example, the substitute is virgin lubricating oil. For used oil that is reprocessed and sold as fuel, on the other hand, the substitute is oil of a similar quality, such as a No. 4 fuel oil for industrial boilers.

The effect of these two sets of assumptions concerning the new lubricating oil demand and the demands for used-oil products (fuel, lubricating oil, and other uses) are to isolate, in a modeling sense, used-oil generation, collection, transportation, and any other activities that assist in making used oil appear at the "door" of a re-refiner or a reprocessor.

As a result, changes in the price of new lubricating oil are completely absorbed by purchasers, whether caused by baseline phenomena or by any of the three policies examined here. Similarly, the value of bringing used oil (potentially of differing quality) to the doors of re-refining and reprocessing facilities is primarily dependent on the costs of the alternatives with which they compete in the market—virgin lubricating oil and fuel oil. Hence, none of the costs or activities involved in used-oil generation, collection, transport, and recycling can be passed either backward to the lubricants market or forward to the fuel and lubricating oil markets that demand recycled used oil.

Given all of this, modeling used-oil generation, recovery, and recycling activities can be done using a fairly simple framework. Figure 3-3 graphically displays the relationships of interest. Beginning with the demand side, the horizontal line at point V on the vertical axis is the value of used oil that reaches the door of a re-refiner or reprocessor. Clearly, V is less than the value of the ultimately re-refined or reprocessed used oil because re-refining and repro-

FIGURE 3-3

Used-Oil Supply—Baseline

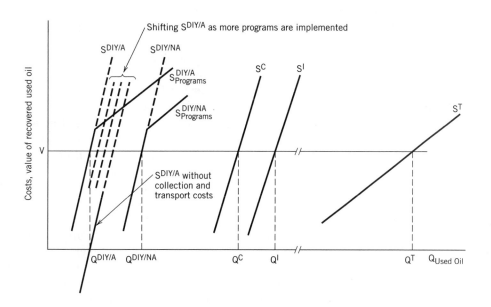

The supply of used oil to the recycling management system flows from a number of sources. Industrial and commercial automotive generators of used oil are mostly insensitive to price due to regulatory and other considerations. For the DIY sectors, V is the value of used oil after collection, consolidation, and transport, as shown by the vertical distance between the automotive DIY *(DIY/A)* supply prior to transport costs and the automotive DIY supply of used oil to the "doors" of recycling facilities. The DIY used-oil supply is not very responsive to the price paid for used-oil returns, but is sensitive to the existence of various collection, information, and other programs that make returning used oil for recycling more convenient. This is shown by shifting the automotive DIY supply function, dependent only on price, to the right as the volume and intensity of these used oil return and recycling programs are increased, to produce the $S_{Programs}^{DIY/A}$ schedule.

cessing are costly. Moreover, the used oil actually generated varies in quality, so Figure 3-3 can be thought of as the market for used oil of a particular quality class. V will thus be different for different quality stocks of used oil.

Abstracting from quality differences, Figure 3-3 shows how the framework models the flows of used oil from generators to recycling facilities. First, there are multiple sources of used oil whose typical volumes and recovery cost conditions differ from one type of generator to another. Larger volume generators, such as industrial facilities and commercial automotive generators, face different used-oil recovery, collection, and transport costs, and may respond differently to changes in the used-oil management system than, for example, the millions of DIYs who generate only a few gallons of used oil each year. Furthermore, the baseline conditions for generators of a given type may vary substantially. For example, the density of locations to which to return used oil affects the rate of recycling among automotive DIYs. Hence, it seems reasonable to divide this population into several different groups based on such factors as the density of return locations.

Based on these and other considerations, the framework groups the subsectors of generators listed in Table 3-1 into four classes: (1) industrial generators (I); (2) commercial automotive generators, such as service stations and lube shops (C); (3) nonautomotive DIYs (DIY/NA), which are remote machinery operations at, for example, mines and farms; and (4) urban, suburban and rural DIYs, referred to as automotive DIYs (DIY/A).

The supplies from these four used-oil generation sectors are shown in Figure 3-3. It is important to explain carefully how these sources of supply are constructed. First, several activities are often performed by different entities to move used oil from generators to recycling facilities; these include generation, recovery, collection, consolidation, and transportation.[2] The approach explicitly models these layered activities, beginning with the supply of used oil from generators, then adding the costs of collection and transport.

Second, in Figure 3-3 the high-volume industrial and commercial automotive sectors' supplies of used oil are shown as steep curves, reflecting the view that, especially in the current environmental regulatory and liability climate, these entities are unlikely to reduce their supply of used oil to the management system even if the value of recovering and recycling used oil falls. This is consistent with the fact that these sources do relatively little improper disposal. They may attempt to increase their supply by undertaking various additional activities (say, by redoubling their recovery efforts) if used-oil values rise, but will not generate substantially more used oil. Hence, the view here is that industrial and commercial automotive supply to the used-oil management system is not very price sensitive. The industrial and commercial used-oil supplies also abstract from the division of V between payments for recovery of oil, and collection and transport costs. For in-house reuse, the value of the recycled used oil is mostly retained by the facility recovering the oil, but for recycling off-site, this value covers both direct payments to generators and the costs incurred to deliver the used oil to recycling facilities.

The other two used-oil generation sources shown in Figure 3-3 differ somewhat from the industrial and commercial automotive sectors. These segments are characterized by large numbers of individual generators with, in most cases, relatively small amounts of used oil in any given period. Both their low volumes of generation per entity and their dispersion geographically make modeling these sources very different from the

---

[2] Of course, used oil that is recycled on-site or used for in-house fuel will not require some of these steps. This analysis, however, focuses mainly on off-site recycling.

higher volume commercial transportation and industrial sectors.

Because of either the low volumes and infrequency of generation or geographical isolation, recycling rates in these sectors are largely a function of considerations other than the prices paid for used oil. For automotive DIY generators in particular, such factors as a predisposition to recycle, the ease of returning used oil, the distance to and convenience of return facilities, possible curbside collection, and the existence of public and private programs intended to enhance the recycling of used oil and other materials, are all probably better determinants of used-oil recycling rates than the prices received (especially because the prices received typically are zero). Similar considerations apply to portions of the nonautomotive DIY sector, although some of these entities may resemble the larger industrial generators. An additional consideration in farm-sector recycling is the value of using the oil in some other productive way—to kill weeds or to oil machinery, for example.

In light of this anticipated price insensitivity, the generator supplies from these sources would be expected to be extremely inelastic with respect to used-oil prices received. Subsets of the other generation sectors presumably also face similar conditions in that the volumes generated are low, and the implicit inconvenience costs of recovery and return are high. This would account for the industrial sector dumping, for example. Thus, where dumping is prevalent, the cause appears to be the very low value of what is periodically generated relative to the fairly high costs of recovery and return.

If this were the end of the story, the prospects for enhanced used-oil recovery from any of these sources would be grim. Another key feature of the supply from these generators, however, is important for the analysis. In particular, the value of recovering, collecting, and transporting used oil from these generators to recycling facilities is not necessarily transmitted blindly through the intermediaries and down to the generators themselves. Because of their numbers, dispersion, low volumes, and intermittence of supply, in many cases it is less expensive to undertake a number of different activities at the collection and consolidation stage to enhance used-oil return than it is to simply offer DIYs higher and higher payments for returning oil. Information and education programs, a greater number of drop-off points, more intensive direct collection systems, and so forth, are less costly and more effective at raising return rates for these generators than offering more money for returning used oil. Therefore, one would expect that as the value of delivering used oil to recycling facilities increases, more and more of these nonprice methods and programs would be instituted by entities in the used-oil collection system. Unless there is a good reason otherwise, the supply from DIY generators should reflect the minimum cost methods for obtaining their used oil. Hence, it is by reference to these nonprice programs and activities that the DIY supply function should be derived.

The automotive DIY sector shown in Figure 3-3 is constructed using two methods, reflecting the absence and the presence of these nonprice programs and activities that encourage DIY recovery and return of used oil. For quantities up to the baseline amount and potentially somewhat higher than that, the analysis assumes that these programs are sparse and generally only undertaken in a few localities. Furthermore, because this is the supply to the doors of reprocessors and re-refiners, the supply curve reflects not only DIY costs of recovery and return, but also those of collection, consolidation, and transport. This analysis assumes that the current baseline payment to DIYs who recover their used oil is zero, so that these other costs consume the entire value of the oil. The supply from DIYs is thus shown in Figure 3-3 as a very steep curve beginning below the quantity axis and intersecting it at the baseline quantity, $Q^{DIY/A}$, to which these collection, consolidation, and transport costs are added to arrive at the automotive DIY supply to the doors of recycling facilities, the steep $S^{DIY/A}$ curve intersecting the horizontal line drawn from V.

While the initial baseline conditions assume relatively modest levels of DIY return programs, higher values of used oil will cause municipalities, oil companies, independent collectors, and other such entities to fund the establishment of more of the nonprice programs and activities that help to enhance DIY recycling. That is, as the value of used oil rises, rather than paying a few cents more for DIY used-oil returns, the higher value is devoted to increasing the density of collection points, to education campaigns, and other such programs to substantially reduce the inconvenience costs of recovering and returning used DIY oil. As with any activity, consumers respond to the total cost involved, not just the monetary component. It simply happens that the nonmonetary costs of returning used oil are very high for automotive DIYs. Hence, measures that directly reduce these time and inconvenience costs will produce the greatest impact on DIY used-oil returns.

The automotive DIY supply function in Figure 3-3 incorporates the fact that higher used-oil values will give rise to more of these convenience-enhancing programs, thus eventually the curve becomes flatter, as indicated by $S_{Programs}^{DIY/A}$. The supply of this used oil to recycling facilities thus reflects the increasing use of convenience-enhancing programs, rather than simply higher price payments to DIYs. Merely raising prices paid for DIY used oil would continue along the dotted portion of the original automotive DIY supply function, $S^{DIY/A}$. Instead, one should think of the DIY supply function with the progressive implementation of these recovery programs as being the locus created by a succession of very steep DIY supplies moving from the baseline to increasing levels of convenience-enhancing programs. This is shown in Figure 3-3 for the automotive DIY sector as several dotted supply curves (inclusive of the costs of collection and transport)

reflecting levels of implementation of those programs that trace the actual automotive DIY supply function, $S_{Programs}^{DIY/A}$.

This construction of the supply functions for low-volume, dispersed generators is roughly consistent with what is known about how these sectors actually behave. But it is also integral to understanding how these sectors might respond to the various approaches considered in this analysis for enhancing used-oil recycling. In particular, because of transactions costs, individual DIYs cannot consolidate any revenues they might receive from used-oil returns and reproduce the activities, programs, and collection systems that are integral to encouraging and enhancing used-oil recovery and return to the management system. Instead, only entities elsewhere in the collection system can convert small amounts of money per gallon of used oil into these recovery programs and activities—oil companies, recycling collectors, municipalities, and so forth. This imposes an important asymmetry in the potential supply responses one can expect under the three different used-oil recycling enhancement policies.

MODELING THE THREE APPROACHES

The basic framework outlined above can be used to examine the performance of the three candidate approaches for enhancing used-oil recycling. Because of the baseline volumes and disposition of used-oil supply, the expected price insensitivity of most generators, and the asymmetry conditions that govern the supply of DIY used-oil, this qualitative analysis reveals significant differences in the performance of the policies.

Impact of a Product Charge on Used-Oil Recycling: In its most basic form, the product charge is the easiest of the three options to analyze. In essence, the product charge is a tax on lubricating oil sales, with the proceeds used to fund the various programs and activities that enhance the recovery and recycling of used oil, especially from the DIY sectors. Because this framework assumes a completely inelastic demand for lubricating oil, the charge is absorbed by lubricating-oil purchasers, with no impacts on any of the flows of interest in the framework.

The central issue for the product-charge approach is determining exactly how the revenues from the charge should be spent. What is assumed here is that the money is devoted to doing the best things possible to enhance used-oil recycling. Here "best" refers to activities that obtain the most used oil for the least cost. Because this analysis does not incorporate risk reduction from increasing used-oil recycling, but is instead confined to estimating costs and assessing success in terms of enhancing used-oil recycling, the best use of the product charge revenues is defined in these cost-effectiveness terms.

The proceeds of the product-charge would thus be allocated to states and localities to use for education campaigns, drop-off centers and collection infrastructure, and other methods to make it more convenient to return used oil. What is viewed as outside the scope of the proper use of the product-charge revenues is making, or causing to be made, direct payments to used-oil generators. While not beyond the government's legal authority, making direct payments for used oil essentially mimics the refund side of a deposit-refund system. There seems little point in analyzing a product-charge system that is in reality a deposit-refund system, especially when the latter is a competing option to be evaluated. Hence, the activities the government would undertake with the product-charge revenues would focus on funding the sets of programs and other measures intended to enhance returns of DIY used-oil and a few other sources of used oil facing similarly high inconvenience costs.

Given the construction of the supplies of used oil, the use of the product-charge revenues can be thought of as moving up the automotive and other DIY supply functions, spending both the price received for additional oil delivered to recyclers and the charge revenues, un-

til the funds are exhausted. For simplicity of presentation, the product-charge revenues are shown as being spent on programs and activities that enhance the recovery and return of both the automotive and nonautomotive DIY segments, and none in the industrial and commercial sectors, although this is not to suggest that DIY-type problems do not exist in other subsectors of used-oil generation.

While it is intuitive to think of the product charge generating revenues moving gradually up the DIY supply functions by creating more of the relevant programs, V, the value of recovered used-oil, remains unchanged. Hence, one can also think of the market effects of these recycling program expenditures as a downward shift in the DIY supply functions, so that their new intersections with V are consistent with the increased amount of DIY-generated used oil collected after funding the additional collection programs. This is shown graphically in Figure 3-4, where the same level of V now generates a larger quantity of used oil from DIY sources.

One can then calculate the costs of levying the product charge and spending the funds on these recycling programs directly. First, the product-charge revenues are a transfer from lubricating oil purchasers to the government, or whatever entity operates the system. Hence, the net cost of the product charge option is simply the total cost of obtaining the additional used oil, including the used-oil recycling infrastructure expenditures, minus the social value of the extra used oil. Graphically, this net cost is shown as the shaded areas above V under the original DIY supply functions between the old and the new quantities supplied.

This measurement of the net cost of the product charge in Figure 3-4 is consistent with the conventional analysis of the welfare cost of a subsidy, which is the essential function of using the product-charge revenues to subsidize used-oil collection programs. In the usual analysis of a subsidy, the supply function is shifted downward by the amount of the subsidy; the net welfare cost

FIGURE 3-4

Impact of a Product Charge on Used-Oil Recycling

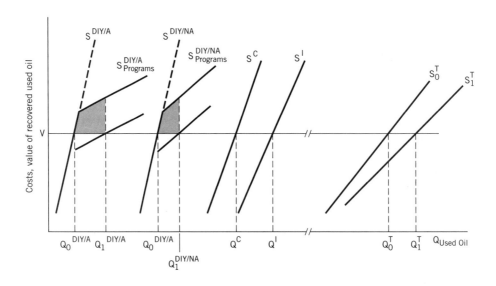

Product-charge revenues are spent on DIY sector information, collection, and consolidation programs. *V* remains unchanged in this process, so that the DIY supplies are best thought of as shifting downward. Net costs are the shaded areas between the original DIY supplies and V, and the baseline and new DIY quantities recycled.

is calculated as the area below the original supply function and above the demand function between the baseline and the new (higher) quantity. In effect, the net welfare cost is the difference between the cost of supplying the extra units minus the value to demanders of the extra quantity. The areas shaded in Figure 3-4 correspond to this concept: *V* measures the value to society of each additional gallon of recycled oil, and the costs of obtaining the extra used oil are represented by the areas under the original DIY supply functions between the old and new quantities.

Finally, this analysis addresses only the costs of the used-oil recycling program. Presumably, collecting this additional used oil reduces the environmental risks of improper disposal, such as dumping. While these have not been calculated here, if one assumes that the risk-reduc-

tion benefits of additional used-oil recycling are worth at least the marginal additional costs spent under the product charge to obtain it, the net social welfare effect of the approach will be positive.[3]

Impact of a Recycling Credit System on Used-Oil Recycling: Recall that the recycling credit system requires sellers of virgin lubricating oil to recycle

[3] The risks posed by used oil, as outlined at the beginning of this analysis, are at best controversial. Depending on the viewpoint of the estimator, improper used-oil disposal is argued to be either one of the nation's worst environmental problems or a benign set of practices largely without any environmental significance. The project on which this analysis is based was confined to the "cost-side" of the used-oil question, and focused exclusively on the operation and effectiveness of the alternative used-oil recycling programs.

an amount of used oil equal to a certain percentage of their virgin oil sales, for example, 40 percent. These oil manufacturers can perform the recycling themselves or they can purchase credits for the required amount from used-oil recyclers. This system operates in the analytical framework in a fairly simple way. As shown in Figure 3-5, the total amount of recycling required in order to sell the quantity of lubricating oil demanded is indicated by the vertical line at the right of the graph. This line intersects the total supply of used oil to the management system at a price above V, as indicated. Tracing back to the individual supply functions along this higher implied price yields the new quantities of used oil supplied under the system from each source.

In essence, the higher value of used oil caused by the minimum level of recycling mandated by the credit system is fed back through the system to achieve the additional used-oil recovery required.

Of course, this graphical exposition of the operation of the credit system tends to obscure the reality of how the used-oil system will meet the recycling target quantity. As discussed, used-oil demanders do not simply call out higher prices and wait for a supply response. Instead, spurred by the higher profitability of used-oil recycling, both sources bid higher prices for industrial and other large-volume supplies and engage in the many programs and activities that encourage additional DIY used-oil recovery and returns. Thus, as shown in Fig-

FIGURE 3-5

Impact of a Recycling Credit System on Used-Oil Recycling

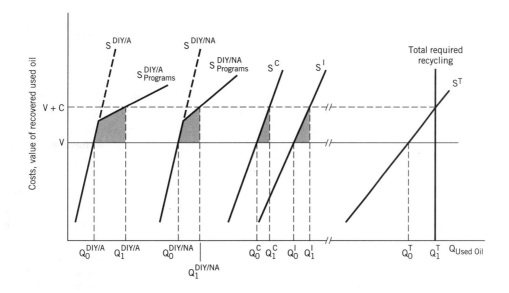

The credit system requires additional used-oil recycling to meet the target percentage. This encourages additional used-oil supply from the industrial and commercial sectors through the higher price, V, plus the value of the credits, C. For the DIY sectors, the higher value of used oil, C, is spent on information, collection, and consolidation programs to generate additional recovery.

ure 3-5, although the credit system's operation equalizes the marginal supply costs of used oil across different sources, the composition of the costs for the industrial and commercial sources is somewhat different from that of the DIY sectors. While transport and other such costs are relevant to all sectors, payments directly to generators are likely to be more prevalent for the former two sources, but uncommon for the DIY sectors, where these funds are instead invested in convenience-enhancing infrastructure. Thus, the actions that underlie the market's ability to achieve the recycling target include both nonprice ways to increase DIY recovery and recycling and price-based incentives to other supply sources, both of which are funded by the credits.

Another interesting observation is that there is an effective maximum value of the credit based on the costs of other virgin products that could be brought into the system masquerading as used oil. That is, if credits become extremely valuable, products that resemble used oil will enter the system to generate credits if the costs of these products are less than the value of the credits. This enforcement problem, of course, applies to any approach that raises the value of recovering used oil.

The cost of the recycling credit system is measured very much the same way as is the product charge. The cost of the credits to sellers of virgin lubricating oil, either to purchase them or to generate them directly through additional recycling, is passed through to lubricating oil purchasers. The unit value of the credit is determined by the cost of obtaining and recycling the marginal unit of used oil to satisfy the recycling target. Hence, as before, the net cost impact is measured by the areas under the supply functions down to the social value of the additional used oil collected, V, between the old and new quantities. Again, the overall net welfare effect of the credit system depends on the risk-reduction benefits of en-

hanced used-oil recycling. As with the product-charge analysis, if one assumes that the value of this environmental risk reduction is at least equal to the marginal credit value, the net social benefits of the system are positive.

Impact of a Deposit-Refund System on Used-Oil Recycling: A deposit-refund system can be modeled in this framework by thinking of the deposit as a product charge on lubricating oil sales, and the refund as a subsidy to certain used-oil-related activities; for example, returning oil to recycling facilities or to local collection centers. As before, the deposit (or charge) part of the system is absorbed by lubricating oil purchasers, so these are thought of as transfers between purchasers and the entity operating the system. The refund (or subsidy) part of the system, if focused on all used-oil returns, can be thought of as subsidizing the costs of moving used oil from generators through the management system and to the ultimate end-users. In general, this will have the effect of increasing the recycling of used oil, although it is critical to determine what activities are subject to a refund and which entities receive them.

Consider first a system in which all lubricating oil sales are subject to a deposit and all generators who supply used oil for recycling receive refunds (paid by the drop-off point or the collector, for example). To keep transactions costs to a minimum, the system does not require proof that a deposit was paid to receive a refund. In general, the rate of throughput of the lubricating oil business is sufficiently rapid that paying refunds for oil for which no deposit was paid (because it was purchased prior to the system's enactment) will not pose an undue strain on the system's finances. Deposit and refund rates could be adjusted initially to account for this if it was a significant issue.

As noted, the deposits are transfers from the users of lubricating oil to the entity operating the system. The refunds are then paid to generators, which encourages them to recover and supply more used oil to the recycling system. It is important to note that the refunds are paid to generators themselves, not to those who ultimately deliver used oil to recycling facilities (if these are different entities). In Figure 3-6, the refund raises the potential value of recovering used oil to the generators themselves. Hence, the refund shifts all of the supply functions downward by the amount of the effective subsidy, including the DIY supply functions. However, the DIY supply functions that are shifted here are the very steep functions drawn under the assumption that the existing recycling infrastructure is not enhanced, regardless of the higher value of recovering used oil. Because the refund is paid to DIY generators, the flatter DIY supply

functions used in the analysis so far are not applicable. Instead, the relevant supply behavior will be the inelastic functions indicated in Figure 3-6, where the flatter segments are now dotted to reflect their irrelevance.

Given this understanding of a deposit-refund system's operation, probably the most important result is the very small increase in the DIY quantities of used oil obtained under this program relative to the other two approaches. The problem is that the refunds paid to individual DIYs who return used oil for recycling are effectively lost from the collection system, because the numerous DIYs cannot pool their refunds to finance a used-oil recycling infrastructure that would benefit them, a problem ultimately caused by high transactions costs.

FIGURE 3-6

Impact of a Deposit-Refund System on Used-Oil Recycling

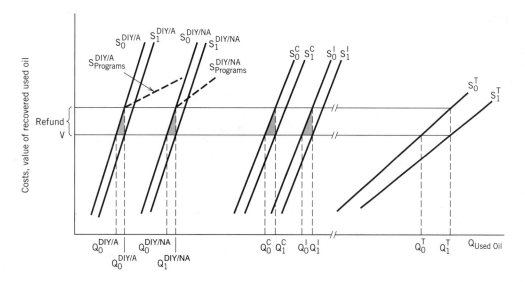

The deposit-refund system encourages additional supplies by offering a higher price for recovering and returning used oil. Because the deposit revenues are returned to DIYs, no additional information, collection, and consolidation programs are undertaken.

The cost of this system is calculated as follows. The deposits are transfers from lubricating oil purchasers to the entity operating the system. The net cost of the program is the difference between the social cost of obtaining the additional used oil and the value to society of the used oil. As before, the net social cost of the program is given by the shaded areas between the old and new quantities under the original supply functions down to V.

Another form of the deposit-refund system could be targeted solely at the automotive DIY sectors. Assuming that used-oil generation sources could be distinguished and the system enforced, the analysis of this system would be the same as above except that only the automotive DIY sector would be included. As with the recycling credit system, there is a limit on the effective value of refunds. This is dictated by the prices of products resembling used oil that could enter the system to obtain the refunds— an enforcement issue that becomes increasingly important the higher the refund rate.

Finally, the only way for a deposit-refund system to encourage the used-oil system to undertake the activities and programs that appear to be better than pure price signals in encouraging DIYs to return used oil is to give the refunds to the entities that can undertake these activities instead of the generators. These entities are likely to be large distributors, oil companies, recycling companies, local governments, and even retail stores. Of course this could be done, but such a system would then look very little like the traditional deposit-refund system for container deposits in which numerous individuals are targeted with a positive incentive to avoid littering. One could still call this a deposit-refund system, but in reality it would be a tax-subsidy system like the product-charge approach, in which the revenues are used to undertake DIY used-oil recovery and return programs. But that is the operation of a competing approach, the product-charge system; it would render the analysis pointless to transform the deposit-refund system into simply another variation of a tax-subsidy scheme to improve its performance.

EMPIRICAL ASSESSMENT OF THE APPROACHES

Given the operation of the three different approaches for enhancing used-oil recycling as analyzed above, it is easy to determine which is likely to provide the greatest benefit at the least cost to the economy. Indeed, two features of the used-oil market and the operation of the different options for enhancing recycling suggest an obvious conclusion. First, the large commercial transportation and industrial generators already recycle the vast majority of their used oil. Relatively modest changes in their incentives are unlikely to produce much additional used oil. This implies that systems that cover all generators of used oil probably will be less cost-effective than others with a tighter focus.

Second, and probably most important, is that the most realistic sources of additional used oil, especially used oil that is currently dumped or otherwise inappropriately disposed of, are the DIY sectors, or other subsectors that share the inconvenience-of-return problems. In addition, because of its generation volume, dispersion, and other factors, the best way to target and ensure the return of DIY used-oil is to establish and expand the many different information and education programs, the common-sense infrastructure investments, and the host of other activities that accomplish this objective.

Hence, the best candidate is the product charge, because it provides a source of revenue to fund cost-effective DIY and related subsector recycling, collection, education, and other investments. The credit system is probably the runner- up because it, too, triggers these cost-effective methods of obtaining additional DIY used-oil. Yet, the credit approach also brings other large generators of used oil into the system, probably unnecessarily, for these other sources already recycle most of their used oil.

It is interesting that the least desirable option—the deposit-refund system—is the one most economists would nominate for the automotive DIY used-oil sector. Ordinarily, the circumstance of many people possessing small quantities of something environmentally harmful would be tailor-made for a deposit-refund system. But the peculiar nature of the generation and collection conditions for DIY used-oil renders the direct refund of deposits to DIYs a relatively weak mechanism for obtaining additional used oil.

A simple numerical model illustrates empirically how much more powerful the product-charge approach is for increasing DIY used-oil recovery relative to the deposit-refund system. The information used in this model reflects the most accurate information currently available concerning used-oil generation and disposition, the existing recycling infrastructure for DIYs, and the best estimates of DIY responses to the various methods of encouraging greater used-oil recovery and recycling.[4] Still, the underlying data are extinct, and a substantial degree of professional judgment, ratified by anecdotal evidence, is necessary to provide any quantitative analysis of the relative performance of these two approaches to DIY used-oil recycling.

Table 3-2 lists the national automotive DIY baseline situation in terms of population, the percentage of households classified as DIYs, the volume of used oil generated by these DIYs, and the amount of that used oil ultimately recycled. These figures imply a national average automotive DIY recycling rate of 33.3 percent.

---

[4] The quantitative inputs used here were developed based on a number of studies of used-oil generation and collection conducted by federal agencies, states, and private industry. Given the scarcity of primary data in this area, a considerable amount of professional judgment on the parts of those with expertise in used-oil collection and management was required to transform sketchy information from widely varying locations and surveys into parameters suitable for numerical analysis. As such, these inputs are more than illustrative, but less than precise. Nevertheless, the information and modeling do yield sensible results when compared to actual used-oil recycling programs.

Table 3-2
BASELINE CHARACTERISTICS OF AUTOMOTIVE DIY SECTOR, 1990

Characteristic	Level
Population	248,243,000
Percent DIY	60%
Used Oil Generated (gal.)	210,000,000
Used Oil Recycled (gal.)	69,873,000
Recycling Rate	33.3%
Education Saturation	10.0%
Curbside Used Oil Pickup	2.0%
Drop-Off Sites	6,500
Drop-Off Sites per Community of 100,000	2.6

Source: ICF Incorporated, 1992. "Evaluation of Alternative Options for Enhancing Used-Oil Recycling."

Table 3-2 also lists the total national number of drop-off sites where used oil can be taken for collection and recycling, as well as the levels of both curbside used-oil pickup and public information and education programs. Curbside pickup of used oil is extremely low, offered to only about 2 percent of the population. The public information and education figure reflects that nationally about ten percent of the population is "saturated" with knowledge of how and why they should recycle used oil.

Finally, the number of drop-off sites is restated in terms of the number per "typical" community of 100,000 people, 2.6, because the cost estimates and effectiveness measures for the various used-oil recycling program activities were developed for this representative size community. Modeling used-oil recovery, collection, and recycling in the context of a community of urban, suburban, and rural residents is necessary to reflect different baseline recycling rates and other relevant factors that vary significantly by population density, and to explore how the cost and efficacy of programs to enhance used-oil recycling are affected by community characteristics.

Hence, conceptualizing a moderately sized community composed of automotive DIYs in a variety of circumstances captures both the baseline distinctions of importance as well as the challenges faced by those communities as they attempt to increase used-oil recycling. For purposes of this numerical analysis, the results of the deposit-refund and product-charge systems for the hypothetical community of 100,000 people are simply scaled up to the United States population total to obtain the national estimates of the effectiveness of these two programs.

To analyze the implementation of the product-charge program, one must first consider how to productively allocate the revenues among the various programs and activities that enhance automotive DIY used-oil recycling. Rough calculations suggest that the most cost-effective expenditures are to add used-oil collection tanks and related equipment to existing curbside collection trucks that do not already have them, which costs only a few cents per gallon of used oil collected. Yet, this allocation is economical only for areas in which curbside separation and collection is already practiced, or about 15 percent of households nationally. Beyond that point, the used-oil curbside-collection option is prohibitively expensive, for it requires purchasing additional trucks and other equipment, rather than "piggybacking" on an existing separation and collection system.

Two other relatively inexpensive and productive uses of the product-charge revenues that increase DIY used-oil recycling are public education campaigns and drop-off centers. Up to a point, the information campaigns yield some added used-oil returns from DIYs at a cost of ten to twenty cents per gallon. Yet, these effects are also conditioned on the presence of drop-off centers and curbside collection of used oil, so that not just information, but also access and convenience are important for recovering additional used oil from DIYs who are not offered curbside used-oil collection service. In general, an additional used-oil drop-off center costs about thirty

to forty cents per gallon of used oil collected, and yields an increased used-oil recycling rate overall of 2 to 4 percent for the representative community of 100,000 people, given the current average density of 2.6 drop-off points.

Based on this rough sense of what activities would be funded from the product-charge revenues, this empirical illustration assumes that 70 percent of the funds will be spent on additional drop-off centers, 20 percent on more DIY information and education campaigns, and the remaining 10 percent on adding the low-cost additions to handle used oil for existing curbside collection systems.

The deposit-refund system is easier to examine empirically, because the only key parameter is the sensitivity of automotive DIY recovery and recycling to the price received for the used oil returned. Figure 3-7 illustrates the change in the DIY used-oil recovery rate as a function of the refund received. From the diagram, it is clear that refunds in the range of tens of cents per gallon raise the recycling rate very little. Of course, this simply reflects the dominance of the inconvenience factor in determining DIY used-oil recycling. A few cents per gallon per return amounts to virtually nothing when compared to the monetary and time costs of undertaking used-oil recovery and recycling in the first place.

Based on these parameters and assumptions, the relative effectiveness of the programs can be computed. Table 3-3 reports the quantitative results of installing a product charge of five cents per gallon on new lubricating oil purchases by DIYs, coupled with funding the various DIY recycling programs discussed above, and a deposit-refund system that collects the same five cents per gallon from DIYs on lubricating oil purchases, but refunds that same amount for used oil returned for recycling.

As shown in Table 3-3, the product charge levied at five cents per gallon of DIY lubricating oil sales generates nearly $27,000,000 for use in these programs. Allocated according to the percentages indicated above, this raises the "satu-

FIGURE 3-7

Price Sensitivity of Automotive DIYs to Refund

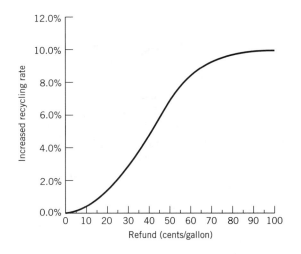

Recycling rate for automotive DIYs is very insensitive to the refund offered. Significant increases in recycling through higher refunds requires large per-gallon payments.

Source: ICF Incorporated, 1992. "Evaluation of Alternative Options for Enhancing Used-Oil Recycling."

ration" level of the education and information programs to 27.2 percent from the baseline level of only 10 percent. Table 3-3 also shows that curbside pickup for used oil now covers all of the preexisting curbside collection programs that service about fifteen percent of the population. Finally, the number of drop-off sites per representative community of 100,000 people rises from 2.6 to 5.1. Taken together, these programs raise the automotive DIY recycling rate overall from 33.3 percent to 46.6 percent, gathering almost 30,000,000 gallons of additional used oil to be recovered and recycled rather than dumped.

In contrast, the deposit-refund system is less effective in obtaining more used oil from the automotive DIY sector. As indicated in Table 3-3, a five-cent deposit and refund for automotive DIYs increases the recycling rate by less than .2 percent. Again, this reflects the fact that this system utilizes none of the funds to add the various programs that far more effectively recover and recycle DIY used-oil. Because of transactions costs, the individual DIYs cannot combine their refunds and cause the added used-oil collection and recycling infrastructure

Table 3-3
PERFORMANCE OF PRODUCT-CHARGE AND DEPOSIT–REFUND SYSTEMS FOR AUTOMOTIVE DIYS

Characteristic	Baseline	Product Charge	Deposit–Refund
Used Oil Generated (gallons)	210,000,000	210,000,000	210,000,000
Funds Generated	n/a	$26,923,100	$26,923,100
Refunds	n/a	n/a	$3,512,873
Funds Spent on Programs	n/a	$26,923,100	n/a
Education Saturation	10%	27.2%	10%
Curbside Used-Oil Pickup	2%	15.4%	2%
Drop-Off Sites per 100,000	2.6	5.1	2.6
Used Oil Recycled (gallons)	69,873,000	96,208,040	70,257,460
Used-Oil Recycling Rate	33.3%	46.6%	33.5%

Source: ICF Incorporated, 1992. "Evaluation of Alternative Options for Enhancing Used-Oil Recycling."

to be established that would increase the convenience of returning used oil.

Table 3-3 also indicates, however, that the very weak response of automotive DIYs to the refund rate implies that a substantial amount of unredeemed deposits will remain under the deposit-refund system. It might then seem reasonable to raise the refund rate until the pool of unredeemed deposits is exhausted. Doing so would result in a refund rate of about thirty-five cents per gallon. But even a refund this large raises the automotive DIY recycling rate only an additional 4 percent, so this system's performance is still far less effective at increasing used-oil recycling than the product-charge approach.

Another way to illustrate the difference in effectiveness of the two approaches is to search for a refund rate that approximates the recycling outcome of a product charge. A charge of only two cents per gallon raises the automotive DIY recycling rate from 33.3 percent to 42.6 percent. Yet, it takes a refund rate of about sixty-eight cents per gallon to achieve roughly the same recycling outcome. Refund rates in this range are at or higher than the prices of other fuels and substances that could be substituted for used oil in order to obtain refunds. This runs the risk of bankrupting the system through misrepresenting the identity of what is returned for refunds. It is not clear that any deposit-refund system can match the success of the product-charge system in practice if the implied refund rate exceeds the cost of products that resemble used oil.

All of this clearly indicates that the deposit-refund system for DIY used-oil is less effective at increasing the used-oil recycling rate than is the product-charge option. Does the same broad conclusion hold if the evaluation criterion is shifted from effectiveness at increasing used-oil recycling to net social welfare enhancement? The answer is yes, as long as the value of risk reduction associated with the increased DIY used-oil recovery and recycling equals or exceeds the additional costs of either of the programs. That is, because the costs of collecting and recycling the additional

DIY used-oil under the product-charge system are less than under the deposit-refund system, if the risk reduction benefits exceed the costs under either program, the net welfare improvement under the product-charge system must be greater.

Finally, shifting the evaluation criteria slightly by observing that while the deposit-refund system is not a very effective method of increasing the DIY used-oil recycling rate, it does appear to generate a significant amount of revenue, in the form of unredeemed deposits, for the operator of the system. Indeed, the five-cent-per-gallon deposit-refund system shown in Table 3-3 provides over $23,000,000 of unredeemed deposit revenues. If these funds were to be allocated to the various DIY used-oil recycling programs as with the product charge, the system's performance would be vastly improved.

While this is true, if these unredeemed deposits were to be so allocated, the system would operate much more like the product charge, rather than a deposit-refund system. But the issue here is the effectiveness of the fundamental features of the two approaches for enhancing DIY used-oil recovery and recycling. The fact that the deposit-refund system is not particularly successful at gathering additional used oil unless it is transformed into a variation of the product charge approach is simply another way to state the overall conclusion concerning its performance relative to other options. The engine that drives a deposit-refund system is the incentive generated by the refunds, and the reality appears to be that this mechanism doesn't function well in the context of used oil. Indeed, even raising the refund rate to exhaust all deposit revenues does not significantly improve its relative performance. This conclusion is not altered by deciding to spend unredeemed deposits the way one would the proceeds of a product charge.

Still, one might observe that the deposit-refund system could generate a large amount of revenue for use by the government for other purposes, as long as political pressures do not force a balance between total deposits and total re-funds. While this is true, the object of this evaluation is to determine the effectiveness of the alternative approaches in raising the DIY used-oil recycling rate, not whether lubricating oil is a good candidate for a revenue-raising tax. One could similarly question whether spending the product-charge revenues to raise used-oil recycling rates is a better use of the funds than retaining them for other uses. This, too, involves an extension of the basis of this evaluation to weighing the welfare enhancement achieved by increasing used-oil recycling against the social benefits of other public expenditures. Both of these observations are beyond the scope of this analysis, although they are clearly important issues from a broader public policy perspective.

Finally, two cautions are appropriate. One is that the relatively weak performance of the deposit-refund system for used-oil recovery is not somehow a serious blow against the approach in general. Rather, it just happens that the conditions of DIY used-oil collection make this method relatively less attractive than other alternatives. Deposit-refund systems have been used quite productively for some years to en-hance returns of beverage containers and other recyclable items. But it is easy to see why the experience with deposit-refund systems for returnable glass and plastic containers has been far more successful than it would be for used oil. Among other differences, returnable container collection-point densities (mainly grocery stores) are high, and this convenience means returns are frequent, while the reverse is generally true for used oil.

The second caution is that, throughout this discussion, the policy goal of enhancing used-oil recycling, especially DIY oil, has not been questioned. Some observers of the used-oil debate, however, suggest that the major environmental problem caused by used oil is not casual dumping of small quantities by numerous DIYs. Instead, they argue that the main environmental harm occurs when inadequately reprocessed used oil, or waste oil that has been intentionally adulterated with hazardous wastes, is burned as a fuel in industrial, commercial, and large residential facilities. If this is so, the problem is primarily one of enforcement of existing regulations, and none of the approaches analyzed here would be relevant to reducing these risks.

Chapter 4

Reconciling Conceptual Tools
and Available Data

This chapter continues to expand on the basic theme of applying the fundamental concepts and technical apparatus of microeconomics in practical analyses of environmental policy and regulation. As with the previous two chapters, the applications of environmental economics presented here focus on developing modeling tools for analyzing real-world policy questions. This chapter, however, emphasizes a slightly different aspect of the interplay between data availability and the design of analytical approaches, which is that theoretical methods must match the type and quality of the information available. There is no sense in designing a highly complex framework for an empirical analysis if there is no hope of obtaining credible detailed data to apply to it. Similarly, it is important to ensure that the information used in an empirical model is indeed what the framework requires.

The first application in this chapter reviews the analytical core of a larger project that evaluated regulatory controls to reduce human exposure to formaldehyde. In this study, the key issue is the practical impossibility of obtaining a key set of input data for the analysis. But something can always be done. The questions are precisely what that might be, and how distant the end result will be from the ideal.

The second application summarizes the analysis and central findings of a project that reviewed and evaluated a large simulation model for predicting the costs and other effects of a regulation tightening restrictions on the use of a particular pesticide. The central concern in this study is the importance of consistency between input data and the requirements of analytical frameworks. Here the economic model was quite extensive and sophisticated, and large amounts of information were available for quantitative analysis. The problem turned out to be that the model's requirements in one small area were different from the nature of the input information used, with serious consequences for the empirical results.

Restrictions on Formaldehyde Use in Textiles Manufacturing[1]

One of the environmental statutes EPA administers is the Toxic Substances Control Act, or TSCA. This statute is unusual for several rea-

[1] While a number of ICF Incorporated staff members assisted in conducting the research project on which this analysis is based, the contributions of Clarence Koo and Sudhakar Kesavan deserve special acknowledgment.

sons, as discussed in Chapter 2. Briefly, other EPA statutes tend to focus on particular media or activities that give rise to human and nonhuman risks, such as hazardous and solid wastes, air pollution, and water pollution. TSCA, however, allows EPA to consider any sources of environmental risks, regardless of the activities that cause them and the media through which they are transmitted. The authority granted EPA under TSCA also allows almost any sort of regulatory intervention, ranging from requiring process controls for reducing occupational exposures to national bans on risky substances or activities. Thus, TSCA is probably one of the nation's most flexible environmental laws, and at the same time one of its most powerful.

Given the statute's title, regulatory activities under TSCA focus on identifying potentially harmful substances, such as toxic or hazardous chemicals, and then assessing specific risks of exposure to them in many different uses. Normally, a host of chemicals or compounds are under study by EPA at any given time, in different stages of EPA's risk management process. At the time the project on which this material is based was conducted, one such chemical was formaldehyde. EPA had reached an initial determination that formaldehyde exposure in certain activities and products posed a significant threat to human health. Formaldehyde is used in many different applications, but one of specific interest to EPA was its use in resins for manufacturing certain types of fabrics. In particular, urea-formaldehyde resins are used to impart a durable-press finish to certain fabrics that are blends of cellulosic fibers, such as cotton, and synthetic fibers, such as nylon and polyester. Fabrics made from fully synthetic fibers normally are already wrinkle resistant, so treatment with resin is unnecessary.

EPA noted human health hazards resulting from the use of urea-formaldehyde finishing for fabrics, mostly to workers who made the fabric or who fashioned garments from them. Under its TSCA authority, EPA explored a number of options to reduce these risks, and produced an array of detailed studies of these exposures and possible measures to control them. This analysis summarizes a few technical issues that arose in the process of exploring ways to reduce the risks of formaldehyde use in textiles manufacturing.

The Question

The central task in this analysis was fairly conventional—estimate the costs of a variety of different methods to control worker and consumer exposure to the formaldehyde used in durable-press textiles. A number of specific control options were considered, but they can be grouped into three broad categories. One class of options was to use different, nonformaldehyde-based resins. Another was to subject the fabrics made with urea-formaldehyde resins to washing or other treatments after manufacture to eliminate the formaldehyde residues. Yet another option was to require the storage of fabrics treated with the resin to allow time for the residual formaldehyde to dissipate. In each case, the basis for the analysis was to determine the costs of these controls, and the degree to which they offer risk reduction, and then to examine how the increased regulatory costs would affect the prices and quantities of these and other fabrics sold. From there, estimates of producer and consumer surpluses gained or lost could be calculated.

As is true with many practical applications of economic analysis to environmental policy and regulation, it is often easy to outline the basic technical approach for conducting the evaluation, but actually using the framework to produce quantitative results often poses significant difficulties. The analysis of formaldehyde use in textiles was no exception. One challenge of particular interest here is that the U.S. textile industry is subject to extremely vigorous foreign competition, often from manufacturers that operate in areas of the world where labor costs are only a fraction of those in the United States. The formaldehyde regulatory options under consideration, however, generally would only apply to U.S. textile operations because most of the formaldehyde exposures of concern were to workers, and EPA has no clear authority over foreign operations unless they create risks for U.S. entities.[2] This would subject the domestic industry to even stronger competition from foreign unregulated competitors. In addition to the existence of substantial imports of textiles not regulated by EPA, an extremely detailed set of regulations and restrictions concerning the importation of textiles to the United States has evolved over the years, further complicating the problem.

Thus, the task in this analysis was to model the costs of the formaldehyde regulatory controls in the context of significant unregulated foreign competition in textiles manufacturing and the complex U.S. system of textile importation controls. Adding these real-world considerations to the problem turned what might have been a "garden-variety" cost-analysis into a very challenging empirical task.

The Analysis

Without the imported fabric and apparel competing directly with the soon-to-be-regulated U.S. textile industry, the analysis would be relatively straightforward. Figure 4-1 shows the standard graphical measurement of consumer and producer surplus changes due to the formaldehyde regulatory costs. In this figure, the supply of durable-press fabric shifts upward by the amount of the compliance costs for the relevant regulatory option, whether the costs involve alternative resins, fabric treatment, or storage. Consumers of this fabric are worse off,

as measured by the decline in consumer surplus equal to areas *A* and *C*. Producer surplus changes as a result of the regulation by the difference between areas *A* and *B*, which could be either a gain or a loss depending on the slopes of the demand and supply functions, and on the amount of the compliance costs. The net cost, however, is areas *B* plus *C* after recognizing that area *A* is transfered from consumers to producers. The risk-reduction benefits of the regulatory option minus these net social costs measure the net benefits of the regulation.

There are some obvious complications in obtaining empirical estimates of surplus changes using this simple theoretical apparatus. For example, the slope of the demand function is critical to determining the price and quantity changes, which in turn help to define the distribution of gains and losses of surpluses and the net social cost of the regulation. If this type of fabric is only a small component of overall textile sales, and if there are good substitutes for it at low cost, the demand function will be quite flat; if not, it will be steeper.

Clearly, the empirical results depend critically on the shapes of the functions in the figure, and obtaining credible estimates of their slopes conditional on the degree to which other fabrics can substitute for the treated fabric, both in consumption and production, is not necessarily easy. But that was not the primary empirical problem presented by the textiles analysis. The main problem was the existence of substantial imports of fabric to the United States from firms not subject to the formaldehyde regulations, and whose economic interpretation and modeling were substantially confounded by the U.S. system of quotas on textile imports.

While it is not difficult to model additional textile supplies from non-U.S. sources, as will be seen presently, determining the sensitivity of imported textile supplies to changes in U.S. durable-press fabric prices, given the U.S. textile import quota system, is quite complex. The central problem is to determine whether or not

---

[2] This analysis simplifies reality slightly in that it is possible that some residual formaldehyde could exist in imported textiles. In this event, EPA's jurisdiction would include regulating these imports for the safety of U.S. workers and consumers. Assume, however, that the amount of time required for shipping is enough to allow the formaldehyde to dissipate sufficiently.

the quotas are binding. A binding quota implies that no additional imports will occur when U.S. durable-press fabric prices increase as a result of the formaldehyde regulations. In this case, the analysis will be very much like that in Figure 4-1, with minor modifications that will be discussed. If the quotas are not binding, then imports of foreign durable-press fabric will increase as U.S. prices rise. The analysis in this situation will be quite different from that shown so far. Hence, it is crucial in modeling imports of textiles to know whether or not the relevant textiles quotas are binding. This proved in practice to be a far more difficult task than expected.

To gain some idea just how complex this quota system is, consider the fact that each coun-

try faces a negotiated quota for importing articles to the United States for each type of garment made from each different type of fabric. For example, a country might face one import quota for men's cotton shirts, and a different import quota for women's skirts made of a specific blended fabric. Thus, there are potentially as many separate quotas as there are exporting nations, times the number of different types of articles, times the number of fabrics used to make them.

But matters are still worse. It turns out that textile import quotas are fairly flexible. A country facing a binding quota for one category can tap an unused quota ceiling for that category from previous years, or it can essentially bor-

FIGURE 4-1

Formaldehyde Regulatory Costs with No Imports

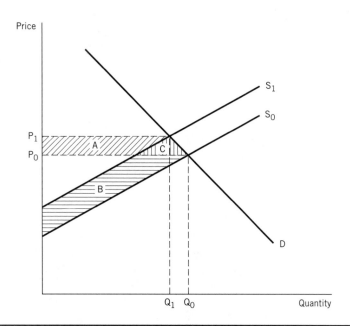

With no imports, formaldehyde regulatory costs can be measured as the net loss in consumer and producer surpluses. Consumer surplus falls by area A plus C, and producer surplus changes by the difference between areas A and B. Area A is a transfer from consumers to producers, so the social cost is area B plus C.

row from future quota allotments. It is even possible to use quota allotments for other textile categories where quotas are not binding. Hence, it is extremely difficult to determine from even the most detailed data whether or not any specific quota is really binding.

In the process of researching the textile quota system, it rapidly became apparent that obtaining a reasonably accurate picture of the actual state of all of the different quotas on the relevant textiles was a hopeless task. This illustrates one important feature of practical applications of microeconomics in environmental policy analysis—weighing the cost of additional research and data collection against the value of the likely increase in the precision of the results. In analyzing the use of formaldehyde in durable press textiles, the cost of producing anything approaching accuracy regarding the actual state of the numerous textile importation quotas was extremely high, and modest levels of effort would not generate any significant or reliable information.

Perhaps more important, however, was the fact that the value of additional information on the quota and supply conditions for imported textiles to improve the precision of the results was also fairly low. While it is perhaps not immediately obvious, it turns out that one can bound the estimated U.S. welfare effects of the formaldehyde regulatory options without knowing the precise state of the textiles quotas, based solely on domestic supply and demand conditions. Fortunately, data from several sources, such as empirical studies of textiles production and consumption, were sufficient to characterize the domestic supply and demand functions for these textiles. Hence, given the high cost of the research necessary to refine the results based on actual quota conditions, this bounding was the best that could be done, and was more than satisfactory for policy makers.

It is fairly easy to see how one can bound the welfare effects of the formaldehyde regulations without detailed information on the numerous textile importation quotas. Intuitively, there are really two sources of supply for durable-press textiles, domestic and foreign. The risks of primary interest arise from the domestic supply source. Foreign workers who are exposed to formaldehyde in the textiles, for better or worse, are not the explicit concern of the EPA's environmental protection process. Hence, social costs of any regulatory strategies to address U.S. formaldehyde exposures would arise only from the domestic supply source.

In light of this, it is clear that to the degree that more imports can be purchased in place of domestic textiles that will cost more under the regulations, U.S. risks can be reduced at lower cost by turning to foreign sources at the expense of domestic suppliers. That is, if imported textiles that pose little risk to U.S. entities can be purchased at current prices, it will be more cost-effective to obtain the required risk reduction through added imports rather than from domestic producers who face higher regulatory costs to control formaldehyde exposures. It then follows that the lowest U.S. social welfare cost of the formaldehyde regulations will be when foreign imports of these textiles are supplied perfectly elastically, and the highest will be when they are supplied perfectly inelastically. In the perfectly inelastic case, no additional imports can be obtained to substitute for domestic durable-press textiles that are more expensive to produce under the regulations. This case corresponds to the extreme situation in which all quotas are binding and inflexible. In the perfectly elastic case, domestic formaldehyde risks can be reduced at a much lower cost by purchasing additional imports at the existing market price.

Any foreign durable-press textiles supply response between perfectly elastic and perfectly inelastic will generate net U.S. costs between these two extremes. Presumably, some quotas are binding and others are not, and one could conceivably estimate the supply elasticities for those nations and articles for which quotas are not binding. But all of that effort would simply yield an aggregate elasticity of supply of imports between these two polar cases. Hence, it is reasonable to bound the results analytically before deciding to spend all of the resources necessary to characterize the actual quota and foreign supply conditions quantitatively.

These two bounds on the social costs of the formaldehyde regulatory options can be shown graphically. Figure 4-2 illustrates the case where imports are supplied perfectly elastically, at least within the range of quantity variation caused by the formaldehyde regulations. Here, the two preregulation sources of supply are S_0^D for the domestic industry and S^I for imports. The total

supply schedule for the United States is the domestic supply up to the baseline price, P_0, and then the horizontal S^I schedule at that price past the demand function. Prior to the formaldehyde regulation, the quantity produced by the domestic industry is Q_0^D, with the remaining quantity demanded supplied by imports, Q_0^I.

With the formaldehyde regulation, the domestic supply schedule shifts upward to S_1^D, reflecting the costs of regulatory compliance—alternative resins, added treatment, or storage. The postregulation total supply to the United States traces the new domestic supply schedule up to the imports supply price, P_0, and then follows the horizontal S^I schedule at that price. Because imports are supplied perfectly elastically, the price remains un-

FIGURE 4-2

Formaldehyde Regulatory Costs with Imports: Quotas Not Binding and Perfectly Elastic Import Supply

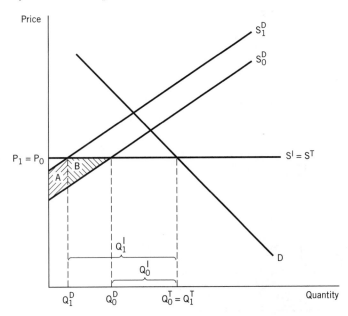

With nonbinding quotas and perfectly elastic import supply, domestic regulatory controls raise U. S. textiles manufacturing costs and reduce supply. Imports increase, leaving the price and total quantity unaffected. The net cost of the regulation is area A plus B, which is borne completely by the domestic textiles industry.

changed, the quantity supplied by the domestic industry drops to Q_1^D, and imports rise to Q_1^I. Moreover, because the total quantity and price are unchanged, consumers are not affected by the regulation. Hence, all of the regulatory costs are borne by the domestic textiles industry. These costs are measured by areas A and B in Figure 4-2. Area A represents the explicit compliance costs imposed by the regulation for the textiles still manufactured domestically, and area B is the extra producer surplus lost due to the fall in the quantity the U.S. industry now finds it economically feasible to supply.

Figure 4-3 shows the other bounding case in which the supply of imports is perfectly inelastic. This corresponds to the extreme situation where all of the import quotas are binding and

inflexible. The graphics are slightly more complex in this case. Prior to the formaldehyde regulation, the total U.S. supply schedule is formed by starting with the domestic supply function, S_0^D, up to the price P_0. At this point, the total supply is augmented by imports, so it becomes horizontal for a distance that equals the maximum amount of foreign supply allowed, $\overline{Q}^I$. Beyond that point, the schedule resumes tracking the domestic supply function. Essentially, this procedure inserts a flat segment representing allowable imports in the domestic supply function at the price, P_0. After the formaldehyde regulation is imposed on the domestic textiles industry, the new total supply, S_1^T, is derived the same way, starting with the new domestic

FIGURE 4-3

Formaldehyde Regulatory Costs with Imports: Quotas Binding

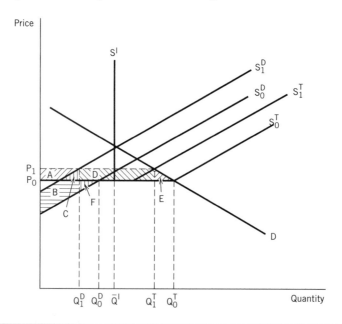

With binding quotas on textile imports, the supply of imports is horizontal at the world price, P_0, up to the quotas allotment, and then vertical. Horizontal summation of import and domestic supplies, before and after the imposition of the domestic regulation, yields the total pre- and post-regulation supply of textiles. The net welfare cost is the sum of areas B, C, D, E, and F.

supply function, S_1^D, inserting the allowable imports at P_0, and then continuing to trace the supply as shown in Figure 4-3. The total quantity supplied and consumed falls and the price of durable-press fabric rises as a result of the regulation. The social cost of the regulation in this case can be measured as follows. First, ignore the foreign suppliers of imports because they are not included in the U.S. social welfare function. Next, the loss of consumer surplus is the sum of areas A, C, D, and E, which together yield a fairly conventional-looking area normally associated with the consumer welfare impacts of a price increase. Domestic producers, on the other hand, gain area A but lose areas B and F. The net loss in U.S. welfare is then equal to the sum of areas B, C, D, E, and F, because area A is a transfer from consumers to domestic textiles producers.

The areas of net social cost have intuitive interpretations. Areas B and C together measure the extra regulatory costs of producing the durable-press textiles still supplied by the domestic industry. Area D measures the surplus losses of U.S. consumers that are transferred to foreign exporters who receive the higher post-regulation price P_1. Areas E and F are remaining domestic producer and consumer surplus losses associated with reduced quantities supplied and consumed.

The total U.S. welfare cost of the regulation in the binding quotas case must be greater than that in the perfectly elastic imports supply situation. Furthermore, the two polar cases also bound the results obtained using import elasticities between these two extremes, which is the equivalent of determining the exact conditions of all of the quotas and foreign supplies in reality. This can be illustrated graphically as follows. Beginning with the perfectly inelastic imports case in Figure 4-3, as the import supply function becomes flatter and flatter, areas A, C, D, and E will decline and eventually collapse to zero, leaving only areas B and F. But this is precisely the social cost of the regulation in the perfectly elastic case as shown in Figure

4-2. Hence, these two cases serve as upper and lower limits for the regulatory cost estimates, regardless of the actual quota and foreign textile supply conditions.

Of course, the range of cost results generated by this bounding exercise might simply be too wide for some policy makers, in which case additional research would have to be undertaken to develop better estimates of foreign supply elasticities and import quota conditions. In addition, the domestic industry's surplus losses under the two extreme cases range from being largest in the lowest social cost case and smallest in the highest social cost case. To see this, note that for domestic producers the major difference between the two polar situations is that they gain area A in the perfectly inelastic imports case shown in Figure 4-3, whereas they do not in the perfectly elastic import supply situation shown in Figure 4-2. Hence, producers are better off when import quotas are binding than when they are not. Thus, to the degree that policy makers weigh individual components of surplus gains and losses due to a regulation along with total costs, this relationship is important to highlight. In the actual formaldehyde project, however, decision makers were satisfied with the range of empirical results and the components of the welfare effects, so the unsavory prospect of trying to actually measure textile quota conditions and foreign supply elasticities to refine the results was avoided.

Finally, an interesting twist can be added to the analysis. Suppose that instead of quotas, the United States levies tariffs on imported textiles, but that imports are otherwise perfectly elastically supplied by foreign producers. In this case it is possible for the formaldehyde regulation to actually generate negative U.S. costs overall. To see this, consider Figure 4-4, which is similar to Figure 4-2 except that two imports schedules are shown, one with and one without the tariff. Clearly, in this case the lower-cost suppliers are the foreign importers rather than the domestic

FIGURE 4-4

Formaldehyde Regulatory Costs with Imports: Imports Subject to a Tariff

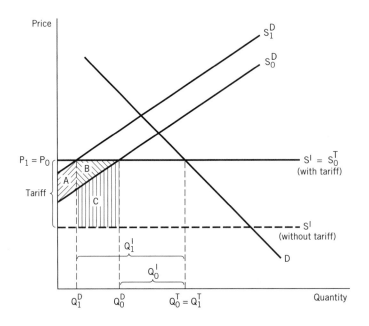

When imports are subject to a tariff instead of binding quotas, the regulatory costs cause domestic production to decline and imports to rise. Because the government collects added tariff revenues, areas B and C, these can more than offset the regulatory costs imposed on the domestic industry, areas A and B.

industry, as indicated by the position of the without-tariff import supply function. Of course, that might be the reason for the tariff in the first place. In any event, prior to the formaldehyde regulation, the domestic textile industry supplies Q_0^D, imports are Q_0^I, and the U.S. government collects revenues equal to Q_0^I times the tariff.

Imposing the formaldehyde regulation shifts the domestic supply function as shown, which yields the new quantities of domestic supply and imports. The social cost analysis here is similar to that illustrated in Figure 4-2. The difference is that while domestic producers still lose areas A and B for the same reasons described earlier, the U.S. government (which is decidedly included in the U.S. welfare function) gains areas B and C

in the form of added tariff revenues. If area C exceeds area A, the United States as a whole will actually experience negative total social costs from the regulation in addition to enjoying its risk-reduction benefits.

Intuitively, this result occurs because foreign suppliers in this situation are socially less costly suppliers of textiles than the domestic industry *and* the U.S. government collects the difference between the high U.S. price and the lower international textile supply price. Hence, while the domestic textiles industry suffers a producer surplus loss due to the formaldehyde regulation, any decline in domestic production that is replaced by imports yields added tariff revenues. This tariff revenue can potentially more than offset the domestic textile industry's losses, which would generate actual welfare improvement to be added to the risk-reduction benefits of the regulation. U.S. producers are nevertheless still unlikely to favor the regulation despite this possibility because, of course, they will not be given the incremental tariff revenue. Net welfare impacts are thus useful in predicting overall efficiency enhancement, but it is the gross gains and losses of specific entities that better measure their reactions to environmental policies.

Cancellation of a Pesticide Registration[3]

Many of the studies and applications in this book focus on welfare effects measurement techniques and interpretation from the theoretical perspective. This study, however, is about evaluating actual empirical estimates of welfare changes, given that the analytical apparatus generating the results is acknowledged to be appropriate for the task. That is, given that the technique for measuring the welfare effects of an intervention is correct, one must still verify that the empirical results produced by the framework make sense. This study shows one example of how even the best microeconomic model will fail if the input data are not what the framework requires.

The particular environmental regulatory policy that gave rise to this analysis was a proposal to substantially restrict the use of some widely-applied pesticide products in agriculture. Some background on pesticide regulation in the United States is useful in understanding the analysis that follows. Although the world of

pesticide regulation is complex, the fundamental idea is fairly easy to understand. Pesticides are regulated by EPA under the authority of the Federal Insecticide, Fungicide, and Rodenticide Act (FIFRA). Use of these substances is controlled primarily through a system of *registrations* of chemicals for application on particular crops in specific regions to control what are called *targeted* pests. A pesticide may only be used in accordance with its approved registration, and only within the limitations of its label, which specifies maximum concentrations, frequency of use, and other application restrictions. All of these use restrictions are developed based on the target pests, applicator and consumer safety, and ecological protection.

Economic analysis typically arises both in the course of evaluating a proposed new registration for a pesticide product and in assessing the desirability of continuing an existing one. Analyses of existing registrations also are necessary when EPA decides to conduct a *special review* of a current pesticide registration. These reviews are referred to as *special* because they fall outside of the major ongoing programs for evaluating new pesticide registrations, and for reviewing the large number of pesticide uses that were "grandfathered" when FIFRA was originally enacted. Because many of these grandfathered uses never received the cost–benefit scrutiny to which new pesticide registrations are subjected, EPA is conducting the necessary studies to perform these evaluations. Special reviews are thus cost–benefit studies of existing pesticide registrations that have been triggered by information suggesting that a potentially serious risk problem exists requiring EPA's immediate attention, thereby accelerating its evaluation relative to the ongoing process of reviewing all of the grandfathered uses.

When evaluating a pesticide registration, EPA typically conducts a risk assessment to determine the human health and environmental threats of the particular substance and application, and an economic analysis of what is re-

[3] This analysis is an encapsulation of a research project conducted jointly with Arun Malik, at the time of the University of Maryland. His encouragement to summarize the project findings here is gratefully acknowledged. Of course, any shortcomings of this abbreviated version are the sole responsibility of the author.

ferred to as the *benefits* of the pesticide's use. A benefits analysis of a pesticide registration is an assessment of the economic advantages of the pesticide over the alternatives, such as enhanced crop yields and potentially lower chemical and application costs. This terminology is somewhat confusing because in environmental economic analyses, the benefit of an intervention is normally the risk reduction that results, which is evaluated using risk and exposure assessments. In the pesticides world, however, the terminology evolved differently because historically EPA was in the business of considering new registrations. An economic analysis of a proposed *new* registration would therefore assess the cost and yield advantages that would be achieved— hence the term *benefits analysis*.

But the same terms are used for the studies necessary to determine if an existing pesticide registration should be canceled. That is, when considering canceling a current pesticide use, EPA conducts a benefits analysis of the cost reduction or increased yields provided by the pesticide that will be lost if it were to be canceled. Hence, the benefits analysis prepared for a pesticide cancellation evaluation is what one would normally think of as the cost of the regulatory action. While EPA's stance in a special review is one of evaluating whether or not a pesticide registration should be canceled, the economic assessment of the costs of such an action is nevertheless referred to as a benefits analysis.

The Question

The project on which this study is based arose in the course of EPA's special review of a major pesticide used on a wide variety of vegetable crops across the nation. Although the central focus was on the risks and benefits of the primary pesticide under special review, EPA also examined other closely related pesticides employed for similar purposes under what is called a *cluster analysis*. The basic motivation behind a cluster analysis is that given the EPA's decision

on the primary pesticide's cancellation, roughly the same results might be reached for other pesticides similar in chemical formulation and use. Widening the focus of the special review to encompass these similar pesticides might offer some economies of scope in the course of conducting the risk and benefit analyses for these substances.

Perhaps more significantly, however, a cluster analysis might lead to slightly different regulatory conclusions than a one-by-one review of the group of pesticides. For example, suppose the results of the special review of the primary pesticide suggest that its risks outweigh its benefits. This finding, however, is presumably conditioned on the availability and cost of alternative pesticides that could be used instead. But if these substitutes are closely related in chemical structure and effects, they too might be canceled upon closer examination. If so, this is cause to think a second time about the cost of canceling the primary pesticide subject to the initial special review.

The objective of the project underlying this study was to review the benefits analysis prepared by a pesticide manufacturer for a special review of a particular chemical and the cluster of pesticides similar to it. The analysis focused mainly on evaluating the methods and results obtained in the manufacturer's benefits analysis for theoretical and empirical accuracy. EPA undertook this review for two reasons. One was that the analysis had been prepared by the manufacturer of the chemical under review, certainly not a disinterested party in the regulatory process. Hence, EPA needed to determine whether it should incorporate the results of that analysis in its deliberations. The other reason for conducting a careful review of the manufacturer's benefits analysis was that its results suggested that large costs, significant transfers among consumers and commodity processors, and a host of other agricultural market disturbances would occur if the pesticide under review, much less the whole cluster of chemicals, were to be canceled. The central question for this analysis, consequently, was whether the manufacturer's benefits analysis was technically correct in terms of its microeconomic foundations, and whether the empirical results the framework generated were plausible.

The Analysis

Evaluation of the benefits analysis for this major pesticide and its cluster of similar chemicals began by examining the basic microeconomic apparatus underlying the quantitative results. What had been developed for the analysis was a fairly extensive partial equilibrium model of numerous different agricultural commodity markets directly and indirectly affected by the possible pesticide cancellations. Directly affected markets are those vegetable commodities on which the potentially canceled pesticides were currently used, so that a cancellation would pose possible yield losses and higher substitute chemical treatment costs.

An example of the effects of a cancellation on a directly affected agricultural commodity market is shown in Figure 4-5. Here the yield losses and cost increases that result from using a less effective, more expensive substitute chemical cause the supply function to shift leftward and upward. Farmers must spend more for the substitute chemicals and still may suffer some reduced yields. Precisely how far the supply function shifts depends on the costs and efficacy of the substitutes, and on the profit-maximizing choices made by growers of this commodity of the best combination of higher substitute chemical costs and their pest-control capabilities.

The welfare consequences of the pesticide cancellation in this directly affected market are fairly conventional. Producers of the commodity experience welfare changes equal to the difference between areas A and B, which measures the change in their producer surplus. The net effect on these producers could be either positive or negative, depending on the relative magnitudes of these two areas, which are themselves ultimately dependent on the slopes of the supply and demand functions, and the magnitude of the shift of the supply function. Consumers of this commodity, however, are clearly worse off by an amount measured by areas A and C, which corresponds to the usual measure of consumer surplus loss because of a price increase. The net welfare cost amounts to areas A and B in this directly affected market.

Other markets can also be affected by the cancellation even if they do not use the pesticides under review. Figure 4-6 shows such a case. Here the commodity is a substitute for one or some of the commodities that use the pesticide under review. Because the pesticide cancellation raises the prices of directly affected commodities, this tends to shift outward the demand for their substitutes. As shown in Figure 4-6, the demand for this substitute commodity shifts from D_0 to D_1, which then raises the price in this market because of the upward-sloping supply function. The welfare effects of the pesticide cancellation in indirectly affected markets are also reasonably intuitive. The demand curve relevant for measuring the welfare effects of an increase in this substitute's price is the one that reflects the higher prices of the directly affected commodities. When a directly affected commodity's price increases, the demands for its substitutes will shift outward. Using D_1, consequently, the increased price in this market causes consumers to lose areas D, E, and F, while producers of this commodity gain areas D and E. On net, the welfare cost in this market amounts to the triangular area, F.

The theoretical apparatus underlying the manufacturer's benefits analysis thus consisted of a large multisector model of agricultural markets, with a full complement of demand and supply functions, as well as cross-price elasticities between the various affected commodities. Cross-price elasticities, of course, are necessary for determining how demands in the various markets are affected when prices for other com-

FIGURE 4-5

Pesticide Cancellation Impact on a Directly Affected Market

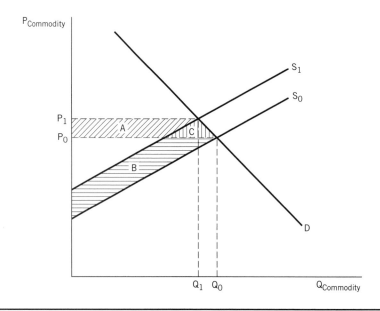

Cancellation of a pesticide used on this commodity results in increased costs and lower yields. This generates reduced consumer surplus, measured by areas *A* and *C*, and a change in producer surplus, measured by the difference between areas *A* and *B*. The net welfare cost is area *B* plus *C*.

modities change. The model was also capable of producing both short- and long-run estimates as much as five years into the future, because supply elasticities were available for both time horizons. Thus, nothing seemed to be amiss with the technical approach for modeling the impacts of these possible pesticide cancellations. But inspection of the empirical results generated by the framework suggested otherwise.

Several features of the quantitative results signaled a potential problem. First, producer surplus losses in the markets directly affected by the pesticide cancellation were relatively small, and consumer surplus losses in those same markets were quite high. Second, there were apparently very large transfers from consumers to producers in indirectly affected substitutes mar-

kets, which suggests large price increases for these commodities. Finally, processors of commodities, or those who purchase crops at the farm level and bring them to the retail market, seemed to be reaping greatly enhanced profits.

All three of these observations suggested that price increases for both directly and indirectly affected markets were large, so that area *A* in Figure 4-5 and area *D* in Figure 4-6 were also large, and that the slopes of the supply functions were quite steep. The problem was that the long-run supply elasticities were, in fact, quite high for most of the commodities involved, whether directly impacted by the cancellation or only indirectly affected. It is easy to see in Figures 4-5 and 4-6 that the flatter the supply functions are, the smaller the price increases will be; therefore, the consumer surplus losses will be lower

FIGURE 4-6

Pesticide Cancellation Impact on an Indirectly Affected Market

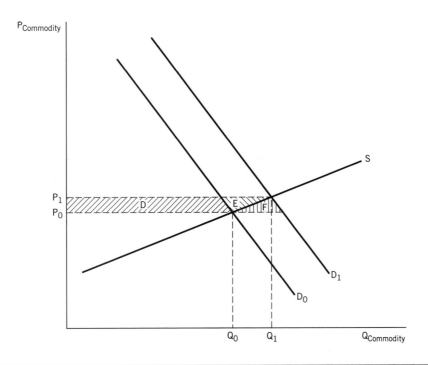

A good that can substitute for the commodity for which the price increases as a result of a pesticide cancellation will experience increased demand. This may raise its price and result in reduced consumer surplus, measured as areas D, E, and F, and increased producer surplus, measured by areas D and E.

in both types of markets, and producer surplus losses in directly affected markets will be higher. But the empirical results generated by the model pointed in quite the opposite direction. Hence, if the long-run supply functions for the commodities were really so elastic, how could the model produce such tremendous price increases and the attendant gains and losses between consumers and producers, especially in indirectly affected markets?

The answer to this puzzle had to do with exactly how cost increases at the farm level were translated from that sector to the retail level to calculate consumer-surplus impacts.

In many applied microeconomic models of markets, such as those for the commodities affected by a pesticide's cancellation, the explicit relationship between intermediate goods and final consumer goods normally is suppressed. As long as the analysis is conducted using supply and demand functions applicable to the stage of production at which the intervention occurs, the relevant welfare effects calculated using surpluses defined by those functions will be accurate.

In the framework being evaluated, however, both the farm and retail supplies for the commodities directly and indirectly affected by the pesticide cancellation were modeled explicitly. There is nothing at all wrong with this, and, depending on the characteristics of the various nonfarm components that are combined with farm-level supplies of these commodities to form the total retail supply, the relationship between the farm and retail levels should be quite straightforward. Reasonable assumptions made in the framework under evaluation included a perfectly elastic supply of nonfarm inputs (e.g., transport) and no substitution of nonfarm inputs for farm-level supplies. Under these circumstances, the retail supply of a particular commodity is simply the farm-level supply plus the cost of nonfarm inputs. Figure 4-7 depicts this situation, with the precancellation farm supply of the commodity, S_0^{Farm}, shown as upward sloping and the nonfarm inputs supply,

$S^{Nonfarm}$, as perfectly elastic, the latter assumption imposed for simplicity. The precancellation retail supply of the commodity, S_0^{Retail}, is then the vertical sum of the farm supply function and the nonfarm input costs. Prior to the pesticide's cancellation, the retail price is P_0^R, and the farm-level price received for the commodity is P_0^F, where the difference between these two prices measures per unit transport and other nonfarm input costs.

The effects of the potential pesticide cancellation are also shown in Figure 4-7. As before, the farm supply function shifts upward and leftward, reflecting higher costs and possible yield losses. Adding the unchanged nonfarm input costs to this postcancellation farm-level supply function, S_1^{Farm}, yields the new retail commodity supply, S_1^{Retail}. Combining this with the demand function yields the new retail price, P_1^R, and the new total

FIGURE 4-7

Pesticide Cancellation Impact on Commodity Retail Price

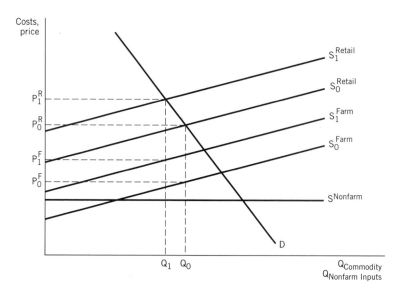

The upward shift of the farm-level commodity supply is translated into the same upward shift of the retail-level supply function. This is because the retail supply is obtained by vertically adding the farm-level supply curve and the costs of nonfarm inputs.

quantity, Q_1. Tracing back down to the postcancellation farm-level supply gives the new farm-level commodity price, P_1^F. Note that because the nonfarm inputs are available at constant cost, the vertical distance between the two retail-level supply functions is the same as that between the two farm-level supplies. This means that the absolute cost increase at the farm level is what drives the shift in the retail supply function, a point worth remembering.

This exercise of explicitly tracing supplies of a commodity from the farm to the retail level does not really add much to the analysis, although it does require more precision about the nature of the demand functions being used. For example, in Figures 4-5 and 4-6, the supply functions are shown at the farmlevel—hence the demand functions depicted there are also demands at the farm level. But the relationship between those demand functions and the retail commodity demand shown in Figure 4-7 is reasonably intuitive. Starting with the retail-level demand function, subtracting the costs of nonfarm inputs, the remainder is the farm-level demand. It is perhaps helpful to think of the demanders at the farm level as processors who then pay the nonfarm input costs in order to bring the commodity to consumers at the retail level. As such, they communicate the consumer demand down to the farm level, net of the nonfarm input costs that must be paid.

Of course, all of this simply shows how the relationship between the farm and retail supplies of and demands for a commodity ought to be modeled in a full representation of both the farm and retail-market levels. But the way the framework under evaluation actually connected the farm and retail markets in the analysis was not done in the explicit structural manner shown in Figure 4-7. Instead, translating between the farm and retail levels was accomplished in the framework using what are called *transmission elasticities*. Transmission elasticities are measures of the sensitivity of retail-level

prices of commodities to changes in their farm-level prices. Thus, if a commodity's transmission elasticity is .25, a one percent change in the farm-level price yields a one-quarter percent change in the retail price. Interestingly, under the assumptions that nonfarm inputs are in perfectly elastic supply and that there is no substitution of nonfarm for farm level inputs, the transmission elasticity also measures the farmer's share of the retail dollar spent on the commodity. For example, when the transmission elasticity is .25, farmers receive 25 percent of the total revenues generated at the retail level.

In the framework under evaluation, consequently, the direct effects of a pesticide cancellation were computed at the farm level, but their impact on retail prices was obtained by translating farm-level cost changes to the retail stage using commodity transmission elasticities, presumably because these estimates were readily available. There is nothing inherently wrong with this procedure as long as the transmission elasticities are consistent with the underlying model structure, the magnitudes of the farm and nonfarm input costs, and retail prices. But this was the essence of the problem with the results the framework generated, because the transmission elasticities were not consistent either with the other market data used or with the structure of the underlying model.

As a general rule, when estimates of parameters needed for empirical modeling already exist, normally it is cost-effective to use them, because the time and expense of trying to estimate them all over again is avoided. But using existing empirical estimates does not mean that they can be imported wholesale into the analysis without at least some critical evaluation.

The problem in this case was that the original estimates of the transmission elasticities for the commodities modeled were produced for entirely different purposes, mostly having to do with studying the myriad of government programs targeting the farm sector, such as commodity price supports. For the most part, the transmission elasticities used were estimated using standard regression procedures applied to historical data on farm- and retail-level prices. As such, the econometric estimates reflect variation in the data from a host of possible sources, *not* just changes in farm-level prices for commodities. Because of this, there was no guarantee that the estimated values of the transmission elasticities would be consistent with the purpose for which they were intended to serve in the pesticide cancellation structural model.

In fact, the econometrically estimated transmission elasticities were grossly inconsistent with the framework and its assumptions. Almost all of the transmission elasticities used were in the range of 0.6 to 0.9, and some were even greater than 1.0, even though the farm inputs as a proportion of the total retail cost of most of these commodities were on the order of 0.1 to 0.35. But transmission elasticities larger than the farm-input proportion of the retail cost of a commodity are not consistent with the assumptions and operation of the model developed for the analysis. To illustrate this, suppose that farm inputs are 25 percent of the total retail cost of a commodity, for example, $1 out of a total of $4. If the pesticide cancellation raises farm input costs by fifty cents, or 50 percent, under the assumptions in the structural model, the maximum increase in the retail-level price would be fifty cents, or 12.5 percent, which is one-quarter of the percentage increase in the farm input price. So the maximum transmission elasticity in this case would be .25. Anything higher than .25 will overstate the retail price increase.

In general, farm-level inputs are only a portion of the total retail cost of commodities, so any given percentage increase in farm inputs will translate into a smaller percentage increase at the retail level, and the smaller the farm inputs are in the total retail cost, the smaller will be the resulting retail percentage price increase. Thus,

the transmission elasticities used in the framework were far too high, two to three times greater than they should have been in most cases, thereby exaggerating the increases in retail commodity prices as a result of the pesticide cancellation. Conceptually, this caused the new retail supply function in Figure 4-7 to be shifted two to three times farther than the shift in the farm-level supply, which is inconsistent with the underlying structural model.

All of this explains the suspicious quantitative results the model generated. The framework essentially imposed the pesticide cancellation at the farm level for directly affected commodities, and then used transmission elasticities to estimate the impact on retail prices. These, in turn, were used to calculate the welfare changes consumers and processors experienced. Because the price increases at the retail level overstated the actual incremental costs incurred at the farm level by several times, the model predicted far higher consumer surplus losses than actually would occur for directly affected commodities. This overstatement of the increase in retail prices also impacted indirectly affected markets, because the cross-elasticity-induced higher demand for those goods was considerably overamplified, leading to higher price increases than would actually occur. This explains the large consumer surplus losses in these markets.

Finally, these overly high transmission elasticities also account for the model's prediction of large profit increases for commodity processors. Retail price increases of directly and indirectly affected commodities were significantly overstated; because the model's estimate of what consumers would lose was based on these retail price increases, the estimated consumer surplus losses were far larger than the actual costs of the pesticide cancellation. Hence, some other party should be gaining the difference between the actual costs of the cancellation and the overstated consumer surplus losses. Those who were profiting significantly at the expense of consumers, at least according to the results the model generated, could not be farmers. This is because the framework computed farm-level price changes due to the pesticide cancellation explicitly using estimated yield losses and substitution cost increases. Of course, the exaggerated retail price increases could still affect the farm sector indirectly because of the linkages in the model from market to market. Nevertheless, the gross magnitudes of the welfare effects predicted for the farm sector were believable. The only other economic sector in the model was commodity processors, who therefore gained the difference between the correctly estimated farm-level cost changes and the overstated retail price increases. Hence, the use of inappropriately large transmission elasticities also explains the model's prediction of large increases in commodity processor profits.

In the end, the model's quantitative results predicting large price increases for many commodities, substantial consumer surplus losses and similar increases in commodity processor profits, and large-scale cross-sector transfers and quantity shifts, all were largely the result of using transmission elasticities that were significantly higher than allowed by the assumptions and foundations of the framework. Hence, it was not the model that caused the problem, but the quality of the input information used to obtain empirical results. It is perhaps ironic that out of all of the volumes of input data used for the model—hundreds of items including quantities, prices, yield changes, substitution costs, and demand, supply, and cross-price elasticities—a single set of some 30 commodity transmission elasticities compromised the quantitative results. The devil truly *is* in the details.

Chapter 5

Modeling and Interpreting Social Welfare Changes

This chapter contains three studies that focus on intuitive modeling and measurement of the social welfare impacts of environmental regulations. As such, they explore in slightly more detail the correspondence between the analytical apparatus typically used—the graphics of supply and demand, and welfare effects measurement using areas of consumer and producer surplus—and real-world market conditions and regulatory effects. The issues examined here include why most analyses are confined to a single market, and exactly what certain graphical areas of surpluses correspond to in practice.

The first application analyzes the welfare measurement implications of the fact that almost any intervention in the private sector will cause numerous and varied changes in a wide range of markets. Almost everything ultimately is connected to everything else in modern economies, so it is unlikely that all of the effects of a regulation will be confined to one market. The relevant question, however, is whether and when one needs to broaden the analysis beyond the market directly targeted by a regulation to examine other markets where conditions are disturbed as a byproduct.

The second study briefly explores the relationship between (1) the *a priori* economic assertion that providing new and correct information to consumers about, say, the environmental or health risks of a product, will have positive net

benefits (or at least cannot result in welfare losses), and (2) the visible and seemingly quite adverse results that providing such information sometimes causes—reduced demand, and idled plants and workers. Policy makers often ask how such clearly negative market impacts are to be reconciled with the economist's conclusion that information provision is socially beneficial.

The final application in this chapter analyzes a proposition encountered fairly frequently in practice. One manifestation is as follows: If one bans a product subject to preexisting mandated environmental controls, the regulatory costs saved can be subtracted from the producer and consumer surplus losses caused by the product ban to obtain the net social cost of the regulatory action. The analysis demonstrates that, as stated, the proposition is false, but that its plausibility flows from other cases in which one does subtract costs of preempted regulatory controls in the process of estimating welfare impacts of new regulations. It is important not to confuse the two types of situations.

Cost–Benefit Analysis and Related Markets

A question frequently encountered in practical applications of economic analysis to environmental policy evaluation is how many markets must be examined to determine the social welfare impact of a particular intervention. For example, if a regulation requiring pollution control devices increases the costs of manufacturing a particular good, this may cause consumers to substitute other products for the more costly item. Hence, less of the regulated good will be produced and consumed and more of other commodities will be purchased. Do these other markets need to be examined to determine the regulation's total social welfare impact?

This question is central to determining the scope and boundaries of practical analyses of environmental programs. Almost any environmental regulation alters conditions in markets other than the one directly targeted. Programs that increase the costs of managing hazardous waste will increase the demand for waste management services and equipment, and will encourage increased use of inputs that generate less waste. Regulations that impose costly controls on pollution associated with electricity generation will cause industry and consumers to conserve power use by purchasing more energy-efficient appliances, and encourage utilities to use a cleaner mix of fuels. In all of these cases, the regulatory costs imposed on one activity affect a myriad of other markets. Practitioners are often asked whether the effects beyond the directly targeted market are reflected in their analyses; if so, how, and if not, why not.

The Question

To make matters more concrete, assume that the activity subject to direct environmental regulation is the supply and use of chlorinated solvents, which pose human health risks, possibly cancer. The relevant regulation might embody various risk-reduction requirements involving both occupational and ambient exposure protection measures, or possibly design or formulation standards for products that use these solvents. Assuming that the costs of these controls are high, the new regulation will certainly affect the price and quantity of chlorinated solvents demanded and supplied. But higher prices for chlorinated solvents are also likely to increase the demand for other substances that can perform the same function, such as nonchlorinated solvents and other processes. The central issue here is whether these other markets must be examined to assess the full effects of the environmental regulation targeting the supply and use of chlorinated solvents.

Conventional analyses of environmental interventions, whether they are taxes, command-and-control pollution abatement requirements, or the host of other regulatory methods by which environmental improvements are sought, normally focus on the market directly affected by these interventions. In most cases, this is accurate and complete, given the assumptions implicit in these studies. Yet, there is no guarantee that any given real-world situation will conform to those often unstated assumptions and conditions. Why is it that normally one can ignore all other markets when analyzing the impacts of an intervention in a particular market? What conditions typically require one to go beyond the specifically targeted market to ensure that the welfare effects measurement is complete? To anticipate the conclusions reached here, the answer generally is that the single-market analysis is fairly robust, but it is critical to understand why this is so and to appreciate the occasional exceptions.

The Analysis

These questions are best answered by carefully exploring the consequences for both the chlorinated and the substitute nonchlorinated solvents markets that result from the new environmental rule. After the imposition of the new regulation, chlorinated solvents supply and use becomes more expensive. The standard way to conceptualize the new environmental regulation is to shift the chlorinated solvents supply upward, as shown in Figure 5-1.[1] The original supply curve, S_0, is shown as the perfectly elastic schedule at the baseline price, P_0^{CS}. The postregulation chlorinated solvents supply, S_1, is also horizontal, but is now at the higher price of P_1^{CS}. The vertical distance between the two supply functions measures the regulation-induced increased costs of chlorinated solvents supply.

Measuring the net welfare effects of the regulation using this diagram follows the conventional procedures. The price rise from P_0^{CS} to P_1^{CS} causes demanders of these solvents to lose areas A and B. Producers of chlorinated solvents, on the other hand, are indifferent because they are assumed to be able to redeploy their manufacturing resources at no cost. They can easily produce other commodities and goods that are made using the chemicals and other materials that go into making these solvents—the central assumption behind a perfectly elastic supply curve. Hence, the social cost of the regulation is measured by areas A and B. Area A represents the extra resources required to obtain the Q_1^{CS} amount of solvents still produced and consumed. Area B measures the remaining surplus losses attributable to demanders turning to less desirable alternatives. Finally, presumably there are benefits of the new regulation, either to workers, the environment, or consumers. These are not addressed here, although if the regulation is socially beneficial, its risk-reduction benefits will exceed its costs as measured in Figure 5-1.

All of this should be quite familiar as the standard measurement of the welfare effects of a regulation in the *primary* chlorinated solvents market where the intervention is applied. The questions of interest really begin with noting that less of these solvents are used than before, following the

imposition of the regulation. In their place, presumably demanders purchase more of other substitute chemicals that can accomplish the same results, such as nonchlorinated solvents. One might think of this as an outward shift of the demand for these alternative solvents, which can be called a *related market*, because its demand rises when chlorinated solvents prices increase.

The question is whether this change in the demand for nonchlorinated solvents, or the ramifications in any market affected by the new regulation on chlorinated solvents supply and use, generates any net welfare effects of concern. Clearly, the demand for these alternative solvents does rise after the increased costs for supplying and using chlorinated solvents work their way through to demanders, but the standard method of calculating the welfare cost of a regulation ignores it. Why this is acceptable, and when it might not be, hinges on two key considerations. The first is whether movements of demands in related markets cause price changes in those markets[2]. The other major consideration concerns whether prices in other markets are accurate measures of social costs.

RELATED MARKETS AND PRICE CHANGES

In deciding whether the market for nonchlorinated solvents must be examined after the chlorinated solvents market experiences the higher regulatory costs, it is best to begin with basics. Figure 5-2 shows the nonchlorinated solvents market before the price of chlorinated solvents increases as D_0, and as D_1 afterwards, where each demand is conditioned on the relevant chlorinated solvents price. The demand shift is shown as an outward one, reflecting the assumption that nonchlorinated solvents are substitutes for chlorinated solvents—as the

---

[1] Here the regulation is viewed as affecting the supply of chlorinated solvents. In reality, the regulation could focus mostly on using these chemicals, shifting upward the supplies of products made with them instead of the supply of the solvents. Assume for convenience, however, that the cost impact of the regulation is confined solely to the supply of chlorinated solvents.

[2] This analysis focuses on shifts in demand as defining related markets that might require examination. The same considerations apply to the "supply side" as well, when the schedules of factor supplies to other activities are affected by a new environmental regulation.

FIGURE 5-1

Regulatory Costs in the Chlorinated Solvents Market

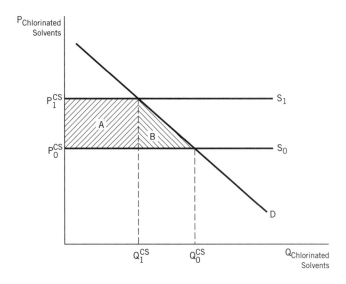

The standard measurement of the welfare costs of an environmental regulation on chlorinated solvents supply identifies areas *A* and *B* as the loss of consumer surplus.

latter become more expensive, people shift to the former. The supply of these alternative solvents is assumed in this figure to be perfectly elastic at the price of P_0^{NCS}.

The obvious question is whether the area between the two nonchlorinated solvent demand curves down to the price has any significance. That is, with the demand for these alternative solvents higher after the price increase for chlorinated solvents, does this somehow mean that the regulation increases the consumer surplus for these other solvents, and that one should "color in" this area as a welfare gain to be subtracted from the welfare cost estimated in the chlorinated solvents market in Figure 5-1?

The answer is no, for an important reason. Returning to Figure 5-1, consider what demanders are imagined to do when higher and higher prices for chlorinated solvents are announced: They observe the price of these solvents and then

decide how much of them to purchase, *and* how much of other factors of production or consumption goods (such as nonchlorinated solvents) to purchase, given their prices. As the price of chlorinated solvents changes, demanders reallocate their expenditures on these products and other goods. It is this process of adjustment, of course, that gives rise to the familiar downward-sloping chlorinated solvents demand curve, as shown.

What happens in other markets when the price of chlorinated solvents changes and demanders adjust their purchases is not directly shown in most analyses, but is essential for actually constructing the original demand for chlorinated solvents. Put simply, as the price of chlorinated solvents rises, the demand for substitutes for them, nonchlorinated solvents for one, shifts outward, as shown in Figure 5-2. A crucial determinant of the slope of the chlorinated solvents demand curve is the availabil-

FIGURE 5-2

Impact of Chlorinated Solvents Regulation on the Market for Nonchlorinated Solvents:
Perfectly Elastic Supply of Nonchlorinated Solvents

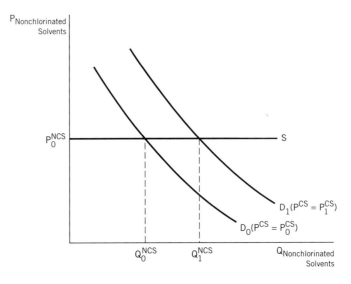

Demand for nonchlorinated solvents, a set of close substitutes for chlorinated solvents, increases when the price of chlorinated solvents rises as a result of the regulatory compliance costs.

ity of substitute goods and their respective prices. Thus, the demand for chlorinated solvents will be very flat if there are many close substitutes at comparable prices, but it will be very steep if there are few good substitutes and they cost significantly more.

It should now be obvious that one should not "color in" the area between the two demand curves for nonchlorinated solvents. The movement outward of this demand curve is envisioned, and demanders allowed to increase their nonchlorinated solvents purchases at the price of P_0^{NCS}, when the original demand curve for chlorinated solvents is constructed. Thus, this area in Figure 5-2 does not represent increasing consumer surplus as the price of chlorinated solvents rises. Instead, the shifting nonchlorinated solvents demand is one reason for the position and slope of the original chlorinated solvents demand curve in the first place. Without the opportunity to purchase more of these alter-

native solvents at the price of P_0^{NCS}, the demand for chlorinated solvents would be steeper and, as is easily verified, the social cost of the new environmental regulation governing their supply and use would be higher.

Therefore, the rise in the demand for these substitute solvents after the increase in the price of chlorinated solvents already is reflected in the estimated social costs of the regulation as measured in Figure 5-1. Hence, while there is indeed more consumer surplus in the nonchlorinated solvents market after imposing the regulation on chlorinated solvents than before, this is implicit in the costs measured in the directly regulated market. In this case, therefore, one does not need to examine this related market.

Consider a slightly different situation as shown in Figure 5-3. Here the demand shift for nonchlorinated solvents is the same as in Figure 5-2, but now the supply is upward sloping. Hence, as the demand for these alternative solvents shifts outward in response to the increase in the price of chlorinated solvents, not only do consumers purchase more of these substitutes, but the price of nonchlorinated solvents also rises. The question now is whether the rising price of these alternative solvents changes the verdict on the need to examine this market to completely capture the costs of the environmental regulation on chlorinated solvent supply and use.

Conceptually, the situation represented by Figure 5-3 differs in an important way from the perfectly elastic substitute supply case. In particular, the rise in the price of nonchlorinated solvents is inconsistent with the original demand for chlorinated solvents, which was constructed assuming that this close substitute could be purchased at a price of P_0^{NCS}. The increasing price of nonchlorinated solvents therefore changes the problem slightly.

What is added by the increasing price of nonchlorinated solvents certainly includes transfers from their demanders to their producers, which generally occur whenever a price increases. Yet, it should also be reasonably intuitive that the cost of the chlorinated solvents regulation should be higher when the price of this close substitute increases than when it does not.

FIGURE 5-3

Impact of Chlorinated Solvents Regulation on the Market for Nonchlorinated Solvents:
Less-than-Perfectly Elastic Supply of Nonchlorinated Solvents

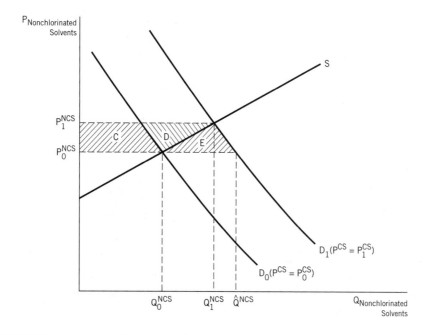

If the supply of nonchlorinated solvents is not perfectly elastic, the price rises when demand increases. The relevant demand curve to use for measuring additional welfare effects of the price increase for nonchlorinated solvents is D_1, which reflects the higher price of chlorinated solvents. Demanders of nonchlorinated solvents lose areas C, D, and E, and producers gain areas C and D. The net social cost of this induced price increase is measured by area E.

Regulatory costs should be lower the easier it is for demanders to substitute other goods. Changing the supply assumption for nonchlorinated solvents from perfectly elastic to less-than-perfectly elastic effectively makes it more difficult for demanders to substitute away from chlorinated solvents. Hence, the welfare cost of the regulation should rise as the nonchlorinated solvents supply becomes less elastic.

Intuitively, the nonchlorinated solvents market clearly does need to be examined to complete the analysis of the welfare effects of the environmental regulation on the chlorinated solvents market. How exactly one should measure welfare effects overall in the face of two increasing prices, however, is not immediately obvious. Recall that any given demand curve generally assumes constant levels of the prices of other goods and that changing other goods' prices will cause shifts in its position and shape. It thus seems reasonable when calculating welfare effects in one market to require that the prices in other markets be at the levels assumed by the demand curve being used.

Therefore, the first step should be to calculate welfare effects of the regulation in the chlorinated solvents market using the demand curve as drawn in Figure 5-1. Analytically, this holds the price of nonchlorinated solvents constant and hypothetically allows additional nonchlorinated solvents to be purchased at the original price of P_0^{NCS}. After computing these costs, the new price of chlorinated solvents is P_1^{CS} But this implies that the relevant demand curve in the nonchlorinated solvents market for purposes of calculating the effects of the increase in the price of nonchlorinated solvents is D_1 in Figure 5-3, not D_0.

Having thus "reset" the position of the nonchlorinated solvents demand curve to reflect the higher price of chlorinated solvents, one can then compute the changes in surpluses in the nonchlorinated solvents market due to the rise in the price there. This is done by continuing with the hypothetical situation in which demanders face a price of P_1^{CS} for chlorinated solvents and P_0^{NCS} for nonchlorinated solvents; so the initial position before raising the price of nonchlorinated solvents is at $\hat{Q}^{NCS}$ in Figure 5-3, not Q_0^{NCS} or Q_1^{NCS}. Now, raising the price of nonchlorinated solvents from P_0^{NCS} to P_1^{NCS} causes demanders to lose areas C, D, and E, this reflects the conventional consumer welfare costs of a price increase. Producers of nonchlorinated solvents, on the other hand, gain areas C and D. Hence, the net welfare cost of the nonchlorinated solvents price increase is area E. This should be added to the estimated cost of the regulation in the chlorinated solvents market as measured by areas A and B in Figure 5-1.[3]

The results are thus consistent with the original intuition that relative to the perfectly elastic nonchlorinated solvents supply case, when the price of nonchlorinated solvents rises, the net cost of the regulation on chlorinated solvents supply should be higher. The less-than-perfectly elastic nonchlorinated solvents supply makes it harder to substitute for chlorinated solvents, so the welfare cost of the regulation increases.

Return now to the original question of whether one must examine markets other than the one directly targeted by an intervention. Clearly, markets that are undisturbed by the intervention—in the sense that their demands and

---

[3] It is possible to argue that if one used a demand function for chlorinated solvents that incorporated the fact that its close substitute, nonchlorinated solvents, will rise in price as the price of chlorinated solvents increases, the nonchlorinated solvents market does not have to be examined to capture all of the welfare effects of the original regulation. This is true, although such a demand function runs counter to what most analysts normally assume about demand relationships—in particular that all other prices are held constant as the price of the good in question is altered. This is why one refers to conventional demand functions as *ceteris paribus* (holding everything else the same). But if one were to use this alternative demand function formulation, termed *mutatis mutandis* (letting things change that need to, such as the substitute's price), the information necessary to obtain that demand curve would be identical to that required to estimate the additional welfare effects in these related markets when using *ceteris paribus* demand functions. As a result, there is no real economy of analysis or information in the alternative *mutatis mutandis* formulation.

supplies do not shift—do not have to be analyzed. Markets that are affected by the intervention—those that are related in the sense that their
demands (or their supplies) shift in response to
price changes in the primary market—must be
examined to measure additional welfare effects
if their prices also change. So far, however, one
appears to be safe in excluding related markets
in which quantities change, say as in Figure 5-2,
but where prices do not. While this is generally
true, there are exceptions, as explored below.

DIVERGENCES BETWEEN PRIVATE
AND SOCIAL COSTS

Consider the same related market for chlorinated
solvents, that of nonchlorinated solvents, as

shown in Figure 5-4. Here, as in Figure 5-2, the
supply of nonchlorinated solvents is assumed to
be perfectly elastic at the price P_0^{NCS}. As before,
because nonchlorinated solvents are substitutes
for chlorinated solvents, when the environmental regulation raises the cost of chlorinated solvents, the price of chlorinated solvents rises, the
demand for nonchlorinated solvents shifts outward, and the quantity of nonchlorinated solvents
consumed rises from Q_0^{NCS} to Q_1^{NCS}. As discussed above, ordinarily one would ignore the
nonchlorinated solvents market when calculating the social costs of the regulations on chlorinated solvents supply and use, because the price
of nonchlorinated solvents does not change.

Consider an added complication. Suppose
that in the process of producing and using

FIGURE 5-4

Impact of Chlorinated Solvents Regulation on Nonchlorinated Solvents:
Preexisting Nonchlorinated Solvents Market Externality

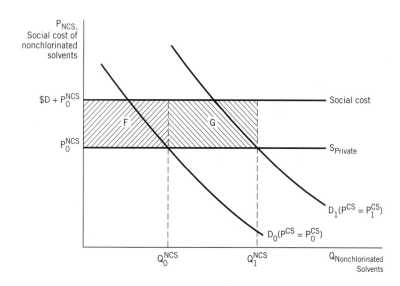

If nonchlorinated solvents production also involves environmental externalities, the increased demand for
these alternative solvents due to the new regulation of chlorinated solvents supply will increase the level of
these harms. Area *F* measures these environmental risks prior to the chlorinated solvents regulation, and area
G is the increase amount of these damages.

nonchlorinated solvents, other significant environmental externalities result, such as flammability due to the petroleum-based nature of some of these chemicals. Assume that the social cost of this risk amounts to $D per unit of nonchlorinated solvents produced. In this case, the actual social cost of nonchlorinated solvents production is measured by the line at the height of P_0^{NCS} plus $D, as shown in Figure 5-4. It is clear from the figure that the preregulation social costs of the original quantity of nonchlorinated solvents produced exceeded the private costs by the amount measured by area F. Of course, the conditions described in the nonchlorinated solvents market suggest the need for some intervention to correct the externality, but assume for purposes of this analysis that these environmental problems will remain uncorrected.

The actual additional welfare impact in the nonchlorinated solvents market due to the chlorinated-solvents regulation is now readily apparent. When demanders purchase more non-chlorinated solvents at the price P_0^{NCS} in response to the increase in the price of chlorinated solvents, the social damages associated with nonchlorinated solvents production rise by the amount measured by area G between the full social cost of nonchlorinated solvents supply and the privately perceived costs, P_0^{NCS}. Hence, this cost should be added to the regulatory costs measured by areas A and B in the chlorinated solvents market in Figure 5-1.

In general, the problem depicted in Figure 5-4 is one in which a related market contains resources or activities the private and social values of which are not equal. When this happens, the changing quantity in a related market, even though the price remains the same, is no longer irrelevant. Of course, this complication is not confined to environmental situations, because many economic activities may be incorrectly priced by the market. Nevertheless, environmental problems often give rise to this complication.

It should be reasonably intuitive why one needs to examine related markets where quantities change and private and social costs are not equal. It is a basic rule that when people do not face the full social costs of their actions, market outcomes will not necessarily be the most desirable from a social perspective. Here, consumers substitute nonchlorinated solvents for chlorinated solvents using the price P_0^{NCS}, which is not equal to the full social cost of producing and using nonchlorinated solvents. Hence, the welfare effects of the regulation measured solely in the chlorinated solvents market will not capture its full impact.

Finally, what of markets in which social and private valuations are different, but where quantities are not affected by the original regulation? The answer here is simple. Although there are preexisting externalities in such markets, they are not increased or decreased by the intervention in the chlorinated solvents market. Hence, they are not relevant for computing the total welfare effects of the regulation.

SUMMARY AND IMPLICATIONS FOR PRACTICAL ANALYSES

To summarize, markets that are unaffected by an intervention in a particular market—in the sense that their demands or supplies do not shift—can be excluded from the analysis. Related markets, or those in which demands or supplies are affected by the intervention in the directly targeted market, can also be ignored if (1) their prices do not change, and (2) social and private costs of the activities involved are equal. But if prices in related markets actually do change, or if social and private costs in these markets are unequal and quantities change, these markets ought to be examined.[4]

So what does all of this mean for practical analyses? Must the analyst scour every related market searching for upward-sloping supplies or divergences between private and social costs?

Clearly, this is not a realistic possibility. But assuming that other prices *always* will not change and that private and social costs in every other market *always* are identical is also not acceptable, because there are occasional cases in which these assumptions fail to hold.

For example, as discussed in the addendum to the asbestos case study in Chapter 2, one of the reasons cited by the appeals court in overturning EPA's rule banning many asbestos products was that, in the court's opinion, EPA did not adequately consider the risks of the substitutes for asbestos. Some of the substitutes consisted of similarly fibrous materials that might pose the same risks to human health as asbestos or even worse.

On a practical level, the possibility of unaddressed risks in related markets is a greater threat to the analysis than the impact of possible price changes in other markets. Recalling the analysis in Figure 5-3, the welfare cost of a price change in the nonchlorinated solvents market to be added to the regulatory costs measured in the chlorinated solvents market is the small triangle *E*. Areas *C* and *D* are transfers from consumers to producers. Thus, the portion of the net cost of the regulation on chlorinated solvents supply attributable to the higher nonchlorinated solvents price normally will be small relative to the total. In general, the smaller the quantity

change and the smaller the price increase in a related market, the smaller will be this component of the total social cost. Because of this, practical applications rarely concern themselves with this source of welfare loss in related markets.

The possibility of preexisting externalities in related markets, however, is more problematic. This may be one reason why practical analyses of environmental policies place considerable emphasis on exploring the details of how markets might respond to a regulation, in addition to estimating total regulatory costs. Indeed, identifying what substitutes will be used if a particular product is subjected to a stringent regulation is important not only for calculating compliance costs, but also for determining whether related markets harbor significant environmental risks of concern to policy makers.

Information Provision, Market Adjustments, and Net Benefits[5]

One useful feature of microeconomic analysis is that one can often reach a useful and robust conclusion using *a priori* reasoning. For example, economists are quite comfortable arguing that the net welfare effect of a correctly designed and implemented externality tax is unambiguously positive. Because the tax is set equal to the marginal social damages of the relevant environmentally damaging activity, this causes polluters to accurately balance not only the private, but also the social costs and benefits of their actions. Under this approach, the economist has confidence that whatever happens—who reduces emissions and who does not, exactly what control techniques are adopted, and so forth—the results must be beneficial from a social perspective.

---

[4] This analysis is intended to provide practical guidance on these issues for use in real-world applications. Hence, a few other conditions that allow one to calculate the effects of an intervention in the directly targeted market have been omitted here. These tend to be fairly technical, such as using compensated demand and supply functions. Perhaps one might be capable of satisfying these conditions in, for example, applied labor economics, where such considerations are often central concerns. But in the environmental arena one is lucky to have demand and supply functions at all, much less have any notion of whether or not they are compensated. Hence, such conditions and restrictions are best thought of as "maintained hypotheses" in the analysis because there is little one can do if they fail to hold. For a much more detailed discussion of the general topic, see R.E. Just, D.L. Hueth, and A. Schmitz, *Applied Welfare Economics and Public Policy:* (Englewood Cliffs, N.J.; Prentice-Hall, Inc. 1982), Chapter 9.

[5] The basic theme presented in this analysis is an outgrowth of a research project conducted by Anne Wittenberg of ICF Incorporated.

While this sort of economic reasoning is powerful and persuasive to many, its impact in reality is often less profound. Indeed, the central focus of the final chapter of this book is why corrective taxation and other economic incentive-based approaches have not been used very often in practice. But this same sort of "it clearly must be better" *a priori* reasoning occasionally arises in contexts other than that of externality taxes. And when it does, the noneconomists of the world often do not accept the blanket predictions of net social welfare gains that easily satisfy economists. Hence, when using these sorts of theoretical arguments, the analyst must be prepared to defend them using the specifics important to decision makers.

This study explores the practical tension between the tendency of economists to conclude that certain interventions will be socially desirable, regardless of the specifics and details, and the desire of policy makers and others to be convinced by visible evidence that these *a priori* pronouncements are really true.

The Question

The background and question analyzed in this study are easy to convey. The issue concerned the welfare effects of providing additional information to consumers regarding the use of chlorofluorocarbons (CFCs), which are ozone-depleting substances, in the manufacture of certain products. The central task here was calculating the welfare impacts of providing the information to consumers. The question and analysis can be generalized, however, to any situation in which previously unavailable information is provided to consumers, which causes them to change their purchasing patterns or otherwise revise their behavior in response.

A priori analysis suggests that if the information is correct and consumers react rationally to the new information, the net social welfare effect of providing the additional information will

be positive, or at least cannot be negative.[6] It is difficult to argue with this reasoning, for it relies on the familiar concept of the sovereignty of consumer demand and the intuitively appealing proposition that correcting a "bad" or a "mistake" has to be good for society.

Yet, the fact is that when consumers purchase fewer of the items now known to contain ozone-depleting substances, producers of these goods may suffer a reduction in the value of their investments devoted to supplying these goods. Those who stand to lose financially are often not very receptive to the economist's *a priori* argument that the welfare effects of the information provision will be positive. Analysts are therefore often pointedly asked, where exactly do these effects show up? If these readily apparent costs are already incorporated into the economist's conclusion that the net welfare effect of providing the information must be positive, or at least non-negative, how is this possible without explicitly measuring them?

The Analysis

It is always best to begin with a vision of what changes when a regulation or other intervention occurs, and then to analyze the welfare consequences and other effects of the policy. It is also generally useful to begin with simple constructs to observe basic principles clearly before seeing how they are modified when more complexity is introduced. Proving that the social welfare impacts of providing consumers with information concerning products' CFC use must be positive (or at least non-negative), regardless of the degree of dislocation of capital and other resources devoted to making those products is no exception.

---

[6] Of course, the term net social welfare connotes the usual economic notion of consumer satisfaction. Thinking in broader terms, however, everyone can imagine circumstances in which telling a slight untruth does less harm than being completely honest. The issue here is not so subtle as to involve these sorts of deeper philosophical concerns.

First, what happens after the information is provided is fairly easy to see. As shown in Figure 5-5, the original demand for a particular product containing or manufactured using CFCs is shown as D_0. The supply of the product in this figure is assumed to be perfectly elastic. After the information provision program takes effect, the demand for this product falls to D_1, but the price remains unchanged. This decline in demand reflects the fact that the benefits of consuming the product are in fact lower than consumers originally thought. Indeed, the actual consumer benefit of the marginal unit of the product at the original quantity, Q_0, is far less than the price, as indicated by the height of D_1 at Q_0.

The *a priori* conclusion that the information provision must generate positive net social benefits (or at least non-negative) can be supported using Figure 5-5. Because the actual consumer benefits from this product are measured by the demand function after the information is provided, D_1, the area between the two demands down to the price has no welfare significance—the extra consumer surplus under D_0 did not in fact exist. Hence, the benefits consumers really obtained prior to the information provision are measured by the difference between the true consumer surplus, area A, minus area B, which represents the excess of consumer expenditures for the Q_0 minus Q_1 units of the product purchased over their actual value, as measured by D_1. In response to the new information, consumers reduce their demand and purchase Q_1, which generates a consumer surplus of A. Hence, the

FIGURE 5-5

Welfare Effects of Information Provision: Perfectly Elastic Supply

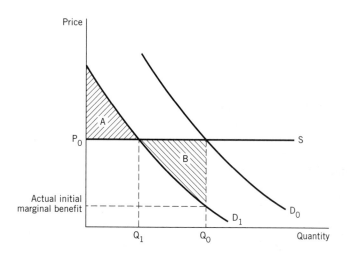

Providing information informs consumers that the actual marginal benefit of consuming Q_0 units of this product is far less than the price, P_0. Demand therefore falls to D_1. The social benefit of providing this information is the change in consumer surplus from area A minus area B, (the excess of consumer expenditures on the Q_0 minus Q_1 units over their actual benefit, prior to providing the information), to area A afterward. Consumer welfare thus increases by area B.

benefit of providing the information is measured by area B.

Another way to grasp that area B measures the welfare gain of providing the information is to imagine that rather than being ignorant of the presence or use of CFCs in the product, consumers were forced to purchase Q_0 units despite their actual demand for the product. In this case, consumers do not wish to purchase the Q_0 minus Q_1 units at the price of P_0, but they are made to do so anyway. There must be a welfare loss in this situation, for the extra units consumers are forced to purchase are worth only the area under their demand function, D_1, between Q_1 and Q_0, but they pay P_0 for them. Hence, the welfare loss imposed by the forced purchase of the extra units of the product must be area B. A rule requiring that consumers purchase units of a product for which their marginal valuation is less than the price thus has the same sort of impact as the lack of information that causes consumers to mistakenly purchase more units than they otherwise would.

So far so good. But what about the question of capital losses suffered by producers who own equipment devoted to manufacturing this product when the information provision causes consumers to reduce their demand? The answer is that there are no such losses in the situation depicted in Figure 5-5. The perfectly elastic supply function assumes that the factors of production involved in making this product can be redeployed at no cost to alternative, equally valuable uses. Hence, the diagram in Figure 5-5 is too simple to analyze the case in which the demand reduction generated by the information provision causes the capital losses of interest.

Consider the situation shown in Figure 5-6. Here the shift in demand following provision of information to consumers is the same as in Figure 5-5. The supply function in this case, however, is upward sloping to reflect the more general situation in which some of the inputs required to manufacture the product are not

immediately and costlessly transferable to alternative, equally valuable uses.

Although there are more consequences of providing information when the supply function is upward sloping, the basic results and intuition remain the same. The key complicating factor here is that as the demand function shifts downward, the price of the product declines. Two consequences result from this drop in the price of the product. First, the quantity decline in this case is less than in the perfectly elastic supply situation, which merely reflects the additional movement down the correct demand function, D_1, from the original price, P_0, to the new price, P_1.

FIGURE 5-6

Welfare Effects of Information Provision: Less-than Perfectly Elastic Supply

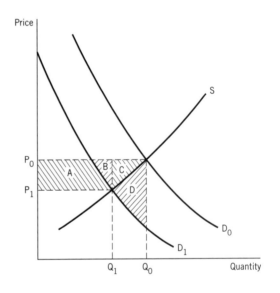

If the supply of the product is less than perfectly elastic, the fall in demand due to providing the information will reduce producer surplus. This tends to reduce the net welfare gain of providing the information. Here consumers gain areas A, B, C, and D, while producers lose areas A, B, and C. The net benefit is area D.

The second consequence of the reduced price is that, as with any change in a price, transfers occur between consumers and producers. In this case, the falling price provides gains to consumers at the expense of producers. For example, areas A and B measure the transfer from producers to consumers for the new, lower quantity actually purchased, Q_1, after providing the information to consumers.

Yet, to answer the central question of exactly where the impact of the reduction in value of idled equipment is felt, one needs to carefully analyze the net welfare effects of the information provision. Begin with consumers, whose welfare gain is measured by areas A, B, C, and D combined. Intuitively, this consists of the transfer from producers caused by the fall in the price for the Q_1 units still consumed (areas A and B), and the welfare gain obtained by reducing purchases of the product that are no longer desired, which is measured by the original price minus the area under their actual demand function, D_1, for the Q_0 minus Q_1 units no longer purchased, or areas C and D. Producers, on the other hand, lose areas A, B, and C because of the price decline. On net, as a result, the welfare gain due to providing the information is area D.

The measure of welfare improvement of the information provision in Figure 5-6 is different from the same measurement in Figure 5-5's perfectly elastic supply case precisely because of the presence of production inputs, equipment in this case, that cannot be reallocated to other equally productive pursuits. The impact of equipment that is idled or otherwise adversely affected by the reduction in demand for the product following the provision of the information can be seen as follows. Note that in Figure 5-6, if the supply was actually perfectly elastic, the net welfare gain would have been measured by areas B, C, and D, rather than only area D, so that areas B, C, and D in Figure 5-6 together equal area B in Figure 5-5. Thus, the welfare gain of providing the information declines as one moves from perfectly elastic supply to less-than-perfectly elas-

tic supply, a reduction in welfare improvement caused precisely by the supply-side rigidities and costly adjustments attributable to the equipment devoted to manufacturing this product, areas B and C.

Intuitively, area C corresponds to the early retirement or otherwise less-than-equally-productive redeployment of some production equipment to alternative uses. Area C thus accounts for the standard interpretation of the portion of producer surplus loss associated with the reduction in quantity after a decline in price. Area B's interpretation is very similar. It measures the degree to which society as a whole would be better off if the associated equipment could be redeployed costlessly to alternative, equally valuable uses, rather than remaining devoted to producing a product whose marginal value turns out to be lower than originally thought. Thus, both area B and area C measure the cost to society of having invested in too much equipment to manufacture this product, investments that cannot be costlessly redeployed. This reduces the net welfare gain generated by the information provision.

Figure 5-7 takes this reasoning another step. Here the supply function is assumed to be perfectly inelastic, so that the downward shift of the demand function after the information is provided translates only into a price decline, with the quantity purchased completely unaffected. In this case, the welfare impact of the information provision is zero, because the price decline simply transfers areas A and B from producers to consumers. Thus, the supply-side rigidities give rise to significant transfers between consumers and producers but nullify any gain in net social welfare. Intuitively, this result flows from the fact that regardless of the provision of the information to consumers, the product still will be produced and consumed, because the underlying inputs cannot be productively redeployed elsewhere in the economy. Of course, the information generates gainers and losers, but it does not, in this limiting case, cause any net welfare improvement.

FIGURE 5-7

Welfare Effects of Information Provision:
Perfectly Inelastic Supply

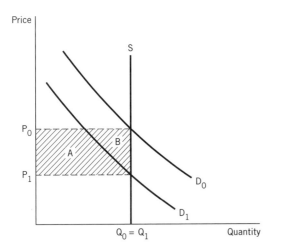

Perfectly inelastic supply of the product completely erases the net welfare gains of the information because producer surplus losses offset the consumer surplus gains.

Figure 5-8 shows yet a different situation. Here, providing the information results in a complete collapse of demand, so that none of the product is produced or consumed after its provision. As a result, the production inputs associated with this product will suffer a total loss of all surpluses. But the welfare effects measurement in this case is really no different. Once again, consumers gain the entire original cost of the now-shown-to-be mistaken purchases of the product, areas *A* and *B*. Suppliers, on the other hand, lose area *A*, making the net welfare impact of the information provision in this case still positive, despite the demise of the industry.

Two final comments are in order. First, as in most real-world situations, one can generally expect that the supply conditions for a product will become more elastic over time as reinvestment and other longer-run production decisions are made. Thus, the welfare gains from

FIGURE 5-8

Welfare Effects of Information Provision:
Demand Decline to Zero

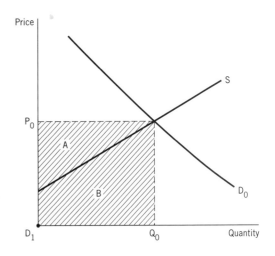

Even if the demand for the product collapses to zero after providing the information, the net benefit will still be non-negative. As shown here, consumers gain areas *A* and *B*, their original expenditures on the product, and producers lose area *A*. Despite the demise of the industry, the net benefit of providing the information is positive.

providing information are likely to rise over time as the underlying supply functions become more elastic.

Second, throughout this analysis, the implicit assumption has been that one is not simultaneously conducting an analysis of the possible risk-reduction benefits associated with the decline in the quantity of the product produced and consumed. Otherwise, there is a risk of double-counting. Suppose the information being provided concerns the health risks to consumers of using a product. The downward demand shift that results already measures the value consumers place on avoiding those health risks, so adding an independent estimate of the health benefits of reduced consumption of the product would double-count the benefits.

Product Bans, Regulatory Cost Savings, and Social Cost Accounting

This study briefly analyzes what seems to many people to be a plausible proposition. As with the other examples in this chapter, the central issue involved turns out to be quite simple once the problem is thought through. Yet, when first encountered, these puzzles can give one pause. The proposition discussed here, for example, has considerable intuitive appeal, but is ultimately false.

The Question

The proposition in question flows from the following stylized facts. Suppose a particular activity currently is regulated to protect human health and the environment. To make matters concrete, assume that the activity is the manufacture of some chemical that is then used in a variety of processes and products. Assume also that making, transporting, and using this chemical involve substantial risks to exposed workers, the general population, and the environment. Because of these risks, assume that various regulations governing the manufacture, transport, and use of the chemical exist, requiring process controls, limitations on releases to the environment, and a host of other protective and preventative measures.

Now suppose that EPA decides that despite the existing network of controls and regulations, this chemical still poses an unreasonable risk to society and that, as a result, the chemical will simply be banned from further production and use. In the process of computing the benefits and costs of the chemical's ban, it is asserted that because the chemical's manufacturers, transporters, and users will no longer have to expend resources to comply with the preexisting regulatory controls, these saved resources should be subtracted from the estimated social costs of the ban.

This proposition is plausible, because one can visualize firms saving all of those costs of compliance, and devoting them instead to other productive activities that ultimately benefit consumers. Indeed, the proposition normally is stated quite loosely, almost in passing, so that unless one pauses to consider it carefully, it might go by unnoticed.

The Analysis

As with many seemingly plausible statements that ultimately prove false, the best way to analyze them is to return to the problem's fundamentals. Here, the correct answer lies in clearly defining the basis for measuring the costs and benefits of the chemical's ban. On the benefits side, matters are relatively straightforward. One should measure the human and environmental exposures to the chemical, given the existence and operation of the mandated controls, and then estimate the damages and other harms that are caused. These are the benefits of banning the chemical from remaining production and use. Of course, for many reasons this can be difficult in practice, yet the focus here is on disproving the proposition that the preexisting regulations' control costs should somehow be counted in society's favor when the chemical is banned.

On the cost side, the fundamentals suggest that the social welfare loss due to banning the chemical is the consumer and producer surpluses associated with making and using the chemical, as seen in earlier chapters. The relevant measure of these surpluses, however, must be consistent with the benefits side of the analysis. Hence, the proper measurement of the consumer and producer surpluses lost when the chemical is banned should also assume the presence of the preexisting exposure and emission controls.

As shown in Figure 5-9, the supply of the chemical in the absence of the preexisting controls is shown as S_0, which would produce an unregulated price and quantity of P_0 and Q_0. The various exposure and emission control costs shift the supply curve upward, producing the actual pre-ban price and quantity of P_1 and Q_1.

Given the pre-ban state of this chemical's supply, the consumer and producer surpluses actually lost when the ban takes effect are areas A and B, consistent with earlier graphical analyses of environmental regulations. The chemical's preexisting environmental control costs are shown as area C in the figure; according to this analysis these are not intrinsically different from the other costs of manufacturing the chemical, or area D. Neither type of cost associated with manufacturing the chemical is subtracted in estimating the welfare effects of banning the chemical.

FIGURE 5-9

Social Cost of Banning a Chemical Subject to Costly Preexisting Environmental Controls

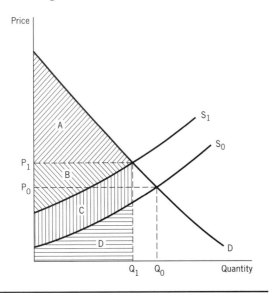

The cost of banning this product is measured by the producer and consumer surpluses, areas A and B, that remain after accounting for the preexisting regulatory costs, area C. Hence, area C is not subtracted from the welfare cost of the ban, just as the other costs of supply, as measured by area D, are not.

That one should not count the saved regulatory control costs as, in a sense, negative social costs, can be seen even more clearly in Figure 5-10. In this representation of the chemical's pre-ban market conditions, the control costs are assumed to be far higher than in Figure 5-9. Indeed, the regulatory control costs are so high that very little consumer and producer surplus remains after accounting for these environmental protection measures. As before, areas A and B measure the total consumer and producer surplus losses that result from banning the regulated chemical. As drawn in Figure 5-10, however, if one were to subtract area C, the costs of the preexisting regulatory controls, the net result would be a negative social cost of the ban. Of course, this would lead one to conclude that even if there were no risk-reduction benefits at all from banning the chemical, society could still gain by banning something that consumers clearly want to purchase and that producers clearly want to supply. That conclusion, of course, makes no sense.

When analyzed this way, the proposition that the compliance costs associated with preexisting regulations that are saved when a product is banned should be netted out of the estimated social costs of the ban is clearly false. Because one sets out to calculate the social cost of banning the chemical as its social value net of its cost of production, the fact that resources originally devoted to compliance with the preexisting environmental regulations are released to other productive uses is already taken into account. This release does indeed happen, but this is already subsumed in measuring the ban's cost as the consumer and producer surpluses lost.

The issue can be stated differently as follows. If one wanted to count the reduced compliance costs as a benefit, one would have to treat all parts of the problem symmetrically. One would first count the welfare cost of the ban as the chemical's total benefit to consumers that is lost—areas A, B, C, and D—minus the cost of producing the chemical that is now released to other produc-

FIGURE 5-10

Social Costs of Banning the Same Chemical Subject to Very Costly Preexisting Regulatory Controls

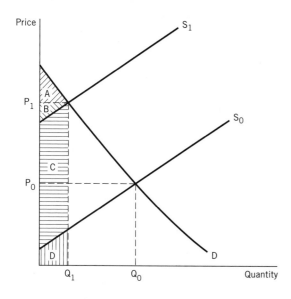

If the preexisting regulatory costs, area C, were subtracted from the area A and B estimates of consumer and producer surplus losses due to the ban, this would yield a negative net cost.

tive pursuits, or areas C and D. But this method still arrives at a net cost of areas A and B.

The plausibility of the proposition that the compliance costs saved should provide a net benefit to society ultimately flows from the fact that these resources do indeed return to other uses. But given how the ban's cost is calculated, this release of compliance cost resources is irrelevant. The example can be changed slightly, however, to yield circumstances in which the process of estimating the net cost of an additional regulation does involve subtracting out preexisting regulatory costs. Suppose that instead of banning the chemical, EPA decides to issue a new regulation that mandates a more expensive and more effective way to reduce the chemical's

environmental harms and that these new controls must be used instead of the older ones. Assume also that the preexisting regulations impose only variable costs, so that the new control methods can be adopted immediately and no investments in compliance are jeopardized.

In this case, one would compute the benefits as the incremental exposures avoided relative to a baseline that includes the old controls. The social cost of the new regulation, symmetrical with the benefits side of the analysis, would be the incremental total costs of producing the chemical. But these can be approximated as simply the costs of the new environmental controls minus the costs of the old requirements. In this case it thus seems acceptable to subtract the preexisting regulatory costs in computing the new rule's net cost increase.

But one should be careful to note the differences in the cost calculation methods between the two examples. In the case of the ban, one seeks to measure the incremental regulatory cost of the new regulation, but because it is a product ban, the obvious way to do so is to compute the consumer and producer surpluses associated with the chemical that will be lost. This also happens to be the net increase in regulatory costs relative to the preexisting controls, but the measurement method—calculating remaining surpluses that will be lost when the product is banned—already accounts for the regulatory cost savings, since these are reflected in the reduced total surpluses in the market. In the second example, however, one directly measures the social cost of the new regulation as the net increase in control expenditures, then treats these conceptually as incremental surplus losses.

The difference between these methods is subtle. In the case of the ban, one knows that all remaining surpluses will be lost, so it seems appropriate to estimate these surpluses directly. In the other case, however, one sets out to measure not the total remaining surplus, but rather the incremental regulatory costs that will then result in additional surplus losses. Analytically, both methods are correct and avoid double counting; they just appear to be different because they attack the problem from opposite ends. The key to correctly estimating the net social costs of new regulations where older ones already exist, and deciding whether or not the preexisting regulatory costs should be subtracted in this process, is in carefully dissecting how one intends to measure these costs. The question as stated for this analysis was whether, after estimating the consumer and producer surplus losses of the chemical's ban, one should subtract the saved compliance costs associated with the preexisting regulations. Put this way, the answer clearly is no.

Chapter 6

The Analytical Significance of Baselines

The two applications in this chapter highlight instances in which specifiying the baseline for the analysis is extremely important in determining the outcome. "Baseline" is the term used to connote the situation in the absence of the regulatory intervention. Many analyses assume a preregulation baseline in which a single externality needs to be addressed and no other regulations exist. Specifying the baseline in these cases is an analitically straightforward data-collection task, perhaps including some projections of market conditions as they might develop over time. This can be complex, of course, but the baseline itself does not have any special analytical interest.

In practical applications, however, matters are often very different. In many cases, regulations may already exist to control some of the environmental damages associated with a substance or activity, but not other sources of risk. Furthermore, regulators often consider imposing multiple types of rules to regulate different stages of the production and use of a toxic substance, or other activities that can generate environmental risks, such as hazardous waste generation and disposal. Regulations already in force, or those about to become effective, sometimes make it problematic to define the baseline and estimate the costs and benefits of additional regulations.

This chapter illustrates these points through several examples in which assumptions about the baseline fundamentally shape the character of the results. In the first study, the task is to compute the costs and benefits of a regulation that is imposed on top of two preexisting rules regulating a particular activity. What is shown in this case is that the costs and benefits of the new regulation depend critically on which of the two preexisting rules governs the marginal economic conditions in the regulated market. Hence, specifying the baseline in this analysis largely determines the nature and magnitude of the quantitative costs and benefits of the new regulation.

The second study illustrates a slightly different point. Here the issue is that multiple regulations are to be imposed on an activity simultaneously. While each rule is different from the others, their effects overlap in the sense that some of the targeted risks will be avoided by more than one of the regulations. Hence, in examining the effects of any one regulation, what one assumes about the existence of the others is very important. The focus in this case is on how to calculate the costs and benefits of multiple rules, separately and jointly.

Mandatory Recycling under the CFC Phaseout and Tax[1]

International concern for the destruction of the ozone layer of the earth's atmosphere caused by chlorofluorocarbons (CFCs) and other ozone-depleting substances reached a crescendo in the mid-1980s. Stratospheric ozone provides protection for the earth and its many resources, terrestrial and aquatic, animal and plant, from the destructive effects of excess ultraviolet radiation from the sun. Ozone depletion increases human skin cancer, causes blindness in aquatic species, and may result in a variety of damages to natural resources, agricultural crops, and even manmade materials, such as plastics. This widespread environmental concern resulted in a multinational treaty limiting the future production of these harmful substances—the 1987 Montreal Protocol.

A vocal proponent of limiting production of ozone-depleting substances, the United States rapidly established the necessary regulatory infrastructure to ensure domestic compliance with the limitations specified in the Montreal Protocol. This took the form of a national schedule for reducing the production of two classes of the most serious ozone depleters, CFCs and halons. Although much of what is reported in this illustration applies to both CFCs and halons, this discussion uses the term CFCs from this point on both for ease of exposition and because the specific regulatory features of interest in this study apply most concretely to CFCs.

The London and Copenhagen amendments to the original Protocol imposed more stringent ozone protection measures under which a schedule for eliminating CFC production altogether was developed and ratified.[2] The CFC phaseout,

as it is called, was originally implemented by issuing CFC manufacturers permits to produce CFCs—based on their past production levels—that declined over time to conform to the schedules in the Protocol and its amendments. These production rights were made tradeable to minimize compliance costs across different manufacturers of CFCs.

Concurrent with the regulatory implementation of the phaseout, a tax on U.S. CFC production was also promulgated. The primary purpose of this tax was to capture for the government and its citizens the additional profits that manufacturers would reap from CFC sales during the phaseout. Estimates at the time placed these excess profits from the rising prices anticipated under the phaseout at some $7 billion or more. As promulgated, the tax is levied at rates that are based on the specific ozone-depleting potential of the different chemical compounds in the CFC family. Over time, as the phaseout targets become increasingly stringent, CFC prices are likely to rise, generating increasing profits from remaining CFC production. Hence, the tax rates are scheduled to increase as well. Table 6-1 lists the CFC phaseout limitations as a percentage of 1986 production and the CFC tax rate for CFC-11, year by year to 1996, at which time the phaseout will be complete.

Table 6-1
CFC PHASEOUT AND TAX POLICIES

Year	Phaseout Quantity (percent of 1986 production)	Tax Rate ($ per pound)
1989	100	None
1990	100	1.37
1991	85	1.37
1992	80	1.67
1993	75	3.35
1994	25	4.35
1995	25	5.35
1996	0	

Note: Tax rates are for CFC-11. Other substances are taxed at different rates reflecting their ozone-depleting potential. Phaseout schedule is for CFCs only, and reflects all Protocol amendments through March, 1993.

---

[1] The central theme of this analysis is based on several ICF Incorporated research projects conducted primarily by John Wasson and Bernard Eydt.

[2] Other ozone-depleting substances are also covered by the agreements. Some of these are subject to different limitation schedules, while others are under study to determine whether their use should be reduced or eliminated eventually.

It is worth briefly analyzing the welfare impacts of the phaseout and tax in their combined form, because this defines the state of the CFC market for additional regulations, the topic of this study. A graphical representation of the impacts of the CFC production phaseout and the tax is shown in Figure 6-1. It depicts a representative CFC chemical, CFC-11, but the results generalize to all of the different compounds. As shown in the figure, the cost of producing CFCs is a constant $1.63 per pound regardless of quantity. Demand is shown in the figure as the usual downward-sloping curve. Of course, what underlies this demand function is a set of increasingly costly substitution actions that would be adopted if the price of CFCs rises. Costly alternative chemicals to accomplish the tasks CFCs perform and ways to reduce leakage from refrigeration equipment containing CFCs would be considered, as would possible retirement of the CFC-specific equipment altogether.

Also shown in the diagram is the phaseout target for this particular year, $\overline{Q}$, which is far below the quantity demanded at the no-regulation supply price of $1.63 per pound. The effective supply function under the phaseout limitation is thus the original supply function over to the maximum allowed quantity under the phaseout, $\overline{Q}$, and then the vertical line as shown. The phaseout's quantity limitation causes CFC prices to rise (to $6 per pound in the diagram) in order to efficiently ration the limited quantity available. The CFC tax levied of $3.35 per pound (the actual tax rate for CFC-11 in 1993) is represented by the difference between $4.98 and the $1.63 cost of supply.

The welfare effects of the phaseout and tax together should by now be easy to diagram. Using Figure 6-1 relative to the no-regulation baseline, consumers lose areas A, B, and C, which is simply the consumer surplus loss caused by the rise in price from $1.63 to $6. The government, or taxpayers, ultimately, gain area B, which measures the tax revenues generated by the sale of the phaseout-limited quantity. Finally, producers gain area C, which is the revenues earned based on the market price of CFCs, minus both the cost of production and the taxes paid to the government.

The benefits of the phaseout can be thought of as reduced current and future ozone depletion. This translates into reduced human and ecological damage caused by ultraviolet radiation. Rough estimates of the benefits of decreasing CFC production range widely, but are in the tens of dollars per pound. Hence, as shown in Figure 6-1, drawing the social cost of CFC supply at, say, $16.63 per pound ($15 for the environmental damages and $1.63 for their cost of production) allows graphical depiction of the benefits of the phaseout production limitation. The area below the *social-cost function*, down to the $1.63 cost of production, between the phaseout quantity $\overline{Q}$ and the *no-regulation* baseline

FIGURE 6-1

Costs and Benefits of the CFC Phaseout and Tax

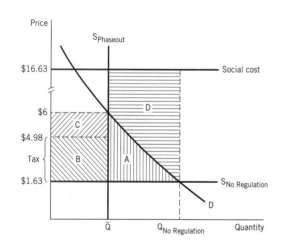

The CFC phaseout in this year produces risk-reduction benefits amounting to area A plus D, and imposes consumer surplus losses measured by areas A, B, and C. The government gains the CFC tax revenues, area B, and CFC producers gain area C. The net benefit to society thus is area D.

quantity, measures the human health and ecological benefits of this year's production limitation. The costs, on the other hand, are simply the net welfare impacts on consumers, producers, and the government. Because areas B and C are transfers from consumers to the government and to producers of CFCs, the net cost of the phaseout in this year is area A. Subtracting that from the total benefits yields area D as the net social gain from this particular year's limitation on CFC production.

Of course, over time as the CFC phaseout targets become more stringent and the tax rate rises, all of these measurements will change. Moreover, while the costs of the phaseout are generally borne in the relatively near future, say during the life of a machine designed to use CFCs, the benefits of reduced ozone depletion will be enjoyed for many decades. Hence, measuring the social costs and benefits of the basic CFC phaseout policy requires a multiyear time horizon and a fairly sophisticated environmental-damage model.

The Question

All of this, however, is background for the question posed in this study. A large-scale effort to estimate the costs and benefits of the phaseout had already been completed and the relevant regulations to implement the phaseout and collect the tax were already on the books when this next phase of CFC regulation arose.

While the phaseout reduces and eventually eliminates CFC production, EPA remained concerned about the ozone-depletion threat posed by the vast amounts of CFCs contained in millions of units of various types of equipment. One of the major uses of CFCs is in heat transfer, particularly air conditioning and other refrigeration applications. These machines generally hold charges of CFCs that leak over time, or are vented to the atmosphere upon servicing or disposal.

EPA wished to avoid venting this stock of CFCs and, instead, sought to encourage its recycling. This would both delay eventual release

of these CFCs and make it easier to meet the phaseout's production limitations. Motivated by these considerations, a rule was proposed requiring the recapture and recycling of CFCs upon the servicing or disposal of many types of equipment. Sales of these recycled CFCs would be exempt from the tax and would not count against the phaseout's production caps.

The central problem posed was to estimate the costs and benefits of this added layer of CFC regulation, given that the phaseout and the tax regulations already exist. Thus, considerable attention was devoted to the correct specification of the baseline prior to imposing this new regulation, and the resulting effects of the baseline on measuring its welfare effects.

The Analysis

As we have seen before, the most productive way to approach analyzing the welfare consequences of environmental regulation is to begin by envisioning the resulting changes in economic and physical activities. In the case of the regulation requiring the recapture and recycling of CFCs, owners of the affected equipment will spend resources to comply with the requirements when servicing or disposing of the relevant machines. Such costs include more expensive techniques that recapture CFCs in the process of recharging equipment, and the need to reprocess used CFCs to appropriate standards of purity before resale. Assume that these costs amount to $8 per pound of CFCs recaptured and recycled.

RECYCLING-RULE EFFECTS IN THE ABSENCE OF OTHER REGULATIONS

Specifying and calculating the costs of compliance with the CFC recycling rule are relatively easy. Determining what else happens in the economy as equipment owners begin recycling instead of venting CFCs is a little trickier, but very important for measuring the rule's social costs and benefits. Ordinarily, in the absence of the CFC phaseout and tax policies, the extra

CFCs supplied by requiring recycling would simply constitute an additional source of CFC supply whose value would be equal to the cost and price of CFCs, $1.63 per pound. In this unregulated state of the world, as more CFCs are supplied from recycling, the supply from virgin sources would decline.

Figure 6-2 shows how the recycled CFCs displace virgin production. Without the recycling rule, virgin production would satisfy the entire demand, Q_T. As the diagram indicates, however, the extra CFCs supplied constitute an additional source offered, regardless of price; these CFCs result from a regulatory mandate to recapture and recycle, so they will be supplied regardless of the price received. As a result, virgin production drops to Q_V, which, when added to the recycling quantity, Q_R equals the total CFCs demanded at the $1.63 price. Virgin CFC production is offset

in this case on a one-for-one basis because of the assumed perfectly elastic supply; anything less than the current market price causes CFC manufacturers to reduce their supply, thus reestablishing the original equilibrium price.[3] In this previously unregulated world, consequently, society would spend $8 per pound for recycling CFCs and save $1.63 per pound in virgin production costs. The net cost of mandatory CFC recycling is shown as the shaded area A, defined by the $8 per pound cost of recapturing and recycling these additional CFCs, minus the cost of virgin CFCs, $1.63 per pound.

In the absence of the phaseout and the tax, the benefits of the recycling regulation would be less ozone depletion, both because CFCs that would have been vented will be recaptured and reused, considerably delaying their ultimate release to the atmosphere, and because fewer total virgin CFCs will be produced as the recycled amounts displace virgin production. Given that the environmental cost of producing and releasing a pound of CFCs results in damages on the order of tens of dollars, it may well be worth the substantial costs of recapturing and recycling used CFCs that would otherwise have been vented, to obtain the benefits of delayed and lower overall releases of CFCs.

FIGURE 6-2

Effects of Mandatory CFC Recycling
with No Preexisting Regulations

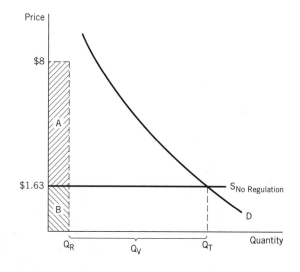

In the absence of preexisting regulations, mandatory CFC recycling costing $8 per pound displaces virgin-source CFCs that cost only $1.63 per pound. The net cost of the recycling mandate is area A.

Two Possible Baselines under the Phaseout and the Tax

For this analysis, however, the baseline state of the world prior to the imposition of the CFC recycling rule already contains the phaseout and the tax. In analyzing the welfare effects of the recycling rule, one cannot ignore the presence of these preexisting regulations. Indeed, far from being the exception, these situations are common in practical applications of economic analysis. In this case it also turns out that the phaseout and tax regulations have a dramatic impact on the consequences and welfare effects of the ad-

[3] Of course, a less-than-perfectly-elastic supply would result in a less than one-for-one reduction in virgin CFC supply, but the essence of the analysis would be unchanged.

ditional rule requiring CFC recapture and recycling. Hence, predicting the economic effects of the new recycling rule requires a careful construction of the baseline for the analysis.

Two possible baselines can be constructed as the backdrop against which to assess the costs and benefits of the new recycling regulation. The conditions in Figure 6-1 form one baseline. In this view of the world, the phaseout limitation on CFC production is the binding condition in the market. That is, the CFC tax is small enough so that it does not affect the marginal supply or demand conditions in the CFC market—it simply redistributes the profits from the allowed production, from manufacturers to the government. Hence, the market price and quantity are determined by the phaseout's quantity limitation.

Another baseline state of the world is also possible. In this alternative baseline, the tax is the binding regulation, not the phaseout's quantity limitation. Figure 6-3 shows this situation. Without the tax, the phaseout-determined market price would be $4, but with the tax the price is $4.98. This implies that the quantity of CFCs produced and consumed will be less than that allowed under the phaseout. This baseline could be the reality if a substantial drop in CFC demand occurred independently of the phaseout and tax rules. Indeed, in the early years of the phaseout, the actual level of CFC production was less than the maximum allowed, which automatically implies that the tax was the binding regulation.

Which of these two possible baselines one should use is of more than casual interest, because both the costs and benefits of the new recycling regulation depend on which baseline applies.

RECYCLING-RULE EFFECTS WHEN THE PHASEOUT IS BINDING

Suppose the correct depiction of the world is as in Figure 6-1, where the phaseout quantity limitation is binding. Once again, the way to analyze the costs and benefits of the new recycling

FIGURE 6-3

CFC Tax as the Binding Regulation

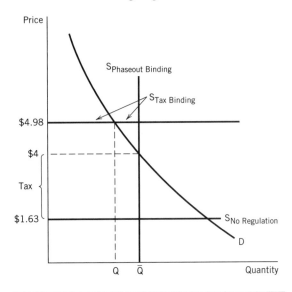

Which preexisting regulation is binding depends on the position of the demand function, the stringency of the phaseout limitation, and the magnitude of the tax in a particular year. Here the CFC tax is binding because the actual quantity is less than the allowed phaseout amount.

regulation is to clearly define what will happen differently relative to the baseline. As before, the recycling rule will force equipment owners to engage in costly recapture and recycling of CFCs, which again provides a new source of supply of CFCs. These added costs are, as assumed earlier, $8 per pound of CFCs recaptured and recycled.

Care is needed to define what happens in response to this new source of supply when the phaseout limitation is binding. Imagine that an additional pound of CFCs is supplied to the market as depicted in Figure 6-1. The equipment owners and CFC recyclers will spend the $8 necessary to recapture and recycle that pound, and will receive the market price of $6 for it. But in this case, virgin CFC production does not fall. Instead the extra pound of CFCs supplied through recycling constitutes a net increase in the quantity available to the market. This means that someone will be able to use that pound of CFCs rather than to engage in costly controls or purchase substitutes, which, at the margin, cost $6. Hence, the recycled pound of CFCs costs society $8, but reduces other control costs by $6, so that on net, the recycled pound costs society only $2.

Figure 6-4 shows how the costs of the recycling regulation when the phaseout is binding can be measured graphically. The costs of the additional CFCs supplied through the mandatory recycling program are depicted by the shaded area A plus B, which is the $8 per pound cost of recapturing and recycling the additional CFCs, multiplied by the quantity involved, Q_R. Netted out of this are the control-and-substitution costs avoided by those who now use the extra CFCs. This is simply the area under the demand function from the original phaseout quantity, $\overline{Q}$, to the new total amount of CFCs supplied to the market, Q_T. Thus, the net cost of the recycling program is area A which is the $8 per pound cost of recycling times the Q_R amount of CFCs recycled, minus the value of the extra CFCs to purchasers, as measured by the demand functions. Note that CFC tax revenues are unchanged because virgin CFC production levels remain constant.

RECYCLING-RULE EFFECTS WHEN THE TAX IS BINDING

The results are very different when the tax is binding. In this case, when the extra recycled CFCs are supplied to the market, virgin production declines. As in the case of no preexisting regulation, when the tax is binding the marginal supply conditions are defined by the costs of virgin production ($1.63 per pound) plus the tax ($3.35 per pound). For increases in supply in-

FIGURE 6-4

Costs of CFC Recycling Regulation: Phaseout Limitation Binding

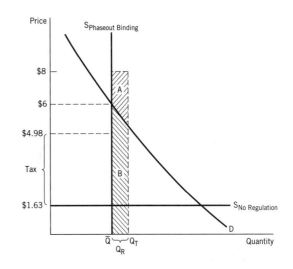

Mandatory CFC recycling provides a net increase in the available CFCs when the phaseout limitation is binding. The total cost of recycling CFCs is area A plus B, but control and substitution costs equal to area B are saved, so the net cost is area A. CFC tax revenues do not change because virgin production remains constant.

duced by the recycling rule, a one-for-one reduction in virgin supply results.

This has important implications for the cost of the CFC recycling rule, because rather than saving society fairly high control and substitution costs, as it does when the phaseout limitation is binding, when the tax is binding, recycled CFCs save society only the cost of virgin production. To see this one must carefully calculate the social cost of the recycling activities. Begin again with the $8 per pound of recapture and recycling costs. Equipment owners and recyclers pay this, but then receive the market price of $4.98. Consumers are indifferent because the recycled pound of CFCs costs them the market price, the same as virgin-source CFCs. Producers of virgin CFCs are also indifferent because, although their revenues fall by the price, $4.98, their costs also fall by this same amount, the $1.63 production cost and the $3.35 tax.

The government, however, is not indifferent, because recycled CFCs are not taxed. Hence, the government loses the $3.35 per pound tax proceeds for the virgin-source CFCs that recycled CFCs displace. Adding up all of the gains and losses, the net cost to society for a pound of recycled CFCs is $8 minus $4.98 (the equipment owners' and recyclers' net cost), plus $3.35 (the government's loss), or $8 minus $1.63. This is simply the explicit expenditure per pound on recapturing and recycling CFCs, minus the cost of virgin CFC production.

Figure 6-5 shows how to measure the net cost of the recycling program under the tax-binding baseline. As in the no-regulation case, the costs of the recycling program are measured by the shaded area A plus B, defined by the $8 per pound cost of recapturing and recycling CFCs and the amount of those additional CFCs, Q_R. Subtracted from this are the avoided virgin CFC production costs, area B. The net cost of the recycling program is thus area A, which includes the decline in tax revenues due to the fall in virgin production.

INTUITION AND RECONCILIATION WITH THE BENEFITS

Clearly, which of the two preexisting CFC regulations is binding in the baseline makes a substantial difference in the estimated costs of the new recycling regulation. In this example, when the phaseout limitation is binding, the net cost to society per pound is $2, $8 of recapturing and recycling expenditures minus $6 of avoided control-and-substitution costs, at least for marginal amounts of extra recycled CFCs. When the CFC tax is binding, however, the regulation's cost is far greater—$8 of recapturing and recycling costs

FIGURE 6-5

Costs of CFC Recycling Regulation: CFC Tax Binding

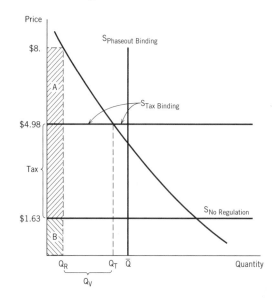

When the CFC tax is binding, mandatory CFC recycling displaces virgin CFC production. The cost of CFC recycling is area A plus B. The extra CFCs are worth the market price, $4.98 per pound, but the government loses tax revenues because the untaxed recycled CFCs displace taxed virgin CFCs. The social cost of supplying the displaced virgin CFCs is only $1.63 per pound, so the net cost of the mandated recycling thus is area A, much higher than when the phaseout is binding.

minus only the $1.63 cost of virgin production, or $6.37 per pound. This result may seem surprising, if not disturbing. How can it be that the same economic activities mandated by the CFC recycling regulation cost two very different amounts, depending on something normally as innocuous as specifying the baseline?

The intuition for this result has to do with fully appreciating the fact that what happens when an additional pound of recycled CFCs is supplied to the market depends on which baseline regulation governs marginal CFC supply conditions. When the phaseout limitation is binding, the extra CFCs displace socially costly control-and-substitution activities as measured by the height of the demand function at the phaseout-limited quantity. The greater these substitution costs are, the higher the value of the extra CFCs provided by the recycling rule. When the CFC tax is binding, however, the recycling regulation forces on the market more costly re-captured and recycled CFCs in the place of so-cially less expensive virgin-source CFCs. Hence, the costs of the new recycling rule will be lower when the phaseout rule is binding than when the CFC tax is binding.

The intuition for the result runs even deeper though. Consider the social benefits of the new recycling regulation under the two different baseline specifications. When the phaseout limi-tation is binding, health and other benefits of re-cycling consist only of delaying the release of CFCs from this year to future years. That is, the recycling regulation avoids current venting by re-capturing the CFCs and then placing them in other pieces of equipment that themselves even-tually will leak. In this case, no change occurs in the total amount of virgin CFCs produced and released over time; the time profile of releases is only shifted toward the future. When the tax is binding, however, the recycled CFCs displace vir-gin production. In this case, the recycling regula-tion will not only shift the time pattern of CFC releases toward the future, but will also reduce the total amount of CFCs produced and eventu-ally released.

Hence, the ozone-depletion benefits of the re-cycling rule also depend on which baseline ap-plies. These benefits will be higher if the CFC tax is binding and lower if the phaseout limitation is binding. Now matters should make more sense, for when the costs of the recycling regulation are higher (*tax binding*) the benefits are as well. When the recycling regulation's costs are lower (phase-out binding) the benefits are also lower.

Baseline specification is thus sometimes more than merely a process of forecasting future mar-ket conditions relative to which regulatory out-comes are described and evaluated. Indeed, the correct specification of the baseline occasionally can be the most important step in practice. This is especially true when preexisting regulations already affect economic conditions in a market, as this study demonstrates.

Overlapping Regulations for Hazardous Waste Disposal

The Resource Conservation and Recovery Act, or RCRA, governs a variety of aspects of solid- and hazardous-waste management. To imple-ment the mandates in RCRA over the years, EPA developed and promulgated a number of regu-lations to control the risks of solid-waste landfilling and incineration, and many rules governing hazardous-waste management and disposal, including treatment standards and dis-posal-facility design and permitting require-ments. Because many of the scientific and policy concerns associated with solid- and hazardous-waste issues are fairly technical, until the early 1980s regulatory activity under RCRA was mostly left to the policy makers at EPA.

In 1984, however, Congress passed the Haz-ardous and Solid Waste Amendments (HSWA) to RCRA. These amendments modified or added approximately 70 provisions of the statute and imposed over 58 specific deadlines requiring ac-tion on the parts of EPA, the states, and the regu-lated communities. In general, the HSWA pro-visions were very detailed and extremely strin-gent, especially regarding EPA's oversight of hazardous-waste management.

Two related developments over the years leading up to the amendments were largely re-sponsible for HSWA's close attention to the dis-posal of hazardous wastes. One was the long and growing list of Superfund sites around the country, where toxic wastes were deposited, often over many years, and then abandoned. In some cases, entire housing developments were located on or very near some of these sites.

In others, hazardous wastes had contaminated ground and surface waters, posing risks to human health and the environment. Estimates of the cleanup costs for these sites ran in the many billions of dollars, with apparently no end in sight. The other factor that greatly influenced the content of HSWA's modification of RCRA's sections on hazardous wastes was a combination of the general "greening" of America and an increased awareness, if not phobia, of toxic substances and cancer-causing agents. Fear of the unseen and unfelt, but deadly, results of exposure to toxics thus provided public backing for far stricter hazardous waste management rules.

Thus, HSWA was profoundly influenced by the huge and growing Superfund problem and the apparent consensus among the voters that hazardous wastes were a significant and imminent threat to the health and safety of the population and the environment. HSWA mandated a host of new regulatory programs, such as a major overhaul of the design and operation requirements for hazardous waste disposal facilities and a complete waste-by-waste reassessment of what should be allowed to be disposed of in hazardous waste landfills. HSWA also included deadlines for implementing the required regulations after which Congressionally mandated "hammer provisions" would be triggered. For example, in the landfill disposal reassessment provision, if EPA failed to meet the statutory deadlines for evaluating different groups of wastes, all such wastes for which EPA had not made a decision would immediately be banned from land disposal.

Facing the many specific Congressional mandates and the various hammer provisions, EPA began to develop and evaluate options for implementing the many programs and policies required under HSWA. As with most regulations, this process included cost–benefit assessments of the different options and programs. This study reviews several basic analytical issues that arose

in the process of evaluating some of the new hazardous waste disposal requirements mandated in HSWA.

The Question

HSWA contained numerous specific mandates relating to many different aspects of hazardous waste management, including standards for certain treatment processes, and manifesting requirements (essentially documentation and notification) for generators and transporters of these wastes. Land disposal of hazardous wastes, however, received intense scrutiny, because it was this practice that produced the huge Superfund abandoned-wastes-sites problem in the first place. Furthermore, to some people, landfilling toxic materials, unless it is done carefully, poses a silent but ever-present threat to humans and the environment. Out of sight is definitely not out of mind.

The hazardous waste land disposal requirements in HSWA were thus motivated by a "never again" sort of mentality. By mandating multiple requirements and restrictions for hazardous waste landfills—*where* they may be located, *what* they are allowed to accept, *how* they are designed and operated, and so forth—the basic intent was to make widespread future contamination of water and land by disposal of toxics as improbable as possible. The stringency of these regulations is not so much of interest here as the overlapping nature of the various land disposal requirements in HSWA, which motivated the analysis summarized in this study. The term *overlapping* signifies the fact that if several regulations each independently targets a set of possible environmental harms potentially caused by landfilling hazardous wastes, at least some of the damages avoided by one regulation may also be avoided by another. Hence, if both regulations are promulgated, the sum of their impacts individually will be different from their combined effect.

This is important from an analytical perspective, because each rule in a series of mandates, such as those in HSWA for land disposal of hazardous waste, is often "packaged" individually, so that each requirement constitutes a separate regulation. When this occurs, a cost–benefit analysis normally is prepared for each. The question then arises precisely how to calculate the costs and benefits of a set of overlapping rules, all targeting the same general set of risks, when they are to be evaluated separately.

To make matters more concrete, and to simplify some of the many details a bit, this analysis focuses on three different major classes of hazardous waste landfill regulations. One is a requirement to undertake and maintain a variety of monitoring activities at and around hazardous waste landfills to detect a release of toxic material from the facility as soon as possible. Loosely speaking, these consist of collecting and analyzing leachate (liquids that seep through the landfill), and groundwater-monitoring wells drilled at a number of locations around the facility. Monitoring requirements typically are used to provide an early warning of a release so that appropriate mitigation measures can be initiated.

A second type of regulation establishes certain minimum design requirements for hazardous waste landfills, such as the number and composition of facility *liners*, which are barriers to waste migration into the soil and groundwater below. Liners commonly are made of compacted clay or other types of nonporous natural materials, as well as various impermeable synthetics. Yet a third type of hazardous waste landfill regulation is often referred to as a *location restriction*. Basically, the purpose of restricting the location of hazardous-waste landfills is to prevent them from operating above groundwater aquifers or too near surface waters, which currently, or may in the future, supply water for human consumption or serve important ecological and economic purposes, such as the habitats and nutrients provided

by wetlands, and the recreational and commercial uses of rivers and lakes.

Clearly, these three types of regulations applied to hazardous waste landfills will have overlapping effects. For example, monitoring requirements clearly compete with design standards in avoiding exposures to toxic substances that may leak from a facility. The former sounds the alarm early to prevent major damage from a release, and the latter makes that release less likely. Similarly, location restrictions on hazardous waste landfills may considerably lessen the amount and severity of any damages from these facilities, regardless of the probability of a release. Hence, the basic question posed here is how to account for the impacts of these overlapping regulations, together and separately.

The Analysis

It is best to begin matters by characterizing the baseline for hazardous waste facilities affected by the various new regulations. For purposes of this discussion, both the baseline conditions and the nature and functioning of the various HSWA regulations are somewhat stylized to highlight the problem's key features. Naturally, as with most other real-world environmental analyses, there are always additional details and complications. Nevertheless, the central focus of this study is on some broad analytical issues, so smoothing over some of the complexities makes the important points more clear without loss of generality.

Unlike many other instances in which new regulations are promulgated to address a currently unregulated environmental problem, prior to HSWA hazardous waste facilities were subject to a variety of rules and standards. In particular, these facilities were subject to design and operation standards at the federal level, as well as the other more conventional methods of controlling the sorts of risks they pose, such as zoning restrictions and traditional property and tort law.

For example, if a hazardous waste facility were to release toxic materials into groundwater, there was some probability that it would be detected and traced back to the facility. If so, existing cleanup rules and liability laws would be triggered, forcing remediation of the contamination and damage payments.

Nevertheless, HSWA embodied the view that existing regulations allowed too much remaining risk. Hazardous waste landfills accept waste over many years and then are intended to store them indefinitely. The worry was that given enough time, releases of toxic substances seemed almost assured. Moreover, in many cases these facilities were located above or near important sources of ground and surface water. Hence, if a release were to occur and not be detected quickly, extensive contamination was likely, with the attendant human health effects and environmental damages. Finally, the probability of detecting and tracing a release back to particular facilities can be fairly low, both because of the timeframes involved from initial release to eventual detection of contamination, and the possibility that some other source, such as an industrial plant, could have caused the pollution problem. Thus, the motivation for the fairly strict mandates in HSWA relating to land disposal of hazardous wastes flowed generally from the view that despite the existing regulatory and legal structures, these facilities still posed unacceptable long-term risks to human health and the environment.

As outlined above, among many other mandates, HSWA called for promulgating three general types of stricter requirements for hazardous waste land disposal: restricting facility locations, tightening their design and operation, and requiring continuous monitoring. To see how the baseline risks would be mitigated by these different regulations, consider the following hypothetical example: Suppose that there are 1000 hazardous waste landfills and that in the regulatory and legal climate of the baseline, the probability of a release from any one of them is 10 percent over some relevant timeframe, say 30 years. Suppose as well that the baseline probability of detecting a release if one occurs is also 10 percent, and that if a release is detected, remediation and other costs associated with avoiding human health impacts amount to $1 million, and that prior to the cleanup, $10,000 worth of environmental harm occurs, such as fish kills, contamination of habitats, and other sorts of nonhuman ecological damages. Finally, assume that if a release goes undetected, a significant amount of human health and environmental damages results, say 10 expected cancers among the exposed population and some $100,000 worth of ecological harm. Toxic materials in the concentrations normally associated with gradual contamination often are not immediately noticeable to those consuming the water or otherwise coming into contact with the affected water and soil, hence the relatively higher levels of damages associated with undetected releases, relative to detected ones.

RISKS AND COSTS IN THE BASELINE AND UNDER THE REGULATIONS

Given these hypothetical baseline circumstances, Table 6-2 shows the expected levels of the various damages and costs for both detected and undetected releases. Given the 10 percent probability of a release and the 1000 facilities, the expected number that will experience a release is 100. These can be divided into *detected* and *undetected* according to the baseline 10 percent probability of detection, so one would expect a total of 10 releases to be detected and 90 to go undetected. Finally, as shown in the table, multiplying the expected number of releases of both types by the respective human and nonhuman damages and remediation costs yields a total of $10 million in remediation costs plus $100,000 worth of environmental damage for detected releases, and some 900 cancers and $9 million of environmental harm for undetected releases. These hypotheti-

Table 6-2
BASELINE AND INDIVIDUAL REGULATION OUTCOMES

Regulatory Case	Number of Facilities Releasing	Detected			Undetected		
		Number of Releases	Remediation Costs ($ millions)	Environmental Damages ($ millions)	Number of Releases	Cancers Caused	Environmental Damages ($ millions)
Baseline	100	10	10	0.1	90	900	9
Monitoring Requirements Only	100	90	90	0.9	10	100	1
Design Standards Only	20	2	2	0.02	18	180	1.8
Location Restrictions Only	100	10	10	0.01	90	90	0.9
All Regulations Together	20	18	18	0.018	2	2	0.02

cal figures reflect the motivation of the HSWA mandates: The baseline appears to saddle the nation with some expensive cleanups and a number of unseen and undetected risks to human health and the environment, even though the probability of a release is not high.

At this point one might ask whether these facility owners would engage in extra protective and preventative measures to avoid these remediation costs and environmental harms. Given these baseline conditions, the answer is probably not, because facilities are likely to be held liable for the damages to human health and the environment only for detected releases, not for those that are undetected. Hence, in the baseline each facility faces a probability of having to pay the $1 million of remediation costs plus the $10,000 in environmental damages for a detected release of only 1 percent, which is the 10 percent probability of a release times the 10 percent probability of it being detected. If the relevant additional protective and preventative

measures cost more than the roughly $10,000 expected cost of this gamble, many facilities might not undertake them. Hence, some type of intervention appears to be warranted.

The impacts of the three different classes of more stringent regulations are also shown in Table 6-2. Consider first the monitoring requirements. By themselves, these do not change the probability of a release, only the probability of detection given a release. The assumption made here is that the detection probability rises from 10 percent to 90 percent with the monitoring requirements. Hence, while the total number of releases remains the same, 90 percent of them will be detected instead of only 10 percent. As a consequence, the costs of remediation activities for detected releases rise substantially, but the number of human cancers and the more severe environmental damages associated with undetected releases falls dramatically. Monitoring requirements essentially convert undetected releases into detected ones. Detected releases pose higher explicit monetary costs, but these are likely to be lower than the human health and environmental harms of undetected releases. Estimates of the value of avoiding one statistical death (where a large population is exposed to a risk that will result in one expected death) vary widely, although figures in the $1 million to $10 million range are common.[4] Hence, in this example, when an undetected release is converted into a detected one, society avoids 10 cancer cases for about $1 million of remediation expenditures. Assuming even a $1 million value per cancer avoided, this seems to be a worthwhile trade.

Facility design standards, however, explicitly reduce the probability of a release. What is assumed here is that the probability of a release falls from 10 percent to 2 percent, which implies that the expected number of releases from the 1000 facilities falls from 100 to 20. This reduction in the total number of releases, detected and undetected, translates directly into a substantial reduction in the level of damages to human health and the environment, as well as in remediation costs.

Facility location restrictions, however, affect neither the probability of a release nor the rate of detection given a release. Instead, this type of regulation changes the level of damages, given that a release occurs, whether it is detected or not.[5] As such, location restrictions function as a kind of insurance policy against releases of toxic materials. The assumptions made here are that for an undetected release the expected number of human cancers drops from 10 to 1, and that environmental damages decline from $100,000 to $10,000. These consequences reflect the fact that if these facilities are located in areas where toxic releases will result in far less exposure of humans and natural resources, the level of damages, even for an undetected release, will be far lower than in the baseline.

For a detected release, on the other hand, environmental damages decline from $10,000 to $1,000 and remediation costs are unchanged. The rationale for no decline in the remediation costs is that existing regulations tend to require costly cleanups, more or less irrespective of the degree of potential harm caused by a release—a result of the no-tolerance posture of hazardous waste regulation. While the location restrictions do not by themselves change the number of releases or their division between detected and undetected releases, the amount of human health and environmental harm that results from undetected releases is considerably less than in the baseline.

Finally, although the results for each of the three types of regulations are instructive, the

---

[4] The literature on the implicit value placed on saving statistical lives is quite extensive. Although several methods are used for estimating the value of saving statistical lives, one popular approach relies on observed compensating wage differentials. The basic idea is to estimate the increased compensation a group of workers requires in order to accept a small increase in the probability of death, usually job-related. Summing this added compensation for the whole group and then dividing by the expected number of additional deaths among them yields the estimated value of avoiding a statistical death. The term "statistical death" is used because the incremental probability of death is small and the population affected is large. Several well-known surveys of this literature include M. J. Bailey, *Reducing Risks to Life: Measurement of the Benefits* (Washington, D. C.: American Enterprise Institute, 1980); M. W. Jones-Lee, ed., *The Value of Life and Safety* (Amsterdam: North Holland Publishing Company, 1982); D. M. Violette, and L. G. Chestnut, "Valuing Reductions in Risks: A Review of the Empirical Estimates," Prepared for U. S. Environmental Protection Agency, Economic Analysis Division, 1983; W. K. Viscusi, *Employment Hazards: An Investigation of Market Performance* (Cambridge, Mass.: Harvard University Press, 1979); and W. K. Viscusi, "The Value of Risks to Life and Health," Journal of Economic Literature, Vol. XXXI (December 1993), 1912–46.

[5] Of course, it may be difficult, if not impossible, to move an existing facility from one location to another. Assume that what happens is that a new facility is built in compliance with the location restrictions and the old one is closed. One could make the same simplifying assumption about the design standards if existing facilities cannot be retrofitted. In both cases, the existence of old facilities presents interesting complications if they cannot comply with the regulations at the same cost as new facilities. But the social cost consequences of prematurely closing old facilities are unrelated to the basic thrust of this analysis. Hence, assume that any closures of existing facilities to comply with these regulations impose no additional social costs.

reality is that all three will be imposed simultaneously. Hence, as shown at the bottom of Table 6-2, the actual residual risks and environmental costs expected, given the operation of all of the regulations, are lower than for any one of the individual options. This is not unexpected, because although the regulations overlap significantly in the sense that they each avoid at least some of the same risks, their joint coverage is far from complete. As the results for all regulations combined in the table indicate, all three regulations taken together end up avoiding most of the cancers by reducing the number of expected releases, by shifting undetected releases into the detected category in which remediation actions avoid cancers, and by reducing the expected number of cancers and environmental harms caused by an undetected release. This process, however, also causes an increase in the total number of detected releases, because the monitoring requirements render most of the far smaller number of releases observable. Thus, relative to the baseline, all three regulations together result in lower total releases, far fewer cancers and other environmental damages, but higher remediation costs.

ALLOCATION OF TOTAL IMPACTS TO INDIVIDUAL REGULATIONS

If all that is required is an estimate of the total benefits and costs of imposing all three regulations at the same time, the *all regulations together* results in Table 6-2 can be used directly to estimate the benefits as simply the difference between the baseline and the entries in that column for remediation costs, environmental damages, and human health effects. Costs would amount to simply the total compliance costs spent by the 1000 facilities for all three of the regulations.

But what if one is required to evaluate each rule individually, providing a separate cost–benefit analysis for each? One possibility is shown in Table 6-3 where the change in risks and costs provided by each regulation individually is computed relative to the *no additional rules* baseline. These are simply the differences between the levels of risks and costs for each regulation alone and those in the baseline, as presented in Table 6-2. This method essentially assumes that the impact of each regulation is unaffected by imposing either of the other two rules.

Table 6-3
EFFECT OF EACH REGULATION INDIVIDUALLY

		Detected			Undetected		
Regulatory Case	Change in Number of Facilities Releasing	Change in Number of Releases	Change in Remediation Costs ($ millions)	Change in Environmental Damages ($ millions)	Change in Number of Releases	Change in Cancers Caused	Change in Environmental Damages ($ millions)
Monitoring Requirements Only	0	80	80	.8	-80	-800	-8
Design Standards Only	-80	-8	-8	-0.08	-72	-720	-7.2
Location Restrictions Only	0	0	0	-0.09	0	-810	-8.1

Another method of computing the results of the three regulations individually is shown in Table 6-4. This is the reverse of the first approach in that here each rule's impact is computed assuming that the other two regulations are already in place. The approach in Table 6-3 assumes that each regulation is *first*, so that the other two regulations are assumed not to be present when each is imposed individually. In contrast, the method shown in Table 6-4 conceptualizes each of the rules as *last*, in the sense that it computes effects assuming the other two regulations exist already. Hence, the impact of the monitoring requirements, for example, is computed by subtracting the results for all regulations together from those for all regulations except the monitoring requirements.

These marginal differences measure the incremental impact of the three sets of requirements according to this approach.

Clearly, neither of these methods provides the right answer. Table 6-5 compares the sum of the impacts of all three regulations predicted by each approach to the actual total changes in health, cost, and ecological effects they generate jointly. As shown in Table 6-5, the first approach suggests that the three rules combined avoid three times as many cancers as there really are in the baseline. This problem arises because this method assumes that each regulation independently attacks the baseline conditions, so that each is credited with avoiding a large portion of the risks present in the baseline. But because these three regulations overlap, once one option

Table 6-4

EFFECT OF EACH REGULATION ASSUMING THE OTHER TWO REGULATIONS EXIST

Regulatory Case	Number of Facilities Releasing	Detected			Undetected		
		Number of Releases	Remediation Costs ($ millions)	Environmental Damages ($ millions)	Number of Releases	Cancers Caused	Environmental Damages ($ millions)
All Regulations Together	20	18	18	0.018	2	2	0.02
All Regulations Except Monitoring Requirements	20	2	2	0.002	18	18	0.18
Change Due to Monitoring Requirements	0	16	16	0.016	-16	-16	-0.16
All Regulations Except Design Standards	100	90	90	0.09	10	10	0.1
Change Due to Design Standards	-80	-72	-72	-0.072	-8	-8	-0.08
All Regulations Except Location Restrictions	20	18	18	0.18	2	20	0.2
Change Due to Location Restrictions	0	0	0	-0.162	0	-18	-0.18

Table 6-5

SUM OF INDIVIDUAL EFFECTS OF REGULATIONS COMPARED TO ACTUAL JOINT IMPACT

| Regulatory Case | Change in Number of Facilities Releasing | Detected | | | Undetected | | |
		Change in Number of Releases	Change in Remediation Costs ($ millions)	Change in Environmental Damages ($ millions)	Change in Number of Releases	Change in Cancers Caused	Change in Environmental Damages ($ millions)
All Regulations Together	-80	8	8	-0.082	-88	-898	-8.98
Sum of Effects Computed Relative to No Regulations in Baseline	-80	72	72	0.63	-152	-2330	-23.3
Error	0	64	64	0.712	-64	-1432	-14.32
Sum of Effects Computed Assuming Other Regulations Exist in Baseline	-80	-56	-56	-0.218	-24	-42	-0.42
Error	0	-64	-64	-0.136	64	856	8.56

avoids a substantial amount of the risks, especially the human cancers, they cannot then be avoided again by the other two rules. The regulation assumed to be first is thus credited with a large amount of the benefits, but obviously, all three rules cannot simultaneously be first. The other problem evident with the first approach is that it predicts a far larger increase in the level of remediation expenditures than is true. This problem occurs because the monitoring requirements taken alone suggests that a large number of releases will still occur but will be detected, and those responsible required to engage in costly remediation efforts. The reality, however, is that with the other regulations in place, far fewer facilities actually experience releases and require remediation.

The second approach also has its share of problems. Here the estimated number of avoided cancers and reduced environmental damages vastly understates the correct levels of benefits. The reason for this is similar to the first

method's gross overstatement of these effects. When each regulation is thought to be last, none of them will account for the bulk of the actual benefits, because these are, in a sense, avoided already by the other two rules that are assumed to be present. The other problem with this second approach is that it predicts a decline in remediation costs for detected releases, when the reality is otherwise. This occurs because when the marginal impact of the design standards is computed, a large number of baseline releases are expected and detected because of the monitoring requirements. The design standards then reduce the implied remediation costs significantly by lowering the probability of a release, so the predicted remediation cost savings are large. But when imposing the monitoring requirements assuming a baseline that includes the design standards, there are far fewer releases to be shifted from the undetected to the detected category, so the increase in remediation costs is much less than without the design standards.

As a result, the marginal monitoring require-ments calculations do not capture these "inter-mediate" remediation cost increases, which the computations for the design standards then as-sume are saved.

Thus, neither of these possible approaches for computing the impacts of the individual rules is satisfactory for situations in which multiple regulations overlap. Depending on the regula-tions and the underlying risks being addressed, either approach could yield over- or underesti-mates of their combined effects on different ben-efit and cost categories, and sometimes by very large amounts.

Sequential Allocation of Effects

The source of the problem, unfortunately, is that there really is no iron-clad analytically correct way to parcel out the total impact of a group of regulations that jointly target a set of risks when all are imposed (at least conceptually) simulta-neously. What is known is the total result of the rules taken together relative to a baseline with none of them. How the total is allocated to the individual rules ultimately is arbitrary.

Arbitrariness, however, comes in many shapes and sizes. For example, with these three hazardous waste landfill rules, one might decide to divide the total impacts equally, allocating to each regulation one-third of the total effects. This is about as arbitrary as one can be when con-fronting these sorts of *imputation problems*, as they are called. It is also not a very satisfactory solution for the analyst who must prepare sepa-rate *stand-alone* cost–benefit analyses for each of the three rules. That is, an analysis of one of the three regulations that estimates its impact as one-third of the effects of that rule plus one-third of the impacts for two others evaluated elsewhere is unlikely to be acceptable.

Allocating the total results of imposing all three regulations simultaneously, however, can be arbitrary in a more structured way. To see this, note that in addition to the baseline and

all three regulations combined, one can also compute the marginal effects of successively adding one regulation after another, starting with the baseline and ending with having all of the rules in place. This process of sequen-tially adding multiple regulations is shown in Table 6-6. Here the monitoring requirements are imposed first, then the design standards, and finally the location restrictions. After each such addition, the changes in risk and cost catego-ries are computed and attributed to the regula-tion just applied. This process incrementally moves from the baseline situation to the fully regulated state of the world as the additional monitoring, fewer physical releases, and lower harms per undetected release are successively provided by the three regulations.

This technique also generates some interest-ing "intermediate" benefit categories. For ex-ample, as shown in Table 6-6, when the moni-toring requirements are imposed first, they pro-vide both risk-reduction benefits by shifting re-leases from the undetected category to the de-tected one, and much higher costs in the form of remediation expenditures. But when the design standards are then installed, in addition to yet more human health and ecological risk reduc-tion, this regulation also provides benefits in the form of reduced remediation costs. These design standard financial benefits largely offset the huge remediation costs associated with the monitoring requirements.

Of course, in purely physical terms, many of the remediation costs "expended" by the moni-toring requirements and then "saved" by the de-sign standards never really occur because all of the regulations will be imposed simultaneously. But this highlights the great advantage of se-quentially applying the different regulations as done here. As shown in Table 6-6, an important feature of this process is that when all of the marginal impacts of the three different regula-tions are summed, the total is precisely equal to the actual combined impact of the rules taken together. This sequential estimation of the mar-

Table 6-6
SEQUENTIAL ESTIMATION OF MARGINAL EFFECT OF EACH REGULATION

Regulatory Case	Number of Facilities Releasing	Detected			Undetected		
		Number of Releases	Remediation Costs ($ millions)	Environmental Damages ($ millions)	Number of Releases	Cancers Caused	Environmental Damages ($ millions)
Baseline	100	10	10	0.1	90	900	9
Monitoring Requirements Only	100	90	90	0.9	10	100	1
Change Due to Monitoring Requirements	0	80	80	0.8	-80	-800	-8
Monitoring Requirements Plus Design Standards	20	18	18	0.18	2	20	0.2
Change Due to Design Standards	-80	-72	-72	-0.72	-8	-80	-0.8
All Regulations	20	18	18	0.018	2	2	0.02
Change Due to Location Restrictions	0	0	0	-0.162	0	-18	-0.18
Sum of Sequential Marginal Impacts of Regulations	-80	8	8	-0.082	-88	-898	-8.98

ginal impact of each regulation thus appears to be a more coherent and structured way to allocate the total impacts of all of the regulations to the individual components than dividing up the total among the three regulations in a completely arbitrary way.

Unfortunately, this process of sequentially adding regulations and then computing the marginal impacts of each successive rule can be conducted in any order, so the specific allocation of the total effects to the individual rules is still arbitrary. That is, the sum of the estimated marginal impacts of each of the three rules computed sequentially will be the same, regardless of the order in which they are imposed, and the total will always be the correct amount for all three taken together. But the method does not itself suggest that any particular order is best, so while the method lends coherence and consistency to the process, ultimately it does not resolve the allocation issue.

Table 6-7, for example, shows the sequential estimation of marginal impacts for each of the three regulations, but in a different order. Here, while the total impact of all three rules is still correct, the allocation to the individual component rules differs substantially from that calculated using the order in Table 6-6. This is especially pronounced for the cancers avoided. Comparing the marginal impacts of the three regulations in Tables 6-6 and 6-7 reveals that the first regulation imposed tends to be allocated most

Table 6-7
ALTERNATIVE SEQUENTIAL ESTIMATION OF MARGINAL EFFECTS OF EACH REGULATION

Regulatory Case	Number of Facilities Releasing	Detected			Undetected		
		Number of Releases	Remediation Costs ($ millions)	Environmental Damages ($ millions)	Number of Releases	Cancers Caused	Environmental Damages ($ millions)
Baseline	100	10	10	0.1	90	900	9
Design Standards Only	20	2	2	0.02	18	180	1.8
Change Due to Design Standards	-80	-8	-8	-0.08	-72	-720	-7.2
Design Standards plus Location Restrictions	20	2	2	0.002	18	18	0.18
Change Due to Location Restrictions	0	0	0	-0.018	0	-162	-1.62
All Regulations	20	18	18	0.018	2	2	0.02
Change Due to Monitoring Requirements	0	16	16	0.016	-16	-16	-0.16
Sum of Sequential Marginal Effects of Regulations	-80	8	8	-0.082	-88	-898	-8.98

of the avoided cancers, leaving relatively few for the other two rules. In practice, when multiple regulations target the same cancer risks, this disproportionate allocation of risk reduction to the first one almost always occurs. This probably explains why there is a general tendency to calculate the risk-reduction benefits of multiple overlapping rules relative to a no-regulation baseline, as in Table 6-3. Although this generally will grossly overestimate the total impact of all of the regulations combined, it will make the best case for each of the regulations independently.

In the end, there is no correct way to impute the total benefits of multiple, overlapping regulations to the individual rules. In practice, the best resolution of this problem would be to prepare a single cost–benefit analysis for all of the regulations combined. When that is not a possi-

bility, other institutional aspects of the rules, such as implementation beginning in different time periods, might suggest a logical order in which to analyze the regulations. In the absence of any such guidance, the best one can do is to conduct the successive analyses using consistent baselines, and to acknowledge the influence of the other regulations on the cost and benefit results for each individual rule.

Finally, although it is true that when multiple overlapping regulations are promulgated simultaneously, the allocation of total benefits to the individual rules ultimately is arbitrary, the entire issue begs a more fundamental question. So far the assumption has been that the three hazardous waste landfill regulations will be promulgated together. But what if the question is whether or not to promulgate any or all of the rules in the first place? That is, when several candidate regulations targeting the same sources of risk have overlapping effects in the sense discussed here, how should decision makers evaluate the costs and benefits of promulgating the rules individually or in combinations?

It is tempting to argue that a foolproof approach for deciding on the optimal set of regulations in such a situation is as follows: Start with the regulation that offers the highest net benefits alone, assess the marginal net benefits of the other regulations when combined with the initial rule selected, add the one offering the highest net benefits, and continue this procedure until no additional regulations offer positive net benefits.

While such an approach appears to offer a rational procedure for sorting through multiple overlapping regulatory options, it will not necessarily lead to the correct answer. To see this, consider Tables 6-8 and 6-9. Table 6-8 gathers from previous tables the total impacts of all seven possible combinations of the three hazardous waste landfill regulations, including the baseline. To evaluate the net benefits of all of these possible combinations, two additional steps are necessary. First, one must finish *monetizing*, or valuing, the risk-reduction benefits. The remediation costs and environmental damages have been carried through in dollar terms throughout this discussion, so what remains is to monetize the cancers avoided. For this discussion, assume that the social value of avoiding these cancers is $2 million per case.[6]

[6] In practice, it seems that no matter what value one uses for saving "statistical lives," someone will be unhappy: Either the figure is too low or too high; or even to entertain the notion that human lives can be valued in monetary terms seems abhorrent. Great caution is thus advised in conducting analyses or in making policy decisions solely on the basis of the dollar value assigned to human mortality risk reduction.

Table 6-8

RISKS AND COSTS OF ALTERNATIVE COMBINATIONS OF REGULATIONS

Regulatory Case	Number of Facilities Releasing	Detected			Undetected		
		Number of Releases	Remediation Costs ($ millions)	Environmental Damages ($ millions)	Number of Releases	Cancers Caused	Environmental Damages ($ millions)
Baseline	100	10	10	0.1	90	900	9
Monitoring Requirements Only	100	90	90	0.9	10	100	1
Design Standards Only	20	2	2	0.02	18	180	1.8
Location Restrictions Only	100	10	10	0.01	90	90	0.9
Monitoring Requirements Plus Design Standards	20	18	18	0.18	2	20	0.2
Monitoring Requirements Plus Location Restrictions	100	90	90	0.09	10	10	0.1
Design Standards Plus Location Restrictions	20	2	2	0.002	18	18	0.18
All Regulations Together	20	18	18	0.018	2	2	0.02

Table 6-9
NET BENEFITS OF ALTERNATIVE COMBINATIONS OF REGULATIONS ($ MILLIONS)

Regulatory Case	Benefits				Regulatory Compliance Costs	Net Benefits
	Remediation Cost Savings	Avoided Environmental Damages	Value of Cancers Avoided	Total Benefits		
Monitoring Requirements Only	-80	7.2	1600	1527.2	10	1517.2
Design Standards Only	8	7.28	1440	1455.28	10	1445.28
Location Restrictions Only	0	8.19	1620	1628.19	50	1578.19
Monitoring Requirements Plus Design Standards	-8	8.72	1760	1760.72	20	1740.72
Monitoring Requirements Plus Location Restrictions	-80	8.91	1780	1708.91	60	1648.91
Design Standards Plus Location Restrictions	8	8.918	1764	1780.918	60	1720.918
All Regulations Together	-8	9.062	1796	1797.062	70	1727.062

Table 6-9 summarizes the monetized benefits estimates for all combinations of these regulations by subtracting their impacts from those in the baseline. As is normally the case in practice, the value of the cancer-risk reduction is far larger than the other monetized effects. Indeed, many actual regulatory analyses only focus on human cancer risks when they are present, because human mortality has tended to dominate most other benefit categories, at least for environmental-policy decision makers. In the future, however, human health effects may become less preeminent as attention shifts toward more concern for ecosystems and other nonhuman environmental risks.

The other item needed to calculate the net benefits of the various possible combinations of options is their regulatory compliance cost. Here the simple assumptions are that the monitoring requirements and the design standards each cost $10,000 per facility, and the location restrictions cost $50,000 per facility. Hence, for the *monitoring requirements only* option, the total cost is $10,000 times the 1,000 facilities, or $10 million. For multiple regulations these costs are additive, making the total cost for location restrictions plus design standards $60 million ($10 million for the design standards and $50 million for the location restrictions). Subtracting these costs from the total benefits for each of the combinations of regulations yields the net benefits as shown. All of the net benefits entries are roughly similar in size, which reflects the quantitative dominance of cancer-mortality risk reduction. One could alter the example to make the differences between the net benefits of the alternative combinations more stark, but these figures will serve adequately to illustrate the basic point.

Using the *net benefits* entries, one can evaluate the suggestion that it is best to add individual regulations sequentially, based on which successive option offers the highest net benefit. Under this procedure, one would select the location restrictions, because this option offers higher net benefits than the other two regulations alone, as shown by the individual option entries in Table 6-9. From there, one would then compute the increase in net benefits of adding either the design standards or the monitoring requirements. The figures in the table would suggest adding the design standards, because this yields higher net benefits than adding the monitoring requirements. Finally, one would assess whether it is worth adding the monitoring requirements by comparing the net benefits of *all regulations together* with the net benefits of *location plus design standards*. According to the figures in Table 6-9, one would decide to move to the *all regulations together* combination.

But there is a problem with this procedure. The net benefits entries in Table 6-9 indicate that the *monitoring requirements plus design standards* combination offers the highest net benefits, not the *all regulations together* option. Somewhat paradoxically, starting with the individual regulation with the highest initial net benefits ultimately leads one to the wrong choice. In fact, the optimal combination does not include the *location restrictions* option at all.

What happened here is reasonably intuitive. The location restrictions alone are effective at reducing cancer risk, as are all of the options. But the location restrictions avoid more cancers than the design standards, and, unlike the monitoring requirements, they do so directly without shifting releases into the detected cat-

egory, where costly remediation expenditures are then triggered. This makes the location-restrictions option the best of the three regulatory options alone. Having started down this path, one is led to the *all regulations together* result.

But the *monitoring plus design standards* combination ends up being a better choice, primarily because the disadvantage of the monitoring requirements—added remediation expenditures—is largely reversed by the design standards' impact on the probability of a release in the first place. Thus, the monitoring requirements portion of this optimal combination offers the cancer risk reduction of the location restrictions, and the design standards offer additional benefits for detected releases, far larger than those provided by the location restrictions. It is thus the interaction between the two individual regulations that makes them jointly desirable.

What all of this suggests is that great caution must be observed in ranking causally overlapping policies individually and in combinations. Indeed, as shown here, using the highest net benefit rule for adding options can lead to the wrong answer, and this will not be apparent unless all of the relevant combinations of options are examined, as in Table 6-9. This example illustrates what is referred to more generally as a *local maximum* problem in conventional welfare maximization. It is possible to move in the direction of welfare improvement and arrive at what one thinks is the best achievable position. But this might not be the global, or overall, welfare maximum. In such cases one must test to be sure that the overall optimum is selected rather than a local, less desirable one. This analysis confirms this problem in the practical context of evaluating hazardous waste landfill regulations.

Chapter 7

The Importance
of Anticipatory Responses

It is not uncommon in practical applications of economic analysis to environmental issues to encounter interactions between the characteristics of regulatory interventions and private sector responses to them that produce unexpected results. Of course, regulations are intended to cause the affected entities to change their behavior. But the focus of this chapter is on changes in private sector decisions that substantially affect the functioning of the regulatory interventions, in some cases frustrating or even reversing the intent of a policy, or altering the nature and magnitude of the original environmental problem of concern.

The first example in the chapter examines a situation in which the private sector's anticipations of, and the revised decisions made in response to, an intervention can, to one degree or another, undo the effects sought by policy makers. The program in question was a proposal to counter global climate change through government-sponsored tree planting. The analysis indicates that private sector profit-maximizing behavior would tend to offset the desired increase in the number of trees, rendering the program less effective than planned, but still costly.

The second application examines the impact of a program designed to increase the energy effi-

ciency of low-income homes. A variety of weatherization measures were installed in these homes to reduce their energy consumption, the program's primary goal. The analysis shows that under plausible conditions, the enhanced energy efficiency of the dwelling could actually result in increased rather than reduced energy consumption.

The third study changes focus slightly by exploring the potential impact of accelerated sea-level rise (due to global climate change) on Yap State, the Federated States of Micronesia, an island nation in the western Pacific. Here the central dynamic feature of the analysis stems from the interaction between how Yap manages its future economic, legal, and cultural development on the one hand, and the actual future threat that rising sea levels pose to the islands on the other. At present, Yap is at no great risk, so the magnitude of the future threat from the sea will be largely the result of Yap's future development.

Carbon Storage through Government-Sponsored Tree Planting[1]

Two areas of global environmental concern are ozone depletion and global climate change. The ozone-depletion issue, as outlined in Chapter 5, has been addressed largely through multinational treaties and associated limitations on production of ozone-depleting substances, and international technology transfer programs to hasten the adoption of substitutes for those chemicals. Climate change is similar to the ozone depletion problem in that it potentially changes the earth on a global scale; however, it embodies a far more difficult set of political, technical, and environmental problems.

Most people probably are familiar with the basic thrust of global climate change. In a nutshell, the earth's atmosphere contains a number of *greenhouse gases,* such as carbon dioxide and methane, that both reflect some heat from the sun back into space and trap radiated heat from the earth's surface. On net, these gases tend to trap more heat than they reflect; hence their name. Greenhouse gases are produced by both natural and manmade sources. Indeed, without the natural greenhouse effect, the earth's average temperature would be some 30°C cooler. The current concern about global climate change is that the human-source components of these gases have been growing rapidly, particularly carbon dioxide from fossil fuels burned in energy production. In essence, such fuels as oil and coal contain carbon that has been stored for millions of years. Burning them releases it again in the form of carbon dioxide, which increases atmospheric concentrations of greenhouse gases.

For several reasons, the policy, economic, and international political issues posed by global climate change make the ozone-depletion challenge appear almost simple by comparison. First, there was general agreement among scientists that chlorofluorocarbons (CFCs) and other ozone-depleting substances were indeed respon-

sible for a measurable reduction in the density of stratospheric ozone. This rough consensus about the source and extent of ozone depletion made it somewhat easier to obtain the political support to go forward rapidly with the measures necessary to address the problem. At least as of the early 1990s, this is far from the case for global climate change. There is considerable debate but no clear consensus about what will happen under global climate change. Moreover, if climate change does occur, it may produce gainers and losers, depending on the effects considered and their location. For example, coastal areas clearly will be adversely affected by accelerated sea-level rise, but other areas might gain through improved agricultural conditions.

A second way in which the global climate change issue is different from the ozone depletion problem is that a major source of greenhouse gases is the burning of fossil fuels. Energy use is a fundamental ingredient in modern economies, and enters into virtually all production activities. By contrast, ozone depletion is largely produced by using specific chemicals, for which substitutes could be developed. The ozone problem thus was confined to certain sectors of the economy, so its solution did not involve potentially widespread and pervasive intervention.

Third, while the ozone depletion problem was not necessarily costless to solve, at least there was a reasonable consensus concerning the expense of addressing it. For global climate change, on the other hand, there is no such agreement. Some argue that substantial progress toward mitigating the rise in greenhouse gases can be achieved virtually costlessly with relatively innocuous changes in lifestyles, and by enhancing the efficiency with which energy is produced and used. Others argue that anything other than very small reductions in carbon dioxide emissions will impose extremely large costs on society. Hence, unlike the ozone-depletion issue, this lack of consensus about the potential costs of addressing the climate-change problem makes

[1] The original ICF Incorporated research project on which this analysis is loosely based was conducted by Frances Sussman and David Howarth. Their encouragement to include this adaptation of a portion of that project is gratefully acknowledged.

policy makers wary of signing international treaties that will require substantial reductions in carbon emissions.

Finally, the global climate change issue involves a much stronger international coordination and compensation problem than does ozone depletion. Because the human-source emissions of greenhouse gases tend to be the result of energy production and other activities, such as agriculture, a substantial disagreement about appropriate responses and their financing often arises between developed and developing nations. The latter are entering the period in which the per capita use of energy rises as these nations industrialize. Heeding calls by environmentalists to decrease carbon dioxide emissions through reduced energy use and higher energy prices may stand in the way of the developing world's desire to enjoy the same lifestyle and wealth as developed nations. Developing nations moreover argue that the developed nations caused the problem in the first place, so those countries should pay for its solution. It is not at all clear when and how this apparent impasse might be resolved, although the emergence of clearer evidence of the effects of climate change could serve as a catalyst.

The difficulties and uncertainties about the extent and severity of global climate change, about the costs and impacts of mitigation measures, and the different perspectives and expectations of the developed and developing worlds, all gave rise to the project summarized here. At the time, the prospects of international agreement on any extensive and binding measures to reduce global emissions of greenhouse gases seemed dim. Hence, the United States investigated a number of unilateral programs to reduce emissions, such as improved energy efficiency standards for appliances and automobiles. It also considered ways to increase the amount of carbon *sinks*, which absorb carbon and store it, thereby reducing overall atmospheric concentrations of carbon dioxide. One common carbon sink is trees, which essentially absorb carbon

dioxide and emit oxygen during photosynthesis. Thus, the United States considered encouraging additional planting of trees as one unilateral strategy to address climate change.

The Question

For purposes of this discussion, a simple and stylized tree-planting program will suffice. The basic idea is for the government to pay landowners to plant trees instead of using the land in other ways, such as cultivating crops. By paying the fair-market rent for the land and the costs of planting trees, the government would in return extract a promise from the landowner that the trees would not be harvested for 40 years. After that time, landowners would be free to harvest and sell the timber and then place the land in whatever use they desire.

The questions relevant to this discussion that arose from this project center on whether such a program will be successful, and if so, what the program's costs would be. In the process of investigating these questions, several interesting analytical and program implementation issues arose. While these are presented in the context of the tree-planting proposal, they apply generally in environmental policy analyses of similar sorts of interventions.

The Analysis

In practical policy discussions of all types, one often encounters propositions that appear to be good ideas, but which after study are revealed to be not quite as advantageous as they sound. Planting additional trees to store more carbon in an attempt to do something about global climate change sounds perfectly reasonable. The problem is not the ultimate goal of planting more trees; instead it is that as presented, the program is likely to be very expensive and generate little added carbon storage.

Several observations about the program's operation and the economics of the timber in dustry contribute to this conclusion. First, consider the basic mechanism by which the program is supposed to operate. The government stands ready to enroll land in the tree-planting program by paying the fair rental value of the land and the tree-planting expenses. Program proponents imagined acres of land currently planted in fairly low-value crops being enrolled first, such as grasslands; lands devoted to higher-value crops, such as vegetables, fruits, and grains, would be enrolled later or not at all. Trading grass for trees to store carbon for long periods of time seemed a sensible idea.

Yet, one particular industry sector would be very keenly interested in participating in the program—the timber industry itself. To the country's timber companies, the government program would be hard to resist as long as the 40-year harvesting restriction was not a major constraint. From their perspective, being paid to keep their lands in the cultivation of trees and letting the government pay the planting costs would be quite a boon. Hence, one would expect that large segments of the timber industry would try to enroll in the program. If they did so, the government would incur the land rental and tree-planting costs without any incremental benefit whatsoever, because those trees would have been planted anyway.

In essence, the government would end up subsidizing baseline timber-management activities under the program, trees that would have been planted without the program. This is not an uncommon problem in government programs that seek to promote more of a private sector activity. For example, offering tax credits for research and development efforts often runs the risk of giving credits for expenditures that would have occurred anyway, which considerably raises the cost. To avoid subsidizing baseline investment expenditures, research and development tax credit programs often are designed to apply only for expenditures above those in the prior year, for example, or only for those in excess of some other benchmark level.

In any event, the first problem with the tree-planting proposal is really a programmatic one: how to avoid the high cost and zero benefits of merely subsidizing baseline timber management activities. Assume, however, that the government can restrict the tree-planting program participation in such a way as to exclude land that the private-sector timber industry would devote to growing trees in the baseline. Probably easier said than done, but assume that this is possible.

Given the restriction of the program to lands that would not have been devoted to timber in the first place, it now seems reasonable to begin calculating the costs and benefits of the program to the government, to private sector program participants, and to society as a whole. Analytically, there appear to be four categories to consider: (1) the direct tree-planting costs, (2) the opportunity cost of the lands enrolled in the program, (3) the value of the additional trees when they are harvested, and (4) the climate change benefits of the extra carbon storage.

Calculating the direct tree-planting costs involves the relatively straightforward exercise of estimating the number of acres of different types enrolled and the associated tree-planting costs over time. The opportunity cost of the land enrolled in the program is also easy to measure, because it is simply the fair market rental cost paid by the government. But it is worth pausing for a moment to review why the land's rental rate is a complete measure of its opportunity cost. From a purely analytical perspective, it clearly seems to be true that whatever payments are required to move lands from their baseline allocation into the tree-planting program should be a good measure of the social opportunity cost of their use in the program. A parcel of land's rental rate reflects its value to society in other pursuits, such as growing crops for human consumption or for other purposes. Yet, some observed that in the process of implementing the tree-planting program, the prices of other agricultural commodities might rise to reflect their increased scarcity as more and more lands are diverted to growing trees. Do these commodity price increases pose additional sources of net social welfare losses that must be examined to arrive at the costs of the tree-planting program, or is one safe in continuing to use the land's rental rate alone?

The answer to this question is that the rental rate is sufficient. If only the net social welfare losses are at issue, the increases in the prices of the various commodities whose supply is reduced by the tree-planting program are already captured in the land-rental rates. Indeed, as more and more land is enrolled in the tree-planting, the increasing scarcity and higher prices of the various commodities in shorter supply as the program proceeds will drive up land rental rates. Unless one wishes to measure the distribution of the gains and losses of the tree-planting program among producers and consumers, the rental rates for land enrolled are sufficient for measuring the opportunity cost of diverting land into the program.

The two remaining components of the costs and benefits of the tree-planting program are the value of the trees planted when they mature, and the global climate change benefits of the additional carbon stored by those extra trees over their lifetimes. Assigning a value to the incremental carbon storage would be extremely difficult, as even casual familiarity with the debates surrounding global climate change suggests. Hence, for purposes of this discussion, assume that the amount of increased carbon storage, say in tons, is an adequate place-holder for those benefits. The amount of incremental storage of carbon, however, depends on how successful the program will be in causing more trees to be planted. This remains unclear because excluding lands that would have been planted with trees anyway does not mean that the timber industry has no other way to react to the tree-planting program.

A conventional analysis of a government program intended to increase the supply of a certain activity would draw the standard demand and supply functions for the activity in question and then depict the extra government supply as a shift rightward of the supply function. Figure 7-1 is such a depiction. In this diagram, the private supply of the good or activity is shown as S_0, and the demand is shown as D. The government provision of more of this good or activity is seen in this formulation as a vertical schedule of supply, which, when horizontally added to the private supply, yields a new total supply to the market of S_1. Passing the new lower market price through the original private supply schedule shows that the quantity supplied privately decreases from Q_0^P to Q_1^P.

These basic results of additional government supply—reduced price, higher total quantity, and lower private sector supply—clearly apply

FIGURE 7-1

Effect of Additional Government Supply on Price and Quantity

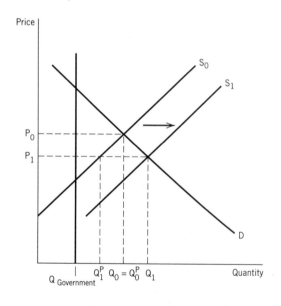

Additional government supply of a good or activity will reduce the price, increase the total quantity, and reduce private supply.

to the tree-planting program. The benefits of the government tree-planting program critically depend on obtaining an increase in the stock of trees under cultivation. Hence, the amount by which the private-sector supply of timber is reduced is an important determinant of the government program's success.

To investigate the fall in private sector tree-planting, however, it is difficult to use a conventional supply and demand diagram. The main problem is that in drawing a timber supply function for a particular year in the future requires a number of assumptions about conditions from the present through the future, such as expected current and future tree-planting, and the price of timber in years before and after the one in question. For example, the supply of timber in some future year at a particular price will be very different depending on the timber prices expected to prevail immediately before and after that year: it will be very low if timber prices in these nearby years are higher than the contemplated price, and very high in the opposite case. Thus, the intertemporal linkages inherent in the timber market preclude the use of the single time-period-oriented supply and demand apparatus.

Because of these complications, different graphical techniques are typically used to analyze the supplies of timber, minerals, and other such renewable and nonrenewable commodities. In this case, Figure 7-2 is useful in trying to measure the ultimate value of the extra trees when they are harvested in the future. As shown by the baseline price and harvests paths, in the absence of the government tree-planting program, the expected price of timber is assumed to increase slightly over time, as is the time profile of timber harvesting in the absence of the tree-planting program. Timber prices need not necessarily rise over time, but they will if the long-run supply of timber is subject to increasing costs and timber demand rises over time as the general economy grows. If the tree-planting program is large, in the absence of any adjustments on the parts of timber producers, the time profiles of timber prices and harvesting will be altered radically beginning 40 years from now as the extra trees are harvested. These are shown as the dashed lines beginning 40 years in the future. Timber prices drop and harvests rise, both quite precipitously.

But this is not the end of the story, for the private sector timber industry will react to the revised expected future prices of timber by planning to harvest slightly earlier and planting fewer trees that will mature after the price drop. As a result of these changes in planting and harvesting plans, the expected prices and harvest quantities in the future will change, perhaps as shown by the dotted lines, which begin to deviate from the baseline significantly earlier than 40 years in the future. Timber producers' profit-maximizing behavior thus tends to redistribute and reverse the expected changes in future timber market conditions that otherwise might result from the tree-planting program. As shown here, they do not completely offset the program's effects, but their actions could well have a significant impact on expected future prices and timber supplies.

It is obvious why the anticipations and actions of timber producers to the future expected impact of the tree-planting program are important to the analysis. Not only do their actions help to determine the value of the extra timber generated by the program in the future, they also significantly affect the magnitude of the net increase in the stock of trees. In reacting to the expected fall in the price of timber, the private sector plants fewer trees. Indeed, in the limit, with sufficient flexibility and adequate alternative opportunities for their land, private timber producers could completely offset the government's tree-planting program by reducing their tree planting by exactly as many trees as the program enrolls, so that no extra carbon is stored and future prices and harvests will be the same as in the baseline. The only way the program can accomplish an increase in tree-planting in this case is to enroll more land in the program, and hence

FIGURE 7-2

Timber Market Response to the Tree-Planting Program

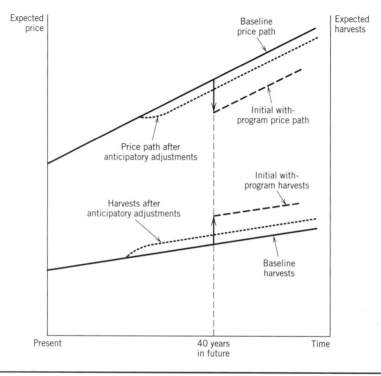

The initial impact of the government-sponsored tree-planting program is to increase harvests. This decreases future timber prices significantly. But in anticipation of this, the private timber industry changes planting and harvesting plans, which tends to redistribute and reverse the impact of the program and reduce its social benefits.

pay to plant more trees than the private sector timber industry can reverse. How much of the government's program the private sector can offset is, of course, an empirical issue, depending on the types of trees involved, the industry's flexibility, and the alternative uses of timber lands. Casual inquiries among the industry indicated that at least some offsetting was a clear possibility.

In the end, the basic problem is that the tree-planting program could cost the government a large sum of money, with a substantial portion devoted to replacing baseline private-sector tim-

ber planting and production. Worse still is that the program only begins to obtain net carbon-storage benefits to the degree that the private sector is unable to offset the government program's effects. It might require a very large tree-planting program before that point is reached and net positive environmental benefits are earned.

The key feature here is that despite restrictions on the participation of the private timber industry (to ensure that only land that would not have been planted with trees can be enrolled), these parties, through profit-maximizing anticipatory responses to the expected changes in future timber prices, can still offset a potentially significant amount of the program's effects. And there is really no way to circumvent this difficulty short of mandating that private timber producers continue to plant trees regardless of the expected future drop in prices.

One final point about of all of this is worth mentioning. To the degree that timber producers cannot divert their land to other uses, the government program will indeed result in greater carbon storage by increasing the stock of trees. But this also implies a drop in the value of the private-sector timberlands and, presumably, the wealth of the timber company shareholders. Thus, the greater the success of the tree-planting program, the greater the negative financial impact on private timber interests. While this may be irrelevant from a purely economic perspective, it might weigh heavily in the minds of policy makers.

Low-Income Household Weatherization Program[2]

The energy crises of the 1970s spawned a variety of conservation efforts, such as more fuel-efficient automobiles, improved household appliance efficiency, and greater insulation of buildings. Both government standards for enhanced efficiency and utility-sponsored programs, such as energy audits, which helped consumers and businesses conserve energy, were common regulatory and nonregulatory measures to reduce energy consumption. Such efforts to achieve energy conservation and improved energy efficiency among users are now known as *demand-side management*.

Although the energy crises of the 1970s seem now to be a relatively distant memory, concerns

about global climate change have sparked a resurgence of interest in energy conservation in the 1990s. The first application in this chapter provided background information on the greenhouse effect, so it will not be repeated here. Suffice it to say that because of the substantial contribution of fossil fuel use to greenhouse gas accumulations, it is easy to understand the recent renewed interest in energy conservation, especially in heating and refrigeration appliances and other space-conditioning devices. Thus, global climate change has replaced the earlier concern about imported oil supplies as the motivation for energy conservation.

One might ask why, in response either to the energy crises or to global climate change, governments and utilities turn to a variety of non-price-based programs to achieve energy conservation and fuel efficiency. That is, why not simply let the price of energy ration its use, or why not simply tax energy use so that it reflects the environmental damage it causes? There are several reasons for pursuing non-price-based strategies. First, energy use is widely held to be a key ingredient in economic growth. Hence, one worry associated with rising energy prices is the possibility that long-term growth will decline. Another related concern is the adverse distributional impact of higher energy prices on lower-income consumers. A slightly different reason for relying on demand-side energy conservation programs is that some energy-efficiency improvements are quite modest for any given consumer or business. Yet, even small increases in energy efficiency when multiplied by potentially millions of individuals can have a considerable impact. The problem is that it would take a very large increase in energy prices to encourage consumers and businesses to identify areas in which these small gains in energy efficiency are possible. Instead, guiding consumers and businesses to these relatively modest potential efficiency gains through these conservation programs helps to provide information that would be costly to obtain individu-

[2] The ICF Incorporated research project on which this analysis is based was conducted jointly with Michael Barth and Louise Sheiner.

ally. Finally, some of these programs are designed simply to try to change people's preferences so that they will voluntarily elect to conserve energy. For these and probably other reasons, efforts to secure increased energy efficiency and conservation seek to reduce energy demand through these non-price-based programs.

The analysis presented here focuses on one particular set of energy-efficiency programs targeting low-income households. A number of electric and gas utilities nationwide observed that dwellings typically occupied by low-income households tend to be very energy inefficient. In many cases, furnaces are old and poorly insulated, walls and ceilings lack adequate insulation, doors and windows fit loosely and lack caulking and weatherstripping, and often are not fitted with storm doors and windows. Furthermore, because low-income households tend to be tenants rather than owners, have little discretionary income, and tend to discount the future at high rates, they have little incentive, much less the resources, to undertake these energy conservation improvements themselves.

These utilities decided to study the need for, and the effect of, energy efficiency improvements for low-income households, particularly weatherization to reduce fuel requirements. Each utility identified a sample of low-income households, conducted energy audits for them, and then provided a variety of energy-efficiency-enhancing weatherization measures for half of the households, with the other half of the sample used as a control group. Typical weatherization measures included furnace insulation, window and door weatherstripping, new thermostat controls, and minor insulation improvements.

The utilities then sought to determine the cost-effectiveness of these weatherization expenditures. That is, was the energy saved by low-income households worth more than the weatherization improvement costs? To answer this question, fuel usage by the households in the sample was monitored for one year before and one year after the

program improvements. After normalizing for weather conditions in the two years, the amount of fuel use saved in a typical year was computed and compared to the weatherization expenditures.

The Question

Ironically, the central analytical question that grew out of this program evaluation was not whether the weatherization improvements were cost-effective; the answer to that turned out to be yes, although payback periods tended to be fairly lengthy—on the order of 5 to 10 years—a long time for these sorts of energy-efficiency improvements. The main question here, however, is related to this finding. Throughout the design and conduct of the utility-sponsored weatherization program, there was a nearly automatic tendency to assume that the weatherization improvements necessarily should result in reduced fuel use. Of course, this is quite plausible, especially to those who have experienced drafty houses and the attendant high heating bills.

But does improving a structure's insulation and other energy use properties necessarily reduce fuel use? This is important because the policy goal of the utility-sponsored weatherization programs was to reduce fuel use, as it is the current goal of policy makers who advocate demand-side management programs to reduce the contribution of energy use to the climate change problem. Hence, the measure of success for these policies is the decrease in the amount of energy use, fossil fuels in particular, that the programs generate. So the question here is whether heating-fuel use should necessarily decline after installing weatherization improvements.

The Analysis

To analyze this question it is helpful to define the nature of the goods consumers purchase as "warmth" and "all other goods." Within a sensible range, individuals presumably prefer more of both *all other goods* and *warmth* when it is cold outside. Thus, households can be thought of as trading quantities of all other desired goods to enjoy warmth in their dwellings.

Warmth is assumed to be produced by purchasing fuel, electricity or gas for example, to heat the interior of the structure. However, the amount of warmth actually generated and retained inside the dwelling, for a given outside temperature, depends on the rate at which the structure loses heat. The poorer the building's insulation, the less warmth will be retained in the dwelling for any given amount of fuel purchased; the better the insulation, on the other hand, the more warmth will be retained for the same quantity of fuel used. Hence, fuel purchases per se by a household must be translated using a *fuel-to-warmth* relationship in order to determine the amount of the actual good of value—warmth—the household enjoys.

Figure 7-3 shows the initial situation for a particular household, not necessarily a low-income one. As shown in the top right-hand quadrant of the figure, this household currently purchases Q_0 of all other goods and enjoys a warmth level of W_0. This is indicated by the tangency of the budget constraint with the indifference curve, IC_0. Of course, what is observable in the market is not warmth itself, but fuel purchases, so defining the position and slope of this budget constraint is somewhat more complex than usual. The other three quadrants in the figure are useful in constructing the household's budget constraint in terms of all other goods and warmth. The top left-hand quadrant shows the budget constraint that is observable in the market, the one that depicts the households trading other goods for fuel. The slope of this *other-goods-versus-fuel* budget constraint is the price of fuel in terms of other goods. The bottom left-hand quadrant shows how fuel is technologically transformed into warmth in the dwelling. As indicated by this schedule, more fuel yields more warmth. Finally, the bottom right-hand quadrant of the figure simply moves the resulting schedule of warmth back into the horizontal axis of the top right-hand quadrant.

Now, to construct the *goods-to-warmth* budget constraint, begin with any particular amount of other goods on the vertical axis and trace leftward to the amount of fuel that can be purchased, which is shown on the left side of the horizontal axis. Next, trace downward from that amount of fuel to find the implied amount of warmth provided, which is given on the bottom vertical axis. Finally, trace from the level of warmth just found through the bottom righthand quadrant's 45-degree line back to the initial level of other goods in the top right-hand quadrant where the process began. This point in the top right-hand quadrant is on the goods-to-warmth budget constraint. Repeating this process for each possible amount of all other goods will trace the entire budget constraint as shown in the figure. Note that the consumption of Q_0 of other goods implies the purchase of F_0 units of fuel, which generate a W_0 level of warmth.

The weatherization program essentially changes the efficacy with which fuel can be translated into warmth retained within the dwelling. Figure 7-4 shows this graphically as a counter-clockwise movement of the schedule that translates alternative levels of fuel use into the amounts of warmth provided. Intuitively, the energy the fuel provides is transmitted to the outside more slowly after the weatherization, so that more warmth can be provided for the same amount of fuel consumption.

The impact of the weatherization program on the household's choice of fuel versus other goods can be observed by tracing out the new goods-to-warmth budget constraint. As shown in the figure, the new budget constraint, BC_1, in the top right-hand quadrant is flatter, reflecting the fact that the weatherization measures make purchasing warmth cheaper in terms of other goods. The household now purchases Q_1 of other goods and enjoys a W_1 level of warmth, as shown by the tangency of the new budget constraint with the higher indifference curve, IC_1. To see the amount

FIGURE 7-3

Household Purchases of Warmth and Other Goods

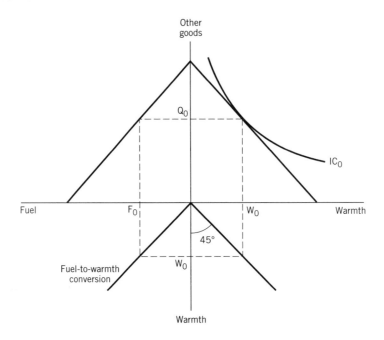

Households initially purchase other goods and warmth based on the total effective price of obtaining warmth. The cost of fuel is one component of the price of warmth, represented by the slope of the line in the top left quadrant, and the rate at which fuel is transformed into warmth, shown in the bottom left quadrant, is another.

of fuel purchased after weatherization, trace leftward from the new equilibrium of Q_1 and W_1 in the top right-hand quadrant through to the goods-to-fuel schedule and read the amount of fuel purchased on the left horizontal axis. As shown in Figure 7-4, F_1 is less than F_0, so this household now purchases less fuel than it did before weatherization. Thus, in this case, the household consumes more of both warmth and all other goods, which implies lower fuel purchases. Here, weatherization improvements do reduce fuel use.

But does this always occur? The answer is no, as shown in Figure 7-5. Here, the initial position of the household is slightly different in that the efficacy of translating fuel purchases into

warmth in the dwelling is less than shown in Figure 7-4. This is shown by the fact that the schedule in the bottom left-hand quadrant is much closer to the horizontal axis than in the previous figure. This makes the initial budget constraint faced by the household depicted in Figure 7-5 steeper than before, which means that it is relatively expensive for this household to purchase warmth.

As before, the impact of the weatherization program is to improve the dwelling's insulation conditions, thereby swiveling the schedule in the bottom left-hand quadrant of Figure 7-5 as shown. Constructing the new budget constraint for the household using the above technique results in the schedule BC_1 and a new consump-

FIGURE 7-4

Effect of Weatherization on Household Fuel Purchases

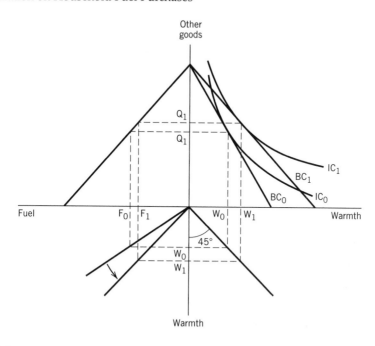

Weatherizing the dwelling changes the rate at which fuel can be transformed into warmth. One possible result is an increase in the household's purchases of both warmth and other goods. In this case, fuel consumption declines, so that the energy conservation objectives of the program are realized.

tion bundle, Q_1 and W_1. In this case, however, Q_1 is less than Q_0, and W_1 is greater than W_0. This implies that fuel purchases rise rather than fall after the weatherization improvements, as shown in the figure.

Thus, the weatherization program need not necessarily reduce fuel purchases, for these can increase without violating any of the usual axioms of consumer choice. Intuitively, this result is more likely for households in particularly poorly insulated dwellings prior to weatherization. In these circumstances, the household might choose to endure relatively low levels of warmth because it is so costly to heat the dwelling adequately given its insulation condition. After the weatherization improvements, how-

ever, the household could find the effective price of warmth so much lower that it might choose to purchase more fuel and enjoy far more warmth than before.

This analysis also signals an important difference between the purely economic approach to policy questions and that of practical policy making. In the latter, the plausibility of the expectation that fuel purchases ought to decline following weatherization stems from the implicit assumption that the household will attempt to maintain the same level of warmth before and after weatherization. If so, it would follow that fuel use would fall in response to the weatherization improvements.

Yet, from the purely economic perspective, the

FIGURE 7-5

Weatherization Can Increase Household Fuel Purchases

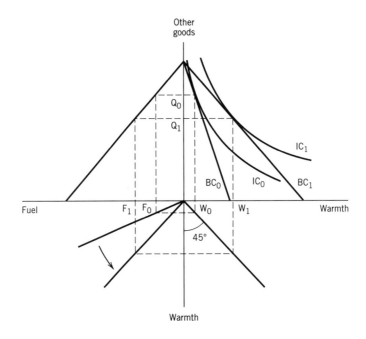

It is possible for fuel use to rise after the dwelling is weatherized. Here the original fuel-to-warmth conversion was so poor that the household consumed little fuel. After weatherization, the household might choose substantially more warmth and actually increase its purchases of fuel. This makes the household better off, but tends to thwart the program's objectives.

real impact of the weatherization program is to make warmth cheaper for households to purchase. Economic analysis thus suggests that, all things being equal, more warmth is likely to be purchased as long as warmth is a normal good. Free weatherization measures also clearly will increase the household's welfare because they reduce the price of purchasing warmth at no cost to them. But while the amount of warmth households consume will rise, it is not known *a priori* whether this will translate into higher or lower purchases of fuel.

Hence, the danger in policy making of relying on the observation that households could achieve the same level of warmth after weatherization improvements using less fuel is that this ignores the behavioral effects of the program. Because households respond to changes in prices, their new purchases of other goods and fuel could defeat the fundamental objective of the policy—reducing fuel use.

Impact of Accelerated Sea-Level Rise on Yap[3]

Although scientific and economic analyses of

[3] The research project on which this analysis is based was conducted with Sally Kane of the National Oceanographic and Atmospheric Administration, and with the assistance of the gracious people of Yap.

global climate change are still in their relative infancy, one of the best-studied consequences of a gradual warming of the earth is its impact on sea levels. A warmer earth will cause polar ice caps to melt faster, causing the mean sea level to rise over time. This phenomenon has received considerable research attention for several reasons. One is that, apart from all of the debate about the consequences of the human contribution to increased concentrations of greenhouse gases, sea levels have already been rising over time as the earth continues to recover from the last Ice Age. Consequently, rising sea levels are not new, uncertain, or hotly-contested predictions solely founded on the science of the greenhouse effect, but something known to have been occurring all along. Rising sea levels, because of the economic and other reasons for considerable development at or near the seashore, are an issue for policy makers independent of climate change.

A second reason for the research attention sea-level rise has received is the potentially enormous financial cost it presents across the globe. Ports, cities, and recreational areas all constitute large investments in significantly threatened positions. However, it is not so much the mean sea level that counts as it is the height and force of storm-generated waves and surge that can literally level a coastal area in hours. With so much investment at risk, studying the impact of rising sea levels clearly makes sense from a public-policy perspective.

Finally, another reason why the impacts of rising sea levels have been studied intensively is that the linkages from a gradual warming of the earth to increased sea levels are far clearer than other anticipated effects of global climate change. Put simply, many of the possible ramifications of global climate change involve a variety of very hard-to-predict changes in weather and rainfall patterns. Not only are these potential climate changes complex, they also may make some areas "winners" and some "losers" as temperature, humidity, and other factors, critical particularly to agriculture, make some areas better and some worse

for human-related activities. As a result, it is not clear exactly what will happen in any given location, given the present state of scientific predictive capabilities. This is less true, however, of global warming and sea levels. Higher mean temperatures, even if they produce a patchwork of differing climate pattern changes across the globe, will tend to cause sea levels to rise. Thus, to some extent, the causal connection from global climate change to this particular effect is easier to model and predict than other weather-related impacts that might result.

In any event, significant research on sea-level rise and its impact on coastal environments has been conducted for understanding and predicting the consequences of accelerated sea-level rise (ASLR), where the term *accelerated* is used to signify the added threat a global warming trend poses. Along with considerable research on other aspects of global climate change, much of this sea-level-related data collection and analysis has been carried out under the auspices of the United Nations' Intergovernmental Panel on Climate Change, or the IPCC. One research effort funded by the IPCC is a series of case studies conducted by a number of member nations detailing the impact of ASLR on various islands, deltas, and coastal regions around the globe. This is a summary of the findings of one such IPCC study on the threat ASLR poses to island environments, in particular to the islands of Yap State, which is part of the Federated States of Micronesia, located in the Pacific's Caroline Islands.

The Question

Of course, anyone familiar with monetary economics will be acquainted with Yap as the Land of Stone Money. The author can verify that there are large pieces of flat stones with holes in their centers virtually everywhere on the island, and anecdotal evidence suggests that they are still in use for a few commercial purposes. Interesting as the many stories about the stone money of Yap may be, however, it is not the central focus of this study, except to the degree that the stones are valued Yapese treasures and threatened by ASLR.

The central questions in this sea-level-rise case study were to determine exactly what magnitude of a threat ASLR poses to Yap, and then to explore the costs and benefits of possible responses. It turns out that Yap represents a significantly different type of ASLR island case study than most of the others undertaken by the IPCC. Most of the previous island studies focused quite understandably on very low-lying atolls and other islands with both extreme current vulnerability to the sea and substantial threatened indigenous populations and infrastructure. In these places, not only are manmade structures threatened, but perhaps more significantly, their agricultural and water resources regularly suffer substantial damage from tropical storms and salt-water intrusion. In these cases, short of full-scale retreat from the islands, expensive protective structures, such as sea walls, tend to be the only feasible responses.

Yap, however, presents a slightly different set of circumstances, in both the present and the future, upon which the threat of ASLR will play. What makes Yap's situation interesting is a combination of both fortunate and unfortunate characteristics. For example, Yap State encompasses a number of islands, with the largest interconnected set of islands (Yap Proper) enjoying substantial land area and height; while most of the other islands (called the Outer Islands) are smaller atolls with virtually no significant elevation. These two parts of Yap have very different potential vulnerability to ASLR, with the Outer Islands far more threatened than the taller main island group. But for some time many Outer Islanders have been migrating to Yap Proper and then on to other countries. Moreover, Western-style structural development near the shoreline on Yap Proper is relatively modest, so at present the conventional ASLR threat to structures and populations is not great.

Hence, as will be shown below, the most interesting feature of this case study is that although Yap faces the most acute threat from ASLR on its atolls, baseline migration trends suggest that these effects will be less serious than for other atolls the IPCC has studied. Where there is a possibility of large-scale harm from ASLR—on a very developed future Yap Proper—this is substantially under Yap's control. If Yap pursues a series of common-sense economic and human-development strategies, it can control the factors that largely determine the extent of its vulnerability to ASLR.

The Analysis

The analysis of ASLR and Yap proceeds as follows. First is an overview of Yap's historical, physical, and economic characteristics. This background information is important, because a clear understanding of Yap's past and present circumstances, especially its level of development and its socioeconomic profile, is essential for properly defining and evaluating Yap's vulnerability and responses to ASLR. Next is a discussion of Yap's future development prospects (the baseline) and the implications of these trends for potential physical and economic threats from ASLR. This is followed by a review of potential response strategies for the threats ASLR poses to Yap emphasizing anticipation, adaptation, and retreat, and highlighting institutional and cultural challenges Yap faces in developing and implementing appropriate responses.

HISTORICAL AND ECONOMIC PROFILE OF YAP

This section provides a snapshot of Yap's current economic situation focusing on its human, physical, and economic development levels, its natural resource characteristics, and some cultural features. This profile concentrates first on the physical characteristics of the islands themselves and on Yap's modern history. It then briefly examines the demographics of the

Yapese and the changing Yap economy, focusing on sources of income, available resources, trade and transfers with the rest of the world, and how these are rapidly evolving.

Yap consists of more than a dozen islands and atolls in the Caroline Islands. Its islands contain relatively little land mass, but large amounts of lagoon areas. Indeed, Yap consists mostly of open ocean between the many islands. Distributed across several million square miles of ocean territory, the mere 46 square miles of land area and the 400 square miles of lagoons essentially form boundary markers for an ocean nation. Because it is located some 500 miles southwest of Guam, all of its islands are tropical in climate and vegetation. With abundant agricultural and reef resources, as well as the vast ocean areas within its 200-mile exclusive economic zone, Yap offers a rich subsistence existence to its inhabitants.

Yap State is commonly thought of as Yap Proper, which is a collection of large islands with significant elevation that contain most of the nation's land mass, and the Outer Islands, which are mostly small, low-lying atolls representing small land areas, large lagoons, and relatively few inhabitants. While there are many other differences between Yap Proper and its Outer Islands, their different geomorphologies, that is, the physical features of the islands, such as elevation and terrain, are of particular importance for assessing the threat of and possible responses to ASLR.

Yap was populated almost two thousand years ago by a variety of peoples from nearby larger land masses. Over the centuries, the Yapese developed a rich culture founded on a traditional form of communal living and tribal governance and a bountiful subsistence economy. Some estimate that as many as 50,000 Yapese lived on the islands prior to their discovery by Western explorers. Yap is best known to the West as the land of stone money. These large pieces of quarried stone, some as much as six feet in diameter, were transported from Palau, hundreds of miles away, and served for years as the islanders' currency.

Yap was discovered in 1526 by the Portuguese explorer Dioga da Rocha, who landed on Ulithi, one of Yap's lagoon islands and the fourth largest atoll in the world. During the next 300 years, the remainder of Yap's islands were subject to occasional visits by Western mariners. Nominally claimed by Spain for several hundred years, like many other island nations during the colonial period, Yap suffered a tremendous loss of population caused by diseases transmitted by their foreign visitors.

Following the Spanish-American War, Yap was sold to Germany largely for commercial interests. Some 15 years later, at the start of World War I, Yap fell under the influence of Japan. Along with most of the western Pacific, Yap was occupied by the Japanese thorugh World War II. From the time of its discovery by the West to the end of Japanese rule, the Yapese population was reduced from an estimated 30,000–50,000 to a low of only 3,000 by 1945.

Yap and many other islands in the central and western Pacific were known collectively as the Pacific Trust Territories of the United Nations after World War II. Administered by the United States military, Yap and its sister island nations were fairly isolated from the rest of the world until the 1960s, when the United States began to inject significant amounts of educational and cultural aid. The Peace Corps, for example, figured prominently in Yap faces during the 1960s and 1970s.

Most recently, virtually all of the original Pacific Trust Territories, including Yap, have negotiated a transition to sovereignty. Yap, Chuuk (formerly called Truk), Pohnpei, and Kosrae together form what is now known as the Federated States of Micronesia (FSM), an independent nation. As will be apparent from the discussion below, however, Yap's new status carries some costs. For example, with the transition from its trust territory status to that of a nation, Yap and the FSM will lose the U.S. assistance payments that in recent years have been its only effective means of supporting an emerging Westernized economy and a large foreign trade deficit.

Similarly, while Yap enjoys the freedom of self-determination, it must also shoulder the burdens of formulating long-range development policies and responding to the threats of ASLR. While not insurmountable, these challenges will require the Yapese to harmonize their existing legal and cultural institutions with the realities of world and local economics. In particular, resolving conflicts between institutions the Yapese possess from their ancestral traditions, and those that were formed during their many years as a trust territory will prove to be a key component in both successful future development and in effectively responding to ASLR.

Table 7-1 lists the 1987 population of Yap by inhabited island and atoll group, the land area of each island group, and the implied population density. This table makes clear that the bulk of the population of Yap occupies Wa'ab, or Yap Proper to Westerners; relatively few people live on the Outer Islands, especially the smallest of them. The table also shows the extreme differences in population density among the islands. For example, given its size, Yap Proper (Wa'ab) could host a considerably larger population than

it presently does. This is fortunate because, as shown in Table 7-2, the age distribution and population-growth-rate projections for Yap through the year 2000 suggest a population that is expanding fairly rapidly.

A clear picture of the Yapese economy can be obtained only by focusing on both the traditional subsistence resources and the emerging market-based arrangements. Yap's subsistence economy is largely defined by the sets of natural resources available to the population: the reef fisheries and the productivity of the land. Tables 7-3 and 7-4 list acres under cultivation, by crop, for land in Yap Proper (Wa'ab), the amount and nature of its cultivable land, and the extent of Yap's abundant water resources contained in its reef, lagoon, and ocean systems. As the tables indicate, the land and sea offer Yap a rich set of resources to use for subsistence. In addition to the aquatic resources and fruit and vegetables available, the Yapese also raise substantial numbers of pigs and chickens; nearly 2,000 pigs and over 25,000 chickens were counted on Yap Proper in 1986. All of this for some 7,000 residents.

More detailed statistics on subsistence agriculture and aquaculture are difficult to obtain,

Table 7-1
POPULATION, LAND AREA, AND POPULATION DENSITY OF YAP STATE 1987

Island	Population (number)	Land Area (square miles)	Population Density (number per square mile)
Wa'ab	6,650	38.670	171.97
Ulithi	847	1.799	470.82
Fais	253	1.083	233.61
Eauripik	99	0.091	1,087.91
Woleai	794	1.749	453.97
Faraulop	182	0.163	1,116.56
Ifalik	475	0.569	834.80
Elato	70	0.203	344.83
Lamotrek	278	0.379	733.51
Satawal	465	0.505	920.79
All Islands	10,113	45.211	223.68

Source: Report on the 1987 Yap State Census of Population, Office of Planning and Budget, Colonia, Yap State, and Yap State's *Draft Second Development Plan,* 1992.

Table 7-2
POPULATION PROJECTIONS FOR YAP STATE, 1988–2000

Age	1988	1992	1996	2000
0-4	1,517	1,567	1,741	1,940
5-9	1,527	1,501	1,483	1,650
10–14	1,290	1,482	1,518	1,450
15–19	969	1,216	1,429	1,515
20–24	828	910	1,137	1,364
25–29	820	809	860	1,053
30–34	792	806	791	819
35–39	636	758	788	775
40–44	360	573	715	765
45–49	308	315	505	665
50–54	282	299	283	431
55–59	264	263	281	264
60–64	210	238	239	254
65–69	208	181	204	209
70–74	136	169	147	158
75–79	79	88	116	107
80+	119	81	67	74
Total	10,345	11,256	12,304	13,493

Source: *Report on the 1987 Yap State Census of Population*, Office of Planning and Budget, Colonia, Yap State, Volume II, p. 52.

largely because these activities do not result in market transactions. The sense obtained from on-site assessment, however, is that Yap Proper contains far more terrestrial resources, and probably aquatic ones as well, than the current population requires for traditional subsistence. The estimated 30,000–50,000 population figure for the period prior to discovery by the West support this view.

Along with other islands in Micronesia, Yap is undergoing a transition from an association of isolated islands housing a mostly subsistence-based and communal population, to the modern Westernized world of market economics, formal employment, and international trade. At present, Yap stands between the traditional subsistence-oriented culture based on family and clan, the land and sea, and communal living, and the new world of a wage-oriented market economy that necessarily requires substantial trade with the outside

world, especially imports. This is evident in Tables 7-5 and 7-6, which present economic-activity-status statistics for the populations of Yap Proper and the Outer Islands. The economic-activity information in Table 7-5 clearly illustrates that Yap is in a state of transition from subsistence to a money–wage economy. Athough many individuals have market-based jobs, others spend their time cultivating, gathering, and fishing. In Yap Proper, in fact, the Yapese tend to participate in both systems. In the Outer Islands, however, the vast majority of inhabitants are listed in Table 7-6 as having the non-market-based socioeconomic status of "Other." It is also clear from the figures in Table 7-6 that the government is the major money-wage employer, suggesting that the market-based portion of Yap's economy relies heavily on public-sector jobs as opposed to private-sector employment.

A number of forces are driving Yap's transition to a market-based economy. One is the edu-

Table 7-3
ACREAGE OF CULTIVATED CROPS,
YAP PROPER, 1986

Crop	Acres
Taro	1,000
Sweet Potato	50
Cassava	25
Yam	10
Vegetables	31
Betelnut	3,050
Coconut	2,500
Breadfruit	40
Citrus	30
Mango	10
Banana	5
Other Fruits	25
Total	6,776

Source: 1986 Agricultural Survey of Yap, as cited in Yap State's *Draft Second Development Plan*, 1992.

Table 7-4
SUBSISTENCE LAND AND WATER
RESOURCES, YAP STATE, 1976

Type	Amount
Land:	Acres
Upland Forest	6,316
Mangrove and Swamp Forest	3,277
Secondary Vegetation	1,366
Agroforest and Coconuts	6,272
Marshes and Interior Waters	517
Grasslands	5,395
Croplands	115
Urban Agriculture	752
Total Land	24,010
Water:	
Lagoon Areas	378.7 sq. mi.
Exclusive Fishing Zone	12-mile zone
Ocean (approx.)	400,000 sq. mi.

Source: Handbook on the Trust Territory of the Pacific Islands, Washington, D.C., 1958, as cited in Yap State's *Draft Second Development Plan*, 1992.

cational system. A large proportion of Yapese men and women have been educated through the high school level using Western texts, teachers, and teaching methods. What Yap has found, however, is that the more educated the population, the less eager are its young to return to their subsistence ways. Education raises expectations and reveals a world that is richer than Yap in certain respects. Inevitably, many look to market-based economic arrangements, not subsistence, as the way to secure a desirable Western lifestyle.

Another force driving Yap toward a market-based economy is the availability of electricity for lighting and refrigeration, and imported Western goods, from foodstuffs to videotapes. Purchasing electricity or imported goods, however, requires that either someone in the family or clan work for wages or that locally produced items, such as fish and copra, be brought to market for sale rather than consumed.

Finally, the introduction of refrigeration and far more productive fishing techniques have begun to erode the traditional clan-based system of resource management, subsistence farming, and output sharing. Communal subsistence in Yap was predicated on traditional cultivation and management of its natural resources, from the reef and lagoon system, through the mangroves and wetlands, and on to the higher land elevations. The ecological and economic success of such a system depends on widespread observance of rules concerning property use, resource management, and the allocation of labor inputs and consumption outputs. For example, the lack of refrigeration in this traditional communal system generates a strong incentive to share a particularly bountiful fish catch, otherwise much of it would spoil. With refrigeration, however, the fish can be stored, thereby weakening the incentive to share the catch.

Similarly, newer techniques of fishing have begun to strain the traditional economics of subsistence in Yap. These methods typically involve purchased inputs, such as lights, batteries, gaso-

Table 7-5

ECONOMIC ACTIVITY OF YAP'S POPULATION, AGE 15 AND OLDER

Economic Activity	Yap Proper		Outer Islands	
	Male	Female	Male	Female
Working primarily to grow, gather, or catch food to eat	363 (17.7%)	810 (43.6%)	459 (51.2%)	858 (80.3%)
Working primarily to earn money	1,138 (55.5%)	464 (25.0%)	191 (21.3%)	30 (2.8%)
Looking for work	86 (4.2%)	19 (1.0%)	18 (2.0%)	5 (0.5%)
Attending school full-time	196 (9.6%)	161 (8.7%)	153 (17.1%)	61 (5.7%)
Primarily engaged in unpaid household work	37 (1.8%)	236 (12.7%)	8 (0.9%)	58 (5.4%)
Unable to work	69 (3.4%)	69 (3.7%)	48 (5.4%)	45 (4.2%)
Other	161 (7.9%)	98 (5.3%)	20 (2.2%)	11 (1.0%)
Total	2,050	1,857	897	1,068

Source: *Report on the 1987 Yap State Census of Population*, Volume 1, Office of Planning and Budget, Colonia, Yap State, Tables 14 and 21.

Table 7-6

SOCIOECONOMIC STATUS OF YAP'S POPULATION, AGE 15 AND OLDER

Socioeconomic Status	Yap Proper		Outer Islands	
	Male	Female	Male	Female
Employed by government	635 (31.0%)	231 (12.4%)	178 (19.8%)	28 (2.6%)
Employed by private organization	412 (20.1%)	160 (8.6%)	8 (0.9%)	2 (0.2%)
Employer	18 (0.9%)	7 (0.4%)	1 (0.1%)	0 (0.0%)
Own account worker	18 (0.9%)	6 (0.3%)	0 (0.0%)	0 (0.0%)
Unpaid family worker	10 (0.5%)	41 (2.2%)	1 (0.1%)	0 (0.0%)
Attending school full-time	196 (9.6%)	161 (8.7%)	153 (17.1%)	61 (5.7%)
Other	761 (37.1%)	1,251 (67.4%)	556 (62.0%)	977 (91.5%)
Total	2,050	1,857	897	1,068

Source: *Report on the 1987 Yap State Census of Population*, Volume 1, Office of Planning and Budget, Colonia, Yap State, Tables 15 and 22.

line for a motorboat, and so forth. Purchased inputs not only require individuals to participate in market transactions, they also spawn and continually reinforce previously weak notions of private, as opposed to communal, property, providing a moral justification for ceasing to participate fully in the traditional subsistence-sharing arrangements.

Newer methods of fishing also tend to weaken the traditional resource-management methods that historically have regulated the Yap fisheries. *Ethnobiology*, as this form of resource management is called, involves a complex system of data collection through the fishermen themselves, a set of customs and rules that allocate the fish to different segments of the population, and fishing practices that avoid overexploiting the reef system. The newer fishing techniques, however, are not only more productive, they also make it more difficult to enforce the traditional Yapese resource-management system of complex exclusions, restrictions, and allocations.

In sum, all of the available statistics, the interviews with Yapese officials, and casual observation on the islands themselves indicate that Yap is moving rapidly toward at least a mixed economy that includes both traditional elements and market-based economic arrangements. What will survive of the traditional features and how much development the Yapese can accomplish in the short term, however, are difficult to predict. Yap's history of subsistence is not a firm base from which to launch a Western-style money economy. Moreover, a market-based economic system tends to erode the traditional ways. Hence, Yap's future development possibilities and options are at best uncertain and problematic.

The positive side of the market-based economy in Yap is represented by the tourism, fisheries, and other export sectors. Although Yap's tourism and fishing exports are on the rise, it is not apparent what additional future growth potential exists in these areas. From the rest of the world's perspective, Yap does not possess unique or particularly precious resources. Furthermore, given the productivity of the land and sea for subsistence activities, Yap is not a low-cost source of labor, so the prospects for large-scale manufacturing or other pursuits in Yap are not good.

Whatever progress Yap has made on the exports and visitation fronts, however, is overwhelmed by its massive quantities of imports. A wide range of goods are imported, including food, machinery, petroleum and other chemicals, and manufactured products. Although the range of imported goods is not surprising, the balance between exports and imports, or the lack thereof, is alarming. Over the past 30 years, Yap has moved from importing 2.3 times as much as it exports to importing more than 34 times as much. Without continuing transfers from the rest of the world, Yap cannot sustain this version of its market-based economy. What has allowed this trade imbalance to continue is the assistance of the United States over the years in both mon-

etary and in-kind forms. Now, after forming the FSM and establishing their independence, Yap State and the other former trust territories of the Pacific face a schedule of transfer payments from the United States that declines to zero just after the turn of the century.

Thus, under current arrangements, in less than a decade Yap will no longer have the substantial assistance payments that currently subsidize its imports. What will happen at that point, no one knows. If the market-based economy is not sufficiently developed to sustain the current level of imports by paying for them with exports, a drastic reorientation of Yap's economy may be necessary. Indeed, it is possible that without these assistance payments, a substantial reversion to the subsistence-based economy of the past may be necessary.

YAP'S FUTURE AND THE IMPACTS OF ASLR

Because Yap consists of a number of islands with different geomorphologies and apparently divergent development paths, a key component of this assessment of the potential impacts of ASLR involves specifying the future conditions that are likely to prevail in the timeframes typically considered in sea-level-rise analyses. Thus, migration and future development are critical determinants of the likely harms from, and appropriate responses to, ASLR.

The greatest threat of ASLR to Yap, at least in physical terms, is on the Outer Islands. Most of these islands possess extremely vulnerable water supplies and coastal agricultural resources. For many of the inhabitants of these islands, life is already a challenge due to typhoons and the lack of electricity and other conveniences common to Western life. ASLR simply worsens their chances for productive existence on their islands. Some of the effects of ASLR on these islands include loss of fresh-water supplies, salt-water inundation of low-lying cultivated lands, loss of land to the sea, and destruction of structures. Of these, the inundation of cultivated land by sea water and the loss of fresh water are particularly serious. Taro patches, a staple of the subsistence diet, require five years to recover completely after salt-water inundation. Similarly, fresh water on these isolated atolls typically is obtained from a thin lens of water that essentially floats on the salt-water. Rising sea levels and severe storms can wipe out the entire water supply. Of course, to some degree the Outer Islands already face these threats from the sea, so ASLR can be thought of as increasing the probability and frequency of their occurrence.

To move beyond these fairly general observations, a detailed economic and physical assessment of the Outer Islands would be required. But the need for such an intensive evaluation is less than clear, because large numbers of Outer Islanders are moving to Yap Proper, and then sometimes on to either Guam or the United States. Moreover, Yap plans little of the infrastructure investments on these atolls that would be necessary to develop and maintain a modern Western lifestyle, including such basics as electricity. Although somewhat speculative, one can argue that an ongoing migration of Outer Islanders to Yap Proper and to other locales is a characteristic of the baseline for the analysis. To the degree that this migration continues, at least the human and economic dimensions of the impact of ASLR on these islands will be mitigated.

Thus, although the Outer Islands stand to suffer the most severe of the physical effects of ASLR, the present trends suggest that these hardships may affect relatively few human and capital resources. Of course, those who remain to bear these consequences will experience them in ways and magnitudes similar to people on other low-lying atolls, such as Majuro in the Republic of the Marshall Islands. While these impacts may not be substantial on a national scale, they nonetheless will be important from the perspectives of the remaining inhabitants of these Outer Islands.

While the Outer Islands of Yap will bear more significant physical effects of ASLR but relatively modest human and economic impacts, Yap Proper faces the opposite set of concerns. On the one hand, Yap Proper physically stands to suffer only modestly under ASLR, precisely because of its significant elevations, its low population density, and the minimal present infrastructure. On the other hand, Yap Proper's baseline should also include both inherent population growth and immigration from the Outer Islands. Accommodating and integrating this additional human load on the islands may cause some stress on Yap Proper's resources, infrastructure, and traditional land-tenure system. As a result, the human and economic dimensions of the impact of ASLR on Yap Proper may be driven by a combination of direct effects of ASLR and indirect results of their consequences on Yap's Outer Islands.

Direct effects of ASLR on Yap Proper potentially include some protection or loss of infrastructure in the main city of Colonia, such as portions of the modest harbor and port facilities, a few office structures, and a petroleum storage facility. In addition, some land may be lost in low-lying areas, particularly in the southern part of the island, although these lands currently appear not to be cultivated. Furthermore, the Yapese tradition—understandable for an island people—of building culturally important structures near the seashore raises the risk of losing a significant proportion of these assets.

Finally, ASLR could potentially damage certain coastal ecosystems, such as the mangroves that line much of the shoreline and the taro patches that lie close to the sea. The mangroves are part of a complex reef and lagoon ecosystem that provides natural resources, such as wood, and a variety of environmental services, such as fish spawning grounds and protection from hurricane winds. Similarly, as in the Outer Islands, taro patches are particularly sensitive to ASLR because inundation by salt water renders them unproductive for a number of years. In general, because of Yap's heavy dependence on the productivity of the land and sea, the primary impacts of ASLR will be on these resources, as opposed to damage to structures and loss of land.

The indirect effects of ASLR on Yap, however, could be more significant than its direct impacts. Yap is a nation in which land is jointly owned by clans, where Western infrastructure is only now being introduced, and where the transition to a market-based economy is occurring, but is only in its infancy. The land-tenure system is particularly important here. Historical land-ownership patterns in Yap consist largely of multiple, overlapping clan-based relationships between people and different clusters of land and sea resources. For example, a number of people might have the right to live on a piece of land; others may have the right to fish a certain area of the reef adjacent to the parcel; others may have the right to gather vegetables and fruits from areas of the land; and still others may reserve the right to return to live on the land. Thus, no one person appears to have clear title to all facets of a parcel of property. Ultimately, the land-tenure system is so complex that it is difficult to delineate even by the Yapese themselves. As a result, Yap is not well-equipped institutionally to accommodate the changes in legal and cultural arrangements, particularly land use, that might be necessary to adapt to ASLR and to the continued in-migration of Outer Islanders.

Finally, the ultimate severity of the threat of ASLR on Yap Proper depends critically on future development. A central assumption in reaching the conclusion that the traditional sources of ASLR damages, for example, land loss and damages to structures, are relatively less important for Yap Proper is that the Yapese will account for the threat of sea-level rise in future development plans; naturally, this is one of the study's central recommendations.

ASLR RESPONSE STRATEGIES FOR YAP

In light of the different types of ASLR threats facing Yap, all of the IPCC response options (no response, protection, adaptation, and retreat) are relevant in one form or another. In particular, *no response* to ASLR seems appropriate for many areas of Yap Proper, where structures are not threatened and where the land is not used for cultivation or habitation, because Yap Proper is a large island capable of supporting a far larger population than it possesses currently. Hence, it is not surprising that in many areas, the optimal strategy is to simply allow ASLR's effects to occur unchecked. For the Outer Islands, no response is probably the best approach as well, particularly in areas of these islands with sparse populations. While any loss of land and destruction of habitats may indeed be unfortunate, it is not clear that any other response strategy is economically justifiable.

Protection is likely to be a viable option in very limited circumstances in Yap. In fact, protection probably is relevant only for a few areas in and around Colonia, where structures of sufficient economic value may be threatened with significant damage from rising sea levels and storm surge. Protection measures that may be good candidates in Colonia include raising the elevations of some existing shore protection barriers, and very selective construction of new structural protection measures, such as small sea walls. For the Outer Islands it is unlikely that any areas economically warrant protection measures, because of their cost and the relatively small populations on these islands. Other responses, such as retreat and adaptation, are likely to be more appropriate.

Adaptation is a strategy particularly relevant for many areas of Yap. Raising threatened structures and modifying critical areas under cultivation to increase their elevation make sense when either the cost of relocating structures makes that not feasible, or when proximity to the sea is particularly important. On Yap Proper, adaptation may be best for some of the structures in Colonia and in outlying areas, as it would be for many areas in the Outer Islands. In almost all cases, elevating taro patches and other important cultivated wetlands are wise investments. As a general matter, when protection or retreat are not technically feasible or economically viable, adaptation is the best approach. Because the costs of adaptation for many of the Yapese structures and resources are relatively modest, this strategy could play a key role in mitigating the impacts of ASLR.

The remaining ASLR response strategy is *retreat*. On Yap, retreat takes two important forms. One is the conventional relocation of resources, activities, and structures farther from the advancing sea. In most cases, this should be relatively easy to accomplish, given the plentiful lands on Yap Proper, the modest construction costs of the traditional dwellings, and the productivity of the tropical lands and resources. The more subtle form that the retreat-response strategy takes is in guiding future development. In particular, it is critical that future development on Yap be undertaken in ways that circumvent threats from ASLR. Thus, the locations of future structures should account for foreseeable future sea levels. Similarly, other structural improvements, such as roads, should be designed in a way to facilitate the migration of natural resources and habitats as necessary. In particular, allowing the mangroves to migrate will preserve the balance of the wetland, lagoon, and reef-system resources. For the most part, this strategy requires more forethought and planning than large financial expense.

Finally, for the Outer Islands, retreat may well take the form of an increased pace of migration to other islands, particularly Yap Proper. In some cases, the advancing sea may make continued habitation all but impossible. The inability to retreat to higher ground, the loss of fresh water supplies, and the frequent inundation of wetland resources all may render particular areas of low-lying atolls unable to support human populations. In these cases, retreat to larger islands or other places may be the only viable alternative.

Clearly, Yap's best options for addressing the problems posed by ASLR center on adaptation and retreat. Indeed, most of the important potential effects of ASLR in Yap can be avoided by human and resource migration and careful planning of the location and characteristics of future development. This is not to say that the potential loss of lands, habitats, and other natural resources, and the dislocation of a portion of the Yapese population are costless. Instead, the main emphasis on retreat and adaptation, as opposed to protection, is that allowing human and natural resource migration and adaptation to ASLR, through careful consideration of future development patterns, will avoid large-scale impacts. Some negative effects are inevitable, but the more profound and intractable threats ASLR poses to other island nations, such as the Marshalls, largely can be avoided.

Although the obvious long-range solutions for Yap are careful planning and gradual accommodation through retreat and adaptation, the individual steps necessary may not be easy to implement. Indeed, the challenges faced in Yap are the considerable complexity of the legal and land-tenure systems, and the inflexibility and rigidity of the public-planning and decision-making process. Thus, to successfully implement the measures necessary to substantially mitigate the impacts of ASLR, Yap must focus on basic institutional reforms.

First, the system of land ownership and tenure may impede the human and natural-resource migration and adaptation required to mitigate ASLR impacts. Land cannot be sold easily or otherwise transferred, especially parcels with the appropriate mix of resources to support subsistence so it is not clear that the necessary population movements can be accommodated easily. To the degree that clans may be required to relocate, an inability to acquire alternative property could make effective adaptation more difficult. This problem is especially acute for the Outer Islanders who migrate to Yap Proper, but then find it virtually impossible to purchase property. Because of this, many Outer Islanders on Yap Proper reside in very crude shelters with no access to the combination of the land, lagoon, and ocean resources necessary for subsistence living. As a result, not only are these people at greater risk of suffering the impacts of ASLR, but they become dependent on mostly government-sector employment. Worse still is that the ability of the Yapese government to pay personnel in the not-too-distant future is in serious doubt after the U.S. assistance payments cease.

A second institutional problem is the traditional caste-based allocation of fishing grounds. This problem is very closely related to the land-tenure system. While this system has historically provided reasonable management of the aquatic resources surrounding Yap, the traditional allocation of fishing areas and species among the population might require adjustment if ASLR differentially alters the abundance or location of these resources.

A third institutional problem area is the current method of public decision-making. In a nutshell, each of the chiefs of the various clans effectively has veto power over virtually any public decision. As a result, it is difficult for the government to undertake public projects or other activities that might be necessary to adapt to ASLR. For example, the new road from Colonia to the northern part of Yap Proper apparently required years of negotiations to secure land rights and to make exact design and location decisions. This planning and public decision making rigidity might make it difficult for the Yap government to enact building restrictions and construction guidelines, and pursue other development policies that will permit natural resources to migrate.

Another institutional problem facing Yap as it attempts to respond to the threat of ASLR is financial resources. To the degree that any of the specific accomodation measures that Yap may wish to implement require significant financial resources, finding the funds for them will be very difficult. The primary source of government revenue is the assistance payments made to the FSM by the U.S. government. Moreover, given the current government structure and the fragility

of the market-based economy at present, it is not clear that any significant revenues will be generated from more traditional sources, such as taxation. Because of this impending shortage of government funds, the importance of guiding future development in ways that will not create new ASLR risks, that must then be protected, is even greater.

Finally, for Yap there is a large premium on preserving traditional knowledge and the historical terrestrial and aquatic natural resource base, one that encompasses more than the normal cultural values of tradition, and historic structures. Responding to ASLR in ways that preserve the option of obtaining a substantial portion of Yap's consumption from subsistence insures against a possible precipitous decline in Yap's ability to import foodstuffs and other items when the U.S. assistance payments cease. If Yap instead permits future development to encroach on large portions of its subsistence resources, there might be little to return to if Yap's progress on its Westernization development path is slower or less successful than many hope.

CONCLUSIONS

The Yap sea-level rise study illustrates two aspects of anticipatory responses important in this type of analysis. One is that where Yap's vulnerability to ASLR is highest in purely physical terms, the expected evolution of these areas over the coming years is likely to substantially reduce the actual threat, at least in terms of its human and economic impact. Hence, while Yap possesses terrain that resembles some of the other IPCC island studies, such as atolls, a continuation of current migratory patterns into the future will make the economic toll of ASLR there far less severe than for other islands studied by the IPCC.

Second, where ASLR could pose significant economic, ecological, and human costs—on Yap Proper—the degree to which it will is largely under the control of the Yapese through future development and land-use planning. In some sense, the future conditions in Yap Proper that will determine the extent and magnitude of any negative effects of ASLR will be the result of Yap's own development decisions over time. Still, it is far easier to prescribe the remedies of informed land-use planning, location restrictions on future structures, preservation of ecosystems, and reform of the land-tenure system, than it may be to follow through on those recommendations. In particular, there is an extreme short-term focus on development in Yap, almost to the exclusion of most other goals. It is hard to overstate the difficulties Yap may have in focusing on the inherently long-term planning issues posed by ASLR. What appear to be relatively simple guidelines for accommodating ASLR in planning future development can be very difficult to implement in the face of almost overwhelming short-term concerns.

Nevertheless, with relatively little existing economic infrastructure to protect and with a comparative abundance of natural resources, Yap can and will survive ASLR. How well it will fare as sea levels rise depends on both streamlining legal and other institutions to facilitate accommodation and migration, and preserving the natural and human resources necessary to derive a substantial amount of economic support from subsistence should this be necessary.

Chapter 8

Incidence of Regulatory Costs

Much of the focus in environmental economics is on the net welfare effects of regulatory policies, or benefits minus costs. This follows naturally from the importance of the goal of efficiency enhancement in economics, which emphasizes that good policy interventions are those under which the gainers, in theory, could compensate the losers, making no one worse off. In practice, however, policy makers also pay close attention to the gross costs and risk-reduction benefits of alternative policies, and on the identities of the parties who bear the costs or enjoy the benefits. Thus, the market impacts and economic dislocations regulations cause are of concern in addition to their net efficiency-enhancing properties. It is therefore important to be able to develop and apply practical methods for assessing the incidence of regulatory costs.

This chapter summarizes three studies that explore how one goes about assessing cost incidence and the economic impacts of regulations in practice. The first study outlines some general procedures for estimating the cost incidence of alternative types of environmental regulations. The emphasis is on practical methods and available data, indicating that qualitative results are sometimes the best one can manage. The second study essentially tailors this framework to assess the potential economic impacts of regulations on small businesses, as opposed to the

entire regulated industry, where the rules apply only in a specific geographical region. Finally, the third analysis shows how even after carefully applying the guidelines outlined in the first two studies, one can still end up with the wrong answer unless one carefully constructs the initial conceptual framework. In this case, the incidence of the particular regulation's costs can be ascertained *a priori*, so further empirical analysis is unnecessary.

Assessing Regulatory Cost Incidence in Practice[1]

In practical environmental policy evaluation, decision makers are almost always keenly interested in who bears the costs and who enjoys the benefits, as well as what other effects a regulation might impose beyond those summarized by its estimated net benefits. Indeed, a regulation's net benefits are rarely the only consideration weighed in policy deliberations. This is at least partially because environmental benefits are often not stated in monetary terms, but are instead presented in their "natural" units, such as can-

---

[1]This analysis is an encapsulation of an ICF Incorporated project on which Arun Malik and Clarence Koo served as principal analysts.

cers avoided or amounts of water and land resources not exposed to hazardous substances.

But even if the benefits were always monetized, decision makers would still scrutinize the incidence of the costs, and the potential magnitudes of any other impacts a regulation might pose, for two major reasons. First, the process of developing and refining a set of regulatory options to address an environmental problem does not occur in a vacuum. There are many opportunities for public comment on proposed regulations, and potentially affected parties, especially the industries subject to the regulations, sometimes lobby intensely for or against particular options and proposals. Decision makers pay attention to the distribution of the financial burden of a regulation because they usually are reluctant to impose potentially very large costs on a small number of entities if this is not absolutely necessary. Thus, in addition to efficiency, policy makers also weigh certain equity considerations in developing and evaluating regulatory alternatives.

A second broad reason for exploring the host of other potential consequences of a regulation is that some effects of considerable importance in public policy can be difficult to capture in the conventional cost–benefit framework used to analyze regulations. In practice, along with cost–benefit studies, analyses of the economic impacts of prospective regulations are often required. These focus on assessing reduced employment or firm closures, especially among small businesses, and evaluating potential negative effects on the balance of trade and possible retardation of innovation. Recently, the impact of regulatory costs on U.S. industry's international competitiveness has become a central concern in public policy making. And any potential for causing job losses has become nearly as important a policy consideration as net economic benefits in evaluating all types of government programs, from taxes and health care, to environmental and other regulations. In reaching a policy decision,

all of these economic impacts normally are considered along with the costs and benefits of regulatory options.

These diverse economic effects of a regulation, however, are clearly directly driven by the increased costs it imposes. Therefore, when one explores the impacts of a regulation beyond its net benefits, the central task is to determine who bears the costs, whether the incidence of the costs changes over time, and what employment, business activity, international trade, and other impacts will be generated by the responses of the affected parties to these costs, given current and expected future market conditions. Thus, the central issues here revolve around a regulation's effects on prices and quantities, as opposed to its impact on economic efficiency per se.

The Question

This study summarizes the results of a project the primary purpose of which was to develop guidelines for assessing the incidence of regulatory costs. The project originally was motivated by the lack of a technically sound, but practical framework for analyzing regulatory cost incidence. In particular, while theory suggests that cost incidence can be measured based on the relative slopes of the supply and demand functions in the market subject to the higher regulatory costs (as will be seen shortly), there appear to be instances in practice in which this method may not be appropriate. In addition, the incidence of regulatory costs is only part of the story, because sometimes very different market impacts on employment and output, for example, can be associated with the same distribution of regulatory costs between producers and consumers.

Finally, it is not entirely obvious exactly how one applies the theoretical proposition that cost incidence depends on the relative slopes of supply and demand when one does not have quantitative estimates of elasticities. A variety of essentially *ad hoc* procedures that do not require elasticities were developed over the years to test for potentially serious economic impacts. Most of these are based on comparing the magnitude of the regulatory costs to various measures of firm size, such as revenues, net assets, and so forth. One such rule, for example, is that a regulation might pose significant impacts if its compliance costs are more than 5 percent of firm revenues. At best, however, most of these tests attempt to determine if a regulation's costs would be a significant burden to complying firms, assuming that the incidence is entirely on those entities.

Thus, the central focus for this project was on developing a basic but systematic approach for assessing the incidence and impacts of regulatory costs that would be consistent with theory, comprehensive enough to be applied to a variety of very different regulations, and less dependent on the existence of numerical estimates of supply and demand elasticities. A framework that could consistently generate quantitative estimates of incidence and impacts was desirable, but not necessarily essential. Fortunately, well-buttressed qualitative assessments of cost incidence and market impacts of regulations are often sufficient for policy makers.

The Analysis

The analysis began by reviewing the conventional elasticities-based method of assessing the incidence of regulatory costs to determine its applicability to the questions of concern and its limitations. This method borrows the traditional analysis of the incidence of an excise tax from public finance economics. Figure 8-1 shows the standard partial equilibrium assessment of the incidence of a tax on a particular activity or good.[2] The supply function is shown shifting upward by the amount of the tax, which results in a lower quantity and a higher price inclusive of the tax. Revenues from the tax are the tax rate times the new quantity, or the rectangle defined by P_1 minus P_1^{NT} (the price received by producers net of the tax), and Q_1.

Who bears this tax can also be seen in Figure 8-1. The top part of the tax revenue rectangle, P_1 minus P_0 times Q_1, measures the reduction of consumer surplus caused by the price increase for the quantity of the activity or good still purchased. It seems reasonable to say that consumers contribute this portion of the tax revenues. Similarly, the bottom part of the tax revenue rectangle, P_0 minus P_1^{NT} times Q_1, measures the decline in producer surplus resulting from the reduced net-of-tax price suppliers receive for the amounts of the activity or good still supplied. Hence, it also seems natural to say that producers pay this portion of the tax revenue.

The incidence of this tax on consumers and producers, therefore, depends on the relative sizes of these two parts of the total tax rectangle. Clearly, the initial equilibrium price and quantity and the slopes of the supply and demand curves determine all four of the relevant pieces of information—P_0, P_1, P_1^{NT} and Q_1. The flatter the demand function, the smaller the consumer share of the tax, and the flatter the supply function, the smaller the producer share of the tax. This suggests that there may be a simple way to determine the incidence of this tax based on the slopes of the supply and demand functions. Indeed, one method for doing so, using elasticities instead of slopes, recognizes that the proportion of the tax paid by consumers equals (1) the supply elasticity divided by (2) the supply elasticity minus the demand elasticity. A few

---

[2] Partial equilibrium tax incidence is an appropriate analogy for the impacts of regulations on markets in most cases. It is possible to argue, however, that the incidence of very large regulatory costs that simultaneously affect many sectors of the economy could be somewhat different. For example, the effects of a large energy tax might be best studied using general equilibrium approaches, or at least macroeconomic models. Here the focus is primarily on the incidence and effects of more modest regulatory interventions confined typically to a single market. For an introduction to general equilibrium approaches for estimating incidence see R. E. Just, D. L. Hueth, and A. Schmitz, *Applied Welfare Economics and Public Policy*, (Prentice-Hall: Englewood Cliffs, N.J.), 1982.

FIGURE 8-1

Incidence of a Tax on an Activity or Good

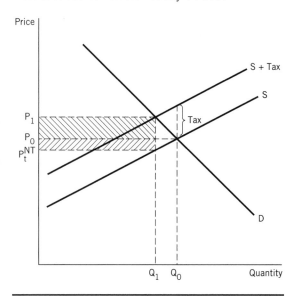

Partial-equilibrium analysis of a tax on a good or activity shows the shares of the tax revenues borne by producers and consumers. The incidence of the tax depends on the elasticities of supply and demand. This approach is useful for assessing the incidence of regulatory costs in many circumstances.

experiments using this formula and Figure 8-1 will confirm this relationship. Hence, if one has the two elasticities, this method provides an easy way to assess the incidence of such a tax.

The *ratio of the elasticities* method has considerable appeal for determining the incidence of costs of environmental regulations. By reinterpreting the upward shift of the supply function in Figure 8-1 as having been caused by the costs of an environmental rule, the method seems to offer an easy way to divide up the regulatory costs between producers and consumers. If the upward shift of the supply function is uniform throughout, the rectangle of tax revenue is the same as the area between the old and the new supply functions out to the new quantity, Q_1, which measures the added regu-

latory costs if this shift is indeed due to an environmental regulation. Hence, the regulatory compliance costs will be borne by producers and consumers in the same way as would be an equivalent tax burden.

But matters are not really so simple because, to be at all accurate, using this method entails making many assumptions about the effects of the regulation and other market conditions that may fail to be true in practice. For example, the vertical shift of the supply function in Figure 8-1 automatically assumes that the regulation imposes additional marginal costs of production for a good or activity. But if the regulation imposes costs unrelated to any specific ongoing market-based production or consumption activity, it is not clear that it can be analyzed using the framework depicted in Figure 8-1. Similarly, if the regulation entails compliance activities that affect long-run production costs but not short-run costs, presumably the situation shown in Figure 8-1 relates to long-run outcomes, not short-run incidence. But this also dredges up the issue of whether the incidence of these costs will change over time, so that a single diagram and a single set of supply and demand elasticities will be inadequate for the task of accurately assessing cost incidence and other economic effects of regulations. Moreover, in some cases economic impacts of importance to policy makers are determined by additional shifts in these functions unrelated to the costs of the regulation, not just their elasticities.

This is not to say that the approach in Figure 8-1 is not useful. Rather, the point is really that predicting cost incidence and other economic impacts of a regulation requires a slightly broader perspective. The basic thrust of the elasticity-based method remains an important conceptual component for assessing the cost incidence and economic impacts of regulations, but in practice it is combined with other considerations in analyses that often have both qualitative and quantitative components. Hence, the approach suggested here is not inherently different from, or more complex than, that embodied in Figure 8-1. Rather, it is designed to address the variety of environmental regulations and market circumstances often seen in practice.

Can Regulatory Costs Be Shifted from Regulated Parties to Consumers?

The approach begins by asking the fairly fundamental question of whether the costs that a regulation imposes on a product or process are even eligible to be passed through to consumers. If not, the incidence will be entirely on the regulated parties. Several types of environmental regulations fit this mold. Many companies have discovered that they are liable for significant sums of money to assist in remediation of contamination at Superfund sites. These costs cannot be shifted to the firms' customers, because they are unrelated to the ongoing economic activities of these companies. As such, the site remediation liability costs simply reduce the wealth of the firm's owners. If these companies attempt to raise prices to recoup those costs, other firms not saddled with these liabilities will be able to undercut the higher prices.

A similar situation occurs when such a liability arises for a firm in the course of conducting its ongoing business, but which can be avoided by other firms in the same business. In this case, even though the costs arise from a current economic activity, if other firms can engage in the same activities without triggering these liabilities, the affected firm cannot raise prices to recover these costs. As a result, in all such cases the regulatory costs will be borne completely by the affected firms and entities.

Although some environmental regulations are of the impossible to shift, wealth-reducing variety, most are of the more traditional type under which all entities engaged in a particular activity are subject to controls or other regulatory costs. These encompass a host of different environmental protection measures, such as mandatory pollution-abatement controls, pro-

tective equipment requirements, hazardous waste and other toxic substances management rules, and restrictions on the uses of certain substances. In all of these cases, the incidence of the regulatory costs generally will be on both producers and consumers, although their relative shares of the burden depend on a number of factors and may well change over time.

The set of regulations whose costs are eligible to be shifted to consumers also includes the costs of a type of remediation liability slightly different from those that simply reduce the wealth of the affected entities. If these liability-triggering events occur with some low but inescapable probability to all who undertake the activities associated with them, the costs of insuring against them will be eligible to be included in the long-run economic cost of these operations. Just as capital investments periodically may be required to sustain an ongoing production process, environmental harms and the liabilities that arise from them also might be an infrequent but unavoidable cost of doing business. In both cases, if these are necessary to continue production, they will enter the long-run cost function. This will be true whether the insurance is purchased explicitly or whether the firm self-insures.[3]

The remainder of this analysis concentrates on regulations with costs that are at least eligible to be shifted forward to consumers, beginning with short-run incidence assessment for both variable- and fixed-cost regulations, and then turning to long-run incidence evaluation.

---

[3] A possible exception to this is when the firms involved are small relative to the potential liabilities. Firms might fail to insure against the liabilities and instead declare bankruptcy if they occur. In a sense, firms in such a position possess the equivalent of put options, where they can shift the excess of the environmental liabilities over their net worth to the rest of society. Presumably this possibility is what motivates various financial-responsibility regulations under which firms engaging in activities with the potential for generating these types of liabilities must either be larger than a particular financial size or obtain third-party guarantees of one sort or another, such as insurance policies.

SHORT-RUN INCIDENCE OF VARIABLE-COST-INCREASING REGULATIONS

Consider first the short-run incidence of a regulation that raises only variable production costs. It is here that the spirit of the *ratio of the elasticities* method is most applicable. In this case, marginal production costs clearly are increased, so that one can confidently shift the short-run supply function upward to model the regulation's effects. Furthermore, when the supply function in Figure 8-1 is interpreted to be a short-run curve, it is easy to explain why it is upward-sloping; investments in plant and equipment, for example, cannot be shifted to alternative uses easily, so their owners are willing to forego some financial returns in the short run. This and similar conditions for other inputs to production, such as relatively immobile labor, suggest that supply-related entities will be more likely to bear some of the regulatory costs in the short run.

Hence, the clearest application of the *ratio of the elasticities* method is to incidence analyses in the short run, and for regulatory costs that increase the variable production costs. At this point, if short-run demand and supply elasticities are available, one could use them to estimate the shares of the costs borne by consumers on the one hand, and by factors on the supply side on the other.

In the absence of numerical estimates of elasticities, one can at least conduct a qualitative study of the elements that substantially influence the responsiveness of supplies and demands to price changes. On the demand side, for example, common sense suggests that demand will be more elastic the easier it is to substitute for the regulated good or activity, and less elastic if close substitutes do not exist or are expensive. Similarly, if the regulated good is a small portion of an entire activity's total cost, such as, say, the brake pads on an automobile, demand will tend to be less elastic than otherwise. Finally, the demand for a good may be very elastic, especially for price increases, if foreign

unregulated imports can be had at prevailing prices. In this case, the relevant demand that domestic regulated firms face is that net of imports. If foreign supplies will flood the market when prices rise, the net demand faced by the domestic industry will be quite elastic. For the supply side, without numerical elasticity estimates, one's only real hope is to investigate the marginal cost conditions in the industry affected, or to try to use short-run supply elasticities for other activities that are roughly similar.

Hence, for determining short-run incidence of a regulation that increases variable costs, one should use the appropriate elasticities if they are available. In most analyses of the incidence of environmental regulations, however, numerical estimates of supply and demand elasticities will not exist, largely because of the nature of the activities regulated and a lack of data. With few obvious options for obtaining quantitative results, one is then typically left to explore "rough-and-ready" qualitative arguments about cost incidence and perhaps a few quantitative avenues. But this is less limiting than one might think, because all of this applies only to the short-run incidence of regulations that increase variable costs.

SHORT-RUN INCIDENCE OF CAPITAL-COST-INCREASING REGULATIONS

Consider a regulation that only increases the capital costs of supplying a good, say a large investment in effluent treatment equipment that requires relatively low operating expenditures. Suppose as well that the affected firms already have significant fixed investments in the relevant plants and infrastructure necessary for supplying this good. In this case, short-run marginal costs do not appreciably rise, so the short-run-industry supply curve does not shift upward, and prices in the short run will be unaffected. Hence, all that happens immediately is that the firms supplying this good are less profitable. The regulatory costs will be completely borne by the producers and there will be no shifting of the burden at all, at least initially. The diagram in Figure 8-1 is thus not applicable to this case, because there is no shift of the short-run supply function, and whether or not one has supply and demand elasticity estimates is irrelevant.

Of course, any actual regulation is likely to impose a mix of capital and variable costs, so that a hybrid of these two cases is probably appropriate for assessing short-run cost incidence. Regulations that impose relatively higher capital costs will tend to be borne proportionately more by producers than consumers in the short run, because the compliance costs that translate into an upward shift of the short-run supply function will be smaller. The incidence of those that lean more toward variable cost increases will tend to be shared with consumers, because more of the regulatory costs will be reflected in an upward shift of the short-run supply function.

Long-Run Cost Incidence

But all of this only speaks to the issue of short-run cost incidence for typical environmental regulations. Long-run outcomes can be quite different. In particular, what distinguishes the short run from the long run is that in the latter, far more adjustments can be made, especially investments in plant and equipment. For example, manufacturing investments eventually wear out and require replacement. In the short run, however, these investments are difficult to shift to alternative uses. Hence, while owners of these assets may be willing to endure reduced profits because of a new regulation in the short run, eventually it will be necessary to replace the investment. If expected future prices are not higher by enough to compensate for the additional regulatory costs, reinvestment is not likely to occur.

Thus, the main distinction between short- and long-run incidence is that in the long run, fewer inputs on the supply side will bear any of the regulatory costs. Given enough time, most production inputs become variable in that they can

be redeployed productively elsewhere. They will not remain invested in the market subject to the regulation unless they earn the same remuneration that they can in alternative pursuits.

Conceptually, this means that long-run supplies generally are more elastic than short-run supplies. Figure 8-2 shows this gradual movement from the short-run incidence of a regulation's costs to the long-run outcome. Here, the initial result is a shift upward of the short-run supply function from S_0^{SR} to S_1^{SR}, which causes a rise in price from P_0 to P_1. Note that the long-run supply function shifts upward as well, and that it is higher than the short-run curve at Q_1. The short-run price increase to P_1 therefore does not fully compensate for the cost of complying with the regulation. This is the essence of how producers bear some of the regulatory costs in the short run. But because the price rise from P_0 to P_1 is not sufficient to recoup the regulatory costs and to provide all of the different factors of production their long-run required rates of remuneration, as time goes by these production inputs become more flexible. For instance, plant and equipment might be allowed to depreciate and not be replaced. This process of "exit" can be represented graphically by short-run supply functions that gradually shift backward until they finally reach the point at which the new long-run supply function and the demand curve intersect. In Figure 8-2, this is indicated by the arrows that show the short-run supply function's initial vertical shift following the imposition of the regulation, and then trace its gradual movement upward along the demand function until it reaches the long-run supply function. This results eventually in a price of P_2, which is high enough to cover all long-run production costs, including these imposed by the regulation.

The eventual incidence of a regulation's cost is thus on consumers and on any inputs to production that are not supplied perfectly elastically to this market in the long run. Hence, if all factors of production are supplied perfectly elastically to this industry in the long run, the

FIGURE 8-2

Short-Run and Long-Run Incidence of Regulatory Costs

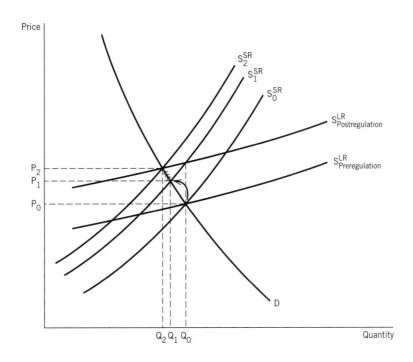

Both the short-run and long-run supply functions shift upward in response to the costs imposed by a regulation. The producer portion of the regulatory costs generally will be greater in the short run than in the long run. The gradual shifting of the short-run supply function over time represents exits that adjust the size of the industry. Eventually, the new long-run equilibrium is reached where most of the regulatory costs are borne by consumers.

incidence must be entirely on consumers.[4] Only if some input is not supplied perfectly

[4] The term "consumers" is used here somewhat loosely. The buyers of this good might well be firms that then use it as an input for producing other items. If these purchasers have fixed capital investments, they might also bear some of the regulatory costs in the short run. Nevertheless, as the short run turns into the longer run, most of the factors of production involved "downstream" from this good will also become flexible, which implies that they too will not bear any of these costs. Over time, as a result, the ultimate regulatory incidence will still tend to shift toward consumers, regardless of how far down the production chain they happen to be.

elastically in the long-run will consumers bear less than the full long-run regulatory costs. The slight positive slope to the long-run supply function in Figure 8-2 allows for this possibility. Here, the long-run equilibrium price increase from P_0 to P_2 is less than the long-run increase from in the costs of production inclusive of the regulation, the latter of which are measured by the vertical shift of the long-run supply function at Q_2.

But simply allowing graphically for some factor of production to bear some of the regulation's costs in the long run does not indicate what input that might be. The usual explanation for why long-run supply functions might be upward sloping is that as an industry expands, prices of some factors of production rise as the demand for them in that use increases. Of course, an industry cannot endlessly expand at constant cost without eventually confronting rising prices for certain inputs.

But this may not be quite on target for determining the identity of any factor inelastically supplied in the long run to a market subject to an environmental regulation, especially given the range of price variation, quantity movements, and the implied change in the demand for inputs that typically result. Normally, changes in the demands for inputs from an industry subject to new environmental regulation are not large relative to the total supply of these inputs. If the use of an input by an industry is small relative to the total supply, any change in demand for the input induced by a regulation is not likely to change the input's price. For example, even a very costly regulation imposed on the entire petrochemical industry—whose main feedstock is petroleum—would be unlikely to change the price oil suppliers receive for their product. Oil prices are set internationally and although U.S. demand certainly is a large component of the total, it would be unusual for a regulation domestically to cause a significant enough change in U.S. demand to alter the world oil price.

As a result, in practice it is usually best to assume a perfectly elastic long-run supply when assessing the incidence of a regulation's costs unless there are strong reasons for overriding that presumption. For example, as outlined in the asbestos case study in Chapter 2, asbestos fiber is obtained by mining and processing the mineral into materials used in construction and other applications. If the United States bans asbestos use, suppliers of the associated asbestos fiber can only attempt to sell to other countries at significantly higher transport costs. In this case, a regulation banning U.S.

asbestos use will cause a significant reduction in the demand and, hence, in the price of asbestos received by these fiber suppliers. Given that the other economic opportunities for these asbestos mines are not very profitable, one would expect this input to bear some of the regulatory costs in the long run. Hence, factors of production that will share the burden of regulatory costs in the long run are those that are substantially devoted to supplying the regulated product or activity and that have few, if any, viable economic alternatives. In practice, these will tend to be fairly obvious once the production activity is specified with some care. Otherwise, assuming a perfectly elastic long-run supply is probably reasonably safe.

Finally, one should be cautious in using elasticities for estimating long-run regulatory cost incidence in the event that any are available. By definition, the elasticities required here are those estimated allowing costs of production that are fixed in the short run to be variable in the long run. Reflecting this in statistical analyses might require, for example, modeling lagged adjustments of quantities to price changes. Hence, if long-run incidence is to be measured using the elasticity-based method, one should ensure that the derivation of the estimates is consistent with their intended use. Of course, cases in which numerical estimates of supply and demand elasticities are available are the exception, rather than the rule.

SHORT-RUN TO LONG-RUN ADJUSTMENT PROCESS

From the perspective of policy makers, the faster that all of the adjustments from the short run to the long run occur, the better, because the eventual incidence of regulatory costs tends to be on consumers. This generally means that the cost impacts are more dispersed than in the short run, which tends to minimize the economic impacts of greatest concern to policy makers. Moreover, it is often the process of adjusting from the short run to the long run that imposes the greatest economic impacts on industries facing potentially large regulatory costs. That is, the economic and financial reality underlying the fairly sterile shifting of the short-run supply functions upward over time in Figure 8-2 can include plant closures and reduced employment.

Because the economic impacts of primary concern to policy makers are precisely the short-run financial losses of the regulated industry and the business, employment, and other dislocations that occur as these short-run to long-run adjustments take place, it is not particularly helpful to say that in the long run the incidence of the regulatory costs will be largely on consumers and hence, not very painful. The old adage "In the long run, we're all dead" would seem to apply here. What all of this really begs is some indication of how these adjustments will occur, how painful they will be, and how long they will take to complete. If they can occur rapidly and with few economic costs and impacts, then this will be welcome news to policy makers. If they will involve a long period of large financial losses to industry, numerous business closures, reduced international competitiveness, and significant unemployment, that is quite a different matter.

Unfortunately, it is not easy to make precise quantitative statements about the process of adjustment from the short run to the long run. But one can identify essentially two paths, one involving the economic dislocations of concern to policy makers and the other potentially avoiding them. It is also possible to define and perhaps quantify the factors that govern the magnitude of these adjustments and how rapidly or slowly they will occur.

One path of adjustment is that shown in Figure 8-3. As before, the short-run and long-run supply functions both shift upward to reflect the regulatory costs, and here the long-run supply is assumed to be perfectly elastic, so that eventually consumers will bear all of the regulatory costs. In this figure, however, two demand functions are shown, one very elastic and the other more inelastic. In either case, there is no avoiding the fact that to reach the new long-run equilibrium, the industry must contract over time. But the magnitude of the adjustment required is very different in the two cases. For the elastic-demand situation, the industry will have to contract significantly before reaching the new equilibrium size. This situation might involve, for example, a costly regulation combined with intense competition from foreign suppliers. Indeed, it is common for industries facing potentially costly regulations to argue that this will put them at a significant disadvantage relative to their foreign competitors.

FIGURE 8-3

Magnitude of Long-Run Quantity Adjustment

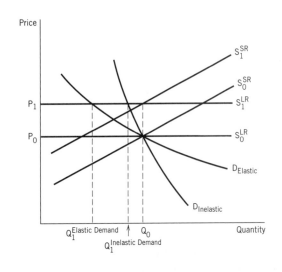

The magnitude of the regulation-induced quantity decline in the long run depends to a large degree on the elasticity of demand. Here, the price increase in the long run induced by the regulatory costs is the same whether demand is elastic or inelastic. The long-run quantity reduction, however, differs substantially in the two cases.

In other cases, however, the size of the adjustment required is not so large. As shown in the inelastic demand case, the magnitude of the decrease in quantity, and hence of the industry's size, is relatively small. One might think of this case as one involving a broad-based regulation on a good or activity with few cost-effective substitutes, such as air emission limitations for industrial facilities and electricity generation plants.

Everything else being the same, consequently, the greater the adjustment required to reach the new long-run equilibrium, the longer it will presumably take and the more painful it might be. And a very important factor determining how great this adjustment will be is the elasticity of the demand function, which depends on the availability and cost of substitutes and the degree to which unregulated competition from abroad can undercut the domestic industry's attempts to raise prices to recoup the regulatory costs.

Given the magnitude of the adjustments required to reach the long run, the other factor that influences how rapidly the process will occur is, loosely speaking, the capital intensity of the affected industry. What signals firms to leave the industry is, of course, the market's reduced short-run profitability. But exactly how much of a reduction in profitability a firm will endure before deciding to exit the industry depends on what proportion of its costs are unalterable in the short run. A firm with extensive fixed costs for manufacturing facilities, long-term rent contracts, and even inflexible labor agreements, will accept lower profitability for longer periods of time than will one with mostly variable input costs. Economically, the *shut down* decision thus depends on whether a firm can continue to operate and still recoup its variable costs of production. If so, it is best to continue in operation despite the reduced profitability and poorer rates of return it receives for its "sunk" costs; if not, the firm would be better off discontinuing production. A related consideration is the underlying pace of routine capital turnover, or reinvest-

ment due to depreciation. In general, the more frequently capital investments ordinarily must be replaced, the more rapid will be the pace of adjustment to the regulatory costs.

Hence, another major determinant of how long this contraction of the industry will take is the amount of sunk capital and investment in the industry and the frequency of its routine turnover. One would therefore expect that, all else being the same, the capital-intensive steel and automobile industries would bear more regulatory costs for a longer period of time than, say, the high-volume retail grocery business or the labor-intensive consulting industry. Note also that the steel and automobile industries face significant foreign competition as well, so that very costly regulations for these sectors are likely to be borne substantially by the producers.

There is a different path of adjustment to the new long-run cost conditions in a market subject to a costly regulation. So far the only variations allowed on the demand side of the analysis have been changes in its elasticity. Indeed, the elasticity of demand is a powerful determinant of the incidence of regulatory costs as well as the magnitude of the ultimate adjustments required to reach the new long-run equilibrium following the imposition of a new regulation. But another variation in the demand is shown in Figure 8-4. Here the demand is shown as shifting outward over time, from D_{t_0} to D_{t_1}, as the market for the regulated good or activity expands. Hence, in the absence of the new regulation, additional investments will be required to supply this market. Two forces are thus at work in determining short-run incidence and the extent of economic impacts. One is the tendency of regulatory costs to reduce profits and to cause the affected industry to contract. The other is the propensity of increasing demand for a good to encourage added investments for its production. If the increase in demand is large enough and occurs rapidly, it might completely eliminate the need for any downward adjustments in response to the regulatory costs. As shown in the diagram,

FIGURE 8-4

Influence of Demand Growth on Cost Incidence

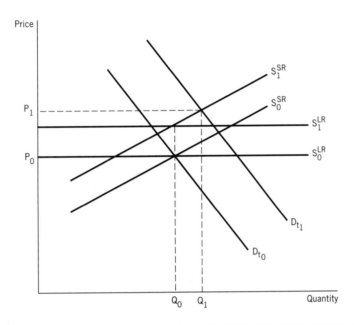

If demand growth is sufficiently strong, the actual adjustment process could result in a rapid shift of regulatory costs to consumers. Here the expansion of demand induces a price increase large enough for producers to recover the regulatory costs even in the short run.

even with the increased regulatory costs, additional investment is required and prices are higher, more than offsetting additional regulatory costs even in the short run. Hence, if demand growth is sufficiently large and rapid, all of the reduced profitability and other economic impacts potentially caused by a new regulation, such as plant closures, unemployment, and so forth, might be avoided altogether.

Summary

This analysis provides several lessons important for practical assessments of regulatory cost incidence. First, some regulations impose costs that cannot be shifted from the entities directly affected. In these cases, the incidence of the costs

is clear-cut and, to a large extent, the economic impacts of concern to policy makers may not occur. With the exception of possible bankruptcies among complying parties, the value of ongoing economic activities are not affected by these regulations. Of course, the wealth of those subject to these sorts of regulations will be reduced, but the types of impacts that often worry policy makers most, such as plant closures, impaired international competitiveness, and unemployment, are less likely to materialize here.

Second, it is usually not sufficient to argue that in the long run, regulatory costs will be borne mostly by consumers, and therefore will be fairly widely dispersed and involve few serious economic impacts. Policy makers are very much concerned about short-run outcomes and the often painful economic adjustments necessary to reach the new long-run equilibrium.

But one should also avoid over-reliance on only short-run snapshots of cost incidence. These can be incomplete and tend to obscure the fact that the question of primary interest is the length and severity of the adjustment process itself. As indicated here, one can say more about the incidence and economic effects of a regulation's costs than simply how they are divided in the short run. There are ways to gain some sense of the magnitude and duration of the adjustment process that gives rise to the major impacts of concern, even if they are only qualitative inferences based on whatever information is available about the market and industry.

Finally, one should avoid focusing on the incidence of regulatory costs exclusively, because neither the short-run nor the long-run distribution of these costs is necessarily a reliable barometer of the economic impacts and dislocations that might occur. As seen here, for example, there are several adjustment paths from the short run to the long run that pose very different risks of significant economic impacts. Moreover, the magnitude of the adjustments required and the speed with which they occur can also vary depending on the underlying circumstances. It is not so much where regulatory cost incidence begins or ends as it is what happens in between that concerns policy makers.

Differential Regulatory Impacts on Small Firms[5]

The guidance for practical assessment of the incidence and economic impacts of environmental regulations summarized in the first study of this chapter contains some important unstated assumptions. In particular, that analysis implicitly

posits that the regulations in question are national in coverage, and that the affected industries contain numerous firms that closely resemble one another, especially in terms of economic size. These assumptions are not unreasonable, given that the project on which that study is based was conducted for EPA, whose regulatory purview is largely national in scope, and whose concerns about regulatory cost incidence revolve mostly around marketwide economic impacts, such as broad-based firm closures, unemployment, and impaired international competitiveness of domestic industries.

This study augments those basic guidelines for assessing the incidence of regulatory costs and their economic effects by narrowing the focus to the impacts of regulations on a subset of regulated firms, small businesses, and by assuming that the regulations in question are regional, rather than national in coverage. This analysis was originally conducted for the South Coast Air Quality Management District (SCAQMD) in California. The SCAQMD is the local air-quality regulatory authority for the large Los Angeles basin, which encompasses several counties and an enormous population. Because of several features of this area, air quality is a major concern. Most transportation is by automobile, and the distances traveled each day, whether for work or leisure, are quite large. Perhaps more important, however, is that the area has weather systems and surrounding geography that tend to trap many precursors to air pollution within the basin. Given the amount of emissions from automobiles and a host of industrial and commercial sources, severe air pollution problems often result, restricting the activities of many people, creating risks of long-term health problems, causing significant degradation of visibility, and damaging natural and man-made resources.

The Question

The SCAQMD traditionally has addressed its pollution-control challenges by issuing detailed

---

[5] This analysis is based on an ICF Incorporated research project to which Cynthia Markert and Michael O'Neil made significant contributions.

industry-specific regulations limiting air emissions, mandating pollution controls, and restricting product formulation and use. Recent years have seen a shift toward some incentive-based systems, such as tradeable permits for emissions of certain compounds. But the issue here is not really what methods of regulation SCAQMD employs, rather it is that the extent of the air quality problems in the region requires extensive pollution abatement by a host of different sources of emissions, regardless of which regulatory instruments are used. Some of these measures even reach down to the level of the individual consumer (banning the use of charcoal lighter fluid, for example).

The central concern that motivated the project upon which this study is based was the possible negative impact the many regulations promulgated by the SCAQMD might have on small businesses within the district. The fact that SCAQMD's jurisdiction is confined to activities within the district itself raised the possibility that vigorous competition from firms outside the area could undermine regulated businesses in the basin. Another source of concern was that compliance with environmental regulations might be relatively more costly for small businesses than for large ones. This would not be detected if SCAQMD's regulations were being evaluated assuming that all members of the regulated community were large firms, instead of the mix of small and large businesses that actually populate many of the industries subject to its rules.

The original project was thus motivated by the need for a framework for assessing whether regulations might place small businesses in a particular jurisdiction at a significant disadvantage. What was required was an approach well grounded in the economics of regulatory cost incidence, but tailored to exploring the differential incidence of regulations on small businesses relative to large ones, and capable of examining rules that apply only to activities in a specific region. In addition to these analytical requirements for the framework, another goal

was to make the approach as clear and step-by-step as possible, so that it could be applied in an almost "cookbook" fashion.

This study summarizes the incidence-assessment framework developed for this project, and briefly outlines the conclusions reached using the approach to predict the possible small business impacts of several existing and proposed air emission regulations in the district. A total of five regulations were examined targeting emissions of volatile organic compounds (VOCs) by a variety of economic activities, including dry cleaning establishments, paint manufacturers, gasoline dispensing stations, and graphic arts shops.

The Analysis

The most productive approach for assessing small business impacts of air regulations promulgated by a locality is to build on the *cost incidence and economic impacts* framework presented in the first part of this chapter. Two key differences here, however, are that the relevant rules apply only within a specific geographic region and that a primary concern is the differential incidence of the regulatory costs on small entities relative to large firms. The geographic limitations of the rules make the threat of competition from outside the area an even greater possibility than foreign competition is to U.S. firms complying with nationwide environmental regulations. The focus on differential incidence shifts attention from industry-wide incidence and impacts to potentially uneven economic effects across different segments of the market.

Aside from the empirical difficulties inherent in the project itself, the desire to develop a cookbook approach posed an even greater challenge. It is quite common to make competing demands on such a framework. One wants them to be generic, flexible, and step-by-step, but at the same time technically correct and empirically precise. The hope is that successive applications of the approach can be conducted at very low cost, but still be accurate. In practice, however, attempts to create cookbooks for technically and empirically complex analyses meet with fates ranging from dismal failure to only the most modest success. The problem is that one must always navigate between the tendency to oversimplify to achieve transparency and ease of use, and the need to incorporate phenomenal detail and complexity to ensure comprehensiveness and accuracy. That tension was certainly felt in this attempt to develop a step-by-step approach for predicting the impacts of local environmental regulations on small businesses.

Framework for Assessing Small Business Economic Impacts

The approach for assessing small business economic impacts summarized here contains a number of steps, each of which either calls for data inputs or definitions (e.g., the nature of the compliance activities required by the regulation) or for various calculations and analyses (e.g., compliance-cost computations). These steps are arranged sequentially for a reason. The framework is designed to focus attention and research resources only on regulations that are likely to impose the burdens of primary concern, so it identifies relatively early in the process those regulations and situations in which severe economic impacts are *less* likely to occur. This means that only those regulations that have a relatively higher probability of imposing such burdens receive full analytical treatment.

Step 1. Determine Regulatory Requirements: The first step in assessing whether a regulation may impose significant economic impacts on small businesses is to carefully catalog what a regulation will require of the affected firms. Clearly, this involves specifying the regulation's explicit requirements for production processes, products, or specific types of equipment, and identifying which industries are regulated. But it is also important to deter-

mine whether all firms in these industries within the jurisdiction are regulated, or only subsets of firms, and whether compliance activities differ within an industry depending on the types of processes used. Finally, if any exemptions to the regulation exist, it is crucial to determine exactly how these are defined; for example, exemptions might be based on firm output or, alternatively, on emission levels.

While collecting these data might seem obvious to many, it is nevertheless important to very carefully determine what types of activities and what sets of firms are regulated. In some cases, a well-defined industry may be affected, but in other cases, it may be only certain pieces of equipment across a wide range of industries that are regulated. Exactly how the regulation's requirements "map" into industry categories and product types is important for determining the degree to which the compliance costs for small firms may or may not be disproportionately large, and hence, the extent to which the regulation may impose economic hardships on those firms.

Step 2. Small Business Definition and Characterization: The second step calls for characterizing the population of small businesses regulated, the methods they may undertake to comply, and the level of financial burden on these small firms at which economic impacts are likely to materialize.

For example, here one should specify the measure to be used for defining a small business and then determine whether any are actually subject to the regulation. If so, one should then roughly determine whether the regulated aspects of these firms' activities are a significant portion of their overall operations, or whether the regulated activities could be discontinued without substantial loss of profits or other undesirable impacts. Finally, for purposes of defining an economic impact, one must decide what magnitude of compliance costs or initial capital and research and development costs should be considered significant enough to cause economic dislocations, assuming they are borne entirely by the businesses themselves.

Step 3. Estimate Regulatory Costs for Small Businesses: Although a regulation may require compliance activities by small businesses, a key determinant of whether the regulation conceivably could cause serious economic impacts for these firms is the size of the compliance costs involved. If the regulation imposes only inexpensive requirements, then it is unlikely that significant economic hardships will result. In such cases, it is not worthwhile to continue the analysis because, regardless of the outcomes of the remaining steps in the framework, no economic impacts are likely to occur. Only if a regulation potentially imposes substantial costs on small businesses should the remaining steps be undertaken.

One commonly used method for determining the costs of compliance for small firms is based on *model plant* process engineering analysis of compliance activities, and estimates of costs provided by suppliers of compliance equipment. Normally these will provide a useful rough estimate of the regulation's costs. Compliance activities that often are important in environmental regulations include research and development, production downtime, and installation costs; additional capital investments; operating and maintenance expenditures; cost offsets, such as the value of recovered product and recycled materials; and the value of equipment that may be scrapped as a result of complying with the regulation. If relevant, one should also evaluate any significant reduced product quality or performance that could result from compliance with the regulation. This can be done either by estimating the reduction in

price likely to be received as a result, or by investigating the increased production costs necessary to avoid this consequence.

If the capital and other initial costs of the regulation are low (less than several thousand dollars), even very small firms are unlikely to experience difficulties in complying. If this is the case, and variable compliance costs are also low, then the regulation is unlikely to generate significant economic impacts. On the other hand, if the capital and other nonvariable costs are high, say, $10,000 or more, small businesses may have difficulty meeting the regulation's requirements even if the implied annualized costs are not very high. This is especially important because small firms may have difficulty generating the necessary funds internally, and may not be able to borrow the funds externally, to undertake the investments necessary to comply. Hence, regulations that impose high initial compliance costs on small firms should be identified as potentially imposing significant economic impacts.

Step 4. Assess Economies of Scale in Compliance Activities: Given that the regulation's compliance costs are high enough to potentially generate significant economic impacts on the small businesses affected, it does not necessarily follow that these hardships will actually materialize. If market and supply conditions indicate that the compliance costs of small businesses might be shifted to consumers of their products or services, high fixed or variable costs will not necessarily produce significant economic impacts on these firms. Whether small firms' compliance costs can be passed through to consumers, however, depends on a number of factors, including the competitive position of small regulated businesses relative to other market participants. In particular, the ability of small businesses to recoup their compliance costs through eventual price increases depends largely on their cost competitiveness after complying with the regulation relative to large regulated firms in the region.

To determine whether the regulatory compliance costs will produce a competitive advantage of large businesses over small ones, first characterize the industry in terms of ranges of output and compliance activities and costs, by several representative firm sizes. In doing so, one should also investigate whether multiplant firms possess an advantage in complying because of regulatory costs that can be shared across all plants—for example, research and development and reformulation costs. Similarly, larger firms might also possess certain economies of scope across several markets in complying with the regulation; that is, large diversified firms may be able to spread some of the compliance costs across several markets.

Based on this information, one can assess the relationship between compliance costs and firm size. If costs are higher for smaller firms on a per-unit basis, the regulation will place smaller entities at a long-run competitive disadvantage relative to larger firms. This is because after the adjustments are made to comply with the regulation, the proportion of compliance costs recovered by small firms will be less than for large firms. Larger firms will be the low-cost producers after the regulation's costs are taken into account, so, compared to the preregulation situation, smaller firms will be less profitable.

But if compliance costs are roughly proportional to the sizes of the affected firms, the regulation will not significantly alter the relative competitive positions of the large and small firms in the affected industry. Still, this does not necessarily imply that undesirable economic impacts from the regulation will not result. Even if the relative competitive positions of the large and small firms in the industry are unchanged, small firms may still experience economic impacts if unregulated competition (e.g., from firms outside of the

jurisdiction) exists and can successfully undercut the abilities of all regulated firms to recover their compliance costs. Hence, even if per unit compliance costs are the same regardless of firm size, the remaining steps in the framework should still conducted.

Step 5. Assess the Degree of Small Business Regulatory-Cost Shifting: To the extent that compliance costs are borne by consumers of the products or services provided by small regulated firms, there will be fewer and less-severe economic impacts associated with a regulation. This, in turn, depends on the degree to which the entire industry can pass on the compliance costs to consumers. Determining the possibility and extent of compliance cost-shifting for small businesses is the most complex and difficult step in the process of assessing a regulation's economic impacts.

Several factors limit the degree to which compliance costs can be passed through to consumers. For example, regulations relating to specialized conditions or problems peculiar to a particular firm are not likely to be shifted to consumers. Thus, one should determine whether the compliance activities are related directly to ongoing production activities of the regulated firms, or whether they are associated with some past problem or condition. In the latter case, other small and large firms without the encumbrance of these problems will prevent the affected business from recouping the regulatory costs through price increases.

Similarly, competition from outside the jurisdiction where the regulation applies may be able to compete with the regulated firms. If so, one should determine whether or not these firms are subject to roughly the same type of regulation in their own locations. If they are not similarly regulated, an important question is whether they can feasibly provide the same products or services in the region as do the regulated firms, at competitive prices.

If so, one should then assess whether this depends on the location of firms in the jurisdiction. For example, gas stations on the periphery of the region might confront vigorous competition from across the border, but not those more centrally located. Yet another factor affecting the regulated industry's ability to eventually shift the cost burden toward consumers that should be investigated is the availability and price of substitutes for the industry's products or services.

Finally, from the previous step, any economies of scale in compliance with the regulation should be considered. If these are substantial, the central issue is how much lower the average costs of compliance of the larger firms are than those of the smaller firms. If larger firms can completely shift their compliance costs to consumers in the long run, this forms the upper bound for small business recovery of regulatory costs.

In general, it will not be possible to shift regulatory costs to consumers if (1) the compliance activities are not tied to the products or services provided (e.g., regulations relating to specialized conditions or problems); (2) competition from outside of the jurisdiction can completely undercut the regulated firms because these firms face no similar compliance costs, and transportation costs into the region are not significant; or (3) there are viable substitutes for the industry's output at highly competitive prices.

But a complete inability to pass compliance costs through to product or service consumers should be considered an extreme case for many local environmental regulations that target ongoing economic activities by all members of a regulated industry. In many cases, competition from substitute products or from firms outside the region will not pose serious problems (e.g., location is not always economically irrelevant) so that, at least in the long run, some of the compliance costs may be shifted to consumers. The more likely result, therefore, will be at least a partial recovery of compliance costs by all businesses in the region, although significant economies of scale in compliance could still pose a long-run burden on the smaller regulated firms.

Step 6. Timing of Small-Firm Compliance-Cost Shifting: Even if small firms' compliance costs eventually can be shifted to consumers, in many cases this can require a long adjustment period before the price of the product or service rises to cover these costs. During this time, the firms in the industry suffer reduced profitability. Larger firms tend to have more substantial sources of internal and external funds to survive this adjustment period than do smaller firms. Hence, the slower this process, the greater the possibility that smaller firms will suffer serious economic impacts. The purpose of this step is to gain some insight, albeit only qualitative, into the length of time during which the additional compliance costs may be borne by the firms in the industry, even if in the long run these costs will be shouldered mostly by consumers.

As outlined in the preceding study, several factors help to determine how long the transition process might be. For example, if the regulated firms have many highly competitive uses for their capital equipment and other such investments, or if the ordinary turnover rate of their investments is rapid in any case, it will take relatively little time for the necessary adjustments to take place. On the other hand, if the industry is fairly capital-intensive and possesses durable capital with few alternative economic uses, this process may occur more gradually. Finally, if the demand for the output of the regulated firms is growing rapidly, the cost incidence will shift more rapidly toward the long-run outcome.

Hence, to gain some understanding of the amount of time it will take for the industry to adjust to the new regulatory costs, one should assess the capital intensity, normal rates of capital turnover, the nature and prices of substitutes for the industry's output, and the rate of demand growth for these outputs. Although quantitative estimates of these timing issues cannot be generated easily, even the qualitative indications provided by these factors can be helpful in sorting regulations into those that will and those that probably will not involve long transition times before the compliance costs can be passed through to consumers, assuming that this shifting is possible.

Step 7. Evaluate Possible Decline in Long-Run Industry Output: Even when all of the compliance costs may be shifted to consumers in the long run, if the demand for the industry's products or services is very elastic, there may be a large reduction in industry output. This could cause many of the industry's smaller firms to contract or close while this adjustment takes place.

To gain some sense of what the possible magnitude of the reduction in industry output might be (assuming that demand is not growing very rapidly), one should compare the per-unit-of-output compliance cost to the price and average unit cost of the products or services of the affected industry. If the per-unit regulatory costs are large, and all else the same, a greater reduction in long-run output will result. The other major determinant of long-run output changes is the elasticity of demand. If there are few cost-effective substitutes, then demand will tend to be more inelastic, so that output will not decline as much as when there are many economically viable alternatives.

In the end, if a substantial reduction in the equilibrium level of industry output is probable because of large price increases induced by high compliance costs, then the industry must contract. It is possible that this contraction may be achieved by a disproportionate reduction in the number of small firms in the industry, especially if the regulation tends to

increase economies of scale in the industry. If so, this also constitutes a small business economic impact of the regulation.

These seven steps are designed to detect whether a regulation might adversely impact small businesses. As the framework suggests, these economic effects can occur for a variety of reasons and in several different contexts. If the steps described are followed, generally it will be possible to determine whether a particular regulation is likely to impose a significant economic burden on small firms. In some cases, exploring many of the empirical analyses and issues outlined above may only be possible in qualitative terms, especially when resources available to study and predict a proposed regulation's economic impacts are scarce. Nevertheless, the framework is designed to generate useful information for predicting economic impacts on small firms as efficiently as possible.

In the ideal case, and with substantial research resources, one might be able to apply the framework quantitatively. With sufficient empirical information on the compliance costs to small and large firms, the elasticity of demand (inclusive of competition from beyond the regulation's jurisdiction), and the amount, rate of turnover, and ease of redeployment of the industry's capital to alternative uses, it would be possible to compute the amount of compliance costs small firms will bear in the short and long runs and to roughly estimate the length of the adjustment period. In most applications, however, a mixture of quantitative and qualitative information will be available to support small-business-impacts predictions, which, in turn, will be couched largely in qualitative terms.

Inevitably, the precision of the estimated economic impacts will be less than ideal. Nevertheless, a useful feature of this framework is that it is fairly effective at detecting when regulations probably will not cause significant small business impacts. One is then left with those cases that might impose substantial hardships. It is often just as important to be able to identify instances in which large impacts are not likely as it is to predict precisely what those impacts will be when they are expected to occur.

APPLICATION OF THE FRAMEWORK TO SPECIFIC REGULATIONS

The *small business economic impacts* assessment framework was used in the original project to evaluate the potential impacts of five air-quality regulations targeting volatile organic compounds (VOC) emissions. Aside from the obvious purpose of predicting the effects of these regulations, the main objective was to test the framework to see if it indeed was capable of sorting regulations into those with high probabilities of causing impacts and those with low potential for resulting in these effects. Verification of the predicted impacts on small businesses was based mostly on interviews with small businesses in the affected industries.

While substantial empirical information was generated in the course of these applications of the framework, what is most interesting is the conclusions generated by applying the approach and how those findings were reached. In addition, the rules examined produced a broad array of small-business-impacts predictions. Hence, this study concludes by summarizing the essentials of each of these five applications of the framework, emphasizing primarily the nature of, and the rationale for, their predicted impacts.

Petroleum-Based Dry Cleaning Regulation: One process for dry cleaning fabrics utilizes a petroleum-based solvent. As with other VOCs, emissions of the solvent to the atmosphere create air pollution. This rule required petroleum-solvent dry cleaners to use a carbon adsorber or other abatement equipment to reduce emissions by 90 percent by weight.

Very little research for this rule was required after a cursory survey of the industry in the region found no small businesses subject to the regulation. Petroleum-based dry cleaning is primarily a large-scale operation typically servicing commercial and industrial clients. Hence, the rule would not adversely affect any small businesses.

Perchloroethylene Dry Cleaning Regulation: This rule contained provisions similar to those for petroleum-based dry cleaning. Specifically, the regulation required perchloroethylene dry cleaners to utilize a filtering system and a carbon adsorber or other control equipment, such that either the equipment reduced emissions to the atmosphere by at least 90 percent by weight, or ensured that the concentration of VOCs vented to the atmosphere would be less than 100 parts per million.

Choices of control equipment for these processes included carbon adsorbers, dry-to-dry recovery tumblers, and refrigerated dry-to-dry machines. Carbon adsorbers, however, were not popular among the industry because they required cleaning and eventual replacement, and garment processing was interrupted when the carbon filters were cleaned. Dry-to-dry recovery tumblers without refrigeration were usually used in conjunction with carbon adsorbers. A complete system of a carbon adsorber, tumbler, reclaimer (for solvent recovery), and distiller would meet the 90 percent control requirements. A newer control technology was the refrigerated dry-to-dry machine, which in theory emitted no VOCs to the atmosphere.

Unlike petroleum-based dry cleaning, the perchloroethylene dry cleaning industry consisted mostly of small businesses, such as the local dry cleaning establishments in many neighborhoods. Hence, the possibility of significant economic impacts on small businesses was high. Nevertheless, after examining the economics of solvent recovery and recycling, it was clear that avoiding venting the solvent to the atmosphere was strongly in the financial interest of these businesses. Installing recovery equipment to recapture and then recycle the perchloroethylene turned out to be far cheaper than the high volume of new solvent purchases necessary to replace those vented. Because the requirements of the rule essentially codified economically profitable practices, no small business hardships would result.

Gasoline Transfer and Dispensing Regulation: This rule established requirements for transferring gasoline from trucks, trailers, or railroad cars to stationary storage tanks (Phase I), and for transferring gasoline from stationary tanks to motor vehicles (Phase II). Phase I requirements included the following: (1) a stationary container (known to most people as a tank) must have a permanent submerged fill pipe, (2) a stationary container must be equipped with a certified vapor recovery system, and (3) all vapor recovery lines must be connected between the dispensing vehicle and the stationary container. Phase I requirements applied to tanks with a capacity of more than 251 gallons. Phase II rules required that dispensing units be equipped with certified vapor-recovery equipment, and that the equipment be operated in accordance with manufacturer specifications and be free of defects. A number of exemptions to this rule existed, mainly to exclude very small-volume sources.

The main focus of concern for small business impacts here was on conventional automobile gasoline stations where vapor-recovery equipment was required at the pump, with connections to a central recovery unit. The equipment necessary to comply with the regulation, while of various possible types, was quite expensive, depending on the number of pumps and nozzles at the station. There also appeared to be modest economies of scale in complying with the rule, because higher-volume stations would face a slightly lower per-gallon cost. Hence, given the magnitude of the regulatory costs and possible economies of scale in compliance, the probability was high that significant small-business impacts might result.

Closer analysis, however, revealed that small-business impacts would not be substantial, pri-

marily because the compliance costs were likely to be shifted to gasoline consumers very rapidly. Gasoline demand within the area was inelastic, and competition from stations outside of the region was not possible except along the fringes of the jurisdiction. Furthermore, the economics of gasoline retailing had already undergone considerable change due to the oil crises of the 1970s. The corner station, where car repair was the more important profit center, had largely been replaced by larger outlets specializing in high-volume gasoline sales. Hence, while the potential economies of scale involved in complying with the regulation would have harmed the very smallest businesses, these no longer existed in any significant numbers. The conclusion reached for this rule, as a result, was that while the regulatory costs were substantial, they would be shifted to consumers fairly rapidly, thereby avoiding serious small-business impacts.

Architectural Coatings Regulation: Architectural coatings, better known to most people as paint, are made according to a wide variety of formulations. Two major types of coatings are solvent-based formulations and water-based compounds. This regulation was designed to reduce VOC emissions from solvent-based coatings. Many of the relevant products contained large amounts of solvents, which according to paint and resin manufacturers were necessary to produce high-quality results. In particular, for areas that experience very high humidity, such as kitchens and baths, solvent-based paints tend to perform far better than water-based formulations.

This rule generally prohibited the sale or application of any architectural coatings and paints containing solvent concentrations that exceeded certain limits. A detailed schedule for compliance was specified in the rule, with various effective dates for different classes of paints and coatings. Exceptions were provided for highly specialized solvent-containing products for which water-based alternatives were not acceptable substitutes. The overall effect of this rule would be mainly to impose substantial costs on paint and resin manufacturers for the research, development, and testing necessary to prepare new low- or no-solvent formulations. For many applications these costs were expected to be relatively high.

The paint manufacturing business prior to the promulgation of this solvent concentration rule consisted of a number of medium and large firms supplying mostly the high-volume market, and a collection of very small firms specializing mainly in high-quality, low-volume submarkets. A large proportion of the sales of small paint manufacturers was derived from solvent-based coatings, a set of products essentially banned by the regulation.

The prediction for this rule clearly was that extensive small business impacts would occur. There were few viable alternatives open to these businesses. One possible response might be to engage in a very costly and time-consuming effort to develop new formulations to replace their older products. But aside from the cost of doing so, even if successful, these reformulated products would face substantially more competition from larger firms' product lines. Furthermore, given that most of the rule's costs would be in the form of reformulating products, the implied economies of scale in compliance were very large. Hence, this rule was likely to result in significant impacts on small businesses.

Graphic Arts Regulation: The graphic arts industry consists of firms that engage in flexographic, screen, lithographic, and gravure printing processes. This rule generally required either the installation of emission-control equipment that was 95 percent efficient for gravure printing operations, and 90 percent efficient for all other printing processes, in reducing emissions of VOCs, or the use of lower solvent inks.

Compliance with this rule was expected to be somewhat difficult, regardless of firm size, for several reasons. The emission-control equipment

for solvent recovery was fairly expensive, and it was not technologically feasible for some processes to switch to lower-solvent inks. Hence, the industry was expected to incur significant compliance costs as a result of the rule. In addition, significant competition from outside of the regulation's jurisdiction appeared to exist, and some potentially regulated members of the industry were contemplating relocating to these unregulated areas. Thus, small graphic arts firms would experience substantial economic impacts, because of both the high compliance costs and very effective competition from beyond the regulated jurisdiction.

Cost Incidence of Mandatory CFC Recapture and Recycling[6]

As discussed in several other studies in this book relating to CFCs, in the late 1980s EPA promulgated a regulation mandating a phaseout of CFCs and other ozone-depleting substances production as agreed to by the United States and other nations in the Montreal Protocol and the London and Copenhagen amendments. By depleting the stratospheric ozone layer that protects the earth from excess ultraviolet radiation, these substances cause serious human health and ecological risks. The phaseout of CFCs was implemented by establishing a schedule of increasingly stringent production limitations that was enforced through a system of tradeable permits originally allocated based on past production volumes. In addition, Congress authorized a tax on the remaining production of these chemicals to transfer the potentially large profits anticipated under the phaseout from manufacturers to the government.

Despite these powerful regulatory measures, EPA remained concerned about the ozone-depletion impact of a significant source of CFC emis-

---

[6] This analysis is based on an ICF Incorporated project conducted by Peter Linquiti and Andre Wakefield.

sions that was largely unaffected by the phase-out or tax regulations. This other CFC source is the large stock of CFCs embodied as *charges* in numerous pieces of refrigeration equipment. In the process of servicing or disposing of these machines, their residual charges of CFCs would normally be vented to the atmosphere, thereby depleting the ozone layer. To address this problem, EPA considered promulgating a regulation requiring the recapture and recycling of these charges of CFCs instead of venting them. The recycled-source CFCs would also make it easier for the market to comply with the phaseout's production restrictions.

The recycling regulation targeted firms that service or dispose of a variety of equipment types, such as automobile air conditioners, building chillers, food-storage units, and a host of other refrigeration devices. Compliance with the regulation required purchasing more expensive machines to service the equipment, adopting more costly and time-consuming servicing and disposal procedures, and training service personnel in the new requirements and methods. The universe of firms affected by the regulation was large, diverse, and contained many small enterprises.

As with any proposed regulation, a cost–benefit analysis of the CFC recapture and recycling regulation was conducted. In addition, the potential economic impacts of the requirements on businesses were explored. A key concern was the requirements' impact on small businesses, which represented a substantial fraction of the firms in the affected industries. Estimates of the annual compliance costs with the regulation were in the $5,000 to $10,000 range. While not particularly problematic for large corporations, these costs could be significant for many small operations, such as service stations. Initially, the conventional tests for economic impacts were computed, as described earlier in this chapter, based on ratios of the compliance costs to sales, net worth, and other measures of firm size and financial strength. The recycling regulation

tended to fail these tests, thereby signaling that it might pose substantial economic impacts on small businesses, possibly causing firm closures and reduced employment.

The Question

It has already been noted that economic impacts tests based on comparisons of compliance costs with firm financial characteristics implicitly assume that the directly regulated firms will bear all of the costs, rather than sharing the burden of the regulation with consumers. Of course, a worst-case analysis might assume that the regulatory costs will be completely borne by the complying firms. But the problem is that while these tests might be reasonable indicators of when a regulation *will not* have severe economic impacts, they are poor predictors of whether a regulation *will* cause them.

Because the usual tests for economic impacts in this case indicated that the regulation was likely to impose a significant burden on small, and even some large businesses, the next step in the analysis, quite logically, was to explore more carefully how much of these compliance costs would actually be shouldered by the firms and how much would be shifted to consumers. Hence, the central task for this analysis was to examine the incidence of the costs imposed by the proposed CFC recapture and recycling regulation. To the degree that these costs could be shifted to consumers, that is, the owners of the affected CFC-containing equipment, the firms directly subject to the regulation would bear less of the compliance costs and would thus be less likely to suffer the economic and financial impacts that EPA feared were possible.

Although the explicit exercise required for the analysis was to provide an estimate of the CFC recapture regulation's incidence, the reason for including this brief study here is to demonstrate that the advice for assessing cost incidence presented in this chapter must be applied carefully. In particular, analyzing the CFC recapture regulation revealed that in some circumstances, a few easy-to-overlook facts can profoundly affect the character of the cost incidence assessment and its results.

The Analysis

Following the guidelines summarized in the two preceding studies in this chapter, the incidence of the CFC recapture and recycling regulation was examined fairly systematically. The scope of application of the regulatory requirements was determined to be national and comprehensive, for example, so that the costs conceivably could be shifted to consumers. On the basis of other criteria that jointly define regulatory-compliance cost incidence, the results were at best mixed, depending on the sector analyzed and other factors. For example, some sectors faced fairly high fixed costs of compliance, while others faced mostly increased variable costs as a result of the new regulation. Moreover, in almost all cases, demand for the newly regulated services was not growing particularly rapidly.

The industry adjustment process, as described earlier, was predicted to be easier in some cases and more difficult in others. An automobile service station will find it far less disruptive to cease offering mobile air conditioning servicing, but still remain in business, than would a refrigeration service company specializing in precisely the actions targeted by the recapture and recycling regulation.

In general, the many factors governing cost incidence differed across sectors and did not appear to favor any particularly robust conclusion. The researchers then turned to the demand side of the issue. Exploring the probable demand elasticity for the activities regulated uncovered a crucial piece of information.

As illustrated in a number of the studies and applications described in this book, practical analyses of markets and policies rarely have access to econometric estimates of elasticities, much less data of sufficient quality and quantity to undertake estimating them directly. Instead, normally one uses various forms of relatively straightforward *use and substitutes* analysis to explore the availability and cost of alternatives to the product or activity in question. For example, if regulation of a chemical used in a particular process or good is being studied, one would examine the alternatives to the chemical, and their cost, quality, and performance in the particular application of interest. This gives a rough sense of the degree to which users of the chemical will tolerate price increases, which is essentially the concept of demand elasticity cast in cruder terms.

In the case of the CFC-recycling regulations, imagining what demanders of the newly regulated services might do instead of purchasing the recharging and maintenance services for their equipment revealed a better and more fundamental answer to the incidence question. First, in many cases, choosing not to have the relevant machine serviced is not a viable option. For example, choosing not to service an office building chiller would mean that the building would have no air conditioning, which is unlikely to be satisfactory to the tenants. Similarly, equipment that refrigerates food during transport or storage must be used to avoid costly spoilage.

Thus, the first observation was that the demand for servicing most of the CFC-containing types of equipment is likely to be very inelastic. But a deeper issue relevant to the incidence question lurked in the background. Suppose an equipment owner decided to scrap the piece of equipment to avoid the additional costs imposed by the recapture and recycling regulation. Presumably two events would be triggered by this decision: one would be the purchase of a new piece of equipment that does not use CFCs; the other, however, would be the disposal of the old unit. Yet, the CFC recapture and recycling regulation also governs this action. This implies that in the process of scrapping the old piece of equipment, the same costs of recapture and recycling would be confronted.

What this means for the incidence of the re-cycling regulation's costs is important. The demand for servicing units of CFC-containing equipment depends upon a number of factors, including the age of the equipment, the costs of alternative types of equipment, *and*, quite significantly, the costs of disposing of it. Upon enactment of the CFC recapture and recycling regulation, the cost of disposal rises. Because disposal is, in a certain sense, a substitute for servicing, the demand for servicing should reflect the increased cost of disposal.

Hence, as shown in Figure 8-5, when the supply of CFC-containing equipment servicing shifts upward by the amount of the regulatory costs, the demand function shifts upward as well. Because the regulatory costs at issue here are those relating to recapturing and recycling CFCs from equipment, and these are the same for both servicing and disposal (by assumption), the upward shift of the demand and supply functions will be the same. The incidence of these costs is now clear and unambiguous: Equipment owners bear the regulation's costs, not suppliers of these services. Moreover, this conclusion is not predicated on analysis of demand and supply elasticities; it results from the fact that the regulation governs not only the costs of servicing these machines, but also the alternatives available to the equipment owners.

Intuitively, the CFC recapture and recycling regulation's costs will be borne by equipment owners rather than by the directly regulated suppliers of these services, because the regulation governs all of the available options open to equipment owners. Given that it is impossible to avoid the recycling regulation's requirements, the incidence of its compliance costs is similar to that of the costs associated with discovering a release from a hazardous waste landfill, the resulting containment and remediation costs of which cannot be shifted away from the landfill's owners. The regulation's costs are best thought of as a reduction of the wealth of the owners of the equipment rather than as the equivalent of a tax on the CFC servicing and disposal activities the regulation directly affects.

FIGURE 8-5

Incidence of CFC Recapture and Recycling Regulatory Costs

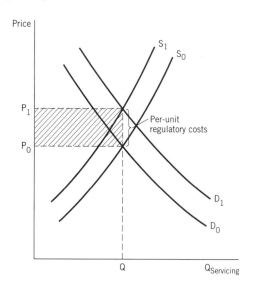

The supply of CFC servicing shifts upward reflecting the costs of the recapture and recycling regulation. But the demand for CFC recycling services also rises by the amount of the regulatory costs because the alternative to servicing, disposal, is subject to the same requirements. Hence, the incidence of the costs of the regulation is entirely on the owners of the affected equipment.

Chapter 9

Intertemporal Issues

The effects of many environmental problems and policies often occur over many years. Hence, in analyzing them discounting and a host of related issues routinely arise, such as determining the appropriate rate of interest to use in expressing future values in present terms, and renewable and nonrenewable resource management and pricing. A host of time-related considerations also figure prominently in the increasingly popular notion of sustainable development. Although the term itself currently defies concrete definition, economic research in the area involves elements from both the environmental and growth fields in economics. Intertemporal considerations certainly raise a larger and more diverse set of specific questions and issues than could possibly be canvassed at one time, so what is presented here focuses on a few of the more basic concepts that are normally relevant in conducting practical environmental policy analysis.

This chapter contains two studies, the first of which seeks to provide a fairly compact review of the conventional literature on discounting from a social perspective, and offers an extension of that analysis to the world of discounting in the context of regulatory costs and benefits. The purpose of this study is to review what one really needs to know about the murky area of discounting in public policy evaluation, not to offer definitive conclusions, for, as the discussion in the study reveals, that objective is at present (and perhaps always will be) an unattainable goal. The second application briefly explores a different type of intertemporal issue that arises frequently in practical policy analysis. Specifically, this study evaluates the plausible proposition that the value of environmental risk reduction ought to increase over time as societies become wealthier.

Discounting from a Social Perspective: First Principles

Economic analyses of environmental policy very often involve intertemporal issues and, hence, discounting. For example, many pollution-control technologies are long-lived investments providing benefits over many years. Similarly, reducing environmental exposures to carcinogens today may avoid human health damages in the distant future. In most policy-making discussions, however, the costs and, perhaps less frequently, the benefits of environmental regulations normally are stated in terms of today's equivalents through a procedure known as discounting. Inevitably, analysts must grapple with the issue of what discount rate is appropriate for computing the present value of a regulation's costs and effects.

In practice, the choice of a discount rate has generated enormous controversy, especially in the area of environmental protection. At least in part, this is because many environmental regulations impose costs in the near term in exchange for benefits that often accrue in the more distant future. In present value terms, the net effects of these policies can be particularly sensitive to the discount rate used to evaluate them, with the estimated net benefits commonly traversing a wide range from very high to quite low, even negative, as the interest rate used to discount costs and benefits ranges from lower to higher values. Hence, proponents of these regulations tend to argue for low discount rates, whereas opponents of these policies tend to favor higher ones.

But the controversy over the correct discount rate to use in analyzing regulations, including environmental ones, runs deeper than simply politics. The literature on discounting in public policy evaluation is voluminous and fairly technical, and discusses several supposedly equivalent procedures for determining the appropriate discount rate. Its complexity and apparent lack of consensus both fuel the debate in the policymaking world over what discount rate and procedures should be used.

The original research project on which this study is based was motivated in large part by the intensity of disagreement about discounting in public policy analysis. One goal in that project was to assess whether or not the disagreements about discounting procedures in practice really flowed from the economic research on the subject. If the literature had in fact reached some consensus on the issue, but had failed to communicate it effectively, a nontechnical summary might assist policy makers in deciding on appropriate discounting procedures. If the research was really divided, understanding the nature of the disagreement nevertheless might help those who still must make choices about discounting in practice.

Two related concerns were also relevant for the project underlying this study. One is that the Office of Management and Budget (OMB) had issued a circular in the early 1970s requiring the use of a 10-percent real (inflation-adjusted) rate

for government discounting calculations.[1] During the mid-1980s, however, interest rates gradually fell from nearly 20 percent during the late 1970s and early 1980s to levels at which long-term rates were below 10 percent. With inflation at the time running 4 or 5 percent, the implied real interest rate was about 3 to 5 percent, less than half the recommended rate. OMB's insistence that agencies continue to use the 10 percent *real* rate, which implies nominal rates of 10 percent plus the underlying inflation rate, became increasingly difficult to justify. Thus, another objective of the project was to determine whether there were strong reasons to argue that OMB's discount rate guidance had become dated and inaccurate.

One final issue that motivated the original project was that the literature on discounting in public policy analysis focuses mainly on discount rates and procedures for situations in which the government extracts funds from the private sector (by taxing or borrowing) and then spends them on a public project, such as a dam for irrigation and hydroelectric power generation. It is not clear that exactly the same discounting procedures developed for public projects should be used to evaluate government regulations. Environmental rules, in part, require private sector entities to engage in costly pollution control activities using their own funds, so it was worth exploring whether the recommendations in the discounting literature could be transplanted to the realm of government regulation.

The Question

The central question for this study is how to determine what discount rate should be used in evaluating the costs and benefits of government

---

[1] Office of Management and Budget, Executive Office of the President, "Discount Rates to be Used in Evaluating Time-Distributed Costs and Benefits," Circular A-94, March 27, 1972.

programs, particularly regulations. A number of other issues are related to this question. For example, does the literature on discounting really argue that several correct procedures exist and that all of them are correct? Also, was OMB's guidance indicating that agencies should use a 10 percent real discount rate ever correct but simply became empirically out-of-date, or is there some more fundamental problem? Finally, is the discount rate choice affected by any significant difference between government programs, in which either taxes or borrowing fund some activity, and private-sector compliance with environmental regulations that require pollution control or other safeguards?

Other issues related to discounting from a social perspective perhaps have even more profound implications than the exact discount rate chosen. For example, when a regulation's anticipated effects may be felt in large part by as-yet unborn generations, significant ethical issues arise. A related question is how one reconciles selecting a single discount rate for a public program, considering that people face many interest rates, often one rate for saving and another higher rate for borrowing, and that different people quite obviously discount the future at unequal rates.

The Analysis

There are two ways to proceed in presenting an analysis of discounting from a social perspective. One is to attempt to describe the development of the literature, from one concept and conclusion to the next.[2] This approach is generally fairly te-

dious and often quite confusing. Such a review must address numerous ideas and issues associated with characteristics of government projects, the structure of interest rates, changes in private investment levels, and a host of other complications. It also tends to lead readers to believe that all of the many digressions and details will somehow terminate in a concrete and defensible empirical answer, when the reality is quite the contrary. The broad answer to the question of the appropriate discount rate to use in evaluating public policies is that, especially for environmental policies involving lengthy timeframes, the issue remains unsettled. Although the literature is capable of yielding a theoretically defensible answer under very restrictive conditions, it is problematic to apply that answer in the real world where these conditions might not hold.

Does this mean that one can then discard the literature and with impunity adopt whatever rate one wishes? Probably not, primarily because what is settled in the literature is enough to exclude some ranges of discount rates. Perhaps more important is that critics will inevitably cite the literature on the subject in arguing against one's discount rate selection. A paramount concern in this analysis is therefore not only what one needs to know to select a discount rate for evaluating government policies, but also the arguments and considerations that make doing so such a messy business.

In light of this, instead of simply trying to summarize the social discounting literature, this encapsulation adopts a different approach, one that hopefully will serve readers better. What follows is first an overview of the current state of the basics of discounting from a social perspective, where the analysis is confined to fairly well-defined and restrictive conditions. The conceptual results are fairly easy to understand and are true, given the simplifying assumptions. Knowing the fundamentals of this topic is thus not nearly as difficult as one might think based on a casual glance at the technical literature on the topic.

---

[2] Excellent summaries of the modern literature on social discounting can be found in R. C. Lind (ed.), *Discounting for Time and Uncertainty in Energy Policy* (Resources for the Future, Inc.: Washington, D.C., 1982) and R. C. Lind "Reassessing the Government's Discount Rate Policy in Light of New Theory and Data in a World Economy with a High Degree of Capital Mobility," *Journal of Environmental Economics and Management* 18, No. 2, part 2 (March 1990): S8–S28. These sources outline the development of the literature to date and include extensive bibliographies.

Next, a different and competing method for calculating a social discount rate—commonly thought to be equivalent to what the literature indicates is the correct approach—is reviewed and found to be incorrect. Experience suggests that in social discounting, it is sometimes as important to know why the wrong answer is incorrect as it is to know the right answer. Following this is an application of the central teachings of the social discounting literature to the world of government regulations, which proves to be reasonably straightforward. Finally, the numerical rate of discount to use in practical applications of social discounting is examined.

SOCIAL DISCOUNTING ESSENTIALS

The basic results in the social discounting literature are actually far easier to understand than the literature's volume and technical sophistication would suggest. To grasp the fundamentals, consider this very simple example. Suppose the government proposes to spend $100 this year on a project that will yield environmental benefits next year. The project might be improved wetlands management, the cost of which includes restoration and other activities this year that will generate economic and recreational benefits next year. Suppose that after careful measurement and analysis, the value of these future benefits is estimated as $120.

Much as private companies and individuals do, the government wants to know whether the net present value of this proposed project is positive. As in any present-value type of problem, the usual private-sector technique would be to discount the future $120 worth of benefits to this year and then subtract from that the $100 current-year cost. Social discounting is really no different from this basic calculation, except that there is no obvious guide for obtaining the missing piece of information needed to perform this calculation: the discount rate to use to express the future benefits in terms of current consumption.

The Consumption Rate of Interest: The general rule throughout the literature on social discounting, to the degree that a rule exists, is that in a sense the government is trading costs and benefits intertemporally on behalf of its citizens. That is, the environmental project described can be thought of as asking individuals to collectively give up $100 this year to purchase $120 worth of environmental and other benefits accruing next year. It then seems reasonable to discount the future benefits to the present using the same rate that the affected citizens would use, for it is on their behalf that the project is undertaken.

So exactly what might that discount rate be? In practice, this turns out to be a question far easier to pose than to answer. Consumers face a variety of interest rates for borrowing and investing, as do corporations and the government. Moreover, interest rates tend to measure at least two phenomena in the real world, the pure *time value of money*, which reflects the facts that individuals require compensation for deferring consumption, and that investing generally yields a positive return; and *risk*, which is familiar to most people as the general proposition that riskier investments should bring higher rates of return.[3]

Nevertheless, to deliver on the promise that the basics can be understood fairly easily, for the moment assume that individuals are homogeneous, and ignore risk and related issues. So circumscribed, the search for the appropriate discount rate for determining the present value of the environmental investment project centers on

---

[3] The term *risk* is used here in its everyday negative meaning. Strictly speaking, any situation whose outcome has a high variance might be called "risky." Some risky propositions, however, are regarded positively. A fire insurance policy for a house involves perfectly certain payments and highly uncertain and infrequent payoffs. Nevertheless, the homeowner will view the "risky" insurance policy positively because the low-probability insurance payoff occurs when the house catches fire, thus serving to offset an otherwise extremely negative financial event.

the rate at which consumers are willing to trade consumption this year for consumption next year. The project can be thought of as costing people current consumption and offering them benefits valued in terms of future consumption. Barring other complications, individuals then should be willing to trade the project's costs and benefits over time in the way they trade consumption over time. In light of this, the question would appear simple to resolve: Simply discount the $120 worth of environmental and other benefits of the project at the rate consumers use to trade consumption over time, and be done with the problem. The resulting net present value will reveal whether the environmental project is a worthwhile social investment. The literature settled on the term *consumption rate of interest* to describe this commonsense approach to discounting in public-project evaluation.

If this were the whole story, one might wonder what causes all of the acrimony and conflict about discounting in public projects, especially environmental ones, aside from the usual political explanations. Indeed, if the issue were only one of trying to obtain a quantitative estimate of the rate at which individuals trade consumption over time, it would seem to be an empirical problem at worst.

Two sets of assumptions employed so far, however, make the analysis appear simpler than it is in reality, one set visible and the other not. The visible assumptions are those concerning the characteristics of the population of individuals on whose behalf one imagines the government to be trading when it proposes and undertakes the environmental project. Exactly who these people are, and even whether they are presently alive, poses an unusually difficult set of problems when trying to choose a discount rate. Similarly, defining even for a specific individual precisely how he or she trades consumption over time in a world of taxable and nontaxable savings instruments, tax-deferred investment opportunities, and so forth, is a very complex task.

These important issues will be revisited later in this discussion. Here the focus is on the other complication that for years has dominated the social discounting literature.

The Source of the Funds Problem: A hidden assumption in the analysis so far is that the cost of the environmental project in terms of current consumption is the $100 mentioned earlier. But how does the government obtain the $100 in the first place? This is critical, because the government can obtain the funds by either taxing or borrowing. Suppose it chooses to raise income taxes. It seems reasonable in this case to suppose (or assume) that the $100 of increased taxes will reduce consumption of other goods by the same amount.[4] As a result, when using taxes, the normal assumption is that the $100 cost of the project is exactly the cost to individuals in terms of reduced current consumption. If so, discounting the benefits at the consumption rate of interest and then subtracting the $100 current cost is the appropriate procedure.

But what if the government chooses to increase its borrowing to fund the project? If the supply of savings is insensitive to the interest rate and the economy is viewed as "closed" in the sense that the United States is assumed not to interact with the rest of the world, the added government borrowing will displace private investment. In the limit, financing the project through borrowing crowds out private-sector investment, dollar for dollar.

One might ask why this matters. It might, according to the literature, because private-sector investment earnings are themselves taxed. For example, the interest earned on a bond or in a savings account, as well as the returns on common stocks, are all subject to income tax. Hence,

---

[4] It is possible to argue that because the marginal propensity to consume is less than unity, a small portion of the taxes might come from savings. For simplicity, assume that income taxes only displace private consumption.

both the government and the individual investor benefit financially from private-sector investments. Suppose a typical, relatively risk-free, private-sector investment yields a total inflation-adjusted gross-of-tax return of, say, 4 percent. If the marginal tax rate is 50 percent, the government will receive 2 percent, leaving the investor the post-tax rate of return, or 2 percent. What this means is that while the $100 of crowded-out private-sector investments are worth $100 to individual investors in a definitional sense, they also have value to the government. This implies that the $100 of private-sector investments displaced by the increased government borrowing are worth more than $100 to society as a whole in terms of present consumption.

This is a confusing point, but a central one in the literature. How can $100 be worth more than $100? The secret is that the measure of value is not dollars, but goods and services, or consumption. Clearly, $100 worth of reduced consumption is worth precisely $100 of consumption, a mere tautology. But $100 of private-sector investment might have a social value different from $100 in terms of current consumption, because investments embody *future* consumption. Here, the $100 of displaced private investments are worth $100 in consumption terms to private-sector investors: This must be true, because $100 of consumption is foregone to purchase the $100 worth of investments. But because the government is also a "partner" in the investment through its taxing power, the total social value of the investment is greater than $100 of consumption. Hence, it is not contradictory to imagine that private-sector investments that are worth $100 to individuals could be worth more than that to society as a whole when their provision of additional future taxes is taken into account, as is the case here.

So what is the social value of the $100 of displaced private-sector investments? Given that the measure of value is consumption, the social value of private investment should be equal to the present value of the consumption stream it provides. To calculate this, first specify the

stream of consumption. Next year the $100 of private investments will yield a total post-inflation return of 4 percent, or $4. Of this, the government receives $2 in taxes and the investor nets $2. Suppose the investor consumes all of this net return and the government uses the tax revenues for whatever public purposes it deems to be appropriate. The $100 of capital continues to be invested, so that it provides the same gross rate of return in the following year. This process of investing, reaping returns, paying taxes, consuming the net-of-tax proceeds, and reinvesting the capital can be thought of as infinitely repeating.

In this simple case, the consumption stream attributable to the $100 of private-sector investments is $4 in each year through the infinite future, where the government receives $2 per year in tax revenues and the investor receives $2 per year in net returns to be consumed. The government's $2 per year can be thought of as avoiding raising income taxes in the future, so this portion of the investment return also represents future consumption. The social value of these $100 of private-sector capital investments is thus the present value of an infinite stream of $4 consumption payments, discounted at the consumption rate of interest. Suppose that the consumption rate of interest is 2 percent. The formula for the value of an infinite stream of annual payments is simply the yearly payment amount divided by the interest rate. Hence, the present value of the future consumption generated by the $100 of private sector investments is $4 divided by .02, or $200 in terms of current consumption. Note that the value of these investments to investors is the present value of the net-of-tax infinite stream of $2 discounted at 2 percent, or $2 divided by .02, which is $100. The investments are also worth an additional $100 to the government because the stream of tax revenues they generate, $2 per year, discounted at 2 percent, is $100. In terms of current consumption, the social value of these private-sector investments is the sum of their value to investors and to the government, or $200.

All of the assumptions made in this simple example can be modified to make calculating the social value of private investments more complex, such as exploring whether or not all of the net proceeds of these investments are consumed by investors. If some of these returns are reinvested rather than consumed, the future stream of consumption associated with the original $100 of private investment is greater and more complex to calculate. The essence of the issue, however, is clear. The private value of capital investments is based only on their net-of-tax returns to investors. But because the government taxes the returns from private investments, their social value should include the tax revenue stream they generate. Hence, the social value of private capital will be greater than the explicit value the market places on them. In this example, the social value of private capital is twice its private value.

Of course, this immediately implies that society would be better off if more private capital investments were made. The private sector invests only up to the point where the net-of-tax returns, discounted at the consumption rate of interest, equal the cost of the investment. At that point, the social, or gross-of-tax, returns on additional investments exceed the consumption rate of interest, so more investment would be socially worthwhile. But this is not so surprising because whenever the government levies a tax on a good or service one generally expects that less of it will be provided. Taxing investment returns, as with any other activity, will cause fewer investments to be made than otherwise.

The impact of all of this on evaluating the net present value of the environmental project should now be evident. If the government borrows the $100 and thereby crowds out $100 of private-sector investments, the actual cost of those displaced investments in terms of foregone consumption, calculated from a social perspective, is really greater than $100. In fact, in the example, the social value of the $100 of capital is really $200 worth of consumption. If all of this is true, the social cost of the project is $200 if the government borrows

the funds and crowds out private investments, because this is the present value of the future stream of consumption foregone.

The discounting literature traditionally has placed great emphasis on determining the methods by which the government obtains the funds to undertake public-sector projects because of their impact on the project's true social cost. The general rule that emerged from the literature was to discount all benefits and costs at the consumption rate of interest, but to adjust these flows first to reflect any changes in private investments that result from either the method the government uses to obtain revenues or the nature of the public project itself. Where private capital is displaced, this adjustment amounts to using the social, instead of the private, value of capital investments in evaluating the costs. Because the social value of $1 of private investment is called the *shadow price of capital*, the overall method recommended in the literature is called the *shadow price of capital-consumption rate of interest* approach, or SPC-CRI.

Given its assumptions, this general approach is both correct and widely acknowledged to be a bit of a mess. There is little guidance on exactly how the analyst is supposed to detect and compensate for changes in private-sector investments as a result of financing government projects. Many hypothetical situations have been studied in which different assumptions are made about the split of a public project's financing between taxes and borrowing. In practice, however, it is unclear how to proceed using this approach even in its simplest form.[5]

Even the magnitude of the shadow price of capital is disputed. The social value of private capital depends on the underlying consumption

---

[5] It is also possible for the benefits public projects provide to cause changes in the level of private-sector investments. Hence, in addition to government financing through borrowing that crowds out private-sector investments, other effects of the public project may increase or decrease private investment activity. This twist adds more layers of complication and computation to what is already a daunting empirical task.

rate of discount, the gross-of-tax rate of return on these investments, and the rate at which the net-of-tax proceeds are consumed or reinvested. In the above example, the shadow price of capital is $2. But that calculation assumes that all of the net-of-tax returns are consumed, rather than reinvested. If this is not the case, the amount of additional investment that occurs must be incorporated into the calculation. Similarly, to compute the shadow price of capital in practice, one must choose from a wide array of rates of return in the economy and select a marginal tax rate. None of this is at all straightforward. In any event, the exact value of the shadow price of capital is not settled in the literature, and it is unclear whether it changes over time and differs depending on the type of project under consideration. Hypothetical examples are easy to specify, but applying them in practice is another matter altogether.

The complexity introduced by the observations that (1) social and private returns on private-sector investments are unequal, and (2) public-project financing can alter the level of private investments, should not be terribly surprising. Recall the earlier discussion in Chapter 5 of the general rules that allow one to limit the analysis to the specific market in which an intervention occurs. There, one condition that necessitates extending the analyses beyond the market of primary interest is when social and private valuations in another market are not the same *and* the quantity in that market changes as a result of the intervention being analyzed. The issue that preoccupies the social discounting literature is essentially an example of this *related market* problem. If a government action changes the level of private-sector investment and the social and private valuations of these investments are unequal, this market must be examined. In the end, the bad news is that if all of this is really true, the literature offers copious caveats and points out many pitfalls, but almost no practical guidance on actually applying these lessons.

Possible Irrelevance of the Shadow Price of Capital Adjustment: The good news is that in practice, no one has ever really followed the SPC-CRI method's requirement to adjust the cost flows (and possibly the benefits as well) using the shadow price of capital. One explanation for this is perhaps that the exact value of the shadow price of capital and precisely how private-sector investment might change as a result of undertaking a public project are both too difficult to calculate in practice. More important, however, is that making these adjustments tends to raise the estimated social costs of government programs, especially environmental rules. Analyses of the costs and benefits of public policies typically are conducted by, or for, policy makers who wish to undertake programs and regulations. They would not eagerly embrace a theoretical recommendation that tends to reduce the economic attractiveness of their proposals across the board.

Even better news is that it turns out that it might not be necessary to worry about the shadow price of capital and its complex adjustments. If not, the basic social discounting procedures would then collapse to simply discounting benefits and costs using the consumption rate of interest. The argument for not bothering with these adjustments is as follows:[6] If the U. S. economy is open in the sense that capital flows into and out of the country, and the world capital market is large enough to render the supply of investment funds perfectly elastic over the range of the relevant quantity variations, then the amount of private investment in the United States will be unaffected by marginal government project financing activities. That is, additional U. S. government borrowing no longer crowds out domestic private investments because the supply of funds is assumed to be provided by large domestic and international sources that stand ready to finance the existing level of private investments and increased gov-

---

[6] This proposition is advanced in Lind (1990). See note 2.

ernment borrowing. In this event, although the social value of private investments is still greater than their private value, because the amount of these investments will not change, the consumption rate of interest can be used to discount benefits and costs without any further adjustments.

It may seem a bit strange that the social costs of public projects can be lowered by simply altering the assumption about whether government borrowing crowds out private-sector investments. Upon reflection, however, this should be reasonably intuitive. The assumptions that the economy is closed, that the supply of capital is very inelastic, and that investments are taxed, collectively impose a significant cost on government debt finance. To borrow another dollar, the government must agree to pay the gross-of-tax rate of return. Although the government also receives tax revenues owed by those to whom it pays interest, if its borrowing crowds out a dollar of private investment, the government will lose an identical amount of taxes that would have been paid on the displaced capital. This implies that the social cost of additional borrowing is the full gross-of-tax rate of return. The present value of this stream of costs is obtained by discounting at the lower consumption rate of interest, which implies that the social cost of an additional dollar of government borrowing exceeds one dollar. These are the circumstances, of course, when the costs should be adjusted upward by the shadow price of capital.

But when the economy is opened and the supply of capital is made perfectly elastic, the impact of an additional dollar of government borrowing will be very different. The government still pays the gross-of-tax rate of return on its debt and gains back the tax revenues owed by those from whom it borrows, but there is no corresponding loss of tax revenues from private sector investments because no crowding out occurs. This means that the social cost of this additional borrowing is only the net-of-tax rate of return, which is the consumption rate of interest. Hence, in this case no adjustment of the costs is neces-

sary. The supply of capital elasticity, therefore, significantly affects the results. An elastic supply allows additional government borrowing without displacing domestic investments that are ultimately worth more to society than the amount of the borrowing itself. An inelastic supply, however, results in this socially costly crowding out of private investments.[7]

The argument that the level of domestic private investment will not be affected by additional U.S. government borrowing is not entirely air-tight, for several reasons. One is that the United States is large relative to the world capital market. Hence, altering U.S. government financing activities could change world interest rates and U.S. investment as a result. Another quibble is that the argument only suggests that government borrowing will not change the level of private investment. But public projects could affect the economic viability of private investments in other ways, thereby generating changes in the level of those investments indirectly.

In the end, it is probably most productive, if not more realistic, to accept the position that the method of financing government programs does not alter total U.S. private investment, because the alternative is to spend the time and effort necessary to try to perform (probably unsuccess-

---

[7] Two further observations are of interest here. First, the open economy assumption is not absolutely necessary because it does not matter whether the additional funds are borrowed from domestic or international sources, or whether this displaces foreign investment and consumption or only domestic consumption, as long as domestic investment is not crowded out. The open economy assumption, however, does make a perfectly elastic supply of investment funds more plausible. Second, what really drives the results is the tax on investment earnings. Without this tax, the cost of marginal additional government borrowing is the same under either assumption about the elasticity of supply of investment funds. In this case, there are no tax revenue consequences of crowding out private investments, so a dollar of displaced private investment is worth one dollar of consumption from a social perspective. Hence, with no taxes on investment earnings, it is no longer important whether the borrowing displaces domestic investment or consumption, so the elasticity of capital supply, in either an open or a closed economy, becomes irrelevant.

fully) the required shadow price of capital and related adjustments. Analytical life is far simpler if the general rule for discounting from a social perspective is to use the consumption rate of interest for both costs and benefits and leave matters at that.

Even with this welcome simplification, there is more than enough unresolved controversy concerning exactly what value one should use as the consumption rate of interest. This will be addressed shortly. But first it is useful to examine an alternative approach to social discounting that is inaccurate, but nevertheless is quite plausible, and enjoys widespread support in the literature and among many analysts.

THE "HURDLE RATE" APPROACH

The "hurdle rate" approach to social discounting is relatively easy to understand. The term *hurdle* refers to the idea that if a public sector project is to be undertaken, it should provide a rate of return that is at least as high as the foregone rates of return provided by the resources it consumes. This sounds very close to the notion of discounting, and it is indeed quite similar. But it is ultimately an incorrect way to discount in public project evaluation.

The hurdle rate approach assumes, as does most of the social discounting literature, that the economy is closed and that the supply of private-sector investment funds is inelastic, so that government borrowing tends to crowd out private investments. As discussed above, in this situation the source of the funds used to finance the public project, taxes versus borrowing, affects the project's net cost.

Under the hurdle rate approach, however, one does not use the shadow price of capital to adjust the costs of the project to account for the full social costs of government borrowing. Instead, this method suggests developing a required minimum rate of return for the public project, a *hurdle rate*, based on a weighted average of the consumption rate of interest and the gross-of-

tax rate of return on private-sector investments, where the weights are the proportions of the project's cost financed by taxes and borrowing, respectively. The criterion for deciding whether a proposed project should be undertaken is whether its internal rate of return (the discount rate that renders the project's *net present value* equal to zero) exceeds this weighted-average minimum hurdle rate.

This approach sounds quite reasonable and intuitive. Indeed, it is quite plausible to argue that if a public project's funding flows, say, equally from taxes and borrowing, then half of the costs will displace consumption directly, and the other half will displace private investments. It seems natural to require a rate of return for the public project no less than a rate equal to the average of the consumption rate of interest (for the tax portion of the financing) and the gross-of-tax social rate of return on private investments (for the borrowing portion of the costs).

Despite its plausibility, the hurdle rate approach in general cannot be relied upon to yield correct project evaluation conclusions. In the numerical example used earlier, if the public project's $100 costs are drawn, say, 75 percent from borrowing and 25 percent from taxes, the hurdle-rate approach would require that the public project yield a rate of at least 3.5 percent, which is 25 percent of the 2 percent consumption rate of interest, and 75 percent of the 4 percent gross-of-tax social rate of return on private investments. Clearly, given the $120 worth of benefits next year, providing a 20 percent internal rate of return, the project more than satisfies this criterion.

But consider a slightly different public project than before. This project still costs $100, which is assumed to be drawn 75 percent from borrowing and 25 percent from taxation. The benefits of this project, however, are $500 worth of environmental improvement to be enjoyed 50 years in the future. Using the hurdle rate approach, this project fails to qualify because its internal rate of return—the discount rate that makes the present value of the $500 of benefits equal to the

$100 privately measured cost of the project—is approximately 3.27 percent, which is less than the required minimum of 3.5 percent.

But is the project really not worth undertaking? To check this, apply the correct SPC-CRI approach (assuming an inelastic supply of investment funds) to the problem. First calculate the total social cost of the project. Because of the financing mix, the cost is $175 in terms of current consumption: 25 percent of $100 from taxes and 75 percent of $100 from borrowing, the latter of which is then adjusted by the $2 shadow price of capital used earlier, for a total of $25 plus $150, or $175. Now discount the future benefits at the 2 percent consumption rate of interest over the fifty-year time horizon. The present value of the benefits is approximately $185.76. Subtracting the social costs of $175 results in a social net present value of about $11. Thus, the project is worth undertaking, contrary to the conclusion one reaches using the hurdle rate approach; the hurdle rate approach may seem plausible, but it is inaccurate and generally cannot be relied upon to yield correct project-evaluation conclusions.

The essence of the problem with this alternative approach is that it attempts to accomplish two tasks with only one instrument. One task is discounting for time itself, which normally is accomplished using the consumption rate of interest. The other is capturing the higher social cost of displacing private-sector investment when financing public projects, assuming that this occurs, a task best accomplished using the SPC-CRI. It is therefore easy to see why the hurdle rate approach runs into trouble. In an attempt to account for the displacement of private investment, it essentially raises the time discount rate, in this case to 3.5 percent, to "over-discount" the benefits. But waiting for benefits to materialize, as in this example, really only costs individuals the consumption rate of interest (2 percent), which is considerably less than the required hurdle rate. The longer the benefits are delayed, as a result, the greater will be this

over-charging for the purely time-oriented element of the problem—the time spent waiting for the benefits. It is not clear, however, that the impact of the higher discount rate on the present value of the benefits is necessarily more or less than what is required to be equivalent to directly adjusting the costs to compensate for displacing private investments. The longer the delay until the benefits are enjoyed, the greater the likelihood that the higher discount rate will "charge" too much, as in this example.

The hurdle rate approach can also be too lenient relative to the SPC-CRI method. Suppose the benefits of this $100 project occur one year after the costs, rather than 50 years in the future, but are worth only $150 next year. Given the project's cost of $100, financed 25 percent through taxation and 75 percent via borrowing, the social cost in terms of foregone consumption is $175, as before. The present value of the $150 of future benefits is $147.06 using the 2 percent consumption rate of discount. Accordingly, the SPC-CRI approach would reject the project because its cost of $175 exceeds the present value of the benefits, both measured in terms of current consumption. But the hurdle rate method would declare the project a positive net social investment, because the apparent $100 cost yields $150 in the following year, amounting to an astronomical 50 percent internal rate of return, clearly exceeding the hurdle rate of 3.5 percent. The relatively modest reduction in the present value of this project's benefits due to the overcharging for time under the hurdle rate approach can thus be far less than the required adjustment for displacing private investments.

It is possible to imagine computing a correct hurdle rate tailored to the specific cost and time dimensions of a particular project, so that the calculated required minimum rate of return would accurately signal whether the project has a positive social net present value. Yet, this would require solving the problem correctly first using the SPC-CRI approach, and then transforming the answer into the implied hurdle rate. For example, two projects with identical costs and financing structures, but with different benefit levels and timing, would have different socially correct required hurdle rates of return. All this would ensure accuracy in applying the hurdle rate method, but it would be ridiculous. To get the correct hurdle rate for any given project, one would have to obtain the right answer directly using the SPC-CRI method; why then bother to back-calculate the implied hurdle rate?

Somewhat ironically, the advantage of the hurdle rate approach was thought to be that it might correctly account for the social costs of projects through a simple computation, based only on the mix of public project financing. The method not only fails to deliver on this promise, but to work properly, it becomes quite cumbersome. It is also worth noting that in the context of an elastic supply of investment funds, the hurdle rate approach to social discounting collapses to the simple consumption rate of interest method. That is, if no domestic private investment is displaced, the weights relevant for the hurdle rate approach are 100 percent for the consumption rate of discount and 0 percent for the gross-of-tax rate of return on private investment.

But at a more general level, the notion of adjusting the discount rate for public project evaluation to account for what is really a preexisting divergence of private and social valuations in a related market—the market for private-sector investments in this case—seems a bit strange. Would one consider adjusting the discount rate to account for other types of preexisting distortions, such as environmental externalities in other markets potentially affected by a public program? Probably not. Then why is it that adjusting the discount rate used in public policy evaluation to account for divergences between private and social valuations in the private-sector-investments market seems so natural? The answer is that this is simply an artifact of the similarity between discounting as an inherently interest-rate-related process and the fact that the

"prices" in the market for private-sector investments are interest rates.

One objection to the consumption rate of interest approach for social discounting is closely related to the rationale underlying the hurdle rate approach. Specifically, it is frequently argued that the government is budget-constrained, so that not all public projects worth undertaking are actually funded. This leaves open the possibility that while a particular project might offer positive net social benefits using the consumption rate of interest to discount costs and benefits, other projects might provide even larger net benefits. Hence, so the argument goes, the higher rates of return offered by those foregone alternatives should be used for discounting instead of the consumption rate of interest.

This is off the mark for two reasons. First, adjusting the social discount rate to capture the higher net benefits of alternative unfunded programs would risk the same errors and inaccuracies as the hurdle rate approach, especially when there is significant variation in the time horizons of different projects. As shown here, one should not adjust rates of time discount to reflect other factors of importance to policy makers.

The basic thrust of the complaint is valid, however, because a limited government budget should be spent on the set of projects that yield the highest net social benefits, perhaps defined broadly enough to accommodate distributional and other such policy concerns. But the way to accomplish that is not by changing the discount rate, but by altering the procedures for choosing projects to fund. Furthermore, even if the more advantageous projects are not selected, this does not imply that the project being evaluated should not be undertaken, which would be the outcome of increasing the social discount rate. If the project is worthwhile from a social perspective when discounted at the consumption rate of interest, society is better off with the project than without it. The fact that programs with higher net benefits *could* be funded is irrelevant if the reality is that they will not be undertaken for reasons outside the control of the policy maker.

Finally, the original project whose findings are encapsulated here was charged with evaluating existing administration discounting guidelines at the time. The analysis revealed that the original OMB guidance directing federal agencies to use the 10 percent real rate of discount in public-project and regulatory evaluation was essentially an application of the hurdle rate of return approach, and thus not technically correct. OMB's guidance was also extreme in the sense that the underlying assumptions were that (1) the cost of public projects are entirely financed by borrowing, (2) the gross-of-tax rates of return on these displaced investments are high in real terms, and (3) the supply of investment funds is inelastic, so that changes in private-sector investment in response to financing government projects are potentially large. OMB recently revised its guidance on discounting issues, arguing that in current economic conditions a 7 percent real discount rate is more appropriate.[8] But the new guidelines continue to use the same inaccurate hurdle rate approach to social discounting, only updating it empirically to the 1990s.

DISCOUNTING AND ENVIRONMENTAL REGULATIONS

All of the analysis so far involves situations in which the government uses taxes or borrowing to finance public projects. In addition to undertaking public projects, however, the government also promulgates numerous regulations governing private-sector activities. Fortunately, applying the basic social discounting principles developed for project evaluation to regulations is relatively straightforward. To illustrate discount-

ing in the context of regulations, three different polar cases are examined in which compliance with the regulation involves only (1) additional operating costs, (2) investments with costs that cannot be shifted to consumers, or (3) investments with costs that can be shifted completely to consumers. Operating costs are labor, raw materials, and other noncapital inputs required for pollution abatement. Regulatory investments include long-lived pollution-control equipment at a plant, or the substantial sums required for cleaning up a hazardous waste site. For reasons that will become clear, the second and third cases—those requiring added investments—are examined under both the closed- and open-economy assumptions regarding the elasticity of investment funds supply.

Regulations Imposing Only Operating Costs: Regulations that impose only operating and maintenance compliance costs are the simplest to examine, because the issue of capital investments, which complicates matters so much in the existing literature, are not relevant. Instead, the regulation adds some production costs to a particular process or product in order to reduce environmental damages. In general, the incidence of these types of regulatory costs is shared in the short run by producers and consumers, while in the longer run they tend to shift more toward consumers. To keep matters simple, assume that consumers bear the costs. In this event, the regulation's costs simply raise the price of the product involved, thereby reducing consumer surplus. Discounting only arises in this case if the analysis involves future years. One might model multiple years if one expects significant changes in the relevant markets, discounting future consumer-surplus losses to the present using the consumption rate of interest. This exactly parallels the social discounting literature's advice.

Regulatory Investments with Costs that Cannot Be Shifted to Consumers: Regulations that require investments with costs that cannot be shifted to product purchasers, while an extreme case

[8] Office of Management and Budget, Executive Office of the President, "Guidelines and Discount Rates for Benefit-Cost Analysis of Federal Programs," Circular A-94 Revised, October 29, 1993.

analytically, are not uncommon in practice. Superfund's pursuit of "potentially responsible parties" who may have contributed even the smallest amount to an abandoned hazardous waste site's pollution threat is an all too familiar problem for many corporations and landowners. In such situations, the liability for cleanups is inescapable and rests solely on the responsible parties or their insurers. Costs associated with past actions are difficult to pass through to current consumers, because other firms without the burden of the historical pollution problem that gives rise to the relevant remediation costs can undercut any attempts to increase prices to recover those costs.

Consider this situation first in the context of a financially closed economy where the supply of investment funds is inelastic. Assume as before, a regulation requiring added investments to abate past pollution problems will displace other private-sector capital investment projects. If so, the explicit cost of these rules will fall short of their actual social burden, so these costs should be adjusted by the shadow price of private capital to arrive at the full social cost of the regulation's requirements. The displaced private investments would have yielded both net-of-tax returns to investors and tax revenues to the government. Allocating the funds to environmental cleanups the costs of which cannot be shifted to consumers, however, provides neither.

Now consider the question in an open-economy context with a perfectly elastic international supply of private capital to the United States. In this case, the level of domestic private-sector taxable investments is unchanged because no capital projects will be displaced by the mandated environmental regulatory investment. Hence, those affected by the regulation are poorer by the monetary cost of the required investments, but the government does not lose any tax revenue. As a result, no adjustment of the costs is necessary. These two different results for inelastic and elastic capital supplies mirror the findings above for public-project evaluation,

where the social cost of debt financing of public projects changes significantly when one alters the assumption regarding the elasticity of investment funds supply.

Regulatory Investments with Costs that Can Be Shifted to Consumers: When regulation-induced capital expenditures can be shifted forward to product purchasers, the analysis is slightly different. The basic idea here is that producers will not make the investments required by the regulation unless they expect to achieve a reasonable financial return on them. This required return, of course, is the gross-of-tax rate on alternative investments.

In the inelastically supplied capital context, the total amount of private-sector investment remains the same, before and after the regulation. What changes in this case is the mix of private sector investment, which moves toward more environmental control and improvement from other pursuits. In the process, some private projects are not undertaken, but investors and the government are indifferent, because the government taxes all of the relevant investment opportunities, and these investments will not be made unless they will yield at least the usual gross-of-tax rate of return. Hence, investors still receive the net-of-tax return and the government obtains its tax revenues, so the impact on all parties except consumers is nil. What happens is that consumers pay more for the newly regulated products or activities, enough to compensate investors at the gross-of-tax rate of return that the environmental investment the regulation mandates must yield.

The social cost outcome here—prices rising by enough to produce the gross-of-tax rate of return for the required investments—might seem different from the earlier findings indicating that when financing a project with debt in the face of an inelastic supply of investment funds, the costs should be adjusted by the shadow price of capital. But the difference is more apparent than real. When the government borrows to finance a project under conditions of inelastic supply of capital to the economy, investors and the government are indifferent as to whether the funds remain in private investments or the government borrows them, just as they are when a regulation draws investments into environmental compliance activities from other productive pursuits. Investors in each case receive the gross-of-tax return and pay the government its tax revenue share. It is future taxpayers who are not indifferent, because presumably they will be the source of the extra taxes needed to service the debt, a yearly liability equal to the gross-of-tax rate of return. This stream of higher future taxes to service the added debt for financing a public project is essentially the same phenomenon as the stream of higher future product prices necessary to amortize the additional investments required by an environmental regulation.

Hence, the findings for the two situations are identical when examined party by party. The traditional social discounting literature normally casts the results for the inelastic capital supply case in terms of the shadow price of capital, so that is the way the analysis is presented here. But the same story can be told more simply in terms of investors, the government, and taxpayers, making it more consistent with this analysis of requiring environmental investments under inelastic capital supply conditions.

Now consider the same regulatory-investment cost question in the open economy, perfectly elastic capital supply context. Rather than reducing or changing the mix of private investments in the domestic economy, the regulation actually encourages more private investment by firms in the business of supplying the regulated product or process. In this case, producers still require the environmental investments to yield the gross-of-tax rate of return, so the costs of the investments will be recovered over time through price increases. The government and consumers, however, are not indifferent. Consumers pay the higher costs of the regulation over time be-

cause prices rise to provide the gross-of-tax rate of return for the capital required to comply. The government collects tax revenue from the additional investments.

What this means is that in an open-economy context with a perfectly elastic capital supply, the social cost of a regulation that requires additional capital investments can be estimated without any reference to divergences between the private and social valuations of private-sector investments. Here the government gains the added tax revenues paid by the mandated investments without suffering any offsetting loss of revenues from other sources. Of course, the increased prices paid by consumers will be high enough to compensate for those tax liabilities, but the government is the recipient of these revenues, making the net burden of the required investments simply their dollar cost. Hence, the *net* social welfare effects in this case can be estimated as if there were no taxes at all. Discounting should be conducted using only the consumption rate of interest with no further adjustments.

This is the same result reached in the discounting literature for the case in which increased government borrowing to finance a project does not displace private investment; the government pays the gross-of-tax cost of borrowing, but regains the tax liabilities owed on those payments. In the case of mandated regulatory investments, there are more parties involved and more transfers among them, but the net social effects are still the same.

THE CONSUMPTION RATE OF INTEREST

Even though what has been presented here is not a formal or comprehensive review of the topic, it should be clear that the social discounting literature is vast, scattered, and analytically fascinated with the implications for public project evaluation of the divergence of private and social returns on private investments. But touching on several of the more prominent branches of the literature does provide the necessary background to arrive at informed conclusions about what is reasonable in practical applications of discounting.

Several basic themes are clear. First, at its core the fundamental recommendation of the discounting literature is to use the consumption rate of interest, where this is thought of as the rate at which individuals are willing to trade consumption over time. The justification and intuition for this choice is that one ought to discount a project's future costs and benefits in the same way as do the individuals on whose behalf the program is undertaken.

Second, if one really should try to adjust the results to account for the impact a government program or regulation might have on the level of private-sector investments, the literature offers little guidance for doing so in practice. Furthermore, the shadow price of capital approach actually has rarely been used, largely because of the uncertainty and complexity of the required adjustments, as well as its tendency to raise the estimated costs of public projects.

Finally, it is possible to argue that the shadow price of capital adjustments may not be necessary after all. In an open-economy context with a sufficiently elastic capital supply, government programs and regulations might not significantly affect total domestic private investment. Hence, it may be safe to ignore what has been a fixture in the literature for several decades. If so, this would validate the standard procedure in the world of practical applications of discounting: Simply use the consumption rate of interest.

So if it is acceptable to directly discount costs and benefits of programs and regulations using the consumption rate of interest, what exactly is this rate and how is it derived? A surprisingly small portion of the social discounting literature is devoted to actually justifying particular numerical estimates as the consumption rate of discount.[9] What advice does exist, however, generally advocates using after-tax rates of return, adjusted for inflation, on relatively risk-free financial instruments. Within these confines there are still many candidates. One of the most popular is federal government bonds of various maturities. These are free of default risk, although they are subject to *inflation risk*, the possibility that inflation in the future will be higher than the expectations embedded in their rates of return. Historical returns on various combinations of these bonds, after tax and after adjusting for inflation, generally have ranged from slightly negative to around 2 percent.[10]

Some argue for including other types of assets in the portfolio used to compute the consumption rate of interest, such as common stocks, corporate bonds, and even housing. Doing so generally increases the estimated historical rates of return, depending on what assets are included and what period of time is examined. In the end, however, there is no clear-cut, easy-to-defend estimate for the consumption rate of interest. Analysts in practice use 2 percent and 3 percent quite frequently, although it not unusual to see rates in the 5- to 7-percent range. In practice, those applying OMB's discounting guidance tend to use rates at the higher end.

It might seem a bit unsatisfactory to have taken so much time to encapsulate this admittedly unsettled literature only to find that no one really knows the exact value of the consump-

---

[9] Lind (1982) provides a fairly extensive analysis of the appropriate social discount rates to use in practice. The discussion of specific numerical rates here is based on this source.

[10] In the United States, nominal interest income is taxed. Hence, the way to adjust pre-tax and pre-inflation interest rates is to first subtract the tax liability from the total nominal rate of return and then subtract the inflation experienced from the net of tax nominal rate of return. Because taxes are levied on nominal, rather than real, rates of return, post-inflation, post-tax rates of return tend to be fairly low. For example, a pre-tax nominal rate of return might be, say, 8 percent. If the marginal tax rate is 40 percent, that leaves 4.8 percent for the investor. If the inflation rate is 4 percent, the net-of-tax, post-inflation-realized rate of return is a mere 0.8 percent. If only real, or post-inflation, rates of return were taxed, the result would be very different. In this case, the post-inflation rate of return is 4 percent, the 8 percent nominal rate minus the 4 percent inflation rate. A 40 percent tax rate leaves the investor with a 2.4 percent after-tax real rate of return.

tion rate of interest. A range from about zero to 4 percent or even 5 percent is fairly large, especially when applied to long time-horizon programs. Unfortunately, this is the state of the literature and its guidance. In practice, analysts tend to pick one rate and use that for most of their research, and conduct sensitivity analysis using various alternative rates.

If it is any comfort, no analysis, much less any specific policy proposal, stands or falls on the basis of the discount rate used. It may also be some consolation to realize that uncertainty about the precise value of the consumption rate of interest is probably the least of the major problems of the social discounting process. There are other issues lurking in the background and hiding in the assumptions. For example, the population consists of a wide variety of individuals, with a range of attitudes toward borrowing and lending, and who face different interest rates at which they can do so. Moreover, the interest rate at which individuals can lend is almost always lower than the rate at which they borrow. Even more problematic is that some people borrow using credit cards that charge double-digit rates, while at the same time investing in savings accounts and similar instruments that yield rates in the 3- to 5-percent range. How should these issues be resolved? The answer is that no one really knows. Should analysts use a different discount rate for the benefits and costs experienced by each well-defined segment of the population that shares that rate? That would be completely impractical.

Worse still is the fact that, especially for many environmental programs, the relevant time horizon is often quite long, sometimes spanning centuries. This means that these programs affect the welfare of people who are not yet born. In this case, the central justification for using the consumption rate of interest—ideally the rate used by the individuals bearing the costs and enjoying the benefits—begins to break down. Since these people are not even alive, how can one know their valuations of these programs' effects, much less the rate at which they are willing to trade consumption across time?

There are many technical problems, quantitative issues, and questions of ethics involved in the social discounting issue. The majority of the literature on the topic developed around the technical implications, and the empirical consequences for public project evaluation, of changes in the level of private investment that financing public expenditures might cause. Much of the literature may now be irrelevant.

The core recommendation that discounting should be done using the consumption rate of interest is still valid. Beyond that simple proposition, however, there is little concrete guidance for practitioners. Questions remain concerning the precise value of using the consumption rate of interest, whether and how the diversity of the population should be addressed, and what to do when future generations yet to be born are affected. Hence, the best course in practical applications is to acknowledge all of these complications and caveats, but then to select a discount rate and conduct the analysis. Where intertemporal issues are particularly important, using a range of rates and reporting the underlying flows of costs and benefits over time often help to avoid what can amount to literally an endless argument about the "true" value of the social rate of discount.

Does the Value of Risk Reduction Increase over Time?

The benefits of some environmental regulatory programs have extremely long time horizons, both because the exposure and other processes that give rise to risks operate over many years, and because many of the health and environmental damages that result can take a long time to manifest themselves. When the delay between the present and the time the benefits of a regulatory action are enjoyed is very large, say hundreds of years, using virtually any positive discount rate will render the present value of the benefits almost nil.

In the project upon which this analysis is loosely based, the benefits in the distant future were reduced numbers of cases of skin cancers and other disorders that result from excess ultraviolet radiation (UV) exposure. The regulation under consideration, of course, was the gradual phaseout of the production of ozone-depleting chemicals, such as chlorofluorcarbons (CFCs). Because ozone-protection issues have been discussed several times in connection with studies and applications contained in Chapters 5 and 6, the background details and context will not be repeated here. Suffice it to say that the time horizon for the benefits was hundreds of years, because of the relatively slow atmospheric ozone depletion and recovery processes involved, and the fact that these skin cancers are the result of cumulative lifetime exposures to excess UV.

The Question

In the course of computing present values for the many sources of benefits of reducing ozone depletion, the value of the cancers avoided in the very distant future, although large in absolute number, were reduced substantially when discounted to the present. The question then arose whether the future values of avoiding these cancers would be the same as the value of avoiding similar types of cancers today. Perhaps more to the point, if the value of avoiding these cancer risks were to rise over time, this might at least partially offset the tendency of discounting to make these future benefits so small in present-value terms.

This question has a very compelling intuitive basis. Casual observation, both of historical U.S. trends and of nations with different levels of income and wealth, suggests that richer societies tend to spend more resources on health care and safety than do poorer ones. At first glance it therefore seems reasonable to conclude that if the nation becomes richer over time, the future value of a given reduction in

risk will be worth more than the same reduction in risk is worth today.

Hence, the central task in this project was to explore whether the value of reducing the risks of UV-related damages should rise over time. This analysis briefly reviews the qualitative considerations that bear on this question, and provides an outline of how one might go about finding an answer. In the end, for reasons that will become apparent, quantitative conclusions would be speculative at best. But the outline of an answer, at least what one would need to know in order to approach the question empirically, is occasionally sufficient for these types of questions.

The Analysis

To explore the proposition that rising wealth over time will cause future values of risk reduction to increase, it is helpful to examine two polar situations between which the value of risk reduction seems to fit. First, suppose that one engages in a program whose benefit is, say, the avoidance of the destruction of one apple in some future year. Suppose further that the marginal cost of apple production is constant and unchanging over time (in real terms, of course, not nominal). In this case, the future value of the program's benefit—the value of an apple—is the same as it is today, regardless of how much wealthier future society may be. At the other extreme, suppose one's regulatory program will prevent the destruction of some unique asset of enduring value to society. Here, one would expect the value of the threatened asset to rise over time as society becomes wealthier.

In the first example, one can think of the supply of apples in every future year as horizontal at the same price as today. Hence, regardless of how great the demand for apples is in any given year, the value of the marginal apple is still simply its cost, which will be the same in every year. In the case of the unique asset, however, the supply can be considered to be a vertical schedule, because there is no more to be had at any price. Hence, if the demand for this asset rises over time as society grows wealthier, the price of the asset will increase as well.

The value of environmental risk-reduction probably falls somewhere between these extremes, but exactly where depends on the circumstances and nature of the risks under discussion. The risks of interest in this analysis are those associated with damage to stratospheric ozone caused by ozone-depleting chemicals, which primarily are cancers and other health effects associated with increased exposure to UV. Focusing only on the cancers, the vast majority of these cases are nonfatal, but require medical treatment. Some, however, particularly melanomas, are fatal. Hence, the health risk posed to humans by ozone depletion consists of a number of different events and outcomes depending on the amount of exposure, self-protection measures, detection and treatment technologies, and the probabilities of recovery or death. All of these components—future protection and medical costs avoided, as well as reduced mortality— are relevant for determining the value of reducing that risk.

Some of the components of this risk reduction, particularly the avoided protection costs and medical treatments for nonfatal cancers, resemble the apple example, in that they involve primarily inexpensive prevention measures, such as more UV-blocking lotions and less sunbathing, and corrective medical procedures, such as the removal of benign tumors. Of course, there are other aspects of nonfatal skin cancers that are also valuable to avoid, such as any discomfort and lost work and leisure time. Nevertheless, much of the social cost of nonfatal UV-related health effects consists of prevention and treatment costs, which are related more to the costs of providing these measures and services than they are to the wealth of the society.

Costs of the more serious health outcomes, such as death, however, have more in common with the unique-asset case. Of course, there is no demand-for-life function to be juxtaposed with a single life's supply to determine its value. Instead, the standard economic approach for determining the value of reducing mortality risk typically focuses on the willingness of workers or other populations to accept small changes in mortality risks associated with hazardous occupations or activities in exchange for increased income or other things of value. Summing the total amount of extra compensation required by a specific population for bearing a particular incremental risk of death, and then dividing by the expected increase in mortality, yields what is referred to as *the value of avoiding a statistical death*. Because the incremental mortality risk is normally small, the additional deaths among a large population are thought of as random, hence the term *statistical*.

All of this simply indicates where one ought to look for the components that define the value of UV-related cancer-risk reduction. But the question here is whether any of the cost or other components that make up the value of avoiding ozone-depletion risks will change over time, and whether or not they do so in a way related systematically to wealth. The question clearly has significantly more texture and complexity than the relatively simple observation that as wealth increases, individuals and societies spend more on health care and safety. In particular, it is difficult to forecast the prevention and medical-treatment components of the value of UV-related cancer risk-reduction. Moreover, few of the most likely changes are in the direction of increasing overall social costs. For example, innovations in detection and treatment technologies could greatly lower the cost of the nonfatal health outcomes of excess UV exposure. Even if new and more expensive technologies are developed, these could still substantially reduce overall costs for these disorders, because they presumably would avoid even worse health effects. Perhaps more important, however, is the potential for innovation to shift the distribution of health outcomes of these cancers away from the mortality category into the nonfatal, treatable types. This would reduce the social costs of excess UV exposure by transforming cancer deaths into less-expensive, medically treatable nonfatal cases.

In each of these cases, however, costs are declining, not increasing. Hence, these factors suggest a lower future valuation of at least some components of the value of this type of risk reduction. Furthermore, all of these possible changes in prevention and treatment costs are associated with increasing wealth in only roundabout ways. Presumably, the fact that wealthier societies spend more on health and safety means that the pressure to innovate will be greater, whether these efforts center on cost-reduction or on new and more effective treatment technologies. Similarly, more intensive monitoring that leads to earlier detection of cancers would be more easily afforded by a wealthier society. Yet, none of these and other imaginable linkages between wealth and the avoided prevention and treatment costs of UV-related cancers is very direct, and they are generally not in the direction of higher avoided costs. So far, then, it seems that if anything, increasing wealth might well produce declining marginal values of this type of risk reduction.

Some of the cost components might be more directly and positively related to wealth, such as avoided mortality risk. But even here the ultimate effect of increasing wealth is not completely clear. On the one hand, it is tempting to think of a far wealthier future society, willing and able to expend vast sums to avoid risks to life and limb and, in fact, doing so. But this should not be confused with the willingness to pay for *marginal* risk reduction given the amount that already is devoted to health and safety. While a richer society may spend considerably more on risk reduction than is spent today, this does not mean that the marginal value of mortality risk reduction will be higher then than now.

The future value of mortality risk reduction hinges to a large extent on whether the risks avoided are relatively small and similar to the risks over which future populations have control. Suppose the future mortality risks avoided by actions taken today are small on a per-person basis after accounting for future protection, detection, and treatment. Suppose further that society in the future is both a far wealthier, healthier, and safer one than today.

It is then possible for the value of a small additional reduction in these risks to be worth less to these future individuals than the same marginal risk reduction is to people today. Intuitively, two opposing influences are at work here. One is that richer people, all else being the same, are willing to pay more for marginal amounts of risk reduction than are those who are less wealthy. On this score, one would say that the future value of mortality risk reduction should rise with wealth.

But all else is not the same, because the levels of risks faced by society today and in the future are not equal; by assumption, the former are higher than the latter. Individuals facing higher levels of mortality risk, all else being the same, will be willing to pay more for a small reduction in these risks than those who face lower mortality risks. This is because the higher the probability of death in the first place, the lower the expected value of income or wealth, and hence the greater the willingness to trade wordly goods for a given increment of mortality risk reduction. Thus, societies that already enjoy low levels of risk, everything else the same, will be willing to spend less for marginal risk reduction than more risky ones. As a result, increasing wealth itself suggests a higher marginal valuation of mortality risk reduction, while the fact that the future richer society will probably already face less risk tends to work in the opposite direction.

It is possible, however, to make a stronger case for a value of avoiding the mortality risks of ozone depletion that increases with wealth. Suppose that these risks are large on a per-person basis, and that there is little that future individuals can do to mitigate them. While this future richer society will have spent considerable sums on risk reduction in all other areas, the mortality risks of ozone depletion will be an area of health and safety over which they have less control. In this case, the marginal value of risk reduction in other areas will be lower than for the UV-related risks, because future individuals will have spent so much to reduce the former but can do relatively less about the latter. As a result, the marginal value of reducing future mortality risks associated with ozone depletion will be relatively high and might well be related in some reasonably straightforward way to the rate of increase of wealth.

Ultimately, whether or not the value of avoiding mortality risks increases over time depends on factors and conditions that are very difficult to assess empirically. The value of reducing risks that are small and similar to those that future richer generations can control or mitigate is governed by the opposing influences of increasing wealth, on the one hand, and the probably lower level of risk already enjoyed by future generations, on the other. For large per-person amounts of mortality risk reduction, and those that rep-

resent, in a sense, gaping holes in a future society's ability to control risks, the argument for a rising value over time is much stronger.

Thus, one can make a case for an increasing value of risk reduction over time, but it is a more complex one than simply observing that wealthier societies spend more on health and safety than those that are less wealthy. Clearly, the possibility that the value of mortality risk reduction is related to wealth underlies the view that the overall value of risk reduction should increase over time as society becomes richer. But mortality risk is only one of several components of the value of UV-related cancer risk reduction. Other elements may actually decline over time, depending on innovation in the areas of protection, detection, and treatment technologies, and their costs. Furthermore, any significant shift in the overall health outcomes of excess UV exposure from mortality to the less-expensive nonfatal category will further reduce the value of this sort of risk reduction. It is thus not obvious that the overall value of ozone-depletion risk reduction rises or falls over time, much less whether any link to increasing wealth exists.

Chapter 10

Recent Trends in Environmental Policy: Some Cautionary Notes

Recent years have seen significant improvements in the condition of the environment due in large part both to several decades of close regulatory oversight and enhanced private-sector appreciation of the environmental consequences of its economic activities. In all, the prospects for continued progress in the environmental arena are quite good. The commitment of the private sector to environmental improvement remains strong, and public policy makers are exploring the use of a variety of more sophisticated methods of regulation, such as cost-sensitive market-based approaches, in place of conventional command and control interventions.

Over the years, much of what has occurred as the nation has become "greener" has been unquestionably beneficial. But this trend has also had a somewhat less desirable impact on at least one aspect of environmental policy practice. Specifically, the high public profile environmental protection now enjoys has spawned a growing tendency to formulate policies and adopt methods of evaluation on the basis of the mere appearance of desirability, rather than careful analysis. This chapter presents two illustrations of this problem. The first study summarizes an evaluation of an analytical technique called *environmental life-cycle assessment*, which purports

to be able to inform consumers and producers of the "full" environmental consequences of specific actions or product choices. In essence, this technique seeks to supplement the price system with information about the environmental results of alternative products or actions so that consumers and producers can choose more environmentally benign alternatives. The analysis demonstrates that, despite its desirable goals, life-cycle assessment is hopelessly complex and inaccurate in practice, so that ultimately it only squanders valuable research resources and yields no significant benefits.

The second application illustrates a more specific manifestation of the underlying problem explored in the evaluation of life-cycle assessment. Here the issue is whether one can develop a coherent analytical basis for estimating the net benefits of requiring municipalities to separate (and then presumably recycle) additional amounts of solid waste, also known as garbage. The analysis shows that although an analytically sound framework for assessing the costs and benefits of mandatory increases in solid waste separation can be constructed, applying it empirically would be prohibitively expensive. Moreover, if one actually did spend the time and resources to make the framework operational, the results would yield quantitative waste separation recommendations that would vary by location and material, and would change over time—advice quite at variance with the one-size-fits-all prescriptions typically mandated by proposed solid waste source-separation rules.

Evaluation of Environmental Life-Cycle Assessment

Recent years have seen a surge of interest in conducting analysis commonly referred to as *environmental life-cycle assessment*, or LCA, which seeks to determine which of several products or processes is the "greenest" from an environmental perspective. In the consumer-choice arena, various studies weigh the environmental costs of disposable and cloth diapers; plastic and paper grocery bags; and alternative packaging materials, such as foam and paperboard. LCA is also used to assist producers in evaluating alternative processes and inputs in their attempts to improve industrial environmental performance.

The central motivation of environmental LCA is the belief that products, processes, and other economic activities cause environmental harms that are not adequately controlled, and use natural resources that are not properly priced. Pollution in the form of releases of toxic substances to air, water, and land, inappropriate use of natural resources, such as forests and other habitats, and excessive use of energy and water, all are thought to be widespread and largely underregulated by environmental authorities. Therefore, the goal is to identify and quantify all of the environmental harms associated with alternative products or processes—essentially, to provide "environmental report cards"—so that consumers and producers can "think globally and act locally" by shifting their purchases and practices toward those that cause relatively less environmental damage.

Attempting to provide these environmental report cards, researchers use LCA to try to summarize all of the different sources of environmental harms caused, and natural resources used, by alternative products and processes. In trying to measure all possible sources of environmental problems, LCA seeks to identify not only the obvious pollution caused by a product or process, such as air emissions of toxic chemicals from a manufacturing facility, but also other, less apparent, sources of these problems; for example, environmental harms caused when fuels are burned to provide energy to make an input used in a particular product. It is perhaps the defining feature of LCA that it tries to ferret out this second set of environmental problems for consumers and producers, who are ill-equipped to locate and measure them on their own.

The Question

The central focus of this study is to evaluate the accuracy of practical applications of LCA and, hence, their ability to correctly guide consumer and producer choices to greener alternatives. The analysis is motivated primarily by several observations. One is that LCA results are the subject of sometimes considerable dispute. Indeed, a study championing one consumer choice for a particular product or activity, such as cloth diapers, seems to be quickly matched by another touting the advantages of the alternative. The apparent lack of robustness of LCA results may suggest a deeper problem.

More importantly, although LCAs are becoming increasingly complex and costly to perform, the caveats and cautions attached to these analyses do not seem to diminish. It is somewhat troublesome that more and more research resources appear to produce little increased confidence in the results. Hence, this evaluation is motivated primarily by the lack of robustness of LCA results, despite their growing complexity and cost.

Unlike some other evaluations of LCA, however, this one does not question the central premise that the prices of products, processes, and other economic activities do not adequately reflect their full social costs, particularly their environmental impacts. Whether the environmental problems that motivate LCAs exist is not the issue. Instead, for purposes of this evaluation it is assumed that many environmental problems are associated with various consumer and producer choices, such as pollution caused by energy use, habitat destruction, occupation of scarce landfill space, and so on. The focus here is on whether LCAs can help to mitigate these environmental harms in practice. From a purely analytical perspective, do (or can) the results of practical LCAs correctly guide consumer and producer decisions toward more environmentally benign alternatives?

The Analysis

The analysis proceeds by first outlining what LCA is in theory and in practice, focusing primarily on the analytical technique itself. Following this brief introduction, the analysis turns to evaluating LCA's ability to provide reliable information to consumers and producers concerning environmentally better products and processes. The study concludes by discussing an alternative, more productive approach for addressing the environmental problems that motivate LCA researchers.

WHAT IS ENVIRONMENTAL LIFE-CYCLE ASSESSMENT?

From a theoretical perspective, environmental LCA grows out of two types of analyses. One is the standard environmental assessment of industrial processes that seeks to identify and, where technically and economically feasible, reduce environmental impacts. The primary concern in these studies is to search out and minimize direct pollution caused by a particular process or economic activity.

The other historical root of LCA is the class of studies originating in the 1970s that sought to measure the full "energy content" of specific products and processes. During the energy crisis, it was held that energy use carried a social cost in excess of its price, so that in addition to the price of a product or process, it was important to know its total energy content. Those studies therefore sought to identify all of the energy inputs required for a product not only directly, but also indirectly, such as the energy required to produce and deliver the inputs necessary to make the particular product in question.

Environmental LCA's roots suggest terminology that is useful for the remainder of the discussion: environmental problems caused by the particular activity under study, say water pollution from a plant that assembles automobiles, are called *direct* sources; environmental harms caused by any other economic activities necessary to produce the automobile, such as air pollution from electricity generation, or water pollution associated with mining and smelting ores to make steel (both of which eventually are embodied in the automobile), are called *indirect* sources. The key distinction between the two sources is not the types of harms caused, but rather the activities responsible for those harms.

Environmental LCAs are thus the marriage of studies of direct environmental harms and the far more ambitious energy-use LCAs of two decades ago. In essence, environmental LCA seeks to identify and quantify all of the environmental impacts of a specific product or process that occur both directly and indirectly, through inputs and other economic activities required to ultimately supply the product.

A couple of key features of LCA are critical for understanding and evaluating the technique as an analytical and policy tool. One is obvious, but important enough to repeat: LCA seeks to identify and weigh the total environmental problems associated with a product or process by trying to link specific products or processes with a list of inputs that potentially lead to environmental problems, including the use of energy, water, renewable and nonrenewable natural resources, air and water emissions, and solid and hazardous waste generation. To do so, LCA works backwards from the product, searching for the pollution caused and the natural resources used by the inputs necessary to supply the product; then, in turn, it examines the inputs necessary to supply those inputs for yet more indirectly caused environmental problems. For example, in investigating the indirect sources of environmental harms associated with cloth diapers, the process of manufacturing pesticides that are used on cotton that is then made into diapers must be examined for any environmental problems that result from, say, its use of energy and chemicals, and hazardous waste generation and management.

This is possible *in theory*, but to do so in practice involves an incredibly large data-collection effort. Although it is easy to list many conceivable environmental problems, it is far more difficult to measure them accurately, especially the indirect sources. Direct environmental harms are those visibly caused by the product use or production process, so identifying and quantifying them is conceptually clear-cut, although often still difficult in practice. Indirect environmental problems are even harder to identify, for these are caused by other production processes or activities necessary to the product or process in question. Tabulating indirect sources of harms first requires that one identify all of these economic activities and then determine whether they cause any environmental problems.

Another important point to keep in mind about LCA is that sponsors of these studies do not commission them out of idle curiosity. Rather, they wish to use the results to make the best choice from an environmental perspective. Thus, the use to which these studies are put is invariably to juxtapose two sets of environmental problems associated with two different products or with two different versions of a process.

The object is to determine which choice causes the least net environmental harm. Because LCAs are intended to inform decisions, their value ultimately flows from providing a net decrease in environmental harms by guiding choices to greener alternatives.

To some extent, the terminology employed by LCA researchers tends to obscure the fundamental fact that LCA seeks to help in making choices between competing alternatives. Indeed, saying that the LCA analytical process is geared ultimately toward defining opportunities for environmental improvement conjures up the image of researchers identifying and mitigating direct environmental harms caused by a product or process, such as direct air or water emissions. This, however, is only part of the story.

Often LCAs explore the tradeoffs between two processes whose environmental differences are largely the result of indirect sources of problems, not direct ones. One process might directly and indirectly, through all of its myriad inputs, use more water and virgin materials, but less energy than another. Thus, obtaining actual environmental improvements by using LCA is really a process of weighing environmental harms from both indirect and direct sources. Trading off environmental damages from all sources is very different from attempting to minimize the direct pollution consequences of an activity, as will be shown later.

In practice, LCAs begin by specifying the *system* surrounding the activity or product in question. In general, the system is thought of as one requiring inputs from the earth, for example, energy and natural resources, and generating outputs of wastes and emissions of chemicals. Activities in the system to be studied normally include raw materials acquisition, manufacturing, fabrication, distribution, use and reuse, and waste management. Most of the effort in life-cycle studies is on specifying numerous linkages from sector to sector and activity to activity, to assess direct and indirect sources of environmental problems.

Practical life-cycle studies use public and private data sources on process technologies and their inputs and outputs, sector by sector, to generate a rough sketch of the total "cradle-to-grave" environmental problems a product or process poses. Given the problem's vast complexity and the nature and aggregation of the available information, LCA researchers normally can only examine "typical" product manufacturing practices and inputs based on national averages, using engineering studies of the processes involved and a significant amount of professional judgment.

While LCAs in practice seek to be internally consistent and generally attempt to be as comprehensive and detailed as possible within time and budgetary constraints, one aspect of these studies is somewhat troubling, even to the researchers involved. Actual examples of LCA always seem to contain a long list of caveats acknowledging the limitations of the available data. But repeated attempts to remedy these deficiencies by delving deeper into details and expanding the sets of economic activities incorporated suggest that the results are not robust. That is, it seems easy to find new sources of significant environmental problems, or to radically alter their magnitude, and thus change the latest "answer," by expanding the scope of the analysis or by further refining and disaggregating the input information.

WHY DOESN'T LIFE-CYCLE ASSESSMENT WORK?

To evaluate the prospects for the practical use of LCA, it is best to return to the fundamental questions these types of analyses seek to answer. Doing so provides a clear sense of the nature of the analytical and empirical efforts required to provide information that is useful to consumers and producers in making environmentally better choices. This discussion introduces and analyzes several fundamental propositions concerning LCA which, taken to-gether, point to fairly strong conclusions about the likelihood that these analyses will ever be sufficiently robust in practice.

There Isn't One Right Answer: To begin with, typically, there isn't one "right" answer to the choice between two products or activities as normally posed in LCA. For example, the environmentally correct diaper decision generally will depend on the location and circumstances of the person making the choice. Proponents of disposable diapers argue that cloth diapers require energy to heat water to wash them and damage waterways through discharges of detergent-laden wastewater. Proponents of cloth diapers claim that disposables use petroleum and occupy scarce landfill space. While all this may be true, it is easy to see that the importance and severity of these different environmental concerns can depend on many factors that vary across the country and change over time. Landfill space is probably a more important environmental issue in metropolitan areas than in rural locales, and the environmental effects of energy production and wastewater discharge depend on the location and existing pollution controls of power generation and wastewater-treatment plants.

It is thus obvious that there isn't one right answer to the diaper question, or really for any of the typical choices LCA researchers investigate. Nevertheless, the LCA industry continues to pursue a single "correct" diaper answer for essentially a "typical" person in an overall "national-average" setting. Worse still, even the emerging LCA guidance literature appears not to recognize this point. As a result, whatever answer an LCA reaches is not necessarily applicable to any specific person or any real-world setting whose circumstances differ from those assumed in the study.

Advocates of LCA might argue that pursuing a single correct answer could still be beneficial overall: if one diaper choice is environmentally better "on average" or for the "typical" individual, the environment will be better off if everyone pursued that choice. This reasoning is faulty. The key issue here is that one should not compare the overall environmental consequences of everyone choosing one product with those that would result if everyone chose the other. Rather, one should compare the environmental effects of any LCA-induced changes in consumers' or producers' decisions with the environmental effects of their *current* choices.

To illustrate the importance and implications of this problem, consider the following highly simplified example of the diaper decision. Table 10-1 lists the levels of environmental problems caused by two different people's decisions about diapers. Mary, who uses disposable diapers, owns an electric washer and dryer system in an area where water tends to be relatively more valuable than is reflected in its price, and power generation involves relatively more pollution than in other locations. John, who uses cloth diapers, lives in a crowded eastern city where the main problem is the high social cost of solid-waste disposal. As the entries in the table indicate, each of these individuals currently makes the environmentally correct choice for her or his circumstances, Mary electing to use disposables and John cloth.

Now suppose LCA produces environmental results for "typical" or "national-average" cloth and disposable diapers, and concludes that one of these options is more environmentally benign. In this example, averaging the environmental problems for both Mary and John over the two choices yields a score of 50 for cloth and 60 for disposables, so such a study would recommend cloth over disposables. Clearly, starting from a situation in which Mary and John are already making the right choice (by accident or otherwise), if they both follow the advice of the study, one will switch from making the right choice to the wrong one, as Mary would here.

The example generalizes to situations with more than two people, and of course one can alter the assumptions to show that in other circumstances, acting on the advice of LCA's single list of environmental problems enhances environmental quality. Yet, the essential point is that it is possible for a one-size-fits-all LCA recommendation to increase environmental harms. Even worse, there is no way to know whether reporting a single LCA "answer" will lead to overall environmental improvement or harm unless the details of specific circumstances are explored. In the example, the life-cycle researcher does not know the levels of specific environmental harms for Mary and John individually, only the national average information is estimated. Hence, unless the specifics of different individuals' circumstances are investigated, it is not clear that the net environmental effects of LCA will be beneficial.

Table 10-1
ENVIRONMENTAL PROBLEMS AND THE CORRECT DIAPER CHOICE: HYPOTHETICAL MAGNITUDE OF ENVIRONMENTAL HARMS

Category	Mary		John		National Average	
	Cloth	Disposables	Cloth	Disposables	Cloth	Disposables
Energy/Air	20	5	10	5	15	5
Virgin Materials	5	20	5	20	5	20
Water	20	0	5	0	12.5	0
Effluent	10	5	10	5	10	5
Solid Waste	5	10	10	50	7.5	30
Total	60	40	40	80	50	60

LCAs Don't Really Measure Actual Environmental Harms: Practical LCAs focus mainly on what is referred to as the "inventory" stage of the assessment, which seeks to tabulate conceivable or possible sources, or precursors, of actual environmental harms. For example, many LCAs report estimates of a product's direct and indirect energy requirements in British Thermal Units (Btus), water use in gallons, landfill requirements in cubic yards, atmospheric emissions of chemicals in pounds, use of virgin materials such as timber in feet or pounds, and water emissions in various units, including pounds or gallons, oxygen demand, and suspended solids.

Thus, contrary to popular conceptions of these studies, practical LCAs do not measure the actual environmental harms of concern, tabulating instead possible proxies for them. But it is not energy use per se that is the environmental problem; rather, it is the harm caused in the process of generating and using the energy that is of concern. Similarly, chemical emissions do not themselves measure any environmental damages. One needs to know, at a minimum, the location, the types, and the numbers of receptors affected to estimate the actual environmental harms these emissions cause. Proponents of LCA will not find this point particularly troubling because, as they maintain, the inventory stage of an LCA is but the beginning, to be followed shortly by the *impacts* and *improvements* stages, which then will address the actual harms caused and the benefits of choosing alternative products and processes.

But practical LCAs never undertake these other stages, probably for the same reason they continue to pursue a single one-size-fits-all answer despite the obvious fact that this ignores the essential texture of the problem. Because tracing the indirect sources of environmental problems for a product even at an aggregated "national-average," "typical-person" level is a challenging task, LCA researchers have more than enough complexity to handle already. But

as soon as LCA researchers attempt to connect actual environmental damages to their lists of a product's use of energy, water, petroleum, trees, landfill space, and other resources, the inadequacies of a single national-average estimate of a product's total environmental impact will become clear. By ignoring all of this, what amounts to a profound methodological problem is disguised as just one of the many standard caveats and limitations of LCA.

Accurate LCAs Are Very Costly and Complex: The empirical task LCA sets out for itself is inherently unmanageable, as even casual reflection reveals. Consider a hypothetical LCA focusing on a bar of soap as discussed in one of the LCA guidance documents.[1] Attempting to define the sectors that need to be included in such an analysis, a variety of activities related to soap manufacturing are mentioned, such as grain production, cattle raising, meat packing and tallow rendering, salt mining, caustic manufacturing, paper production, and postconsumer waste management. The analyst is supposed to examine each of these economic activities to assess all of the possible environmental problems each could cause. Many items of potential importance, such as whether the two soap products require different amounts of transportation or water, are not even explicitly mentioned. Thus, what at first seems to be a simple tallying of environmental harms instead escalates into a major data-intensive investigation.

But matters are even worse. The guidance document indicates that even the energy needed to make the tire on the combine used to harvest the grain to feed the cattle to supply the tallow to make the soap can be considered an input into the process. This should give one pause. The complexity of the analysis appears to be limited only by the ingenuity of the researcher and his

[1] B. W. Vigon, D. A. Tolle, B. W. Cornaby, H. C. Latham, C. L. Harrison, T. L. Boguski, R. G. Hunt, and J. D. Sellers, *Life-Cycle Assessment: Inventory Guidelines and Principles*, prepared for U.S. Environmental Protection Agency, November 1992.

or her research resources. The main problem is that this backtracking through inputs to inputs that "fan out" through the entire economy quickly gets out of hand unless one can confidently decide just how much detail is sufficient and just how far away from the product an input can be before it is safe to exclude it from the analysis. And all of this is still only in service of merely identifying the constellation of inputs for a product, however remote, not the actual environmental damages they cause.

"Associated With" Is Not the Same as "Caused By": Another problem similar to that posed by the inherent complexity of LCA is often ignored in the literature, but is extremely important. Specifically, it is not enough to identify environmental problems "associated with" products or processes as many LCAs indicate they do. Instead, one must conceptualize altering consumers' or producers' choices, deciding between plastic or paper grocery sacks for example, and then determine to what extent the environmental harms of concern change in response. This is not an easy task, because often the actual changes in economic activities that result, and the changes in the levels of environmental problems of concern, may require significant detailed information to predict, and can be different from what one might expect based on casual analysis.

For example, if a less energy-intensive product is recommended over a more energy-intensive one, less power will be required. But exactly what fuel will be saved and what environmental harms will be avoided are difficult to determine. Electric power is routinely traded across transmission grids, so it is not clear precisely where lower electricity generation will occur or exactly what environmental harms will be reduced. Similarly, suppose significant environmental problems of concern in a particular LCA include the erosion and water-quality effects of logging in the United States. But if the U.S. timber industry participates in a large international market for timber, pulp, and paper products,

shifting consumer choices toward products that use less virgin timber will not necessarily reduce the amount of U.S. logging and its attendant damages. Under plausible conditions, the same amount of U.S. logging continues, regardless of any changes in consumer and producer choices as guided by LCAs. Predicting what will actually happen to the levels of economic activities remotely connected to the decision under study, much less any changes in the environmental problems of concern they cause, is a very tricky business that, to its detriment, is largely ignored in the LCA literature.

Complexity Is Unavoidable: That seeking to catalog all (or at least "enough") of a product's direct and indirect environmental problems is complex and costly should not be surprising. LCA researchers essentially seek to develop an information system that provides the same type of data normally summarized and communicated by the price system. Prices of economic goods and services summarize the costs of their supply, regardless of how remote those costs are from the product or service in question. As goods move through the chain of production and commerce, the cost of the primary inputs (labor, capital, land, and raw materials) incorporated at successive stages of a product's supply are added to its price. All of this information transmission is accomplished without the guidance of any single entity, but as the result of the anonymous functioning of the market and the price system.

LCA, however, is motivated by a fundamental belief that many environmental problems are not adequately captured in prices, or at least that social concern for environmental harms and natural resource use surpasses merely their prices. As a result, LCA practitioners must attempt to trace from products and processes back through layer upon layer of other economic activities associated with them to identify and quantify indirect sources of environmental problems. Thus, the real problem for LCA is not measuring environmental concerns for known processes and activities, for one can reasonably expect that once the activity, its location, and other relevant features are specified, experts can judge whether it causes significant environmental degradation or other harms. Instead, it is the need to trace through so many of the economic activities connected to a product or process, stopping to determine whether harms are caused at each point, that makes LCA so complex and difficult.

Setting Practical Boundaries for LCA Precludes Accuracy: All of these issues raise the obvious question of just how much disaggregation and how wide a scope are really required for LCA to ensure accuracy. This is the central tension in LCA today, pitting the detail, scope, and accuracy of such studies, which determine whether their results have any real value, against the cost and feasibility of conducting them, which govern their practicality.

On the one hand, practical LCA researchers labor hard to incorporate whatever details and complexity they can, and generate large amounts of information. Despite the inevitable caveats, limitations, and omissions, it is assumed that what can be (or, perhaps, might be) accomplished in practice still has value to consumers and producers in helping them choose environmentally more benign products and processes. This is the sense conveyed by many statements concerning boundary setting in the life-cycle literature. For example, in the section pertaining to the raw materials and energy component of LCA in SETAC's *A Technical Framework for Life-Cycle Assessments,*[2] the following discussion is revealing:

> A fundamental concept that must be accepted by anyone undertaking an inventory is that the raw materials acquisition system not only extends all the way back to the source for each primary raw material, but also extends laterally to include all

inputs of energy, materials, and equipment necessary for executing each step of acquisition. Obviously such an analysis soon becomes intractable without some methodology for screening insignificant contributions. It may be necessary to extend the analysis of material inputs beyond the first level to second or even multiple levels to identify all significant contributions. In some cases such secondary contributions are the source of the most crucial impacts of all.

The issue from an analytical point of view is how to define the criteria that will determine what is insignificant and can be discarded or ignored. In the absence of superior logic, an analyst must rely on professional judgement or must establish an arbitrary threshold (e.g., components comprising less than 5 percent of the inputs will be ignored). [2]

On the other hand, the guidance literature states that setting arbitrary boundaries on LCAs imposes limitations on the accuracy and comprehensiveness of their results. Therefore, when arbitrary boundaries are set, one cannot make statements about the total level of, or change in, any environmental problems of concern that might be affected outside the system examined. For example, EPA's *Life-Cycle Assessment: Inventory Guidelines and Principles* states the following:

> Depending on the goal of the study, it may be possible to exclude certain stages or activities and still address the issues for which the life-cycle inventory is being performed. For example, it may be possible to exclude the acquisition of raw materials in a life-cycle inventory without affecting the results. Suppose a company wishes to perform an internal life-cycle inventory to evaluate alternative drying systems for formulating a snack food product. If the technologies are indifferent to feedstock, it is possible to assume the raw materials acquisition stage will be identical for all options. If the decision will be based on selecting a drying system with lower energy use or environmental burdens, it may be acceptable to analyze such a limited system. However, with this system boundary, the degree of absolute difference in the overall system energy or environmental inventory cannot be determined. The dif-

[2] Society of Environmental Toxicology and Chemistry and SETAC Foundation for Environmental Education, Inc., *A Technical Framework for Life-Cycle Assessments*, January 1991, 34.

ference in the product manufacturing stage, although significant for the manufacturer, may represent a minor component of the total system. Therefore, statements about the total system should not be made. [p. 19]

The source of the tension is obvious. What can be done in practice necessarily involves setting limitations on the study's boundaries, reining in the scope, and neglecting the immense complexity and details of the real world. Still, one would think that what can be done in practice, albeit imperfect, is still valuable. However, if one cannot make statements about total changes in the levels of particular environmental problems if some of those changes occur outside the boundaries set for the study, what does this mean for the value of practical LCAs? Can nonarbitrary and defensible boundaries be defined to make LCA both feasible and accurate?

The key issue in setting analytical boundaries for LCA is whether in doing so, one has any confidence that excluded elements, or any lack of disaggregation and detail, could harbor environmental problems great enough, or sufficiently different, that consumers and producers would wish to know them before revising their product or process decisions. But setting boundaries is problematic for practical LCA researchers, because there is little *a priori* basis for assuming that the elements excluded from the analysis necessarily are smaller than those included. Indirect sources of environmental problems that LCA seeks to quantify usually are not incorporated in prices. Hence, economic measures of remote or small activities related to a product do not necessarily translate directly into conclusions about the significance of the environmental problems associated with those activities. It is entirely possible for a remote activity that constitutes a small portion of the overall cost of a product to harbor an environmental harm of great significance.

This tension between accuracy and feasibility largely explains the results of practical applications of LCA. For example, several recent attempts to assess the relative life-cycle environmental impacts of cloth and disposable diapers devote considerable effort to tracing the indirect impacts of each alternative in greater depth than previous studies, although they arrive at mixed and different conclusions. One study in particular devotes nearly six pages out of a total of 40 pages in the summary report to describing why its results are superior to previous attempts: because its "boundaries" are more expansive than earlier assessments. Similarly, according to one observer of the diapers debate, one set of researchers is said to have used the national-average cotton production characteristics in evaluating cloth diapers. Apparently, unknown to those researchers, the cotton required to manufacture cloth diapers is a particular variety grown only in the southwestern United States. The social cost of water in this region is presumably far higher than in the nation as a whole.

Finally, a recent LCA report on packaging prepared by the Tellus Institute gives an indication of just how wide the gulf is between what is required for definitive LCA results and what really is possible even with an extremely large commitment of resources.[3] This report, some 900 pages long, summarizes several years of research. Unfortunately, even a study of this magnitude and obvious expense still must admit that it is far from complete and accurate. A few of the limitations enumerated in the report include out-of-date information; omission of the package-forming, filling, and transportation stages; omission of the industrial solid-waste sector; absence of the plastics-recycling sector; and no explicit accounting for habitat destruction, old-growth forest cutting, and other considerations related to timber production.

The Tellus study suggests that readers "who are concerned about virgin materials depletion should consider that factor in addition to the

---

[3] Tellus Institute, *CSG/Tellus Packaging Study*, prepared for The Council of State Governments and the U.S. Environmental Protection Agency, May 1992.

analysis presented here, when evaluating materials recycling options." One wonders how the reader is supposed to do this if the voluminous and expensive study in his or her hands failed to do so. Even this extremely data-intensive effort, focusing only on inventorying national-average estimates of inputs that might conceivably cause environmental harms still cannot arrive at the level of detail and comprehensiveness necessary to give consumers and producers definitive information to improve their choices.

Summary Evaluation of LCA: While LCA's underlying motivation is laudable, and LCA researchers are capable of generating large quantities of numbers, the prospects for ever obtaining accurate advice for consumers and producers at practical levels of effort is really just a hope based only on remote theoretical possibility, not on any real evidence of feasibility. What LCA can reasonably accomplish in practice is very limited: pursuing a single correct answer when there are multiple ones that change over time, seeking problems "associated with" rather than "caused by"; setting boundaries based on practical feasibility rather than on the belief that a wider scope and more disaggregation are not necessary for accurate results; and never really identifying and measuring the numerous location-dependent environmental harms that actually occur. Because of all this, additional research using this approach is unlikely to result in any increased confidence in the results.

Future LCAs will become increasingly complex and expensive, but will never really deliver on their promise to confidently guide consumer and producer choices toward environmentally more benign alternatives. To be sure, more details will be included, and more pages of results will be generated, but the sense that any significant progress has been made toward conclusive, widely applicable, and durable results of value to consumers and producers will be an illusion.

The problem is not that nothing can be done

within the practical limitations of financial feasibility, for the reams of results LCAs can generate are a testament to the creativity and commitment of these researchers. Instead, it is that what generally can be done within practical levels of effort shows that all products and processes are potentially associated directly and indirectly with a host of environmental problems, so that making choices between alternatives is already problematic. LCAs then so severely qualify the results with caveats, limitations, simplifications, omissions, and other problems, that one has no confidence that more details and wider boundaries will not reveal more substantially important environmental problems. Practical applications of LCA, therefore, do not provide conclusive results of any use in guiding consumer and producer choices toward greener alternatives.

But nothing in this evaluation of LCA indicts individuals' everyday common sense attempts to avoid harming the environment. Reducing litter, reusing resources such as grocery sacks and aluminum foil, and conserving energy and other natural resources to minimize one's direct contribution to harming the environment are all laudable and worthwhile pursuits. Traditional notions of environmentally friendly consumer behavior are uncomplicated and are likely to result in the environmental benefits that motivate them.

It is the extension of this notion to product choices not involving obvious differences in direct environmental harms that causes problems. As soon as consumers try to purchase greener products based on both their indirect and direct contributions to environmental harms, they are confronted with a host of competing claims and counterclaims. Aware that "green" is also profitable, marketers then begin to expand the environmental and analytical criteria by which products are evaluated. Claims about the indirect environmental characteristics of products then become the weapons with which an expensive war is waged for the consumer's environmental conscience (and dollar).

Of course, all of this provides a perfect garden for a classical "prisoner's dilemma" to grow, one in which a manufacturer who does not engage in studies to prove the environmental friendliness of his or her product will be at a disadvantage relative to competitors who do make these claims. Unfortunately, these parties probably all know that these green claims are on shaky ground, but they nevertheless must defend themselves at significant private and social expense.

A More Productive Approach

The conclusions reached about LCA seem to leave researchers without any recourse for addressing the environmental problems they consider so serious and widespread. Indeed, for several reasons, this conclusion may seem somewhat depressing. First, and probably most obvious, is that the hope that LCA will generate meaningful and accurate guidance for consumers and producers, at least at some point in the future, will never be fulfilled. It is difficult to accept that all of the honest and diligent efforts to improve LCA techniques, data, and results will not yield beneficial results.

The evaluation's findings are all the more troubling, because LCA might be viewed as the culmination of what has been a long process of public education concerning the environment. The past several decades have seen a significant change in public awareness of the natural world and the impact of human activities have on it. Concurrent with this shift in public attitudes, many environmental improvements, great and small, have occurred. LCA's ultimate motivation is to empower individuals so that they can help the environment by altering their choices. That LCA cannot fulfill that goal is sad, but true. But if LCA cannot help to address the environmental problems that motivate these analyses, does this mean that we can do nothing at all about them?

Fortunately, there is an alternative approach for addressing these environmental harms, one that avoids LCA's insurmountable difficulties of tracing and tabulating the economic activities remotely associated with a product or process to detect and measure indirect sources. This more productive approach is simple and quite conventional: Attack the environmental harms and inappropriate resource uses where they occur, using the variety of tools at the disposal of the environmental authority. That is, if one believes that these environmental damages exist, they should be identified and corrected with the arsenal of regulatory and nonregulatory approaches normally used to attack pollution problems.

For example, if one of the important environmental concerns is habitat destruction, erosion, and turbidity caused by logging forests, the suggested approach calls for developing regulatory policies that strike at the heart of the problem directly. Limitations on logging, standards for cutting and preservation, even taxes on the damaging consequences of logging, all might be considered good candidates for addressing these problems. The results of directly applying corrective environmental regulations of one sort or another will be both a reduction in the actual damages caused by logging and, in general, an increase in the prices of products for which logging is an input.

Similarly, if another environmental concern is potential harm to human health and the environment caused by over-using fertilizers and pesticides, the traditional approach would suggest attacking these problems at their sources by developing stronger regulatory and other programs to limit these risks. These might include additional restrictions on pesticide application procedures, limitations on using certain types of fertilizers and pesticides in particular areas or in certain circumstances, and so forth. Again, the result of these direct approaches would be a reduction in these environmental risks and increased prices for items whose supply causes the pesticides and fertilizer use in the first place.

Of course, the suggested approach offers no magic wand that will easily wipe away the nation's environmental problems. It is no more and no less than the traditional recommendation that successful environmental management and stewardship generally flow from clear problem definition and careful development and application of regulatory and nonregulatory mechanisms to address problems. But the advantages of the suggested strategy are many.

First, it immediately focuses efforts directly on the problems of concern in LCA—widespread environmental harms and inappropriate or underpriced natural resource use. Practical LCAs never really arrive at the ultimate harms of concern. Instead, all of the resources are expended in attempting to trace particular consumer and producer decisions back through the almost infinitely complex interconnections of the economy to those harms, and then hoping that the responses to the answer generated will wend their way back to the problems exactly as predicted. There are obvious advantages to beginning with the environmental problems to be solved rather than leaving their identification and measurement for later.

Identifying, quantifying, and mitigating specific environmental problems directly where and when they occur offers a second advantage. Under this approach, the costs of the controls or other pollution abatement measures used to reduce environmental damages caused by even remote economic activities will be reflected in prices faced by consumers and producers for all the products and processes that are associated with those harms, not just the few consumer and producer decisions that LCA researchers elect to examine.

Third, as actual sources of environmental harms are identified and successfully addressed, the underlying need to assist consumers and producers in making the best environmental choice among products and processes will fade. Bolstering the public's confidence that environmental problems are being addressed and that the consequences of doing so will be incorpo-

rated into prices will ultimately eliminate the original motivation for conducting LCAs.

Fourth, the information requirements for the suggested approach are a small subset of those needed for accurate and definitive LCAs. The traditional approach requires the environmental authority to locate and quantify environmental harms and inappropriate resource use. Armed with this information, regulators then can promulgate rules of whatever type seem appropriate to address these problems. LCA, on the other hand, requires that the input–output matrix of the economy be traced and retraced periodically, location by location, and that the ultimate environmental harms of concern be identified and quantified in order to provide useful information to consumers and producers. In practice, the task of even crudely tracing all of these economic activities and linkages consumes all of the resources in LCA.

Finally, the suggested approach allocates responsibilities for environmental stewardship more appropriately than does LCA. In essence, the traditional approach charges individuals, in their roles as consumers and producers, with ensuring that they cause as little direct environmental damage as is feasible. Thus, individuals should strive to reduce the environmental problems they cause directly, based on their specific situations and activities. Though LCA is motivated by a distrust of prices and the market, consumers and producers nevertheless should accept prices of inputs and goods at face value in making their choices. To do otherwise throws one into the world of LCA in which neither prices nor lists of environmental harms can be trusted to guide one to greener alternatives.

The inability to make rational choices in a world in which one does not trust prices is a particularly important point to understand. Suppose one identifies a cost-saving change in an industrial process that also reduces its direct environmental damages. Ordinarily, this would be a clearly desirable process change to make. But suppose further, as does LCA, that there are many indirect environmental problems that are not accounted for in prices. In this event, one cannot decide rationally that undertaking the process change will reduce total environmental harms. Presumably, the process change will affect many other activities throughout the economy, so until one investigates these indirect sources of environmental harms, the conclusion that the process change is environmentally beneficial overall cannot be supported. Of course, this is a ridiculous situation, but precisely what results from a lack of confidence in prices. Hence, the role allocated to individuals under the suggested approach allows them to trust prices.

The environmental authority under the traditional approach is charged with ensuring that people actually do act in environmentally responsible ways. Its obligation is to correct failures of the market to adequately protect the environment or to price natural resources to reflect their full value to society. If the environmental authority successfully accomplishes its part of the task of managing the impacts of humans on the environment, it will validate the trust that individuals must place in prices.

One objection to discarding LCA and undertaking the difficult, but ultimately more productive, traditional approach to correcting environmental problems is that doing so still does not give consumers and producers information about the environmental content of the products and processes they choose. This complaint goes to the very core of the motivation of LCA. Proponents of LCA assume that prices do not reflect many environmental harms and inappropriate natural resource use, so they seek to provide this information in parallel with the price system. Taken literally, the belief that prices cannot be trusted to reflect the full social costs of products and processes indicts all economic decisions, not just the few that are commonly the subject of LCA. That is, no economic decisions can be trusted to be socially correct if the prices upon which they are based do not reflect vital information about costs.

Unfortunately, it is not possible in practice to provide accurate information on all of the environmental inputs to processes and products or, for that matter, for any set of economic inputs. One can collect and disseminate information about the nature, seriousness, and extent of the environmental problems of concern. Indeed, environmental performance data are very useful, for they direct efforts to monitoring, measuring, and perhaps mitigating actual environmental harms at their sources. Recent attempts to supplement the national income accounts with information on the change in the nation's stock of natural and other environmental resources represent productive first steps in this direction.

What is not feasible in practice is to analytically allocate these environmental problems to particular products and processes, which is the goal of LCA. Some may think this an unfortunate limitation of reality. Perhaps so, but it is the inevitable result of the complexity and diversity of modern economies in which, fortunately, the price system communicates necessary information efficiently, rapidly, and anonymously. Indeed, it is perhaps the most profound benefit of the price system that it coordinates economic actions by communicating remotely and diversely held information, for this could not be accomplished by a single entity.

While there is no *analytical* way to trace from products back through the virtually endless complexity of a modern economy to the environmental problems of concern, there is one way to cause the market to provide this information. Suppose that, for some reason or another, using energy causes environmental damages that are not incorporated in its price, and assume that this harm is the same regardless of the type of the energy. If on pain of death one had to supply information to consumers and producers about the amount of energy (and, hence, damages of concern) embodied in specific products or processes, the only feasible way to do so would be to establish two colors of money, say, red and green. Red money would be the only currency accepted for purchasing energy and green money would be used for all other goods.

Under such a system, all goods and services in the economy would end up with two prices—a red price summarizing energy inputs and a green price reflecting all other factors of production. This example could be extended to other environmental harms by simply expanding the number of colors of money, where each color would be used for a specific environmental problem. In the end, products would have many prices, one for each color of money and its associated environmental harm, which would then supply the detailed environmental information desired.

It is noteworthy that the multiple-currency method of obtaining the desired information still fundamentally relies on the price system, not analysis of the economy and its interrelated sectors. It also emphasizes the fact that doing anything to mitigate the environmental problems of concern requires one to begin with the sources of the harms themselves, not with consumer and producer choices about products and processes. It further reveals that, at its core, the ultimate solution to the environmental problems that motivate life-cycle researchers lies not only in attacking these harms directly, but also in restoring confidence in prices. As shown above, if one does not believe prices, it is difficult to make any rational choices, environmental or otherwise.[4]

Finally, some might still argue that the environmental authorities cannot be relied upon to

address the many environmental problems that still exist. This is a valid concern, but it still does not point to LCA as the solution, because in practice LCA will not reliably advance the goal of guiding choices to greener alternatives. Hence, those who hold this view should consider other ways to affect policy outcomes, such as paying people to lie down in front of logging trucks, for these are more likely to result in environmental improvement than conducting LCAs.

Mandatory Solid Waste Separation and Recycling

The first study in this chapter explored why what is called environmental *life-cycle assessment* of products and processes does not really work in practice. There the discussion focused on analyses that are obviously *product life-cycle assessments*, such as studies intended to determine which type of grocery sack is the least environmentally harmful, and which diaper choice is the most environmentally benign. But a variety of policy proposals in recent years suffer from essentially the same pitfalls and problems, although they often are not immediately identifiable as life-cycle-type studies. This study explores one example showing how some regulatory policy proposals are really LCAs in disguise.[5]

The roots of this study are in the environmental statute under which EPA regulates solid waste disposal—the Resource Conservation and Recovery Act, or RCRA. Traditionally, EPA has focused primarily on developing and enforcing regulations governing technical aspects of solid waste landfill and municipal combustor design and management. EPA's regulations in this area mostly focus on ensuring that solid waste landfills do not accept prohibited mate-

---

[4] To students of the history of economic thought, this may sound much like the Economic Calculation debate during the 1920s and 1930s in which one issue was the ability of a central planning authority to successfully direct economic production activities in the absence of a price system. The results of this evaluation of life-cycle assessment are identical to the conclusions reached over half a century ago. In particular, it is theoretically possible to imagine computing the solution to the economy's production and allocation problem, but it would be absurd to contemplate actually trying. Similarly, it is possible to imagine calculating the full—direct and indirect—set of environmental harms caused by a product or process, but trying to do so in practice would be a waste of time.

[5] This analysis is a summary of an ICF Incorporated research project to which Anne Wittenberg and Abyd Karmali made significant contributions.

rials, such as hazardous wastes, and, through liner and leak detection requirements, that they avoid contaminating water and land resources. Solid waste combustor rules focus mostly on air emission regulation and residual ash management.

In the late 1980s, however, the high public profile of environmental issues, and a few well-publicized incidents involving solid waste disposal difficulties fostered the widespread belief that there was a "garbage crisis." Images of piles of trash with nowhere to go, and a general distaste for locating landfills anywhere near residential communities, both fed the view that the nation was running out of landfill space. In response, EPA began to evaluate possible federal government intervention to solve the supposedly declining solid waste disposal capacity problem. EPA settled on a preliminary recommendation requiring all municipalities to separate at least 25 percent of their solid waste to enhance the rate of recycling. This was intended to stretch the nation's solid waste disposal capacity and thus avert what the public perceived to be the impending garbage crisis.

Most economists at the time viewed the supposed solid waste disposal crisis with considerable skepticism. Indeed, from the purely economic perspective, it is not surprising that solid waste disposal costs are high in densely populated areas. Urban and suburban land is expensive, and the noise, odor, and other unpleasant characteristics of solid waste disposal facilities cause them to be located well away from the more highly populated areas. Along with the increased operation costs associated with tighter environmental regulations on these facilities, those factors caused solid waste disposal costs to increase substantially. But simply because something is more expensive does not mean that we are running out of it. It might be costly to ship waste significant distances for ultimate disposal, but this is an issue of financial expense, not an environmental crisis. Furthermore, recent evidence suggests that landfill space is far from scarce. Indeed, much of the nation now possesses considerable excess solid waste disposal capacity, enough to last for many decades in many cases.

The Question

But the question of interest in this analysis is not whether the push to promulgate federal rules requiring more solid waste separation and recycling was grounded on fact or fiction. Instead, the project on which this study is based was undertaken after the preliminary solid waste separation rule was well into the regulatory decision-making process. While the regulation had considerable support within EPA and in Congress, the problem EPA faced at the time was that no clearly enunciated, analytical justification for the solid waste separation rule existed. Proponents of the separation requirements argued mainly that increased recycling would be beneficial, because it would save landfill space and conserve on natural resources, such as forests. They also argued that because the markets for products made with recycled-source inputs were "thin," it was better to force more of the waste stream into recycling than to wait for the fairly weak demand for products made with recovered materials to encourage more separation and reuse.

The regulatory process, however, involves a number of decision-making hurdles, both inside and outside of EPA. At one of those hurdles, a less anecdotal, more analytical rationale for the separation rule was needed—one based on the economic costs and benefits of its results. Hence, the request that motivated the project summarized here was to try to articulate a theoretically coherent rationale for federal intervention to enhance solid waste recycling.

For several reasons, the challenge this project posed politically was far more serious than its analytical difficulty. First, as shown below, it is possible to construct a theoretically consistent rationale for federal involvement in local solid waste recycling decisions based on purely economic cost–benefit considerations. But the empirical difficulties involved in actually obtaining quantitative results to buttress such a regulation based on that rationale would be insurmountable. This is, of course, the same conclusion reached in the analysis of practical applications of life-cycle assessment presented earlier in this chapter. Perhaps worse, however, is that even if the empirical difficulties in applying this framework could be overcome, the quantitative results would be unlikely to validate a uniform mandatory minimum separation requirement for all localities and solid waste components. Thus, while a coherent rationale could be developed, its empirical results (if they could be obtained) would still not support the specifics of the preliminary waste separation rule.

While disappointing proponents of the waste separation requirements thus seemed unavoidable, bad news nevertheless can be delivered productively in some cases. The approach adopted for the project was to draft a report that began with the most basic issues, and then built layer after layer of arguments and considerations, allowing readers to conduct an evaluation of the preliminary regulation themselves. The hope was that readers would be more receptive to the findings of the analysis if they reached those conclusions on their own.

The Analysis

The analysis of the mandatory solid waste separation proposal began by posing a very fundamental question: Precisely why is federal involvement in a traditionally local government matter necessary? The rationale for federal rules governing possible pollution of land, water, and air in the course of solid waste management is fairly easy to understand. Loosely speaking, the market and the legal systems sometimes fail to adequately protect against such problems, largely because of uncertain detection and difficult-to-prove causal linkages from emissions to health effects and environmental damage.

But imposing a federal rule regarding how much solid waste must be separated and recycled has no obvious risk-related explanation, so it is worth asking what exactly is the problem to be solved by the intervention. Exploring this basic question at the outset might seem a bit naive, but this was an intentional device to try to shift the posture of the policy discussion from one centered on searching for "good things" that might happen as a result of promulgating the waste separation rule, to one focused on the fundamental economic and environmental basis for the regulatory intervention.

Hence, the initial step in the inquiry is to explore why, given the overlay of existing federal and other rules regarding solid waste management, local governments make incorrect choices about waste separation and recycling. Presumably, if the federal government seeks to impose higher waste separation requirements than those chosen by local entities, EPA must believe that these governments are making mistakes, at least from an overall social perspective. Although there are probably many possibilities, three different reasons for federal involvement in this traditionally local government responsibility provide conceivable statements of the problem to be solved. One is that local government decision makers and their constituents are irrational in the sense that they perversely make decisions that are contrary to their interests. Another is that these decision makers have the wrong preferences, or at least ones different from those that drive federal environmental policy.

If either of these two rationales is true, economists have little to offer. It does seem highly unlikely, however, that local governments are irrational. They are perhaps shortsighted, but there are reasons to believe that they may be more attuned to their constituents' long-run interests than is the federal government. Similarly, arguing that local government decision makers and their constituents have the wrong preferences is not really something that economics is equipped to address. Preferences of individuals for the most part are taken at face value in conducting economic analyses, and governmental decisions normally are thought of as syntheses of individual preferences, although there certainly are other ways to characterize them.

A third possible rationale for federal involvement in local decisions about solid waste separation and recycling is more consistent with traditional microeconomic analysis. Under this view, local governments are viewed as being rational and possessing or representing preferences that are consistent with those that guide overall environmental policy. The problem is that the prices and costs these decision makers face might not adequately reflect all of the various environmental problems and concerns about natural resource depletion that are related to their local solid waste management actions.

For example, suppose that enhanced recycling of waste paper reduces logging and the attendant habitat destruction. If the demand for waste paper for recycling, however, does not include the social value of the associated preservation of natural habitats, then the amount of waste paper separation and recycling is likely to be too low from a social perspective. Similarly, suppose that recycled-source aluminum requires far less energy to produce, and that this translates into lower environmental damage from energy production. But if the demand for recycled aluminum does not reflect its lower environmental harm, there will be too little aluminum recovered from the municipal solid waste stream. Finally, if the prices of certain virgin materials are affected by subsidies related to their procurement, say, depletion allowances under the tax code, this also might unfairly tilt the scales against recycled-source materials.

When these divergences of social and private costs or valuations exist, rational and well- (but not completely) informed decision makers may pursue strategies at variance with socially optimal policies. This could provide a possible rationale for federal involvement in these local

government decisions as long as the former can determine what the truly correct choices ought to be for the latter.

This possible justification for the waste separation rule clearly is consistent with the regulation's underlying motivation at the time. For example, one attempt to buttress the waste separation rule argued that the result would be reduced energy use overall. Indeed, most of the explanatory materials surrounding the rule argued that enhanced recycling would somehow decrease the use of valuable natural resources and other social environmental assets. Hence, this justification for federal intervention not only provides an explicit potential rationale for the separation rule based on measurable consequences, but also avoids pinning any blame on local government officials for being intentionally environmentally destructive.

If this is the best way to express the underlying analytical rationale for the waste separation rule, three observations are in order. First, the justification operates in terms of the difference between the social and private values of the environmental effects of activities connected to local waste management decisions, not the absolute amounts the activities themselves. Thus, it is not the energy saved by recycling aluminum per se that is of interest, because the value of this energy saving will already be incorporated in the demand for scrap aluminum. Instead, it is the external environmental damages energy production causes that matter for the analysis. Similarly, it is not the total change in logging that matters here, rather it is the value of the avoided habitat destruction and water-quality impacts.

Second, if these divergences between private and social valuations exist, it would seem more appropriate for the federal government to act to correct them where and when they occur. Presumably, these environmental problems enter into any number of products and activities, not just local government decisions about solid waste separation and recycling. So the obvious solution would seem to be to address them directly and to allow the costs of those regulatory and other corrective actions to filter through the price system, thereby signaling individual consumers and government officials to incorporate these considerations into their decision making.

Finally, one should not expect that requiring increased waste separation and recycling will result in only decreased environmental harms. Recycling is similar in many respects to other production activities, so it may well increase pollution and thus harm the environment in some cases. For example, transporting scrap paper to a mill that can accept it, recycling it using a de-inking process, and then carrying through with the other aspects of paper manufacturing, all can harm the environment. Hence, it is the net change in the level of environmental damages, the decreases minus the increases, that should determine whether federal rules to require additional separation and recycling yield overall environmental improvement.

By now it should be clear that searching for the net social benefits of mandating higher levels of municipal solid waste separation and recycling is really just another manifestation of life-cycle assessment. If one assumes that it is not possible to directly correct the various divergences between social and private valuations and costs that are conceivably connected to local government solid waste management decisions, one is left with the unfortunate second-best task of tracing through all of the direct and indirect consequences of different solid waste recycling actions, as outlined in the evaluation of life-cycle assessment, a task that requires a hopelessly large volume of information. Just as in more explicit life-cycle assessments, there is no apparent end to the search for the possible environmental ramifications of boosting a locality's solid waste separation and recycling rate. Every item in the waste stream whose disposition is altered by the rule will change the host of economic activities and environmental consequences that are associated with it.

Consider just some of the data requirements for assessing the environmental results of diverting more waste paper to recycling markets. First of all, one must determine exactly what things change when more scrap paper is channeled to recycling markets. For this, one must assess where all of the additional waste paper goes in the international paper market; which paper mills in the United States will use more waste paper and less virgin inputs; how the use of water, energy, and other resources, by each mill, is affected; exactly what forests will not be harvested; and what changes occur in the transport of both virgin and secondary inputs. In essence, one needs a "map" of how the additional waste-paper supplies alter other flows and activities throughout the economy.

Second, one must identify and measure the environmental harms caused by economic activities that change as a result of mandating the additional waste paper separation. Here what is required is a catalog of all of the increased and decreased environmental damages that result from the changes in activities caused by the additional waste paper recycling. Note that this step calls for determining environmental *effects*, not simply changes in effluent and emission levels. Estimating effects requires information on the location of the emissions, as well as other factors that determine the nature and extent of harms from pollution. Finally, one must value the changes in these environmental effects, or to at least attempt to array them using a few well-defined metrics for policy makers, such as changes in air concentrations of toxic chemicals, number of fish killed, or changes in biological oxygen demand in waterways.

Of course, one would also have to undertake the same sort of empirical research at the same level of detail for each material involved in the waste separation rule before one could say whether the regulation actually does reduce the overall level of environmental damages. To obtain any reliable results, a vast amount of resources would have to be devoted to the study; of course, as conditions change over time (e.g., the linkage of economic activities to pollution), these studies would have to be updated.

There is, however, a more important point to be made here than merely the expense of actually trying to determine whether these divergences between social and private costs really can justify the waste separation rule. In particular, *if* the existence of these divergences implies that local solid waste decision makers do not face the correct price signals, it is not at all clear that the socially correct level of recycling will be the same across localities and for different elements in the waste stream. For example, from a social perspective, a town very far from any paper mills probably should not be recycling very much paper. The transportation costs, let alone any resulting environmental harms, would likely swamp any net decrease in environmental harms. But a locality close to a new and very environmentally benign paper mill perhaps ought to considerably expand waste paper recycling.

As a general matter, the *divergences of social and private costs* framework for determining whether private actions are socially optimal will yield different implications for different localities and for each waste material. But this implies that although this framework could conceivably provide a justification for additional federal intervention in solid waste management decisions, the analysis suggests that the appropriate recycling levels will not be the same for all localities and materials. The actual preliminary separation rule, however, was to apply uniformly across the entire country. Hence, the mandated increased separation and recycling could be too high or too low for any given locality and material. In fact, it is even possible that the correct direction for the recycling rate for a particular material in a given location could be negative. There is no reason why recycling in a specific instance could not be environmentally more damaging than landfilling or

incinerating. It is not at all clear, therefore, that the uniform waste separation rule would provide overall environmental improvement, much less whether it would offer sufficient net environmental benefits to outweigh the added waste-management costs.

Upon reflection, none of these conclusions is really all that surprising. The solid waste separation rule was buttressed mostly by the belief that requiring additional recycling simply had to be a good idea. The term *recycling* indeed does conjure up images of resource conservation and environmental stewardship. But this implies that the motivation for the rule flowed not from a clearly defined environmental problem to be solved, such as measurable pollution caused by a production process, but instead from the view that recycling was inherently desirable. Hence, when one sets out to calculate carefully all of the positive and negative consequences of such a regulation, it is not surprising that the sign of the net benefits is unclear.

Finally, does this imply that it must always be difficult to justify added recycling efforts by localities in purely economic terms? Not necessarily. The key issue has to do with whether the justification for the additional recycling flows from a clear-cut environmental problem to be solved. In general, the best policy interventions are those that closely focus on the particular problem to be solved. Thus, a regulation directly targeting the pollution caused by the effluent discharged by a particular industrial plant generally will perform better than, say, a tax on the plant's output. The same point applies for the environmental harms regulators hope to address by mandating increased solid waste separation and recycling. If these environmental problems exist, it is best to attack them at their sources using whatever means seem appropriate. Trying to correct them by altering solid waste flows is a particularly blunt, largely ineffective, and possibly damaging approach.

But if the rationale for a locality's desire to increase recycling is that the intervention is an imperfect, but the best available, substitute for pricing solid waste generation and management optimally, the policy may well pass a cost–benefit test. That is, if the best policy instrument—in this case setting the price of waste generation and management equal to its full social cost—is not feasible, a policy of encouraging additional separation and recycling could be the next-best approach. Of course, a recycling policy based on such a rationale would probably be more complex than an across-the-board waste separation mandate. It might focus, for example, on particular waste stream components and specific generators. In general, second-best policies tend to be more complex than the first-best policies they replace. In the end, however, a proposed regulatory intervention is much more likely to survive a critical cost–benefit examination if it is developed as the best available policy to address a clearly defined environmental problem than if it simply sounds like a good idea.

Chapter 11

Environmental Policy
in Theory and Practice

Throughout this book, the focus in all of the studies and applications has been fundamentally on cost–benefit evaluation of environmental policies and the many twists and turns practical analyses take in studying real-world problems and issues. As noted at the outset, the nature and content of much applied environmental economics as illustrated in this book differs somewhat from the traditional teaching in environmental economics; in particular, that the instrument of choice ought to be some form of a tax on the activities that give rise to pollution damages. The project on which this study is based sought to identify the reasons why the remedy most often recommended in textbooks is so rarely applied in practice. Hence, the analysis and conclusions reached here provide at least some of the explanation for why practical environmental economics centers so much on cost–benefit analysis of a wide variety of regulatory and nonregulatory interventions instead of focusing more exclusively on applying the primary guidance offered in most textbooks.

Why Policy Makers Don't Use Environmental Taxes

For over half a century economists have recommended using taxes to correct externalities and other failures of the unregulated market to appropriately manage environmental resources. The inherent logic behind this method of intervention has profound appeal to economists. If the regulator levies taxes on environmentally harmful activities equal to the damages they cause, polluters will then account for these harms in their production and consumption decisions. Once polluters face the full costs of their actions, the externalities will be *internalized* by the relevant decision makers, and the appropriate levels of pollution control and environmental harm will result. The instrument is referred to by a variety of names, such as corrective taxation, environmental or pollution taxes, or Pigouvian taxes, after the economist A. C. Pigou who first developed the notion.

Although environmental taxes have enjoyed widespread support among economists for many decades, economic incentives in general, and corrective taxes in particular, have become increasingly attractive to policy makers in recent years. In part, this new emphasis on economic incentives is driven by the view that, compared to more traditional command and control forms of regulation, they potentially offer some added efficiency and cost savings in achieving the nation's often stringent environmental quality goals. Command and control interventions typically are

219

thought to be insensitive to, and incapable of accommodating, wide variations of control costs and other factors that largely determine the burden of satisfying increasingly stringent environmental improvement goals. Incentive systems, if properly constructed, might provide substantial benefits by harnessing private-sector profit-maximization efforts in pursuit of these goals.

Probably a more important explanation for the recent interest among policy makers in using environmental taxes, however, is that these levies could provide much-needed government revenues. According to this view, not only do environmental taxes appear to be better than the traditional regulatory approach, but a byproduct will be tax revenues that can be used to fund existing or new government programs, or reduce other burdensome taxes. The possibility of generating tax revenues in the process of protecting the environment seems an irresistible lure.

The Question

Despite all of the vigorous support for environmental taxes economists have offered over many decades, much less the more recent desire to use them to generate revenues for cash-starved governments, true corrective environmental taxation has rarely, if ever, been used. Much of environmental policy making is still of the conventional standard-setting command and control variety. Moreover, although there have been attempts lately to use some economic incentive systems, such as marketable permits and deposit-refund systems, environmental policy making has yet to embrace taxes as the regulatory tool of choice. Of course, governments do levy fees on various activities related to the environment, such as fees for the use of waterways and national parks, and charges for waste disposal, but these are primarily intended to cover the cost of providing services, not to correct distorted price signals in the economy. As such, these are not true corrective taxes. To date, much to the dismay of economists and the frustration of policy makers, attempts

to use environmental taxes have been largely unsuccessful.

This lack of progress in using corrective environmental taxes in policy making has spawned numerous reports summarizing incentive systems' characteristics, their advantages and disadvantages, and a host of practical implementation issues they raise. At least implicitly, the underlying motivation for conducting these studies is that the less-than-stellar success in actually using market-based approaches, especially environmental taxes, is attributable to a lack of understanding of their merits, structure, operation, and implementation on the part of those responsible for formulating and analyzing policy options. While this may have been true many years ago, given the number and volume of studies describing incentive systems and indicating when and how they can be used, it seems highly unlikely that ignorance is the primary reason these approaches are not widely used in practice.

It also has been argued that incentive systems go beyond the authorities embodied in the various statutes that govern environmental policy making. Many of these laws do indeed seem to impose rigid and detailed instructions on how to address various sources of environmental risk. Nevertheless, ambiguous legal authority for using incentive systems in the environmental arena probably is not the central reason for their lack of use. Recent assessments of the statutory authority for using incentive systems, particularly environmental taxes, in environmental policy making suggest that these laws are not nearly as unreceptive to market-based strategies as originally thought. Furthermore, if a lack of legal authority was really the binding constraint, there has been plenty of time and inclination to alter the relevant statutes to ensure that incentive systems legally can be used as environmental regulations.

Of course, theory is almost always ahead of practice in any field, so the fact that the latest research techniques and findings take time to find their way into policy making is not surprising. But the gulf between theory and practice in environmental regulation is too vast to be explained by communication delays between the journals and textbooks, on the one hand, and regulatory policy development on the other. Instead, the reasons for the lack of wholesale adoption of corrective taxes as environmental regulations are deeper than ignorance of their operation and advantages, or a lack of legal authority. This study focuses on identifying some of the more significant impediments to using corrective taxation in practice.

The Analysis

The point of departure for this analysis is quite different from previous studies of how economic incentive systems can be used as regulatory instruments. Most existing analyses focus largely on why regulators *should* use economic incentive systems such as environmental taxation. Taking the opposite tack, this analysis attempts to diagnose why corrective taxation *is not* used in practice. The view here is that those responsible for basic environmental policy development are already familiar with the characteristics and operation of economic incentive systems, and that legal authority is not really the central impediment to their use. Hence, the central question is why incentive systems, particularly environmental taxes, are not used more often in practice, given that everyone seems to agree on their advantages.

Many of the issues discussed here are touched on in the literature, particularly the careful summary of the state of environmental economics by Cropper and Oates[1] and the classic comprehensive text by Baumol and Oates.[2] Hence, the primary contribution of this study is that it attacks

[1] M. L. Cropper and W. E. Oates, "Environmental Economics: A Survey," *Journal of Economic Literature*, (June 1992): 675–740.

[2] W. J. Baumol and W. E. Oates, *The Theory of Environmental Policy* (Cambridge, England: Cambridge University Press, 1988).

the question from a fresh perspective and lays out more systematically the various reasons why corrective taxes are seldom used in environmental regulatory policy. The hope is that by making these major stumbling blocks clearer to everyone—students, researchers, and policy makers—the infrequent use of these taxes in practice will be less mysterious and perplexing. Obviously a more ambitious goal is that by diagnosing why attempts to use environmental taxes fail in practice, perhaps some of these major impediments can be overcome.

The analysis is organized as follows. The first portion reviews the basics of corrective taxation as applied to environmental problems. The focus here is not only on the instrument's characteristics and operation, but more fundamentally on the way economists justify its use. Next, a number of reasons why corrective taxation is rarely, if ever, used in environmental policy are explored in some depth. Various reasons are examined, ranging from unrealistic expectations about the operation and effects of incentive systems as regulatory policies, to conflicts between the goals underlying environmental taxation and the mandates governing regulatory policy. Following that is an examination of a variation on environmental taxation prevalent in the literature, the *standards and charges* approach under which environmental taxes are used to achieve predetermined policy goals. Here the focus is on a slightly different set of reasons for the failure to use even this more limited version of environmental taxation in environmental policy. Finally, the conclusion provides some tentative observations about, and suggestions for, using environmental taxes more successfully in the future.

CORRECTIVE TAXATION IN THEORY

The operation of corrective environmental taxes traditionally is depicted using diagrams such as that in Figure 11-1. This figure shows the benefits and costs of an activity that results in emissions of a pollutant that damages the environ-

FIGURE 11-1

A Corrective Environmental Tax

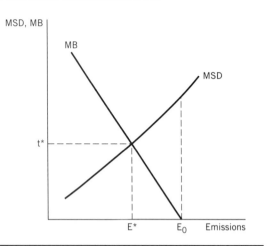

In the absence of regulation, total emissions are E_0. The optimal level of emissions is E^*, where the marginal benefit in terms of avoided control costs, is equal to the marginal social cost of the damages. A corrective tax equal to t^* will achieve the optimal level of emissions and pollution by ensuring that each source reduces emissions up the point at which its marginal control cost equals marginal social damages.

ment. The *marginal social damage* (MSD) function measures the environmental cost of the various types of harms that result from these emissions. The MSD curve rises with increasing emissions, reflecting the assumption that damages rise as the level of emissions increases. The *marginal benefit* (MB) function measures the "value" of emitting rather than undertaking costly controls or other actions to reduce these harms. It may seem a bit confusing to think of emitting pollutants as having value to anyone. But this is simply another way of saying that controlling emissions is costly. The curve thus indicates that marginal control costs are very high when allowable emissions are zero, but that as emission levels rise, marginal control costs fall.

In the absence of any regulation, emissions from all sources amount to E_0. It is no coinci-

dence that E_0 occurs where the MB function crosses the horizontal axis. When faced with a zero cost of polluting, sources are assumed not to engage in any emission control other than those other economic reasons dictate. For example, recapturing some chemical pollutants can be more profitable than allowing them to escape if they can be recycled and reused cost effectively. Hence, the situation in the diagram does not assume that without regulatory intervention there will be no controls on emissions, but only that whatever controls do exist are undertaken for reasons unrelated to the external environmental damages emissions cause. Clearly, in the absence of regulation, the marginal social cost of emissions exceeds their value to polluters in terms of avoided control costs, as shown by the vertical distance between the MSD and MB curves at E_0, where the latter crosses the horizontal axis.

A corrective tax for this situation will operate as follows. First of all, following the usual rule of economics, emissions *ought* to be at the level at which their marginal social damage equals the marginal social cost of avoiding them. This level is shown in the figure as E*, where the MSD and MB curves intersect. Levels of emissions higher than E* would cause more damage (as measured by the height of the MSD curve) than the control costs saved (as measured by the height of the MB function). Similarly, emission levels lower than E* would avoid damages that cost society less than the added control expenditures.

Given that E* is the optimal level of emissions, the challenge for policy makers is to translate that goal into specific actions pollution sources must take. One method might be for the environmental authority to dictate to each source the level of emissions it can generate. This traditional *command and control* approach essentially requires the regulatory authority to parcel out the optimal level of emissions, source by source, providing each polluter with an allowable amount.

Corrective taxation, however, offers a different way to translate the optimal level of emissions into specific guidance for individual sources. Note the striking resemblance (fully intended) of the situation in Figure 11-1 to conventional supply and demand functions for any ordinary economic good. In the latter case, the optimal production and consumption of a good is found where its marginal social cost equals its marginal social benefit. In normally functioning markets, the competitive behavior of profit-maximizing producers and the utility-maximizing decisions by budget-constrained consumers achieve the optimal level of production and consumption of a good. In the case of pollution, however, there is no market interaction between the *suppliers* of emission reduction and the *demanders* of a clean environment by which to establish the optimal emissions level. Hence, if the government can intervene and set the correct "price" for emissions, market interactions should cause the optimal amount of emissions to result.

As shown in FIgure 11-1, setting the tax on emissions at t^* will encourage just the right amount of control by all sources collectively to reach the optimal emissions target of E^*. This must be so, because sources will prefer to control emissions as long as the marginal cost of doing so is less than the tax rate, and will prefer to pay the tax when marginal emission control costs exceed the tax. Setting the tax rate equal to marginal damages at the optimal level of emissions causes each source to reduce its contribution to the point at which its marginal control cost equals marginal pollution damages, precisely the condition that defines the optimal result from a social perspective.

In addition to achieving the optimal level of emissions, the corrective tax approach also ensures that this goal is attained at a lower social cost than command and control style regulations that impose the same performance standards for all sources. To see this, suppose that only two sources emit equal amounts of pollutants in the relevant geographical region and that both are subject to command and control regulation, which requires each to reduce emissions to one-half of the optimal total level, E^*. If the two sources face different costs of controlling emissions, this regulation will be inefficient, because the optimal total level of emissions could be achieved at a lower cost.

This situation is shown in Figure 11-2 where the two marginal benefit schedules reflect the different control costs for each source. Under the command and control standard, each source reduces its emissions to the prescribed level, $.5E^*$. But the marginal cost of controlling emissions differs significantly across the two, as measured by the height of the marginal benefit schedules at the allowable level of emissions, MB_A^0 and MB_B^0. Because of this, the social benefits will be higher by increasing emissions from the high-cost source and decreasing emissions from the low-cost source.

This is precisely what the tax approach accomplishes. Setting the emissions tax at t^* for each source will result in emission levels of E_A^1 for the source with lower control costs and E_B^1 for the source with higher control costs. Total emissions are still equal to the optimal level, E^*, but the amounts contributed by each source will no longer be equal, as they are under the command and control approach. As indicated by the shaded areas in Figure 11-1, the efficiency enhancement of substituting the corrective tax for the command and control regulation can be measured by the difference between the additional control costs incurred by the low-cost source and the reduced control costs saved by the high-cost source. The former are more than offset by the latter.

In general, corrective taxes achieve the optimal level of emissions at the minimum cost by equalizing the marginal cost of control (instead of emissions) across sources and by setting that equal to the marginal social damages of emissions. It is significant that corrective taxes accomplish all of this privately and in a decentralized way as the regulated firms respond to the newly created price signal. Once the price of polluting

FIGURE 11-2

Efficiency Enhancement Under Corrective Taxation

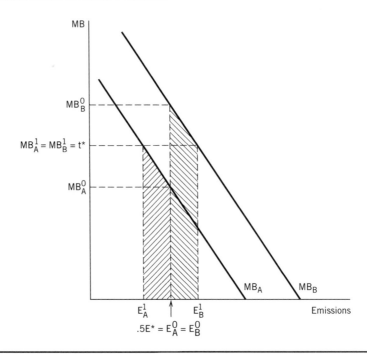

Total emission control costs can be reduced relative to the command and control outcome by encouraging the lower-cost source to control more, thereby permitting the higher-cost source to control less. The corrective tax, t^*, accomplishes this result by allowing the higher-cost source to increase its emission, by paying taxes instead of incurring the more expensive control costs, and by encouraging the lower-cost source to reduce its emissions by an identical amount, thus incurring additional control costs instead of paying the higher tax rate. The costs saved by the former are larger than the added burden on the latter.

is set correctly, the polluters' self-interested decision making will cause not only the optimal level of emissions and damages to materialize, but also ensure that they are achieved at minimum cost to society. This is what economists mean by *harnessing market forces* in the pursuit of environmental improvement.

The conventional illustration of the superiority of corrective taxation thus demonstrates that the essence of the approach is elegant and disarmingly easy to understand. But, as will be seen later, it is very important to distinguish

between the simplicity of the analytical core of corrective taxation and the simplicity of the illustration itself. Indeed, a number of assumptions are necessary to describe the operation and advantages of corrective taxation using the diagrams and analysis presented so far. In particular, the situation depicted in Figure 11-1 is one in which environmental damages depend only on the total level of pollution, so that emissions from different sources cause the same damages regardless of their location. Because of this, it is possible to use emissions on the quantity axis instead of damages and, in turn, to specify the tax rate in terms of emissions rather than the harms caused. Perhaps more important, the assumption that damages depend only on total emissions also implies that only one tax rate is needed regardless of the characteristics of the individual sources. As will be seen, when this assumption fails, matters become considerably more complex for environmental taxation, as they do for all regulatory approaches.

Corrective taxation also requires valuing environmental harms, setting the tax rates based on marginal social damages at the optimal level of pollution, levying taxes directly on the activities that cause the harms, and incorporating in the tax rates all policy goals significant to regulators. As discussed in the following section, the tasks of targeting the required tax appropriately, obtaining agreement on the value of environmental harms, and reflecting all of the myriad real-world policy goals in monetary tax rates should not be taken lightly in practice. Nevertheless, these and other implicit simplifying assumptions are quite appropriate for demonstrating the power and effectiveness of using corrective taxation to address environmental problems. By stripping away all of the complexities normally present in the world, the basic operation of the tax approach can be seen most clearly.

The appeal of corrective environmental taxes thus runs quite deep in terms of economic efficiency, and resonates strongly with the basic faith economists place in free-market outcomes. After all, a well-functioning market requires no special attention or oversight to achieve optimal outcomes. Intervening with a corrective tax thus seems a reasonable intrusion to obtain possibly large gains in economic efficiency; this is especially true relative to command and control regulations, historically the policy instrument of choice among regulators.[3] Seen in this light, the corrective tax remedy is really no more than an exercise in supplying the *missing prices* of environmental harms caused by pollution when the market fails to generate these signals on its own. Hence, over the years economists have championed the tax approach for addressing environmental problems, largely based on efficiency-enhancement grounds.[4]

But viewed from a public policy perspective, using environmental taxation requires more than an efficiency-based justification. In par-

---

[3] It is worth noting in passing that, in some sense, actively intervening in the market to set the appropriate price for pollution is viewed by economists as a last resort. When the market fails to price or manage something correctly, most economists would first suggest that the property rights involved be better defined. Under this more passive approach, whoever ends up with the clarified "title" to the resource being harmed would have an incentive to defend its value using the standard legal mechanisms, such as tort, property, and contract law. This *property-right-clarification* approach will not work for many environmental problems, however, primarily because large numbers of entities are often involved. Many people might be harmed slightly by the degradation of air quality due to emissions from many different sources. Even if the "right" to clean air was clearly allocated to the affected population, it is difficult to imagine each person pursuing each of the emission sources that cause him or her harm. Thus, many market failures that give rise to environmental externalities require more interventionist remedies, such as corrective taxes.

[4] The popularity of corrective taxes also stems from a few of its more subtle features. One is that taxes ensure that the long-run profitability, and hence entry, conditions facing polluters are optimal. Approaches that do not charge polluters for residual emissions and damages will tend to encourage excessive entry. That is, if firms can use the environment for disposal without paying for that right, too many firms will attempt to use this common property resource, reducing the efficiency of the outcome. Another benefit of the corrective tax over the command-and-control approach relates to the incentive to develop new emission-control technologies. Under command and control standards, this incentive is generally confined to seeking lower-cost innovations that meet the requirements of the regulation, because polluters gain nothing by reducing emissions below the current standards. Under taxes, however, the incentive is not only to develop less expensive pollution control methods, but also to explore technologies that achieve even greater emission control than presently, because firms save taxes by further reducing their emissions.

ticular, relative to other regulatory approaches, environmental taxes entail distributional or "equity" outcomes that must be justified. Under command and control regulation, for example, pollution sources incur costs to reduce their emissions to the required levels, but any remaining emissions are allowed without charge. Under corrective taxes, however, emission sources incur not only the costs to control their pollution, but also taxes on their remaining emissions. Of course, all approaches remove from polluters the right to unlimited free use of the environment for disposal purposes, so polluters will be worse off than under no regulation. But corrective taxes further alter the distribution of rights in the economy by charging polluters for their remaining emissions, which under most other regulatory approaches would be allowed free of charge.

Public policy makers may well decide that stripping polluters of the right to use the environment for free disposal of any emissions at all is a reasonable thing to do, especially if the mechanism that generates this outcome (corrective taxation) also improves the efficiency of environmental regulation. But this is a policy choice that almost always must be buttressed by considerations other than economic efficiency, a point often obscured in purely efficiency-based evaluations of alternative regulatory instruments. In theory, other regulatory instruments can achieve similar levels of pollution abatement (perhaps less efficiently), but impose only the costs of controlling emissions, thereby preserving polluters' right to free disposal of residual emissions. For example, in some instances marketable permits can provide the same efficiency enhancement relative to command and control as do corrective taxes. In such cases, taxes and marketable permits both achieve the optimal outcome in every short- and long-run sense of the term. If the permits are distributed free (or grandfathered as this is sometimes called) to emission sources, setting aside implementation and transactions cost issues, the choice between the two approaches rests solely on equity concerns. Corrective taxation charges sources for residual pollution and the marketable permits approach does not, but both achieve the same level of environmental protection.

Of course, the general proposition remains that while corrective taxes are not always superior on efficiency grounds to other approaches, they certainly can be in many instances. Nevertheless, the point is not whether environmental taxes are theoretically more efficient, but whether the potential efficiency enhancement they provide over other forms of regulation is sufficient to justify the distributional outcomes they entail. That is, in practice taxes must be chosen not over *no* regulation, but instead over *other* regulatory options, so the environmental improvement and gains in efficiency provided by taxes must be measured relative to the outcomes those other instruments provide. The better the performance of alternative regulatory approaches relative to that of corrective taxation, the smaller will be the incremental environmental improvement and efficiency enhancement that can be used to justify the equity outcomes taxes produce. It is easy to imagine cases in which the efficiency improvement taxes provide over other alternatives is quite modest, but the added tax burden on emission sources is very substantial. As a result, successfully advocating corrective environmental taxes over other approaches generally requires more than efficiency-based arguments.

One strategy for addressing this equity issue is to sidestep the matter by arguing that it is not the intent of the corrective tax to collect revenue on the residual pollution; it is merely a side effect of the policy's operation. Hence, in keeping with the more traditional economics of public finance, one might try to "lump sum" the tax revenues back to the polluters to mitigate the pure transfer effects of the tax. Doing so would still reap the efficiency benefits of correctly pricing the environment, but at a reduced distributional impact. But no one seriously believes that any revenues from an environmental tax will somehow be returned to the polluters, so the distributional effects of using corrective taxation over other forms of regulation cannot be dodged so easily.[5]

Fortunately for advocates of environmental taxation, sentiment in recent years has been that polluters have no right to the free use of the environment in the first place. According to this view, polluters should not only pay for emission abatement measures, but also for any residual environmental damages they continue to cause. This *polluter-pays* principle is the fundamental argument typically used to justify the equity implications of corrective environmental taxation: It is reasonable to require polluters to pay for even the residual damages they cause the environment if they have no right to pollute for free anyway. This resolution of the equity issue essentially denies that the tax payments are a loss suffered by polluters relative to other regulatory approaches; instead, it views them as eminently reasonable liabilities polluters should face for damaging environmental property owned by others.

Economists are thus reasonably comfortable with the polluter-pays principle as the equity justification for using environmental corrective taxation over other regulatory approaches. If public policy makers have decided that polluters should pay for all of the harms they cause, a corrective tax equal to marginal environmental damages is the regulatory enactment of that principle.[6] From

an equity perspective, environmental taxes are simply the equivalent of presenting polluters with a bill for the damages they do to the environment that they are not entitled to cause in the first place. As long as there is a close connection between the tax rate and the social damages pollution causes, corrective taxation thus seems to be a nearly perfect embodiment of the underlying polluter-pays philosophy.

WHY CORRECTIVE TAXATION IS NOT USED IN ENVIRONMENTAL POLICY

Despite all of its widely acknowledged advantages, corrective taxation has rarely, if ever, been used in environmental regulation. This section seeks to diagnose why attempts to use corrective taxes have been unsuccessful. Although there probably are others, five major reasons why environmental taxes are not used are summarized here. These are: (1) a host of expectations policy makers often have concerning the operation of market-based approaches that are rarely satisfied in practice; (2) unfair comparisons of incentive systems' performance with that of other regulatory approaches; (3) incompatibility of the revenue generation objective and environmental policy goals; (4) conflicts between environmental policy objectives and the goal of corrective taxation; and (5) the difficulties frequently encountered in providing

---

[5] It is conceivable that revenues from an environmental tax might be returned to industry if the funds were dedicated to pollution-control expenditures. A few such programs exist in several European nations, but these are not true corrective taxes, because the rates are not set with reference to the values of environmental harms caused. Moreover, returning the funds on the condition that they be spent on pollution control suggests that the programs are really nonregulatory methods of achieving environmental improvement, combined with, in a sense, a pooled financing mechanism. A good survey of these charge systems and other programs is *Economic Incentives for Environmental Protection*, Organization for Economic Cooperation and Development, 1989.

[6] It is possible for a firm's aggregate tax payments to be greater than the actual environmental damages caused by its pollution. This could happen if the marginal social cost of damages rises as the firm's contribution to pollution increases. If the contribution of each firm to the pollution is "small" relative to the total, however, the marginal social damages will not change over the range of any particular firm's emissions, so that each firm's tax bill will equal the actual damages it causes. Of course, in the aggregate, the total tax collected from the entire industry might exceed the total damages it causes. Nevertheless, as with any input supplied to an industry less than perfectly elastically, the difference between the total tax payments of the industry and the total amount of environmental damages is a "rent" that accrues to the environmental resource's owner. See Baumol and Oates (1988), *supra* note 2, pp. 52–54, and the references cited there, for a complete treatment of this issue.

the necessary equity justification for using corrective taxes. The first two apply generally to using all economic incentive systems, not just corrective taxation, in place of traditional command and control approaches. The other three impediments, however, are specific to using environmental taxes in place of command and control regulation and, in some very important cases, other incentive systems.

Unrealistic Expectations: One reason for the infrequent use of economic incentive systems—all market-based approaches, not just corrective taxation—is that many policy makers believe that these approaches will be universally preferred to, and simpler to use than, other regulatory methods. These expectations stem largely from having inundated policy makers over the years with persuasive, but highly simplified demonstrations of the advantages of market-based approaches. A classic example contrasts an inefficient command and control regulation (one that is insensitive to control-cost differences among multiple sources of pollution) with a marketable permits system under which the aggregate pollution level is the same, but firms trade emission rights, thereby achieving the regulatory target at a lower social cost. The permits are initially granted to individual polluters in amounts equal to the emissions each would be allowed under the command and control regulation. Hence, this example shows that marketable permits can reduce total control costs without making anyone worse off. Perhaps more significantly, from the regulator's perspective it is far easier to use marketable permits to obtain this efficiency enhancement than to try to further refine the command and control regulation. The incentive system utilizes information about the regulated firms' control costs that is not known by the environmental authority. Although this is a useful way to illustrate the powerful results of using incentive systems, repeated exposure to this example leads many people to believe that economic incentives will always be socially less costly than other approaches, that they will be preferred by all of the affected parties, including the polluters, and that they will be easier to use. None of these expectations is warranted in practice.

Theoretically, incentive systems such as corrective taxes will be less costly from a social perspective than traditional command and control approaches as long as the policy target is the same. They also will be better—in the sense that their net social benefits will be greater than under other approaches—if the explicit goal is to achieve the economically optimal outcome; that is, where marginal social costs and benefits are equated. But much of environmental regulatory policy is not formulated the way textbook comparisons of alternative interventions would appear to suggest. Regulators often have in mind a somewhat vague goal of *risk management* for a particular environmental problem and then fashion a variety of regulatory and nonregulatory mechanisms to address it, alternatives that typically result in different degrees of risk reduction.

In light of this, an economic incentive option need not impose lower social costs than a command and control approach if their levels of stringency are different. For example, a weak command and control option could well impose lower social costs than a more stringent corrective tax aiming at the optimal outcome. The costs of the corrective tax might indeed be the minimum amount required to achieve the socially optimal result, but these could well exceed the costs of a command and control option that targets a less-strict level of pollution control.

In practice, because more than purely economic considerations enter into policy making, it is not uncommon for traditional command and control regulations to target a less stringent degree of environmental improvement than could be justified simply on the basis of costs and benefits. Comparing the resulting lenient command and control regulation with a corrective tax that seeks the optimal (and more stringent) level of environmental improvement will show the latter to be more costly than the former. It is thus unrealistic to expect that incentive systems always will be socially less costly than command and control regulations.

The expectation that everyone will prefer incentive systems over command and control approaches is obviously misguided, but seems to be an unwarranted generalization of the results of substituting marketable permits for command and control regulations. When using marketable permits in place of traditional command and control approaches, assuming that the initial free allocation of permits to emission sources is identical to their allowable emissions under the command and control option, any trades of these allowances would be voluntary, and thus could not make anyone worse off.

While this distributional outcome is particularly helpful in selling the advantages of incentive systems to regulators, the problem is that this result does not apply to corrective taxes, or really to most economic incentive systems other than marketable permits. Corrective taxes may well achieve environmental goals at lower total cost than command and control approaches, but the tax bill for the remaining emissions also must be paid. Hence, members of the regulated industry could easily prefer command and control to environmental taxes.

Another unrealistic expectation concerning the use of economic incentives is that they will be easier to design, administer, and enforce than other forms of regulation. This belief is fostered by the sense that "all you have to do is set the tax rate, or decide the total level of emissions and distribute the permits, and the market will handle everything else." While using market-based regulatory strategies can provide some administrative and other benefits, their use still requires regulators to make often difficult policy choices and to grapple with complex causal relationships between economic activities and pollution damages. In designing a marketable permit system, for example, one must decide the

total permissible level of environmental damages and determine what activities will require permits. Similarly, when using corrective taxes, deciding what exactly will be taxed and at what rates are still necessary policy-making steps.

In general, the task of tracing from environmental harms to economic activities to decide where to impose a regulation, setting the boundaries of a regulation's scope, and deciding its stringency can be just as difficult when using market-based approaches as in formulating traditional command and control policies. Economic incentives can help to improve the efficiency of regulatory outcomes, but they do not obviate the need to make policy choices, and they will not magically simplify real-world environmental problems. These approaches do not erase the challenges of real-world risk management; they only add options for addressing them.

Indeed, in some cases, especially those that require frequent and accurate monitoring of emissions, using incentive systems, or any approaches that require detailed information on emissions, can be even more cumbersome and difficult than traditional technology-based command and control. When emissions from many sources at a facility are expensive to monitor, it may be far easier to specify controls based on technologies with known pollution-control properties.

Finally, attempts to use economic incentives in practice often founder on the reality that regulators must give something up in exchange for the efficiency-enhancing benefits of these approaches. In particular, regulators must cede some control over the exact outcome of incentive approaches to polluters. Under marketable permits systems, for example, cost-minimizing trading among the polluters determines the ultimate distribution of emissions. Consequently, while the total quantity of emissions is fixed, the regulator does not know with any certainty exactly how much pollution will be generated by particular facilities. This problem is even more pronounced for corrective taxation, because regulators must completely relinquish control over the total amount and the location of emissions to the polluters.

Thus, for regulators to be confident in using incentive systems, they must find it acceptable for market forces, supplemented by altered incentives, to determine precise outcomes. But this is not necessarily an easy shift of policy-making stance for regulators, given both the the tight control over outcomes offered by command and control regulation and the underlying mandates of the nation's various environmental statutes. Regulators are charged with protecting the environment, so using corrective taxes and accepting whatever results emerge—despite being efficient from an economic perspective—seems to run counter to their fundamental responsibilities.

Some of this sentiment underlies a familiar criticism of corrective taxes: that they make damaging the environment simply another cost item for polluters, rather than something that is, in some sense, fundamentally wrong. This is perhaps why successful attempts to use economic incentives in environmental regulation in recent years have focused on marketable permit systems as opposed to taxes. Because the marketable permits approach offers certainty concerning at least the overall outcome, policy makers tend to be more receptive to allowing the market to determine the details.

Unfair Comparisons of Policies: Another major reason why economic incentive systems are not widely used is that policy makers often implicitly employ different criteria for comparing the outcomes under market-based policies to those of alternative approaches. In part, this also stems from the fact that real-world environmental problems are far more complex than the simple situations depicted in the usual demonstrations of the superiority of market-based approaches. For example, the environmental damages attributable to emissions of a particular substance might de-

pend on the amount and concentration of emissions; on the medium into which the emissions occur; on the nature and value of the activities potentially injured by the emissions; and even the location of the emission source. Similarly, many pollution problems are caused by nonpoint sources, such as agricultural runoff, which can be very difficult to measure and regulate. Pollution problems that fit the description of textbook examples are the exception, not the rule.

Hence, in many real-world applications, policy makers quickly realize that applying incentive systems such as corrective taxes and marketable permits to achieve the optimal result requires a large amount of data collection and analysis. A host of other complications of real-world pollution problems abound, raising design, measurement, implementation, and enforcement issues, all of which can expand the dimensions of the optimal corrective tax or efficient marketable permit problem.

The result is that the apparently simple-to-use and powerful-in-effect advantages of economic incentive systems, so often demonstrated to policy makers, succumb to a "death by a thousand cuts" when applied to real-world problems. Regulators discover that to accurately use environmental taxes or marketable permits requires so much study and analysis that they are often discarded as being mostly the province of theoretical economics, not the day-to-day business of environmental management.

The economic literature on the issue unfortunately has served to reinforce this view by focusing nearly exclusively on what is required to achieve the economically optimal result. Designing a marketable permits system, for example, becomes a very data-intensive exercise when the damages of a particular source's emissions depend on its location and concentration, and the distribution and characteristics of pollution recipients. Complex trading ratios for emissions from different sources are then necessary to account for these heterogeneous harms. For example, if one source's marginal emissions cause twice as much damage as another's, in order for the first source to increase its emissions by one unit, it would have to purchase permits amounting to two units of emissions from the other source.[7] Using corrective taxes in such situations will similarly require a large matrix of tax rates. Under either approach, deciding exactly what is taxed or permitted—emissions or damages—and how to translate between the two, remains an information- and computation-intensive task.

An even more troubling finding for corrective taxation, however, is that the tax rates should be set at the level of marginal social damages at the optimal level of pollution, *not* the marginal social damages that occur in the initially unregulated state of the world. That is, the damage caused by a unit of emissions from a particular source might be, say, $1 prior to any regulation, but at the optimal level of emissions, marginal damages from this specific source might be $.50 per unit. Hence, in general the regulator must compute the optimal set of tax rates based on the damages caused by each source at the optimal levels of emissions. But doing so requires information not only on how environmental damages vary as emissions change, but also the abatement costs of all of the different sources.

This finding erases what regulators initially consider to be the great advantage of using corrective environmental taxes: that all one must do is estimate damages and then promulgate taxes based on them. In reality, using taxes to achieve the optimal result requires a complete computation of the efficient emission and pollution outcome in order to define the correct set of tax rates, a task most practitioners view as hopelessly complex. In theory, with all of that information, regulators could promulgate highly cost-sensitive command and control regulations

and be done with the matter. Corrective taxation was supposed to avoid the need to gather all of this abatement-cost data.

The major practical consequence of the literature's attempts to analyze marketable permits and corrective taxes in more realistic circumstances thus has been to demonstrate that using them correctly and accurately is extremely difficult. As a result, practical applications have been confined to marketable permit systems for a handful of simple cases. For example, permit systems have been, or will be, used to implement the phaseout of chlorofluorocarbons (CFCs) and the nationwide limitation on SO_2 emissions from power generation and other sources. In these situations, the reality (or the assumption) is that the damages attributable to emissions from any particular source are the same, so that complex trading ratios between sources are unnecessary. This homogeneity makes using tradeable permits far more tractable. Moreover, in these few instances, marketable permits are used to achieve pollution-control targets dictated by what really is a political process, so the larger issue of overall economic optimality of the policy targets has been avoided.

Most economists would argue that the literature's emphasis on what it takes to achieve optimality is not intended to preclude the compromises between feasibility and efficiency that are inherent in addressing complex actual environmental problems. Indeed, they would agree that it is not practical to aim for developing a truly optimal set of tax rates when this might require numerous different rates to address the spectrum of actual marginal damages that different emission sources cause, rates that might also have to be routinely updated to reflect changing market and environmental conditions. Instead, one might devise a smaller set of tax rates and then sort the emission sources into a few classes. Of course, this will not achieve the completely optimal result, but such a compromise could be an improvement over the relevant alternatives.

[7] One could also achieve the same result (with the same degree of complexity) by using ambient pollution permits under which, instead of permitting emissions that are then traded in various ratios, permits relate to the right to impair environmental quality at particular locations.

Although it is easy to imagine developing practical applications of economic incentive systems for complex real-world pollution problems, there is considerable reluctance to do so. This is somewhat peculiar, given the track record of environmental policy making using admittedly inefficient command and control regulations. This apparent double standard appears to flow from a subtle difference in the intellectual points of departure for command and control regulations, on the one hand, and economic incentive systems, on the other. When regulators evaluate command and control approaches, their goal is environmental improvement. They recognize that their interventions inevitably will be imperfect, but whatever ultimately is done will at least be some improvement over the status quo.

But when regulators consider economic incentive systems, especially marketable permits and corrective taxes, the major advantage of these systems—improved economic efficiency over command and control—is foremost in their minds. When it becomes apparent that any feasible use of incentive systems in practice will also be imperfect and thus *inefficient*, these approaches seem less appealing. For traditional forms of regulatory intervention, imperfection is part of the messy business of addressing real-world environmental problems. For economic incentive systems, however, their much-touted advantage in improving the efficiency of outcomes is somewhat at war with their less-than-perfect performance in practice.

Unfair as they may be, these inappropriate comparisons of incentive-based and other regulatory policies do occur. To some degree the literature has helped to perpetuate this problem because of its focus on the difficulties of achieving optimal outcomes in complex circumstances. Policy makers are offered little practical guidance on how to construct imperfect, but workable, forms of incentive systems and then compare them to other, also imperfect, regulatory approaches. Thus, the literature's emphasis on the goal of attaining the optimal outcome is at cross-purposes with the fact that all regulatory approaches in reality will be less than perfect. In practice, the best is the enemy of the good.

Incompatibility of Revenue Generation and Environmental Policy Goals: The reasons discussed so far for the infrequent use of corrective taxation in environmental policy making apply to all incentive systems. Other impediments, however, relate specifically to problems that arise in trying to use corrective taxes in environmental policy. One such problem occurs when policy makers seek to use corrective taxes not just as regulations, but also to raise government revenue as a byproduct. The possibility that one can raise revenue and acheive environmental improvement at the same time is indeed a tantalizing prospect. But there are profound differences between taxes intended to raise revenue and taxes used as environmental regulatory instruments.

Good revenue-raising *excise* taxes, from both the economic and political perspectives, are those that are small enough on a per-entity basis not to cause large distortions in economic behavior, but are also spread over many payers, so that they raise large amounts of revenue. Thus, one normally tries to tax a large-volume, widely used economic good or activity that is inelastically demanded and supplied. In addition, to make these taxes easy to administer, one also focuses on goods or activities that are traded or otherwise well documented by the private sector. A good revenue-raising tax collects large amounts of revenue, does not pose a substantial burden on individual entities, and is easy to implement.

But the criteria that define a good environmental tax are quite different from those that characterize good revenue-raising taxes. Corrective environmental taxes are supposed to be noticed by polluters, because the whole point is to internalize the costs of the environmental harms. True corrective taxes are thus environmental regulations, not revenue-generation policies.

Moreover, corrective environmental taxes often must target activities that are not traded in, or well-documented by, the private sector. For example, discharges of toxic wastes to air, land, and water are disposal activities involving products with negative economic value, so levying taxes on these emissions is a very different administrative task than taxing, say, gasoline or some other traded commodity.

Perhaps more important, however, is that the tax revenues produced in total and on a per-entity basis, as well as elasticities of demand and supply, are largely irrelevant for true environmental taxes, because the purpose is to correct the incentives of polluters, not to raise money for the government. Revenues generated by environmental taxes are a byproduct of their operation, not their object. In fact, the best outcome under a true corrective tax is to collect no revenue at all. In this case, the cost of not polluting at all turns out to be lower than the social cost of the environmental damages, so completely eliminating the pollution and collecting no tax revenue is the optimal result.

Because the circumstances that define good revenue-raising excise-tax opportunities are completely different from those that call for using a corrective tax as a regulatory intervention, it is not easy to find environmental taxes that also manage to produce significant revenues and are easy to implement on top of existing market transactions. This is certainly the lesson learned in the various attempts during recent years to levy so-called environmental taxes to raise revenue for the federal government. These proposals tend to fail in practice for quite understandable reasons. To be sold as environmental taxes, they must at least minimally satisfy some commonsense requirements for any environmental regulation, such as providing risk-reduction benefits to society. But because these proposals do not begin with an environmental problem to be solved, the policy justification for these taxes as regulatory instruments amounts to a search for "good things" that

might happen as a result. Of course, clever analysts can always find some good results in any intervention.

The problem is that after identifying some environmental benefits that might result from these sorts of taxes, it usually turns out that the "environmental taxes" as proposed are not particularly efficient regulatory instruments for obtaining those environmental benefits. This occurs because whatever is located in the process of searching for desirable environmental results is not the original motivation for promulgating the tax. Hence, other regulatory instruments could be focused more closely on the underlying environmental problem and thus would be more effective at obtaining the environmental benefits in question. Furthermore, as these tax proposals are studied further, the reality that they do not provide "money for free" sets in; identifiable entities must pay the tax liabilities and normally they are not happy about it. Thus, revenue-raising excise taxes masquerading as environmental taxes usually fail to be used because they encounter significant difficulties in satisfying the basic requirements of environmental regulations: targeting a real pollution problem, being relatively efficient at addressing the problem, and possessing a convincing equity rationale.

Of course, it is conceivable that a true corrective environmental tax could yield large revenues. But proposing such a tax as an environmental regulation would first begin with the pollution problems to be solved and, after careful study and deliberation, the tax would be found to be a reasonably sound environmental regulatory intervention. Tracing from an environmental tax developed in this way to its environmental benefits would be direct and coherent, and would not reveal other, far superior regulatory policies for addressing those environmental concerns.

Somewhat ironically, it is probably accurate to say that the desire to use corrective taxes in environmental policy making to raise government revenue has likely done more to discourage than to encourage their use. In the end, however, the inability to justify environmental taxes when the real goal is to raise government revenues should be viewed not as a failure for true corrective taxation, but as the natural result of attempting to promulgate an environmental policy without a compelling regulatory rationale.

Conflicts between Environmental Policy Objectives and Corrective Taxation Goals: Another reason why corrective taxes are not used is that the fundamental policy goals underlying environmental regulation and corrective taxation sometimes conflict. Hence, even overcoming the hurdles outlined so far, environmental taxes still will not be used when the basic goals of the regulator are at variance with the policy objective pursued by corrective taxation.

True environmental taxation calls for taxing pollution at a rate equal to the marginal social damages caused. The beauty of this approach is that it achieves the optimal level of pollution at the lowest cost, and it does so by ensuring that the incentives of private-sector market participants are consistent with social goals. The problem is that the beauty of this approach is in the eyes of the beholder. Economists find the operation of corrective taxation particularly attractive, not only because of its optimality properties, but also because they are generally in agreement with other policy objectives that are satisfied by taxes. One is the *polluter-pays* principle, which most economists find a reasonably sound equity justification for the distributional results of environmental taxes relative to other regulatory instruments that do not charge polluters for residual legal levels of emissions and their associated harms.

Economists also are attracted to the proposition that policy makers should strive to maximize net social benefits in developing and promulgating environmental regulations, another policy criterion satisfied by corrective taxation. But here there is often some controversy. Although improving the cost-effectiveness of environmental regulations and requiring polluters to pay for the environmental harms they cause are both themes that resonate with many non-economists, there is far less agreement that a purely economic assessment of the net social benefits of environmental regulations should be the primary guide to successful environmental stewardship.

Indeed, it is often observed that many of the nation's environmental statutes do not call for weighing the costs and benefits when setting goals for pollution control and environmental risk management. Instead they direct regulators to reduce pollution risks to reasonable or acceptable levels, to set such goals as minimizing the risks of harm to human health, or to apply available pollution-control technologies, regardless of the risks avoided. For example, regulations for hazardous waste management seek to achieve extremely low levels of risk often at great cost. Hence, the guiding principles embodied in environmental statutes and their legal interpretation are often at variance with the underlying premise of corrective taxation—that public policy should balance costs and benefits to arrive at economically *optimal* regulations.

At first glance, making decisions on any basis other than marginal costs and benefits might seem irrational. Upon reflection, however, setting more stringent targets for pollution control than economic analysis would dictate based on quantified costs and benefits could be simply a crude, but pragmatic way of accommodating a host of other social goals and considerations. For example, society's concern about pollution may extend beyond the expected value of pollution-related harms to the distribution of those impacts among different segments of the population. Similarly, many environmental regulatory programs affect the welfare of generations yet to be born. It is reasonable to adopt a more conservative stance on issues that affect one's distant descendants, especially when environmental effects are somewhat uncertain and possibly irreversible.

For a variety of reasons, therefore, the full set of relevant environmental policy objectives can conflict with the more narrow goal of maximizing net economic benefits. In some cases, at least some of these other policy concerns might be relatively easy to incorporate into estimates of costs and benefits through more sophisticated economic analysis. This suggests that there is potentially some benefit to broadening the definition and inclusiveness of costs and benefits to encompass additional concerns normally considered by public policy makers. For example, one could introduce weights or other factors to reflect the equity implications of environmental outcomes. Similarly, uncertainty and irreversibility concerns might be accommodated using risk aversion and option value adjustments to environmental benefits estimates.

But all of these adjustments must be introduced quantitatively and monetarily when using corrective taxation in order to accurately reflect them in the actual tax rates. This is no small feat in light of the fact that, at least presently, valuing the estimated benefits of environmental regulations in monetary terms is a rare event. Moreover, some policy goals cannot reasonably be embodied in corrective tax rates; for example, the tax rates necessary to satisfy the objective of zero risk of exposure to hazardous wastes essentially would be infinite.

It is thus unlikely that even far more sophisticated economic analysis will systematically, much less quantitatively, capture all of the myriad goals and factors that are actually weighed in practical environmental policy making. Because of this, the costs and benefits typically captured by economic analysis of a regulation will often be a subset of the criteria used by regulators in arriving at policy decisions. If so, this has profound implications for using corrective environmental taxation as a regulatory tool. The great advantage of corrective taxes is that they cause private-sector decision makers to weigh the social costs and benefits of their actions by inserting the missing social values of pollution damages into their calculations. As long as the explicit social goal is to balance economic costs and benefits, corrective taxation is indeed a powerful tool.

But when public policy decisions are guided by a broader set of concerns that are difficult to reflect in dollar-denominated tax rates, the great advantage of corrective taxation becomes somewhat of a liability. This problem is similar to the discomfort policy makers express about the necessity of ceding control over outcomes to polluters when using economic incentive systems. Here, corrective environmental taxes require the regulator to embrace as the overriding policy goal a direct balancing of costs and benefits as measured and monetized in practice, and essentially to ignore other policy considerations that are more difficult to express in terms of monetary tax rates.

Equity Justification for Corrective Taxes Often Fails in Practice: Yet another reason for the infrequent use of corrective environmental taxation in practice is that satisfying the need for an equity justification for taxes is far more difficult in reality than in theory. Recall that more than efficiency enhancement is required for policy makers to be comfortable and confident in using corrective taxation. In particular, taxes impose different distributional outcomes than do other available policy instruments, because they charge polluters for the residual and efficient levels of pollution. The traditional justification for this is the *polluter-pays* principle, which casts the tax liabilities not as an added tax burden on polluters, but as an "invoice" for the damages they cause.

This is all fine in theory. As noted above, however, a significant problem in practice is that quantifying and valuing pollution damages is expensive, difficult, and often extremely controversial. Even on its own terms, trying to convert numerous hard-to-measure impacts of pollution on environmental resources that are often very far removed from goods and services traded in the market is a task fraught with significant uncertainties and substantial information requirements.

Moreover, applying even the best techniques for valuing many of the damages pollution causes often results in a wide range of monetary estimates. Someone has to undertake the unenviable task of selecting and defending a specific value to use in forming the environmental tax rate. For example, estimates of the value of avoiding a statistical death among a large group of people range from hundreds-of-thousands to tens-of-millions of dollars. It matters a great deal in setting the actual corrective tax rate whether figures from the bottom, the middle, or the top of this range are used: several orders of magnitude, to be specific. Those paying the tax naturally will argue for the low end, while defenders of the environment will press for the higher end. There are few proponents of compromise in this debate.

Perhaps more significant is that some participants in the policy-making process disagree with the basic notion that many environmental resources harmed by pollution can or should be valued by the methods and procedures economists currently use. Hence, in many cases the debate is less about the monetary estimates themselves than the fundamental ethical stance implied by placing dollar values on environmental resources and human lives.[8]

Even if some agreement on rough dollar values of environmental damages can be obtained, still more controversy surrounds the practice of discounting future benefits to the present. Many environmental regulations reduce risks far into the future. The present values of these benefits are significantly affected by the discount rate used, sometimes by orders of magnitude. Hence, uncertainty about the precise discount rate, even what appears to be a relatively small range of possible values, say 2 to 4 percent, can radically alter any tax rates based on discounted benefits. Even more troubling is that some question the entire ethical foundation for discounting over long time horizons when future generations are not present to participate in policy decisions. All of this introduces yet more sources of uncertainty about the appropriate magnitudes of environmental taxes and an additional reason for extremely wide ranges of defensible rates.

Throughout all of this, as economists repeatedly and correctly point out, policy decisions must be made. Regulators weighing different alternatives will need estimates of the value of environmental harms to assist them in choosing, otherwise the process of making those decisions without explicit values for environmental damages will reveal implicit values for these effects. Nevertheless, the issue is not so much that the controversy and difficulty of placing values on environmental damages adds another dimension to an already complex policy-making task. Rather, it is that significant uncertainty about the values of environmental damages translates directly into uncertainty about whether the tax liabilities are really accurate "invoices" for environmental damages. This renders what was a very powerful theoretical equity argument in favor of taxes—that the taxes are really only charges polluters must pay for the damages they cause—far less convincing in reality.

USING ENVIRONMENTAL TAXES TO ACHIEVE PREDETERMINED REGULATORY TARGETS

The fact that true corrective taxation seldom, if ever, has been used in environmental policy has not been ignored by economists. Indeed, recognizing that there are often fundamental conflicts between the way policy makers usually approach environmental regulation and the way traditional corrective taxes operate, economists have developed a more restrictive type of environmental taxation. The hope is that this new

---

[8] For a thorough review of the philosophical arguments against the use of corrective taxation see S. J. Kelman, *What Price Incentives? Economists and the Environment*, (Boston: Auburn House, 1981), .

version might avoid some of the more significant problems that have plagued attempts to use true corrective taxes in practical policy making.

This new incarnation of environmental taxation is referred to as the *standards and charges* approach.[9] Because environmental regulatory policy tends to be formulated by establishing acceptable outcomes and then exploring various possible approaches to achieve them, the standards and charges ("taxes" in the terminology of this analysis) approach suggests that taxation could be used as an alternative to command and control to achieve a predetermined regulatory goal. For example, if the acceptable overall level for a particular pollutant has already been decided, taxing sources of emissions at a rate sufficient to attain the specified level of pollution could offer the advantage of cost minimization relative to command and control regulations.

This new version of environmental taxation normally is advanced in the context of a pollution problem to which a number of sources contribute. For example, suppose 10 sources emit a total of 200 units of a particular air pollutant in a specific region. To enhance air quality in the area, the regulatory authority might decide, based on a number of policy criteria, that total emissions from these sources should be only 100 units. One way to achieve this would be to mandate a 50 percent reduction in emissions from each of the 10 sources. Another way to accomplish this goal would be to tax emissions from these sources at a rate sufficient to reduce the total by the required 100 units, basing the tax rate not on the value of marginal environmental damages, but instead setting it at a level that encourages sufficient controls by all sources collectively to meet the predetermined emissions target.

Of course, both approaches will achieve the regulatory objective. But when emission control costs differ across the various sources in ways not known by the environmental authority, the across-the-board command and control approach will impose compliance costs greater than necessary, because marginal control costs will not be equated across sources. As seen earlier, however, the tax approach will minimize the cost of achieving the target reduction in pollution by equating marginal control costs across sources. This will ensure that emission controls throughout the industry are undertaken in a least-cost manner, but does not require the environmental authority to gather and process detailed information on compliance costs source by source, which would be necessary to accomplish the same result using command and control regulation.

Admittedly, the predetermined policy target might be either too stringent or too lenient relative to the fully optimal solution. For example, the optimal amount of emissions actually might be 80 units, so that a true corrective tax aiming to achieve this result would be greater than that necessary here to reduce emissions to the target level of 100 units. Alternatively, the optimal level of emissions might be greater than 100 units, say 120, so that the true corrective tax in this case would be less than that used to meet the predetermined regulatory target of 100 units. But given that the acceptable overall level of emissions from these sources has already been decided, setting a tax at a rate sufficient to attain this goal may not be truly optimal, but will nevertheless have a potentially significant cost-minimization advantage over command and control.

One objective in formulating this new version of environmental taxes is to avoid some of the more troubling difficulties encountered in trying to use true corrective taxation in environmental policy. And taxes intended to satisfy a predetermined regulatory goal do indeed skirt the difficulties in practice of setting tax rates based on hard-to-value environmental damages, and the often intractable conflicts between overall policy goals and the single net-benefit-maximization objective that underlies true corrective taxation. Because the target is no longer the full social optimum, tax rates need only be those

[9] See Baumol and Oates (1988), note 2, Chapter 11.

necessary to call forth from the industry sufficient emission control to reach the environmental improvement goal. Using taxes in this way makes no reference to valuing damages and, by explicitly adopting the predetermined target, completely erases any conflicts between multiple policy goals and the operation of taxes as regulatory instruments.

Of course, in using even this more limited form of environmental taxation, one must still wrestle with many complexities of the world, such as differences in the amount of damages depending on the location of pollution sources, and the difficulties inherent in mitigating non-point-source pollution problems. Moreover, most environmental policy goals tend to be specified in terms of tangible and relatively easily monitored outcomes that are best described by quantitative environmental indicators and measurable emissions of pollutants or by the application of technologies that are understood to achieve a particular quantitative goal. Hence, command and control regulations tend to be written in terms of the ways these policy targets are specified and measured; for example, the maximum concentration and volume of a particular pollutant from a specific plant per day, or the use of particular air-emission-control technology.

Environmental taxes, however, are monetary charges that influence the behavior of polluters, but do not constrain the physical outcome. Finding the tax rate that will attain the overall target level of emissions and pollution, therefore, could require considerable study. Indeed, some experimentation and adjustment of the tax rates would probably be required to reach satisfactory results under this standards and charges redefinition of environmental taxes.

Nevertheless, the empirical challenges one faces in using this new version of environmental taxation are not inherently different from or more difficult than those regulators confront every day in the process of fashioning workable policies to address real-world environmental problems. For example, deciding exactly what to tax and determining whether a single tax rate or several will be required to account for the unequal environmental impacts of different sources are complexities mirrored in one form or another in any practical approach to addressing the underlying environmental problem. When multiple tax rates might be needed, the same circumstances would also require a marketable permit system to establish more complex rules than one-for-one permit trading across emission sources; they also would suggest more complex command and control strategies than one-size-fits-all.

The efficiency case for using environmental taxes as redefined by the standards and changes approach to achieve predetermined policy goals is thus a reasonably strong one. These taxes can generally achieve an environmental target at a lower cost than command and control approaches that do not account for differences in control costs across polluters. Such taxes also offer regulators significant administrative benefits over more traditional source-by-source, command and control regulation. Under the latter approach, trying to achieve the regulatory goal at the minimum cost requires the regulator to collect large amounts of information on each source's control costs, and then to promulgate standards tailored to individual sources to reflect differences in marginal emission control costs. When using taxes, however, the regulator simply searches for the tax rate that is sufficient to achieve the policy target, relying on the individual emission sources to compare their marginal control costs to the tax rate, thus helping society to reach the minimum-cost solution.

With all of these advantages, and far fewer of the problems that have hobbled attempts to use true corrective taxation, one might expect this new incarnation of environmental taxes to have received a warm welcome from policy makers. Unfortunately, this version of environmental taxes also has some practical problems and limitations that significantly affect its attractiveness to environmental regulators. The most important of these are the loss of the equity justification for using taxes as opposed to other forms of regulation, and the somewhat restricted applicability of the approach.

Loss of the Equity Justification for Environmental Taxes: Although the efficiency advantages of using taxes instead of command and control to encourage multiple polluters to achieve a given environmental policy target cost effectively are clear, regulators still must defend environmental taxes on equity grounds. As before, the efficiency enhancement provided by taxes in this case usually is not sufficient to justify their selection over other regulatory instruments because it forces polluting firms to bear the burden of both additional taxes and emission control costs. In general, the smaller the efficiency gains of the tax approach relative to conventional command and control regulation, the less compelling will be an efficiency-based argument for imposing the extra tax burden on currently regulated firms. Put another way, it is difficult to choose taxes over command and control regulation when the cost savings are small and the added tax burden is large.

Far more important, however, is that the cost-minimizing property of taxes in encouraging multiple polluters to reach a predetermined environmental target at the minimum cost is possessed identically by a marketable permits system. The two incentive systems—price-based taxes and quantity-based permits—each achieve the policy target by presenting polluters with the appropriate incentives. Taxes do so by explicitly pricing pollution. Permits accomplish the same result by allowing trading of pollution rights.

Because the tax rate necessary to achieve the regulatory target will be the same as the ultimate market price of the permits, both approaches will attain the overall regulatory goal at minimum cost, and both will equally outperform traditional command and control regulations by improving on the insensitivity of command and

control to variations in control costs across different sources.[10] The choice between these two systems on efficiency grounds, therefore, revolves around subsidiary considerations, such as favoring taxes when transaction costs involved in trading permits are high, and using permits when there are severe difficulties and uncertainties in adjusting and fine-tuning the tax rate to achieve the policy target.

In the absence of any clear efficiency-based reasons for using taxes instead of marketable permits to achieve a predetermined policy objective for multiple pollution sources, it becomes paramount to have a convincing equity justification for taxes. But it is at this point that the new version of environmental taxes runs into deep trouble. Recall that the confidence regulators have in defending the tax approach flows mainly from the *polluter-pays* principle. For true corrective taxation, the theoretical equity argument is strong, because a polluter's tax bill is essentially an invoice for the environmental damages caused.

The problem with taxes that seek to achieve a predetermined policy goal is that the rate necessary to achieve the regulatory target may bear no obvious relationship to the marginal social damages the pollution causes. Hence, when taxes and permits both achieve the overall target level of environmental improvement, the equity case for using taxes instead of marketable permits is weak. The regulator cannot easily use the polluter-pays principle in support of taxes, because there is no basis for arguing that the tax bill equals the environmental damages. This is especially troublesome when marginal

---

[10] Taxes and marketable permits are also superior to command and control regulations in the long run because these incentive-based options price pollution still allowed. If this is not priced, too many firms will enter the industry in the long run, which will then require tighter per-source standards to meet the policy target. For a discussion of this and related points see D. F. Spulber, "Effluent Regulation and Long-Run Optimality," *Journal of Environmental Economics and Management* 12 (June 1985): 103–116 .

benefits fall short of marginal costs at a predetermined policy target. Using an environmental tax in this case would impose a tax exceeding the value of the pollution damages.

This is not to say that one cannot mount an equity justification for using taxes in pursuit of a predetermined policy goal. Rather, the problem is that the tax rate is set to achieve the regulatory target, so it bears no explicit or necessary relationship to the level of environmental damages. Hence, to successfully defend the distributional effects of using taxes, the regulator must develop a secondary and independent equity justification, based presumably on the value of environmental damages at the predetermined policy target. But this is at least some of what the recasting of environmental taxes into the standards-and-charges framework was designed to avoid.

By comparison, the equity case for using marketable permits is quite straightforward. The permits normally are assumed to be distributed to emission sources based on their allowable emissions under a command and control regulation that achieves the same overall level of pollution control. Hence, no one will oppose using these grandfathered marketable permits instead of command and control, because voluntary trades of permits cannot make anyone worse off. Therefore, no equity justification is required for using marketable permits relative to command and control.

But in substituting taxes for a command and control regulation, there is no guarantee that individual emission sources will not be worse off. In fact, relative to command and control, taxes seem to impose almost perverse equity consequences. Consider how a *low-control-cost* emission source fares when taxes are substituted for command and control. Under the latter approach, this source reduces emissions at a modest cost to meet the relevant emission-reduction requirements. When taxes are then substituted, this source reduces emissions even more *and* pays taxes on any residual pollution. This source

clearly must be worse off under taxes than command and control. *High-control-cost* sources, on the other hand, could be either better or worse off under taxes, depending on how much they save by paying taxes instead of reducing emissions and the size of the tax bill they now owe for residual pollution. Thus, in the process of enhancing efficiency—shifting controls from more- to less-expensive sources—taxes effectively penalize low-cost firms and potentially reward high-cost ones.

It is thus easy to understand why marketable permits will be preferred over taxes by regulators and the affected industries. Marketable permits are a direct quantity-based method of achieving target levels of environmental improvement at minimum cost, and if the permits are initially distributed without charge, the approach does not require any equity justification relative to command and control. Taxes similarly enhance efficiency, but require an independent equity justification. In a sense, grandfathered marketable permits dominate taxes because they accomplish the efficiency enhancement regulators seek, without the need to search for the appropriate tax rate and, probably more important, without the burden of defending potentially large distributional consequences, a task rendered quite difficult because there is no necessary relationship between the tax rates necessary to achieve predetermined policy goals and the resulting levels of environmental damages.

Restricted Applicability of the Approach: Recasting environmental taxes into the standards-and-charges framework has another more subtle consequence. As noted earlier, this new version of environmental taxes is most appealing when policy makers establish an overall target level of emissions for multiple pollution sources. For example, many individual sources of CO_2 contribute to the overall global climate-change problem, and reducing emissions from them clearly could benefit from approaches that take advantage of possibly large differences in control costs. Similarly, multiple sources of pollution in an airshed all combine to damage air quality in the region, so it makes sense to use taxes or permits to achieve predetermined air quality improvement targets at lower cost.

Although situations in which multiple sources contribute to a given harm are common, they nevertheless are only a subset of all environmental problems. For example, setting safe drinking-water standards or developing risk-reduction guidelines for pesticide use, much less regulating hazardous waste management, do not fit the *multiple-sources single-harm* mold. In these cases, policy makers are more concerned with risk management at the level of individual occurrences or pollution damages caused by a particular source independent of those generated by other sources. In such situations, the primary mechanism by which taxes provide efficiency-enhancement—cost minimization across multiple sources that contribute to a single harm—is no longer relevant.

For example, when the desired result is for all hazardous waste disposal facilities to undertake various design and other measures to reduce the probability and environmental impacts of toxic substances releases, it makes no sense to try to cast this in terms of a single harm to which all such facilities contribute. Instead, each source poses independent risks. Similarly, when an environmental problem is caused by emissions of pollutants from a single industrial source, no other facilities contribute to the problem, so the across-sources cost minimization provided by taxes no longer applies.

Of course, in all cases it still makes sense to try to achieve policy goals at the lowest cost, so one can imagine using the tax approach to encourage individual polluters to reach their specific policy targets cost-effectively. But incentives to cost-minimize will be present under command and control regulations that directly specify those source-specific targets. As long as

regulators are equally flexible in defining and setting standards under command and control as they are in determining what to tax and at what rates, both approaches will attain largely the same environmental goals.

What all of this means is that in a host of real-world circumstances, regulators gain little by doing anything other than promulgating their policy targets in the terms in which they are formulated. If the goal is to reach a given reduction in the amount and toxicity of the emissions from a particular pollution source, specifying this as an emission standard will accomplish this directly. The regulator could also tax the facility at a rate sufficient to achieve the policy goal, but the result would be the same. Thus, when across-source cost minimization is not relevant, the major advantage of the standards-and-charges version of environmental taxes evaporates. Theoretically, to satisfy a predetermined policy target for an individual polluter, a marketable permit system collapses to a performance-based standard because only one permittee exists, and a tax, after fine-tuning to meet the predetermined policy goal, offers little, if any, efficiency enhancement over intelligently conceived command and control.[11]

Because the compelling efficiency advantage of the standards-and-charges version of environmental taxes applies only in multiple-sources single-harm situations, the case for using such taxes is largely confined to this subset of circumstances. It is therefore somewhat ironic that the great advantage of these taxes only applies in precisely a set of circumstances where another incentive-based instrument, grandfathered mar-

[11] It is possible to argue that an additional reason for the greater efficiency of taxes relative to other approaches is that taxes charge for residual pollution. This ensures the appropriate long-run entry conditions for polluting industries. In practical policy making, however, this is not a very compelling argument. Moreover, it is not clear that these considerations are relevant in the single-source/predetermined target case, especially if the policy goal is more stringent than is economically optimal.

ketable permits, tend to be more attractive to regulators. It is even more ironic that only in these multiple-source single-harm circumstances does it make sense to use marketable permits at all, because, for marketability to mean anything, there must be multiple sources.

Where Do We Go from Here?

Given the many reasons for environmental taxes not being used in policy making, the prospects for their adoption as environmental regulations in the future might seem quite bleak. This impression is partially the result of having dwelled at such length on all of these practical difficulties. But the ultimate goal of the analysis is not just to diagnose the problems regulators encounter in using environmental taxes, but also to indicate how at least some of the many policy and economic issues must be resolved before using taxes as environmental regulatory policies can become a reality.

Prognosis for the Use of Environmental Taxes: The practical difficulties of using taxes as environmental regulations that have been identified here suggest that any reasonable expectations of their adoption in the future will require regulators to approach matters in a number of ways fundamentally different from those used in the past. The first step, of course, will be to ensure that regulators have realistic expectation concerning the operation and effects of corrective taxes. But even after that, however, it still is unlikely that taxes will be the environmental regulation of choice in all circumstances. There will always be some tension between multiple policy goals and the fundamental properties of corrective taxation, depending on the situation, and taxes will require hard work to implement and justify on equity grounds. Nevertheless, approaching their use with realistic policy expectations will go a long way toward making tax-based environmental regulations a reality. Upon reaching that point,

the central issue will be where economists and policy makers might find the best candidates for environmental taxation.

Considering first the use of taxes in pursuit of predetermined regulatory goals, the outlook is reasonably optimistic if the dominance of marketable permits can be overcome. Admittedly, the central advantage of these cost-minimizing taxes is limited to situations in which multiple sources together cause a pollution problem of concern. But within these confines, taxes could be used if they can be defended as superior to marketable permits. Hence, good candidates for these sorts of taxes are situations in which the transactions costs involved in marketable permits are high, both in initially allocating the permits and in accomplishing trades among permittees.

Assuming that there is an implementation-based reason for using taxes instead of permits pursue a predetermined regulatory target, the distributional outcome of taxes will still require justification. From this political perspective, taxes are thus less likely to be chosen over permits when a relatively small number of sources face large tax liabilities. On the other hand, when large numbers of sources face relatively small individual tax bills for emissions, taxes probably will be more acceptable. They will also be more attractive to regulators and polluters when the cost savings over command and control are substantial.

But multiple-source single-harm situations are only a subset of all practical environmental problems. The prospects for using environmental taxes in more general circumstances must therefore lie in returning to the original corrective environmental tax formulation. Recognizing this, it is sometimes argued that one way to avoid some of the major difficulties in using true corrective taxation is to supplement existing command and control regulations by charging taxes on the residual emissions that are allowed under the standards. The command and control regulation achieves the emission reductions the regulator desires, while the tax charges sources for the damages that remain. Clearly, this would be consistent with true corrective taxation as long as the tax rates approximate the social damages the residual pollution causes.

This hybrid system does indeed avoid some of the major problems in using environmental taxation in practice, such as the loss of control over outcomes, and conflicts between multiple policy goals and the exclusive maximization of net benefits pursued by taxes. But it should be readily apparent that it would be difficult to argue for such an arrangement unless one could point to plausible environmental improvements that might result. After all, the extra environmental tax is supposed to be an environmental regulation.

One possible environmental benefit of adding taxes to existing regulations might be that these taxes will be even more stringent, so that additional controls and environmental improvement will result. But this seems unlikely, because there is little reason to think that regulators who are unwilling to promulgate sufficiently strict command and control regulations will somehow be comfortable doing so using environmental taxes.

Because conventional proposals to add taxes on top of existing regulations often do not have strong regulatory arguments in their favor, proposals to use these hybrid arrangements tend to be viewed as obvious ploys to gather more revenues rather than produce significant environmental benefits. This is not to say that using multiple regulations is unwise. Rather, it is that without a clear regulatory justification for supplementing existing rules with environmental taxes, doing so appears to be motivated by the tax revenues generated, not the environmental improvements that will result. Hence, although using corrective taxes in tandem with other regulatory instruments is perfectly legitimate, successfully defending them as regulatory tools is really not much different from justifying their use alone.[12]

Ultimately, to make any tangible progress in applying true corrective taxes in practical environmental policy making, regulators will have to pick their battles wisely. Some situations simply are not realistic candidates for corrective taxation, so it is best to avoid wasting financial and political resources on them. For example, regulators are not likely to be comfortable ceding control to polluters when the environmental problem involves highly toxic substances that produce serious harms to human health and the environment. Similarly, when policy makers consider and weigh a number of policy goals other than measurable costs and benefits, unless these can be incorporated into the actual tax rates, environmental taxation is unlikely to be favored. Regulators should therefore focus attempts to use corrective taxation in situations where policy makers are relatively comfortable with outcomes based substantially on a private sector weighing of costs and benefits, supplemented of course by the taxes. Positive amounts of residual pollution that are uneconomical to avoid must be acceptable, as must be the uncertainty about exact outcomes inherent in ceding control to polluters.

Policy makers should also focus on situations in which using taxes over other regulatory approaches is likely to generate significant gains in efficiency. There is little point to investing

[12] To see this, consider a more realistic example of a hybrid regulatory system under which traditional command and control standards are supplemented with the opportunity to exceed the specified limits of those regulations by paying a fee per unit of pollution. The attractiveness of this arrangement is that it allows flexibility to sources when full compliance is unexpectedly costly for some reason or another. But this is ultimately the same as the general advantage of using taxes over command and control in that it uses private, decentralized decision making about emission control based on a "price" of polluting instead of centralized and information-intensive decision making by the regulator. Hence, this situation will not be any easier to justify than using a corrective tax by itself.

large efforts in using a new regulatory approach where the gains from doing so are small. Hence, the case for using taxes will be easiest to make when there is strong evidence that decentralized decision making about pollution control based on corrective taxes will substantially reduce total costs and increase overall environmental benefits. In practical applications, the blanket theoretical assertion that taxes will be superior to other approaches generally is not a good substitute for a convincing empirical demonstration that identifies the source and magnitude of efficiency enhancement to be gained.

Attempts to use corrective taxes in practice will also meet with greater success when regulators are reasonably confident that tax rates can be devised that bear some relationship to the pollution damages, and certainly that they are not vastly greater than the harms caused. Hence, what is needed in the environmental policy-making arena is a more concerted effort to focus on benefit-valuation issues earlier in the regulatory process, to avoid foundering later for lack of confidence in the tax rates. While this is not new advice, it is worth emphasizing. If policy makers have deep reservations about "pricing" environmental harms, they will not use taxes as regulatory instruments.

In addition to focusing on regulatory situations that are compatible with corrective taxes and where there is a reasonable expectation that tax rates can bear some discernable relationship to pollution damages, policy makers must then engage in fair comparisons of alternative policies. As is true of any regulatory intervention in practice, real-world corrective taxes inevitably will be inefficient relative to the optimal textbook outcome. But because corrective taxation's claim to fame is its efficiency, the approach seems to fail on its own terms in policy makers' eyes.

But correcting the problem of unfair comparisons involves more than convincing policy makers that parallel evaluations of alternative approaches are critical to using taxes in practice.

At least part of the problem is that many observers of environmental regulation tout the superiority of corrective taxes in general, but then criticize specific attempts to use them in the messy and imperfect world of policy practice. An extreme example of this is the insistence that to obtain the truly optimal solution, one must set the tax rate equal to the marginal social damages at the optimal level of pollution, not the current level, which requires regulators to know all of the control-cost information for polluters as well as how the value of damages changes as pollution levels vary.

Of course, regulators never have enough information to ensure that interventions are necessarily optimal, whether command and control approaches or market-based systems, but this does not prevent them from acting. Moreover, worrying about any differences between the value of marginal environmental damages initially versus at the optimal result seems overly cautious, given the current state of quantitative benefits analysis. Regulators consider themselves lucky to have quantitative estimates of risk reduction, uncertain and imprecise as they often are in practice, and monetization of benefits is a rare occurrence. Hence, although there may be exceptions, it is probably reasonable to assume that marginal social damages, initially and at the optimal level, both probably lie within the wide confidence bands provided by attempts to quantify and value environmental harms.

Finally, there is little to be done about the fundamental conflict between by the desire to use environmental taxation to collect revenues for the government and the need to justify such taxes as sound environmental regulatory policy. In general, situations ripe for collecting large revenues using excise taxes are unfortunately quite different from circumstances in which a corrective tax is most useful in addressing an environmental problem.

The resulting tension will never be resolved. On the one hand, the desire to collect revenue will always pull policy makers toward broad-based taxes levied on existing market transactions that spread (hopefully) a large tax burden over many entities. But these are very difficult to defend as beneficial environmental regulatory policies. On the other hand, policy makers wishing to use true corrective taxation as a regulatory tool primarily for its efficiency properties will view revenue generation as an incidental, perhaps even a politically unwanted, byproduct.

It is tempting to argue that perhaps some middle ground can be found where taxes that raise significant revenues are also sound environmental regulatory policies. This is an empirical issue, of course, but one should never lose sight of the fact that one is trying to satisfy two goals with a single instrument, in this case raising revenues and improving the environment. Although it is conceivable that a corrective environmental tax could fulfill both objectives, the record to date is not encouraging.

Hence, rather than setting out to try to find instances in which one can generate large amounts of revenues with an environmental tax, it is probably more productive to discard the goal of revenue generation initially so that practical attempts to use corrective taxation can first be justified as beneficial environmental regulatory policies. Once experience with using this regulatory approach is sufficiently broad and deep, some attention to its revenue-raising potential might be entertained, but never to the point of eclipsing the basic requirement that environmental taxes first be prudent and effective regulations.

Why Bother with Environmental Taxes? In light of all of the problems policy makers confront in attempting to use environmental taxes in practice, much less the hard road that lies ahead for those who continue to pursue this approach to environmental regulation, it is perfectly legitimate to ask why regulators should bother with taxes at all. After all, policy makers have been reasonably successful over the years using traditional command and control regulation. Moreover, while there certainly are some exceptions,

many applications of command and control regulation are not nearly as obtuse and insensitive as the pictures painted by detractors would indicate. Hence, given that command and control is not quite as bad as its opponents suggest and that economic incentives are not quite as good as their proponents wish, the gains to be had by shifting from the former to the latter are normally are overstated.[13]

Nevertheless, there are several reasons for continuing to try to use corrective taxes. First, while substantial environmental improvements have occurred over the past several decades, further gains are likely to be obtained at possibly rapidly increasing costs. Hence, the efficiency-enhancing properties of incentive systems in general will become more important in the future. Furthermore, as the emphasis on efficiency in obtaining environmental improvement intensifies, policy makers will soon learn that the applicability of many incentive systems other than corrective taxation is confined to subsets of environmental problems. For example, marketable permits are really only applicable to situations in which multiple sources contribute to a single harm. Similarly, deposit–refund schemes, such as beverage-container return systems, are useful when one needs to discourage actions by numerous entities that are often individually insignificant but collectively harmful, and enforcing other regulatory approaches is prohibitively expensive.

But the only incentive system with general applicability across the wide spectrum of actual pollution problems is corrective taxation. At least in theory, the approach can be applied to any individual- or multiple-source pollution problem. As a rule, if the harm can be measured and the chain of causation can be traced back to the entities responsible, a corrective tax conceivably

[13] For a discussion some of the biases in empirical estimates of the superiority of incentive systems, see W. J. Baumol "Toward Enhancement of the Contribution of Theory to Environmental Policy," *Environmental and Resource Economics* 4 (1991): 333–352.

can be used to address the problem. Hence, to the degree that policy makers turn to incentive systems more often in the future for their efficiency properties, they will be driven by necessity to corrective taxation because of its broad applicability. Of course, attempts to use taxes still may fail because of the many policy conflicts and practical difficulties discussed here.

A second advantage of corrective environmental taxation in the long run is its inherent ability to tap detailed and diverse data, information that would be very costly for the regulatory authority to gather, in pursuit of social environmental goals. Of course, this is the advantage most often cited in support of market-based approaches. As argued here, however, the benefit of "harnessing market forces" in environmental policy is not entirely unqualified. In many cases, policy makers are not willing to cede control over the environmental outcome to polluters, or are uncomfortable trying to reflect certain policy concerns in monetary tax rates. But where regulators are comfortable with outcomes generated purely by weighing quantified costs and benefits, delegating the detailed decision making down to the individual polluter level does seem to offer significant advantages over continuing to rely on regulatory standards to accomplish the same goals.

This is not to say that developing tax rates for specific circumstances will necessarily be simple. Instead, the point is that if the overall policy goal is to make individual pollution-control decisions based on quantified costs and benefits, it seems an appropriate division of labor for the regulatory authority to focus on developing information about, and monetary estimates of, the environmental damages pollution causes, and to allocate the task of making numerous individual decisions about pollution

control to those in the best position to do so.

Realizing the fruits of this widely touted advantage of corrective taxes, however, depends critically on the willingness of regulators to allow the system to function as intended. Whether the net-benefits-maximization property of corrective taxation is an advantage or not therefore depends fundamentally on whether policy makers believe that their objectives can be satisfied by setting prices for environmental harms and allowing polluters to make their own choices.

Finally, of all possible regulatory approaches for addressing environmental issues, corrective taxation focuses most clearly on the benefits side of the problem. Economists criticize many environmental regulations as being too costly, at least from the perspective of the net social benefits they produce. Hence, by making the benefits almost the point of departure in environmental policy making, the corrective tax approach better reveals cases in which proposed regulations impose far higher costs than the benefits they provide.

Of course, one can argue that many benefits of environmental regulations are difficult to quantify, much less to value, but that they nonetheless do exist. Furthermore, one can note that regulators often weigh more than just quantifiable costs and benefits in making real-world environmental policy. While both points certainly are valid, the emphasis corrective taxation places on the benefits of regulatory interventions indicates what those unquantified environmental effects and other policy considerations must be worth to justify these actions in economic terms. In the longer run, therefore, using corrective taxation could have the side effect of clarifying, if not quantifying, the economic and non-economic tradeoffs regulators face in making practical environmental policy for the nation.

Index

Accelerated sea-level rise:
  economic consequences, 139–51
  effects on State of Yap, 138–51
  environmental consequences, 138–39
Agriculture industry, impact of pesticide registration cancellation on, 77–83
Air pollution, regulations regarding, *see* Environmental protection statutes
Asbestos:
  analysis of environmental regulatory policy on, 8
  analysis of EPA regulatory options for, 38–44
  baseline growth rates for brakes markets, 27 *table*
  baseline growth rates of products containing, 26 *table*
  perpetuities resulting from ban of, 32 *table*
  current regulation banning, 9–10
  exposure of populations to, 37–38
  health risks associated with, 8
  history of federal regulations regarding, 8–9
  producer surplus losses resulting from ban of, 32 *table*
  products that contain, 24 *table*
  results of implementation of product regulation, 43–44
  substitutes information for products containing, 28–30 *table*
  uses and markets, 8, 11–13, 12 *table* , 24 *table*
Asbestos, vertically related markets, 13–16
ASLR, *see* Accelerated sea-level rise

Baselines:
  analytical significance of, 103–25
  definition of, 103
Benefits analysis, of pesticide registration, 75

Chemicals, toxic, *see* Toxic chemicals/substances
Chlorinated solvents, impact of regulation on related markets, 84–93
Chlorofluorocarbons:
  cost incidence of mandatory recapture and recycling, 173–76
  economic impact of dissemination of information on, 94–99
  mandatory recycling and, 104–11, 173–74
  and ozone depletion, 104
  phaseout of, 104–11
  economic value of health risk reduction, 173–74
  tax on, 104–11
Clean Air Act, 8
Consequences, welfare, *see* Regulatory cost–benefit analysis; Regulatory options development analysis; Social welfare
Conversion costs, in producer surplus estimation, 30–31
Corrective taxation, *see also* Taxes, environmental
  reasons for not using in environmental policy, 227–36
  standards and charges approach, 237–46
  theory of, 221–27
    marginal benefit concept and, 222–23
    marginal social damage concept and, 221–23
Cost–benefit analysis:
  for asbestos regulatory options, 11–44
  of chlorofluorocarbon regulations, 104–11, 174–76
  cost perpetuities in, 31
  discounting rates used in, 177–94
  for formaldehyde regulatory options, 71–75
  of government-sponsored tree planting program, 128–33

247

Cost–benefit analysis (continued):
   and imports of foreign products, 71–75
   intertemporal issues in, 177–97
   of low-income household weatherization
     program, 133
   overlapping regulations and, 103, 111–25
   and pesticide registration, 77–83
   private *vs.* social costs, 91–93
   product bans *vs.* regulations, 99–102
   and provision of risk-related information to
     consumers, 93–102
   regulatory benefit analysis:
     dose–response function, 36–37
     framework for estimating benefits of
       regulatory options, 31, 32–38
   regulatory cost analysis:
     basic structure of, 13–20
     data input for, 20–31, 75
     regulatory cost simulation model, 19–20
   in regulatory development and implementa-
     tion, 9
   and related markets, 84–93
   and risk reduction value over time, 194–97
   risk assessment and, 36
   role of economist in, 34–36
   significance of baselines in, 103–25
   and solid waste management separation
     requirements, 199, 212–18
   summary of EPA regulatory options on
     asbestos, 38–44
Cost incidence:
   framework for assessing small business
     economic impacts, 166–71
   guidelines for assessing, 153–63
     in small businesses, 164–73
     long-run-cost incidence, 158–60
     short-run incidence of capital-cost-
       increasing regulations, 157–58
     short-run incidence of variable-cost-
       increasing regulations, 157
     short-run to long-run adjustment process,
       159–63
   of mandatory chlorofluorocarbon recapture
     and recycling, 173–76
   practical assessment of, 152–76
Cost perpetuity(ies):
   resulting from asbestos ban, 31, 32 *table*
   in regulatory cost–benefit analysis, 31

Demand function(s), use of data in cost–benefit
   analysis, 20–25
Demand-side management, 133–38
Deposit–refund incentive system, 49
   and used oil recycling, 58–60
Derived demand and price determination, in
   vertically related markets, 13–15, 18
Discounting, and environmental regulations,
   189–91
Dose–response function, 36–37

Economic impacts, *see* Cost incidence
Economist(s), role in regulatory cost–benefit
   analysis, 34–36
Elasticities, *see* Ratio of the elasticities method
Environmental economics:
   available literature on, 2
   challenges to practical application of theory,
     2–3, 7–8, 67–68
   discounting in, 177–93
   issues and topics in, 2, 3
   and practical analyses of regulatory policies,
     7–8
   time-related issues in, 177–97
Environmental life-cycle assessment, 198–218
   alternative to, 209–12
   definition of, 200–202
   evaluating accuracy of practical applications
     of, 202–09
Environmental policy:
   analysis:
     discounting in, 177–93
     intertemporal considerations in, 177–97
   making, incentive systems in, 9
   recent trends in, 198–218
Environmental Protection Agency:
   and asbestos regulations, 8–9
   and formaldehyde regulations, 67–68
   and hazardous waste disposal regulations,
     111–13
   methods of regulation, 9–10
   types of regulations, 9–10, 66–67
Environmental protection regulations, *see* Regulatory policies; Environmental Protection Agency;
   Environmental protection statutes
Environmental protection statutes:
   of U.S. government:
     Clean Air Act, 8

Federal Insecticide, Fungicide, and
    Rodenticide Act, 8
Resource Conservation and Recovery Act,
    45–46, 111–12
Toxic Substances Control Act, 8–9
of South Coast (California) Air Quality
    Management District, 164–73
Environmental taxes/charges, *see* Incentive
    systems; Taxes, environmental
EPA, *see* Environmental Protection Agency
Equipment conversion costs, in producer surplus
    estimation, 30–31
Ethnobiology, 145
Exposure evaluation analysis, in regulatory
    development and implementation, 9
Externality tax, *see* Tax

Federal Insecticide, Fungicide, and Rodenticide
    Act, 75
FIFRA, *see* Federal Insecticide, Fungicide, and
    Rodenticide Act
Formaldehyde, uses and markets, 67

Global climate change:
    effects on sea-level rise, 138–51
    and government-sponsored tree planting,
        127–33
    and ozone depletion, 104
Greenhouse gases, impact on global climate, 127–28

Halon, and ozone depletion, 104
Hazard assessment analysis, in regulatory develop-
    ment and implementation, 9
Hazardous and Solid Waste Amendments, 111–13
Hazardous waste(s):
    dose–response functions and, 36
    EPA regulations controlling, 45–46
    regulation through Resource Conservation and
        Recovery Act, 45–46, 111–12
    overlapping regulations regarding, 111–25
    used lubricating oil as, 46
Hurdle rate approach, 185–89

Impacts assessments, in regulatory development
    and implementation, 9
Incentive systems:
    deposit–refund, 49
    empirical assessment of approaches, 60–65
    in environmental policy making, 9

environmental taxes as, 219–46
for increasing recycling of lubricating oil, 46–65
product charge, 49
recycling credit, 49
Information provision regarding risks, social and
    economic costs and benefits of, 84, 93–99
Intergovernmental Panel on Climate Change,
    138–39
Intertemporal issues, 177–97
IPCC, *see* Intergovernmental Panel on Climate
    Change

Journal of Economic Literature, 2
*Journal of Environmental Economics and Man-
    agement*, 2

LCA, *see* Environmental life-cycle assessment
Life-cycle assessment, *see* Environmental life-cycle
    assessment
Lubricating oil, used:
    classification of by EPA, 46
    disposition of, by economic sectors, 48–49
    disposition of, by region, 49
    generation of by economic sectors, 47, 50–54
    incentives for increasing recycling of, 46–65
    management system for, 46–65
    non-UOMS disposition of, 48
    supplies of, 50–54

Marginal benefit, 221–23
Marginal social damage function concept, 221–23
Market adjustments, resulting from provision of
    risk-related information to consumers, 93–99
Microeconomics, applicability of basic techniques
    to environmental economic analysis, 7
Montreal Protocol, 104
    Copenhagen Amendment to, 104
    London Amendment to, 104
Multiple regulations, impact on regulatory cost–
    benefit analysis, 103, 111–25

Office of Management and Budget, government
    discount requirements from, 178
Ozone depletion:
    and global climate change, 104
    and government-sponsored tree planting,
        127–33

Pesticides:
    benefits analysis of registration, 76

Pesticides (continued):
   regulation of, 75
      cluster analysis for, 76
Policy analysis, design of models for, 45–65
Producer surplus estimation:
   and chlorinated solvent regulation, 86–93
   and formaldehyde regulation, 71–75
   and pesticide registration cancellation, 77–83
   and product bans *vs*. product regulation,
      99–102
   of losses resulting from asbestos ban, 31,
      32 *table*
   product reformulation costs in, 30–31
   use of data in cost–benefit analysis, 25, 30–31
Product charge incentive system, 49
   and used oil recycling, 54–56
Product reformulation costs, 30–31
Public policy issues, challenges to economic
   analyses of, 7–8

Ratio of the elasticities method, application in
   assessing regulatory cost incidence, 157
RCRA, *see* Resource Conservation and Recovery Act
Recycling:
   of chlorofluorocarbons, 104–11
   credit incentive system, 49
      and used oil recycling, 56–58
   incentives for, 49
Regulations, multiple, impact on regulatory cost–
   benefit analysis, 103, 111–25
Regulatory cost incidence, *see* Cost incidence
Regulatory cost–benefit analysis, *see* Cost–benefit
   analysis
Regulatory Impact Analysis:
   and asbestos regulation, 9
   in regulatory development and implementa-
      tion, 9
Regulatory options development analysis:
   and asbestos regulation, 9–10
   consideration of domestic *vs*. imported
      products, 13
   in formaldehyde regulations, 70–71
   in regulatory development and implementa-
      tion, 9
   and vertically related markets, 13
   welfare effects of, 13
Regulatory options, for asbestos, summary cost–
   benefit analysis of, 38–44

Regulatory policy(ies):
   impact of private-sector responses to,
      126–51
   public, procedures for developing and
      implementing, 9
   scope of impact, 84–93
Resource Conservation and Recovery Act, 47–48,
   111–12
   and mandatory solid waste separation and
      recycling, 212–13
RIA, *see* Regulatory Impact Analysis
Risk assessment, role of, in regulatory cost–benefit
   analysis, 36
Risk reduction:
   as a benefit of product regulation, 32
   calculating value of over time, 194–97
   estimating monetary value of, 32–34

SCAQMD, *see* South Coast Air Quality Management District
Small businesses, effects of environmental regulations on, 164–73
Shadow price of capital-consumption rate of
   interest approach, 183–85
Social discounting, 177–97
   and consumption rate of interest, 191–97
   and environmental regulations, 189–91
   hurdle rate approach, 185–89
   shadow price of capital-consumption rate of
      interest approach, 183–85
Social welfare:
   changes, modeling and interpreting, 83–102
   costs, reduction of through product regu-
      lation, 32
   effects of chlorofluorocarbon phaseout and tax
      on, 105–11
   effects of regulatory options on, 13
   gain, through product regulation, 32
   setting monetary value on regulations affect-
      ing, 32–34
Solid waste management, cost–benefit analysis
   considerations and separation requirements, 199,
   212–18
South Coast Air Quality Managment District,
   164–73
SPC-CRI, *see* Shadow price of capital-consumption
   rate of interest approach
Substances, toxic, *see* Toxic chemicals/substances

Substitute products, economic impact of environmental regulation on, 88–93
Substitute products, impact on cost–benefits analysis, 93
Supply function model, for estimating costs and effects of regulatory interventions, 45, 47–65
Surplus estimations, *see* Producer surplus estimation

Tax, externality, as environmental correction method, 10, 11, 219. *See also* Incentive system; Product charge incentive system; Taxes, environmental
Taxes, environmental, 219–46
 reasons for not using, 227–36
 redefining, 236–46
 standards and charges approach, 237–46
 theory of corrective taxation, 221–27
Textile industry:
economic impact of foreign imports on, 71–75
economic impact of formaldehyde regulations on, 71
Theory of externalities and common property resources, 2
Time-related issues in environmental economics, 177–97
Toxic chemicals/substances:
 characterizing the nature of exposure to, 37–38
 dose–response functions and, 36
 pest-management substances, 8

Toxic Substances Control Act, 8–9, 66–67
 asbestos and, 8, 9
 EPA powers granted by, 8–9, 66–67
 formaldehyde and, 66–67
Toxicological studies, and dose–response functions, 36–37
Toxins, *see* Toxic chemicals/substances; Solid waste(s)
TSCA, *see* Toxic Substances Control Act

UOMS, *see* Used oil management system
Use and substitutes analysis, in cost–benefit analysis, 21–25
Used oil management system, 47–48

Vertically related markets:
 derived demand and price determination in, 13–15, 18
 effects of regulatory options on, 13
 for asbestos, 13–16

Waste(s), hazardous, *see* Hazardous wastes
Waste(s), solid, *see* Solid waste management
Welfare effect(s)/impact(s), *see* Regulatory cost–benefit analysis; Regulatory options development analysis; Social welfare

Yap, State of, effects of accelerated sea-level rise on, 138–51
Yap, State of, historical and economic profile of, 140–46